For Gini, who made it possible for me to write . . .
then, and now.

—Joseph D. Harrington

I-BOAT CAPTAIN

BY ZENJI ORITA with JOSEPH D. HARRINGTON

MAJOR BOOKS • CANOGA PARK, CALIFORNIA

PREFACE

In the late 1940s, when Japan was recovering from her defeat in the Pacific War, the weekly publication *Shukan Asahi* announced that it was seeking stories dealing with actual war experiences.

As one of the few submarine captains who lived through that war, I felt it my duty to prepare a record of those who fought so valiantly under the sea, helping each other and often facing death together, and also about the *kaiten* pilots who sacrificed their young lives in defense of their country. But, when I started to write, I found I had no reference material. On the day of Japan's surrender in 1945, nearly all records had been destroyed. I had only my memory on which to rely. Using that, I wrote about the *kaiten* operations. The article was titled "Human Torpedoes."

Until then, war stories of that time generally dealt with Japanese as cruel, and emphasized incidents of atrocity and starvation. They were extremely self-critical. My story was different. It detailed how young men of Japan had stood to their duty, dying with bravery and grace. I received many letters from persons commending it as not carrying the ugly emotion of defeatism. On the other hand, certain reviewers and journalists who wanted to get along with the Occupation authorities castigated me as someone who approved wars, calling me a fascist.

Years passed, and in the mid-fifties a Japanese production company made a film featuring the human torpedoes. Its contents were far afield from the facts as I had known them. The motion picture depicted them as fanatics, although I had known them as young men who'd loved their parents, families and sweethearts, along with their country. Nonetheless, these did not deter them from the sacrifices they made in the cause of their country. A determination grew in me to write about those *kaiten* men again.

Just then Kennosuke Torisu, one year senior to me at the Japanese Naval Academy, came to me with a proposal. He wanted to write a book telling about the *kaiten* pilots as they really were, admirable young men, and suggested to me that we could do it together. In the form of 16 articles, the tale appeared in *Maru*, a monthly specializing in war stories. Later, the collection appeared in book form. I felt then that my writing duties were completed.

More years passed, and quite unexpectedly I received a letter from an American, Joseph D. Harrington, who was writing a book about Japan's human torpedos. He asked for my first-hand experience for one of its chapters. During our exchange of correspondence, he wrote: "There has been more than one book published in the United States, laden with falsehoods and old distorted impressions of Japanese people, carried over from the Pacific War. I have lived in Japan, and did not find the Japanese people to be anything like I had been led to believe they were. Most books, for example, refer to the 'traditionally warlike Japanese.' I don't think that any nation is a 'traditionally warlike' nation." Mr. Harrington, who had written much about the Imperial Japanese Navy, suddenly made me feel that here was a man who might understand just what it might be like to be a member of it, since he had been a member of the United States Navy for 20 years.

He eventually proposed that we write a book about my experiences for American readers. It would deal with the Japanese submarine fleet as a whole, while centering on my personal experiences. "I have never agreed with the assumption," he said, "that your submarine fleet was not a very good one. Nor with the assumption that the strategic use of it was poor, in and of itself. I think that you Japanese submariners knew your jobs and fought well, but that you had some lousy luck. Bravery, ingenuity and courage are universally admired, as I have found from my successes in writing about the Imperial Fleet. I propose to do a book that will tell the story of the Japanese submarine fleet as it really was."

While reading his letters, I felt as if I had been given a reinforcement of 1,000,000 men.

We set about the task. While he delved into American sources, Mr. Harrington shot out to me over 400 detailed questionnaires about Japanese submarine activities. Since I was still on active duty with the Japanese Maritime Self-Defense Forces when we started, I had to work at it in my off-duty time. After scanty official sources had been exhausted, I began collecting material from old shipmates and friends. I was continually encouraged by Mr. Harrington's attitude, however, and kept on with the work, because I felt that men like him could help foreigners gain a true understanding of the Japanese, and thus help the new Japanese "Navy" . . . the JMSDF . . . come to play a trusted role in the defense of the free world.

It was never my intention to make this book an "official version," like Roscoe's *Destroyer* or *Submarine,* I wanted the work to be accurate so that "experts" would not question it, but also to hold appeal for a wider range of readers. I have tried to describe the life of Japanese submariners, their problems as well as their tactics so that readers might perhaps even feel that they were "living" with the men who fought under the seas for Japan.

I could not have written this book without Mr. Harrington's assistance and expertise. He has blended it expertly with material he gathered from beyond my limited reach. This is a very valuable blend. I think it will make the book interesting for civilians as well as military men.

I must also express my heartfelt appreciation to Mr. Masuru Fujimoto, of the *Mainichi Newspapers* of Japan, who had worked with Mr. Harrington on other works about the Japanese Navy. Mr. Fujimoto kept in constant touch with me, encouraged me, and did a great deal of special translating so that Mr. Harrington would grasp my exact meanings. I owe both men a great deal.

Zenji Orita
Yokosuka, Japan, 1976

This book had its genesis more than 20 years ago, when I used my off-duty time at the Navy Department to dig into naval archives and the Library of Congress. Since writers are naturally neurotic, all of my writings about the Japanese Navy of World War II had begun in anger. Upon starting to write about the "other side of the war," I found that nearly all available material had been "classified," to be reserved for the sole use of a Reserve naval officer so that an "official history" could be written. A history, incidentally, that required a full additional volume after publication to correct its errata, in addition to its original dozen or so volumes. I was not surprised at this, however, my historical work at the Navy Department having shown me that earlier "official" versions, including that of the Civil War, were not reliable, either.

My real opportunity came later, when I was assigned duty in Japan. With the help of Kichisaburo Nomura, a man who'd had his heart broken by Japanese and Americans, I was able to contact members of the former Imperial Navy, and get their stories. I came to learn that atrocities are always commited by "them" and never by "us," an attitude documented by capable journalists in Vietnam, although Eric Sevareid had commented markedly on them in Europe two decades before.

This book has been long in the writing. It has spanned nearly half of my Navy career, a stint as a government flack in Washington, D.C., and more than six years of business, plus part of my present "career," in which I do what a writer should . . . namely anything that will feed me while I pound on the typewriter.

Like Captain Orita, I, too, owe Masaru Fujimoto a great deal. He thinks internationally, which has melded well with my own efforts to think historically.

When the long history of the world is finally written, the best that can be said of any man who lived in it will be that he did his utmost. I hope that, when the chronicle of the Imperial Japanese Submarine Fleet of the Pacific Naval War is slipped in among that history's many folios, that such might be said of Zenji, Masaru, and me.

Joseph D. Harrington
Hollywood, Florida, 1976

Chapter 1

EAST TO WAR

The sun had fallen below the western horizon. Ahead the smoky plume of Mt. Mihara, on the island of Oshima, could no longer be seen. Far astern, the lights of Tokyo and Yokohama cast a glow upon the sky. Cdr. Nobuo Ishikawa, commanding officer of His Imperial Majesty's submarine *I-15,* told me to have all hands fall in on deck, aft of the conning tower.

I was Ishikawa's executive and torpedo officer. All day I had been wondering when he would give us word of *I-15's* mission. That morning, Nov. 21, 1941, he tersely told me. "We will sail this evening. Get her ready for sea." He had then gone to the training cruiser *Katori,* flagship of Japan's submarine fleet, for final instructions, without telling me any more.

Of course I knew that something important was happening. The 6th Fleet, Japan's submarine force, had undergone intense and severe battle exercises from June to August of that year, in areas as far apart as the icy Kuriles and the torrid Mandated

Islands, as well as off Japan and Formosa. During September, all boats returned to their home bases for full refit.

The international situation had already tightened by the time I came aboard *I-15* in March of 1941. Our commander-in-chief, Adm. Isoroku Yamamoto, had told his superiors he thought it was reckless to wage war against the American and British navies, but nevertheless he was determined to do his best if war did come. In January he thought of the idea for an attack against Pearl Harbor, stronghold of America's Pacific Fleet. In that same month, top military men of the U. S. and Britain conferred in Washington, D.C., about the possibility of a war with Japan.

Early in February, Vice Adm. Takejiro Onishi, chief of staff for our Navy's 11th Air Fleet, called Cdr. Minoru Genda to Kanoya for discussions. Genda was considered one of our finest pilots. The top group of fliers he gathered about him was called "Genda's Flying Circus," and they were largely responsible for the high state of training of our naval air arm.

"Here, Genda," said Onishi, showing him a letter from Yamamoto, "Make a study of this Pearl Harbor idea, and let me know if you think it can be accomplished." Genda was back with an answer in two weeks. "It can be done," he said, but listed three absolute requirements, without which success was impossible. Six of our large aircraft carriers would be needed, and these staffed by our very best pilots. And the attack would have to be brought off with complete surprise.

In February, also, our 4th Fleet was established at Truk, in the Carolines. Contrary to what most of the world believed during World War II, the Mandated Islands were *not* heavily fortified when the war began. Their lack of fortifications, in fact, was one of the major factors in deciding to attack Pearl Harbor. Both Japanese and American naval men had long thought that a war between their two countries, if it came, would begin in the areas south of Japan. The American navy expected to have to slam its way across the central Pacific, through the Mandated Islands, to join up with its Asiatic Fleet in a mass assault on the Imperial Navy. Our navy had to plan to block such an approach, and prevent such a rendezvous. It had little chance of blocking it, though, so long as runways, anchorages, and fortifications in the outlying islands were nonexistent. The attack on Pearl Harbor, therefore, dangerous as it was, seemed the logical answer to our main problem, stopping the American fleet in its tracks. If American warships were sunk, or immobilized for many months, Japan would be free to exploit the southern areas, seizing their resources, and to prepare for the day when the American fleet was built up again. The 4th Fleet, meanwhile, with its force of 4 cruisers, 8 destroyers, and 16 submarines, would be sufficient to defend the outlying islands if the Pearl Harbor attack were successful.

During March, when I came on board *I-15* as executive officer, Japan obtained a monopoly on Indochina's rice crop, which was badly needed, and the right to use the French airfield at Saigon. During that same month President Roosevelt signed the Lend-Lease Bill and made the speech in which he said, "When your neighbor's house is on fire, you lend him a hose." He meant that America would help Britain against Germany, but not go to war.

In April our Navy established the 1st Air Fleet, composed of six carriers, and our best aviators were ordered to its air squadrons. The U. S. occupation agreement with Greenland was signed in that month, too. Some American experts on international law described the agreement as "legally indefensible," and claimed the man who signed it for Denmark, which owned Greenland, had no authority from his government to sign. Japan and Russia signed a non-aggression pact that month, too. Our national leaders decided to open negotiations with Washington, in an effort to settle what they called "The China Problem," and to avoid war with the United States if at all possible. At Singapore that same month, men of six nations that opposed Japan's policies met to discuss how Japan should be handled in a war. Their final decision was that Great Britain would send a striking force to Singapore as soon as possible. Should war come, the U. S. fleet would contain the Japanese fleet with strikes in the Marshalls and Carolines, while the Dutch, together with the U. S. Asiatic Fleet, would take care of local defense and convoy escort until all the Allied forces were massed together for a strike against our navy.

In May our Adm. Yamamoto told the Naval General Staff of his plan to attack Pearl Harbor. Adm. Osami Nagano, Chief of the Naval General Staff, vigorously opposed the plan. He felt that Japan should secure the vast resources and raw materials of the southern area first. The aircraft carriers Yamamoto wanted for the Pearl Harbor attack represented 60% of what we had. If we lost them, Japan would be at the mercy of other Pacific naval powers.

In June, the submarines of 6th Fleet were allowed to fire one torpedo each against the steep shoreline of Oshima Island, due south of Tokyo Bay. These tests proved out the mighty Model 95 torpedo. She was the underwater sister to the surface-carried Model 93, the weapon that would hurt the enemy so badly at Java Sea, Savo Island, Tassafaronga, and in other battles. The midget submarine carrier *Chiyoda*, publicly listed as a seaplane carrier, carried out tests with her tiny submersibles off the eastern shore of Kyushu and the western shore of Shikoku, in areas that resembled Pearl Harbor. At that time, midget submarines were a secret kept not only from the Japanese public, but also from nearly all of the Japanese navy as well.

Germany attacked Russia that month, an action that tended to make the northern flank of Japanese defenses more secure. Top Japanese planners decided to stay out of the Russo-German war, concentrating instead on gaining full control of Indochina. Not only would its great food output solve some of Japan's internal problems, but its location would provide bases for a great southern advance when the right time came.

On July 2, 1941, the famous "risk of war" Imperial Conference was held, with Emperor Hirohito present. Fearful that the ABCD powers (America-Britain-Dutch-Chinese) were tightening a noose around Japan's neck, the conferees decided to rush ahead with efforts in the south, and strengthen Japan's position in Asia, even if it meant war. Japan was to press ahead in Indochina regardless of the consequences. A powerful attempt would be made to end the China difficulties, and it was also decided that "Japan will not decline a war with Great Britain and America" in the process of achieving its national objectives. More than a million reservists were called to arms right after that, and all Japanese merchant ships in the Atlantic Ocean were ordered to their home ports.

The Americans had broken Japan's diplomatic code by July. They knew Japan had pressed Vichy France and received for approval our complete occupation of Indochina, which was then French territory. President Roosevelt (although he knew that France had given approval secretly) proposed that Indochina be allowed to remain a neutral area. When Japan rejected his proposal he made loud public issue of it, and ordered Japan's assets in the United States frozen. Holland followed suit, freezing Japan's assets the next day, and Great Britain gave Japan notice that she was terminating all commercial treaties.

It was obvious that the tempers of all national leaders concerned were being heated to the point of hysteria. Unless someone calmed down, yielded, or retreated soon, it would be too late. Practically all of Japan's trade came to a halt when her overseas funds were tied up. Her supplies of oil, the life blood of any industrial nation, were cut off. She had to reach an accommodation with those who opposed her, or go ahead and fight for what she felt she needed to survive. She finally chose the third course.

Very little of these high-level matters was known to the Imperial submarine service, except what we heard in news dispatches over the wireless during maneuvers. We were concentrating on shaping the world's finest submarine navy. Though small in numbers, the 6th Fleet's construction plans were ambitious, and we were very powerful for our size.

In August the one move that might have prevented the Pacific naval war was proposed by Prime Minister Winston Churchill to President Roosevelt at Newfoundland during their famous Atlantic Conference. The cigar-puffing British bulldog proposed that America, The Netherlands, Britain and Russia make a joint declaration to Japan that any further southward movement on her part would automatically mean war with these four nations. Churchill knew that a Russian threat from the north would temper Japan's ambitions. Mr. Roosevelt rejected the suggestion. He reasoned that American public opinion was not yet strong enough to support such warlike statements. Actually, his fellow-citizens considered happenings in the Far East extremely remote from American interests. As one reporter put it, "Americans couldn't get very excited about what 70 million Japs were doing to 6 times that many Chinks."

After Mr. Roosevelt got back from Newfoundland, he and his Secretary of State conferred with our ambassador, Mr. Kichisaburo Nomura, about resuming talks, and arranging for a Pacific conference with our Foreign Minister.

On August 27, Japan protested the shipment of Lend-Lease goods through Japanese waters to Vladivostok, from which port they went overland to Russia for use against our German allies. The next day, a joint conference in Tokyo decided that war, if it began at all, would have to begin in November or December, 1941. November was better because tides, phase of the moon, and typhoons were more favorable. Winter snows would hold back the Russians in either month, if they got any ideas about attacking Japan. After December, however, we would have dipped very far into our critical oil reserves. In any case, a decision would have to be made by early October, so plans could be completed and executed no later than December. After that month, Japan's enemies would be too powerful for her to challenge.

All this information, of course, was knowledge a Lieutenant

less than 10 years out of the Naval Academy at Etajima could not possibly have had at that time. It has taken much reading and study on my part to ascertain these facts. During this period high-level maneuvering and note-exchanging was going on. I worked very strenuously at the only trade I knew, whipping a submarine and its crew into top readiness. Our 6th Fleet had three squadrons of submarines at the time the war started, including one made up of obsolescent boats that were used for training practice in home water. My boat, *I-15*, was in Submarine Squadron (SubRon) 1, and I was one of 3000 officers and men who manned the boats of what was called The Advance Force. Basic pre-war strategy centered around my squadron's advancing deep into enemy waters, and keeping watch on his naval ports. Should he sally forth to attack the Japanese homeland, we were to attack him, then use our high surface speed of 23 knots to dash away and set up a second ambush for him, repeating this tactic until we were out of torpedoes. If, in spite of the damage we did to his fleet, the enemy kept advancing toward Japan, our Combined Fleet would sortie to meet him with boats of SubRon 2 and SubRon 3 screening far ahead of it. Those submarines would repeat the tactics of SubRon 1. Theoretically, by the time the enemy closed with our Main Body for "the one decisive sea battle" admirals dream of, he would be so weakened that he could be crushed. Japan would win control of the Pacific Ocean!

In September 1941, about 40 of Japan's highest-ranking naval officers shut themselves up in the Naval War College at Tokyo for nearly two weeks. There they worked out table-top maneuvers for the opening of a war they were sure was coming. The Pearl Harbor attack was only one part of a plan of operations that would span nearly one-third of the world's circumference, and not many were in favor of the thing. Even Vice Adm. Chuichi Nagumo, who was to command the Pearl Harbor strike force, opposed the idea as drawing too much naval support away from the main southern effort. But Adm. Yamamoto insisted that his scheme be included. In more or less these words he said, "Our island ring defense is very weak. It is far from completion. The Americans could easily take one or more of those islands then come right across the Pacific into the heart of the Empire. Our best course of action is to deliver a knockout blow to the American fleet at the very start. Then Japan can operate in the south without fear of effective opposition. We can build up our island defense ring, and strengthen our fleet for the day when the recovered American navy tries to move westward. At that later meeting, with our strength at its peak, we can destroy it completely."

Yamamoto knew the U.S. better than the others present. He had served in Washington, D.C., and had seen America's industrial might. He thought it reckless to fight a war with her, and had advised against it. He had earlier said that "for six months or a year" he could run wild against the Americans, but could hold out no hope after that. The final decision to prepare for war was made at an Imperial Conference on Sept. 6. The admiral felt that so long as he had to go to war, he intended to begin in a way that gave the best chance of victory. He insisted that the Pearl Harbor portion be included, and threatened to resign if it were not.

Isoroku Yamamoto was "old Navy," having fought in the Battle of Tsushima Strait under Admiral Heihachiro Togo, while a very junior officer in the Russo-Japanese war. He was also "new Navy," being one of the leaders in development of Japanese naval aviation. Because of Yamamoto and men who thought as he did, Japan started the war with 10 aircraft carriers rather than the 3 or 4 most other nations thought we had. We also had the Zero fighter, best plane in the world. We had pilots who could fly missions more than twice as far as pilots of any other Navy. Should Yamamoto suddenly resign from his post as chief of our fleet, there would be great public wonderment as to why. And great public outcry as well. Within the Navy itself there was no telling what might happen by the time rumors had finished spreading. So, in a few weeks, all opposition to his plan vanished. The strike against Pearl Harbor was approved.

While admirals pounded on tables and shouted in each other's faces, 40 miles away, in Tokyo, I labored under Yokosuka's hot summer sun. Sweat made my clothing cling to me as I performed the myriad duties of any ship's executive officer. A final check of *I-15*'s hull and fittings had to be made as well as her weapons. I had to re-check the spare parts stored to be sure we would lack nothing necessary for combat repairs. While I reviewed these matters with officers and petty officers, much rumor was going the rounds. No one had any accurate information about what lay ahead of us, but every man on all 14 first-line submarines moored at Yokosuka was sure in his heart that the next time he put to sea it would be to combat the enemy.

And we were truly ready for it. All 14 boats were 16,000-milers with surface speeds of more than 20 knots. All could steam to the U.S. west coast and back without refueling. Confident we could meet and beat the best, we worked with a will.

15

One sad note sounded through the 6th fleet on October 2. *I-161*, commanded by Lt. Cdr. Takashi Hirokawa, hit a gunboat while steaming in home waters, and sank with the captain and most of his crew. That was the third submarine disaster in 20 months—all due to the rigors of intensive training that was standard policy with the Imperial Navy in the late Thirties. *I-163* had gone down in Bungo Strait, after colliding with another submarine, on February 2, 1939. Only her captain, Takashi Sano, and a few crewmen on her bridge were saved. We also lost *I-167* plus Cdr. Tadashi Okata and 86 crewmen, on August 29, 1940, during Fleet maneuvers in the Bonins Islands.

Also, during October, the portion of SubRon 1 under Hanku Sasaki was suddenly ordered into Kure Naval Arsenal for installation of "special fittings." No one, including Sasaki himself, was told what these fittings were for, but he learned soon afterward. During October a special conference of senior officers was called by Adm. Yamamoto on board his flagship, the battleship *Nagato*, anchored off Kure. There he told them to consider themselves and the forces under them on a war footing.

November came. In its first week, after an Imperial Conference, the special Combined Fleet Top Secret Operations Order No. 1 was issued to a few high-ranking naval officers. It commanded them to complete final preparations for war by early December. The expanded part of this plan spelled out everything, including the details of how Pearl Harbor, Malaya, Guam, Java, the Philippines, and the south seas areas would be attacked. Vice Adm. Mitsumi Shimizu, who commanded all Japanese submarines, passed the word to men who captained his boats Nov. 10.

Part of SubRon 1 and all of SubRon 2 were at Yokosuka then. The rest of SubRon 1, and all of SubRon 3, were at Kure. These, soon to total 30 submarines in all, were the finest Japan had. All would soon be sailing eastward.

From November 10 through November 12, I scurried back and forth along the hull of *I-15* like a water beetle up and down a puddle. My hardest task was calculating just where to stow the great mass of materials coming aboard. We were loading provisions for 90 days. It had to be done in a way that would not reduce her fighting ability. Trim, buoyancy and balance had to be considered while I directed the storage of goods.

It took three days to get the job done. When we were finished, the entire deck space inside *I-15*, except for the diesel engine room, was covered with bags of rice, boxes of dried food, and tins of provisions, to a depth of two feet. It looked like our crewmen were living in a tubular food warehouse. Especially crammed was the torpedo room, near the bow, with a full wartime load of twenty Model 95 torpedoes, fantastic weapons that could make nearly 50 knots enroute to a target. Men in that compartment not only had a two-foot thick floor of food, but had to squeeze between it and the "steel fish," in order to get needed rest.

On order of Vice Adm. Shimizu, the hulls of all submarines were painted black, and their hull numbers white. "*I*" is the first character in the Japanese phonetic alphabet, and looks something like the Greek "*lambda*." Followed by the number "15," it was painted on both sides of our conning tower. It meant *I-15* was a first-line, Class A submarine. "*RO*" type, of which I will tell later, might be called Class B boats, and "*HA*" types Class C, since those are the second and third characters of the alphabet.

The final major item I had to check was the reconnaissance aircraft carried on board *I-15*. This was first inspected thoroughly at Oppama, the nearby naval air base, then hoisted on board. It was test-launched from a catapult forward of the conning tower then stored in a special hangar at the tower's base. No other Navy carried aircraft on its submarines, so far as I know. *I-15* and the other boats of her class carried a single-engined "*Geta*" biplane capable of about 100 knots air speed. Its wings, tail and floats were removable. They were fastened to the inside of the hangar's walls, and were attached to the plane when it was on its catapult, ready for launching, then removed and re-stowed after an air mission was completed. More than 20 Japanese submarines carried airplanes. One of them made two bombing attacks on mainland United States.

By the evening of Nov. 20, all necessary work was completed. Taking one final turn through *I-15* with our "Chief of The Boat," I made a last check of everything. When I turned into my bunk, I was satisfied I had done my work well, and had seen to it that others did their work well. So, Captain Ishikawa now had a submarine that was ready in all respects for combat operations. Right after breakfast next morning he ordered me to prepare the ship for getting underway by evening.

Fourteen submarines had already slipped quietly out of Yokosuka, perhaps the world's most security-tight base. American sailors who have been there since the war's end know of the nine tunnels along the road between it and Yokohama forming the only land approach to the base. And

17

Yokosuka base is surrounded on three sides by water making it easily patrolled by small sentry craft. Before and during World War II, no one was allowed to approach or live within a radius of the base that extended out to the third tunnel unless he had an official connection, or business, with the base. And no one at all in that area was permitted to own a camera. For these reasons, there were no cheering crowds to see us off as we slipped away. Only crews of training submarines waved their caps in circles over their heads to us in the traditional Navy farewell. *I-1, I-2, I-3, I-4, I-5, I-6, I-7, I-9, I-15, I-17, I-19, I-21, I-23,* and *I-25* glided slowly out into Tokyo Bay, and headed south through Sagami Bay without any other fanfare.

My question, Captain, where are we headed, had not received an answer that morning when Ishikawa left *I-15* for the flagship. "I will tell all hands once we are clear of land," he had promised. Now nearly 100 men were in ranks on the after deck when he spoke.

"*I-15* is now beginning her first war mission. Our station has been established at a point 40 miles north of Pearl Harbor in the Hawaiian Islands. We will arrive there on December 7. Unless there is a drastic change in the international situation, Japan will go to war the following day against the Americans, British, and Dutch. A great attack will be made on Pearl Harbor. I hope that you will, under my command, do your best, and show the skills you have trained so hard to acquire these past months and years. I hope that what you do will achieve a glorious name for *I-15!*"

So, I thought. *It has finally come!* My immediate reaction was a deep sense of responsibility. As my captain's chief assistant, I must do my best to discharge my duties efficiently. I was filled with elation that the navy in which I took so much pride would take on an operation so vast. At the same time I was a little apprehensive as to whether we would be able to win out over the world's two greatest naval powers.

Within 48 hours I had something else to think about other than my own personal survival. Planners had selected a northern approach to Pearl Harbor so that bad weather would cover the aircraft carriers making the weather another weapon in our arsenal.

Two days out of Yokosuka, we steamed right into a storm that covered our movements completely. It covered us with plenty of water as well. For many hours I felt I was at the bottom of a watery valley, staring up the sides of two liquid mountains as *I-15* wallowed in the trough of giant crests. Over and over again, with a mighty smash, the spuming wave tops would crash down on my submarine. We, at stations on the open bridge, clutched at any projection available to avoid being washed away in the boiling sea.

We were in that storm a long time, and the nights were especially bad. They were pitch black, and we dared show no lights, for fear of being sighted by some plodding merchantman. In the blackness we had to fight our fear, as well as cold and fatigue. All hands soon fell into a state of near-exhaustion, both mental and physical. With the massive load we carried, *I-15* had only slightly positive buoyancy. This would prove advantageous should we need to submerge quickly, but it made for sluggish movement along the ocean's surface. The only bright aspect was that since we were out of the range of Midway and Wake Island patrol planes we could concentrate all our efforts on fighting the storm and repairing damage.

Topside wasn't the only place where men suffered. A submarine on the surface "breathes" as a swimmer does. Air is sucked to the engines through a large induction valve set in the bridge structure. When a great sea crashed over *I-15*, it covered the induction valve opening. The engines then had to get their "breaths" from elsewhere. So they inhaled them from within the submarine causing rapid fluctuations in our internal atmospheric pressure, and this gave men terrible ear pains. Also, when seas covered the exhaust tubes with water, exhaust gas would be forced back into her interior, making the engines give off a loud, popping noise, and filling the engine room with choking gases. Our engineers suffered terrible ear pains, and had trouble breathing. It was a wonder they could go about their duties.

I-15 pressed on. The weather improved somewhat as we continued east, and I had time to scan Top Secret Operations Orders No. 1 and No. 2. Y-Day, the *tentative* date of attack, was Dec. 8, Japan time. X-day, the *actual* date of attack, was to be transmitted to us later, if war could not be avoided.

The submarine operation was very complicated. *I-19*, *I-21*, and *I-23* moved ahead and rendezvoused at a spot in mid-ocean, then formed a three-submarine screen 50 miles ahead of the Nagumo force. The rest of us took up stations in another screen maintained 300 miles ahead of Nagumo's formation. SubRon 3, meanwhile, headed for Kwajalein atoll, then to stations south of Oahu. *I-8* was flagship of SubRon 3, the other boats being *I-168* through *I-175*. *I-10* had departed Japan before any of us. She was swinging south to check the Fijis and Samoa, before approaching the U.S. west coast. *I-26* was also heading for America, but along a northerly course as she had to first check the Aleutians.

Five more submarines made up the Special Attack Force. They were *I-16, I-18, I-20, I-22,* and *I-24.* The "special fittings" whose nature had so mystified Capt. Hanku Sasaki when he was ordered into Kure to get them were midget submarines, one to a boat, each manned by a crew of two. Each of the midgets mounted two torpedoes. These five Fleet-type submarines were to move in close to Pearl Harbor's entrance. From there the midgets were to penetrate the anchorage before the air attack, and rise to join in once it was launched.

Besides SubRons 1, 2, and 3, Japan had SubRons 4, 5, 6 and 7, totalling 27 more submarines. The 14 boats that made up SubRons 4 and 5 were heading for the China Sea area, there to cooperate in the capture of Malaya and Java. SubRon 6, consisting of the 4 mine-laying submarines, was to mine the waters of the Philippines and off Singapore then move south to harass shipping from Australia. SubRon 7, consisting of 9 RO-class short-range boats, would operate out of the Marshalls, helping attack Wake and other islands.

By December 1, every one of our 57 active duty submarines was on its way to an appointed position. As for the surface fleet, all but one of its 166 ships (a destroyer in drydock for overhaul) were ready for action. On the next day our wireless intercepted a special message from Adm. Yamamoto to all units of the fleet. "Climb Mount Niitaka." it read, "X is to be Y."

War would begin on December 8 (December 7. U.S. time)! The tentative date had been made the actual one. The first portion of the message had spiritual meaning. Mount Niitaka, a peak on Formosa, is taller than Mount Fuji, and is considered the highest point in the Japanese Empire. By using it as his code phrase, Adm. Yamamoto was urging all of Japan's fighting men to strive toward heaven. Throughout that day, and the five that followed, the same thought raced through my mind again and again.

"The arrow is loosed from the bow! The arrow is loosed from the bow!"

* * *

Chapter 2.

THE MIDGET SUBS GO OUT.

While *I-15* laboriously made its way toward the Hawaiian Islands over a course that at first swung north to place it in front of the Nagumo force, five other boats of SubRon 1 were also enroute, each carrying a very special weapon. Just as the German navy had "pocket battleships," Japan had pocket submarines. Shrink a regular submersible to one-seventh of its size, divide its crew by 50 and its armament by 10, and you have the weapon that penetrated Pearl Harbor four hours before the Pacific war began.

The idea for midget submarines originated with Capt. Kaneharu Kishimoto. In 1933 he said, "If we could launch big torpedoes with men on board them, and if those torpedoes went deep into enemy areas and launched smaller torpedoes, there would be practically no chance of a miss." He received permission from Admiral of the Fleet Prince Hiroyasu Fushimi, who was then Chief of the Naval General Staff to construct two prototype midget subs. One condition had to be met. They were not to be *tokko* (suicide) weapons.

Assisting Capt. Kishimoto were four officers who, like himself, later rose to flag rank. Cdr. Toshihide Asama specialized in torpedoes; Cdr. Takeshi Nawa, batteries; Cdr. Kiyoshi Yamada, motors; and Cdr. Ariki Katayama, hulls. The project was classified Top Secret from the start, and work began in a special, closed shop at the Kure Naval Arsenal. During its design and construction the weapon was called "*A-Kanemono*" (Metal Fitting, Type A). Years later, when it began to appear in the Fleet, it was called "*Ko-Hyoteki*" (Target, Type A). Right up until the government broadcast telling of midget submarine operations at Pearl Harbor, most Japanese Navy men thought these bulbous, cigar-shaped hulls were special targets for use by submarines during firing practice. Trials of the pioneer midgets, in 1934, saw them reach the unbelievable for that time underwater speed of 25 knots.

Work on the weapons began in earnest in 1938, when two models of an advanced version were built. Pioneer pilot for these was Lt. Naoji Iwasa. He became entranced with their possibilities. When they proved to be very satisfactory, mass production was approved. To insure continued secrecy, hulls and frames were made in a private yard, then taken to a small island just outside Kure harbor for final assembly. Access to this island was forbidden all who did not know of the weapon.

The mass-produced version was a two-man type with which the world has become generally acquainted because of Pearl Harbor. It displaced 46 tons, mounted a pair of 18-inch torpedoes, and made 24 knots both on the surface and underwater. By changing its battery connections, it could be made to run at 10 knots, 8 knots or, for a 25-hour period, 4 knots. It could also move in reverse at 4 knots. Another type of midget submarine was also built which carried 3 torpedoes and 11 men. It was called "No. 71 boat," and was generally considered the best means of defense for outlying islands. But it proved unwieldy, complicated to handle, and not very well suited to mass production, so it was discarded. Every No. 71 made was completely dismantled for fear that word would leak out that Japan was building midget submarines.

The trainees lived on board IJN *Chiyoda*, one of four ships designed to carry midget submarines. Training was done at Ourazaki, a small island about 12 miles southeast of Kure. It was designated "Base P." Before pilots went out on training missions, officials would clear the area of all fishing boats and commercial steamers. There were numerous accidents with pilots crashing into the sea bottom or hitting target ships accidentally, but they perfected their skills as time went by, doing so in complete secrecy. Even the ships designed to carry these weapons were secret. Our naval listings, and foreign magazines, described *Chiyoda, Nisshin, Mizuho,* and *Chitose* as "seaplane carriers." Foreign navies thought they were floating bases for amphibious aircraft. Actually, these four ships were fitted to transport and to launch 12 midgets each over a specially designed stern. We also had several destroyer-type midget transports which could also launch them over specially sloped sterns.

During the 1941 summer fleet maneuvers *Chiyoda* took out the midget pilots who would later attack Pearl Harbor. They trained in terrain that resembled Oahu. The enthusiasm of Lt. Naoji Iwasa for his weapon grew and grew. It infected others. They had high hopes for their special craft, and were anxious to prove them in battle. But they wanted to do more than simply sortie with the Combined Fleet and form a submarine network around an enemy force in mid-ocean. Iwasa was convinced that his submarine could penetrate enemy anchorages, even an enemy's home ports, and do widespread damage. He proposed this to Capt. Kaku Harada, commanding officer of *Chiyoda.* Harada liked the idea so much that, when Lt. Cdr. Ryunosuke Ariizumi, a submarine member of the Naval General Staff, came to the *Chiyoda* to inspect the training, Iwasa was permitted to present his proposition to him.

"Sir," he said, "our weapon can do far more damage to an enemy on his doorstep than in the middle of the ocean." He pointed out that destroying an enemy warship in its own port was much better than striking it at sea where it might already have hurt some of our forces in battle. Besides, it was a stationary target while in port. There was a greater chance of making hits.

Ariizumi was infected by Iwasa's enthusiasm. He saw that the proposal was passed to Adm. Yamamoto. Yamamoto liked the idea at first, then cast it aside for two reasons: there was very little chance of recovering the midgets after such an attack; if one was detected before the hour scheduled for the air attack all surprise might be lost. And Cdr. Genda had listed surprise as one of the three essentials for a successful attack on the enemy's main base. As a matter of fact, one of our midget submarines actually *was* detected off Pearl Harbor several hours before Japanese planes appeared overhead. Poor American communications, caution, doubt, and hesitation made the warning worthless. Bombs were about to fall on Pearl Harbor when the senior American admiral received word of the submarine contact.

As I said earlier, part of SubRon 1 was in southern Japanese waters while the rest of it was at Yokosuka, refitting. It was under command of Capt. Hanku Sasaki. About October 21 he was suddenly ordered to take *I-22* from Saeki Bay, Kyushu, to Kure Naval Arsenal, for installation of "special fittings."

"We left that same day," he told me, "and had no sooner moored at Kure than a dozen technicians came on board. They began making sketches of *I-22*'s after deck. Naturally I was curious, and asked them what they were doing. But they just muttered something about 'special work,' and went on about their business."

No warship's commander is going to let things be done to his vessel unless he knows what they are. So Capt. Sasaki took Cdr. Kiyotake Ageta, skipper of *I-22*, along with him to 6th Fleet headquarters to find out what was happening.

"There we learned for the first time," he said, "of the midget submarine, and that it was to be transported and launched from Fleet-type boats. No one else was told at that time. Both of us were tremendously surprised. Even though we were submarine men, neither of us had ever heard of the 'special underwater attack craft.' That's what the midgets were called."

Between June and September (after Lt. Iwasa had his talk with Lt. Cdr. Ariizumi) several approaches were made to Adm. Yamamoto with the proposal that midgets be launched from submarines, rather than from *Chiyoda* and her sister ships. Then, in September, Iwasa and several other young officers were able to arrange for a personal meeting with the admiral. Yamamoto was a gambler at heart, and partial both to aggresive spirits and novel ideas. But he was a realist, too. He had no use for futile sacrifice of men who could fight again. Yamamoto finally approved inclusion of midget submarines in his Pearl Harbor plan, but made it a requirement that the midget pilots were to be rescued after their mission was completed.

Yamamoto's decision to include the midgets was made in October barely leaving time to complete construction arrangements. *I-22* was the first submarine ordered into Kure for alterations. *I-16, I-18,* and *I-20* arrived a few days later. On Oct. 31 a fifth submarine, *I-24,* was completed at Sasebo, our third major fleet base. She was immediately ordered into Kure, without any shakedown or sea trials.

Five pilots for the midgets reported aboard the submarines. They were Lt. Naoji Iwasa (*I-22*), Lt. (j.g.) Masaharu

24

Yokoyama (*I-16*), Lt. (j.g.) Shigemi Haruno (*I-18*), Ens. Akira Hiroo (*I-20*), and Ens. Kazuo Sakamaki (*I-24*). On Nov. 13-14, division commander Sasaki, the commanding officers of the five submarines, and the midget pilots received a full briefing on the proposed mission.

The submarines were to depart Kure early on Nov. 18, stop at Ourazaki to load midgets, and depart that same evening on a direct course for Pearl Harbor. The five would travel in line abreast with 20 miles between ships, and the flagship, *I-22*, in the center. While within 600 miles of Wake and Midway, they would travel submerged during the daytime to avoid detection by patrol planes. They were scheduled to arrive at a point roughly 100 miles south of Pearl Harbor after sunset, two days before the date tentatively set for opening the war. Under cover of protective darkness, the submarines would surface so the midget craft could be given a final, thorough check. All five Fleet-type submarines were then to start moving in, until they would be 5-10 miles off Pearl Harbor's entrance. There, they would be arranged in an arc in the same formation (left to right; *I-16*, *I-24*, *I-22*, *I-18*, *I-20*) they had maintained while crossing the Pacific.

Beginning from the left, *I-16* would launch her midget three hours before sunrise. The others would follow at 30-minute intervals. *I-20*'s midget, the last, was to pass through the harbor's entrance 30 minutes before sunrise. All midgets were to drop to the bottom, and lie there until the air attack began. Then they were to rise and join in contributing to the enemy's general confusion and overall damage with their 10 torpedoes. Each pilot had the option, however, of letting the air attack pass, and waiting until dark to rise and fight. After making his attack, at whatever time, each pilot was then to circle Ford Island in the center of Pearl Harbor, keeping it to his left, and depart the harbor. It was felt that the antisubmarine net would pose no problem at that point because of enemy ships running to safety in the open sea. Surely, it would be open for them. Once outside the harbor, the midget pilots were to steer for the predesignated pickup point.

Mother submarines, after launching midgets, were to clear the area. They were to move off as quickly as possible to a point 7 miles off the western tip of Lanai Island in the Hawaiian chain. They would take positions about one mile apart there, and scuttle each midget as its crew was recovered.

At the time of the briefings, the five petty officers who would serve as crewmen in the midget submersibles knew nothing of the plan. They were Naoharu Sasaki (*I-22*), Teiji

Ueda (*I-16*), Harunori Yokoyama (*I-18*), Yoshio Katayama (*I-20*), and Kiyoshi Inagaki (*I-24*). The quintet were given the details later, on the way out from Japan.

"On November 14," Capt. Sasaki later said, "we were visited by Captain Takayasu Arima, the torpedo staff member at Combined Fleet Headquarters. He came with an urgent message from Admiral Yamamoto. The commander-in-chief wanted it positively understood that under no conditions were the midgets' pilots to *force* their way into Pearl Harbor. Everything had to be ideal for them, or else they were to abandon the penetration attempt and retreat to the pickup point. Adm. Yamamoto didn't want to lose the element of surprise just because some young officer became eager for glory. Captain Arima also passed on another order. Everyone involved was to direct his every effort toward rescuing the midget submarine crews, after the attack."

Once underway, Capt. Sasaki found his mind full of worries. He was very concerned about *I-24*, which was only 18 days in commission when she loaded her midgets on board. There hadn't been time for *I-24* to have a shakedown cruise and pass the Fleet acceptance tests. Any of a hundred things could go wrong with her, things that under normal conditions would have been detected, and remedied. If she broke down enroute to Pearl Harbor, she would simply have to be left stranded in mid-Pacific. With radio silence being strictly enforced, she could not communicate with her sister ships, nor they with her.

Hardly any foreigners, and very few Japanese, truly recognize what a tremendous gamble the attack on Pearl Harbor really was. Four of the submarines employed in the operation were completed only weeks before they sailed. The aircraft carrier *Zuikaku* was brand-new. She finished her shakedown cruise only 7 weeks before she left for the attack. And the 1st Air Fleet's aerial torpedoes, which had to be fitted with special fins that would let them run in the shallow waters of Pearl Harbor without nosing into its muddy bottom, were barely ready in time for use. One of the six aircraft carriers, in fact, was actually delayed more than 48 hours in sailing until these aerial torpedoes were delivered on board. Add things like these to the necessity of the Nagumo's force having to navigate most of the way without benefit of celestial observations, and having to refuel enroute in some of the world's worst weather, it seems a miracle that the attack was the success it turned out to be.

On Nov. 20, flagship *I-22* passed Hachijojima, an island well south of Tokyo Bay, giving Lt. Iwasa and Petty Officer Sasaki, crew of the midget submarine, the last view of their homeland that they would get. Each submarine sailed eastward on its lonely way, out of sight and sound of its sisters in the Special Underwater Attack Force. Once inside the patrol areas of Wake and Midway aircraft, no one in those five submarines could see anything but the clouds and green seas as viewed through periscopes. The seas broke over the periscopes constantly, so the horizon was rarely seen. In the evenings, when the submarines surfaced to recharge batteries, replenish air supplies, and make repairs, the clouded view was just as monotonous. Special maintenance men went out on deck nightly, assisted by midget sub crew members, to check the condition of the midgets, a task made extremely difficult by the frightful weather. All had to wear lifelines about their waists.

Cdr. Hiroshi Hanabusa, whose submarine *I-24* was to distinguish itself later with midget attacks at Sydney, Australia, and in the Solomon Islands, probably had the worst time of any of the 30 submarine captains. At one point the forward section of his air pressure system refused to work, almost causing the submarine to sink. This was an item that would have been discovered early on any shakedown cruise, but *I-24* had come straight from her construction berth to Kure, for fitting of the midget submarine rack before sailing eastward. So, during a routine dive, the boat refused to answer when Hanabusa ordered forward air tanks partially blown to level her off. She kept going down by the bow. She was out of control, and almost past her safety depth when Lt. Mochitsura Hashimoto, her executive officer, (who was to sink USS *Indianapolis* during the last weeks of the war,) managed to hammer open the control valve that freed air to blow the forward ballast tank free of water. Once this was done, the submarine was able to regain the surface.

On board Capt. Sasaki's flagship, pioneer midget sub pilot Iwasa was nearly lost overboard. Determined to make certain that his submersible was in top condition, Lt. Iwasa ran out on deck without a lifeline. He was saved by pure luck, frantically reaching out and clutching a section of the mounting rack while a giant wave was sweeping him from the submarine's deck. Capt. Sasaki angrily ordered him not to show his face on deck again until *I-22* reached its launch point.

Except for Iwasa and Lt. Saburo Akieda, who would later attack a British battleship at Madagascar, no man in the midget submarine program was a volunteer. All others, including the petty officers, were routinely ordered to midget submarine training by the Navy Ministry. All, however, were hand-picked. Akieda and Iwasa began training in earnest during the fall of 1940. They were joined by 10 other officers and 24 petty officers the following spring, when enough midgets were on hand to move ahead with practice missions. Men were selected for midget submarines only if they were superior physical specimens, showed evidence of determined temperament, were single, and had light family responsibilities. Ens. Kazuo Sakamaki, of *I-24*, for example, was one of eight sons. Should he die in battle, it was reasoned that there would be seven sons still remaining to revere their parents and carry on the family name.

In spite of countless hardships endured along the way, both the 1st Air Fleet, which had several men washed overboard, and the Advance Submarine Force arrived at designated stations on schedule. But the attack almost missed fire.

All six aircraft carriers were pitching so badly in heavy seas 230 miles north of Pearl Harbor that Admiral Nagumo gave orders none of the cumbersome torpedo planes would be launched. He was afraid they would roll off downward-sloping flight decks right into the sea, or would not have enough power for an uphill takeoff when the carrier's bows reached for the skies again. This caused a great outcry among the pilots. They had been flying 12 hours a day for weeks, much of their training being done at Kagoshima, my birthplace, near the southern tip of Kyushu. All were eager to get into battle.

Nagumo changed his mind after some violent urging by his aviation advisors, and torpedo bombers flew in the Pearl Harbor attack. They did extensive damage. The battleship strength of America's Pacific fleet suffered badly at their hands. This would not have been the case had not Nagumo been influenced to change his mind at the last moment, which is more evidence that the plan to attack Pearl Harbor rested on many small straws. Failure of just a few would have made this daring attack a disaster, rather than the resounding success it became.

At midnight of December 6 (American time), all submarines were in position. The 14 submarines from Yokosuka were to the north of Oahu, ranged roughly in three concentric arcs. *I-15* was in the center arc. The outer ring was composed of *I-19*, *I-21*, and *I-23*. They were still screening for the Nagumo force, and also standing by as warning sentries. They had the additional duty of providing rescue for any pilots who crash-landed in the sea after the air attack. Like the rest of us, they were also supposed to intercept and sink any American warships that escaped the bombs and torpedoes of our sea eagles at Pearl Harbor.

The assault on Pearl Harbor is usually referred to as a "sneak attack." The truth is hard to determine. But, on December 7, 1941, as I took my turn at *I-15*'s periscope, I was doing so in the belief that Japan would mount an overwhelming attack on the U.S. Pacific Fleet just minutes or hours *after* a declaration of war had been handed the American government in Washington, D.C. This belief is still held by some former Imperial Navy officers. Maybe, as some writers have argued, the assault *became* a sneak attack only because American officials who, through code-breaking, already knew what Ambassador Nomura was going to tell them, delayed his meeting with Secretary of State Cordell Hull. Or because Nomura's staff took so long decoding the lengthy message sent him from Tokyo. Foreign and Japanese writers have often pointed out that had Nomura been able to deliver his ultimatum from Tokyo on schedule, Mr. Hull would have known that a state of war existed about 30 minutes before Cdr. Mitsuo Fuchida, flying from carrier *Akagi,* gave the command "Attack! All planes go in!" at Pearl Harbor.

The argument will probably continue among historians for generations. Except, perhaps, British ones. To the old argument I would like to add a quote from *The War with Japan.* Published by Her Majesty's Stationery Office, it is Great Britain's official naval history of the Pacific War, and contains the statement: "Governments brought face to face with the grim possibility of national subjugation are irclined to pay small heed to the niceties of international law." In other words, the British, knowing that America, Britain and Holland had shut off Japan's foreign funds and her oil supplies, were surprised that Americans could be indignant about Japan's reaction.

In any case, by midnight of the day before the attack, there were also 12 submarines arrayed in two arcs to the south of Oahu. The five midget carriers were creeping to within 10 miles of Pearl Harbor's entrance. Well beyond and behind them were *I-168, I-169, I-170, I-171, I-172, I-173,* and *I-175. I-8,* fitted as flagship and carrying extensive communications equipment stood to the southwest of these boats. In Kauai Channel, well northwest of Oahu, was *I-174.* She roamed back and forth on lonely sentry duty, watching for American aircraft carriers thought to be westward of Oahu.

Cdr. Yasuchika Kayahara, in *I-10,* had sighted an American cruiser but nothing else below the Equator. He could have sunk her easily had he not been ordered to pass up any attack until X-Day. Cdr. Minoru Yokota, in *I-26*, had checked the Aleutians. He was now enroute to the Seattle area, and would shortly make the first Japanese submarine kill of World War II. *I-15* was still on the surface, awaiting the sunrise, when I went to bed. I could not sleep. So, after much tossing and turning, I arose and went to the conning tower. I was still there when *I-15* submerged leaving only its periscope and radio antenna above water. We waited anxiously for a signal that meant the surprise attack had been brought off.

The submarines of the Special Underwater Attack Force had surfaced shortly after sunset, and boldly moved in. They could see lights at Waikiki and on the hillside behind it very clearly, twinkling brightly in the blackness. On board all five subs, as in most of the task force, listeners to wireless sets could hear all-night jazz music coming from radio station KGMB, Honolulu. Fuchida's pilots would use it later for a homing beam to bring them over their target from the aircraft carriers. On board *I-22*, Cdr. Ageta's lookouts could see red and green lights, marking the opening to Pearl Harbor. They could also watch the sweep of headlights as automobiles wended their ways up and down the hills of Honolulu.

Around 3 A.M. pilots and crewmen began getting into their midgets. Each solemnly thanked the crew of the submarine that carried him out from Japan, as well as the pair of specially trained technicians sent along to keep his weapon in perfect condition. Then, bowing to senior officers, each pilot got into his midget. After that the submarines dipped slightly below the surface. Now only a telephone communications and a battery charge line tied each midget to its mother submarine. Capt. Sasaki teased Lt. Iwasa as the pilot and his crewman got into *I-22's* midget. "Are you sure you can get inside with that thing sticking from your waist?" he asked, pointing at the special short sword Iwasa was carrying. Iwasa, a white *hachimaki* tied tightly about his forehead to signify his great resolve, and a faint scent of perfume coming from his uniform, took this in good humor. He spoke his last words over the telephone line to Lt. Tetsuaki Sugamasa, navigator for *I-22*. "Take care of my belongings," he told him, "I left them all bundled up." Then, at the appointed time, he started his motor and was cast loose to carry out his mission.

At 3:30 A.M., Tokyo time, which was 10 minutes before 8 o'clock at Honolulu, the signal for which thousands of men in the task force waited came over the wireless. From Cdr. Mitsuo Fuchida's bomber, 10,000 feet over Pearl Harbor, all ships could clearly hear the signal "dot-dot-dash, dot-dot-dash" repeated many times. In our code this was *"To . . . To . . . To . . ."* the word to attack. Three minutes later it was followed by the message "We have succeeded in a surprise attack at 3:23 A.M."

As other writers have told, the signal carried, possibly through some atmospheric freak, all the way to Japan's Inland Sea, where wireless operators on board Adm. Yamamoto's flagship picked it up. On board *I-15* my commanding officer kept saying over and over again, "This is good! This is good!" and ordered me to pass the word throughout the boat.

I did. The crew went wild. I could hear *"banzai's"* ringing everywhere. Men were shouting at the tops of their lungs, throwing their arms around one another, and weeping for joy. It is characteristic of my countrymen that their tears flow freely on occasions when they are filled with a sudden happiness, almost as freely as when they are suddenly sad. That is the way it was with the men of *I-15,* including myself, at that moment.

This excitement soon stopped. All of us became intent upon listening to the American radio, especially the naval circuits. Our monitoring had picked up only coded messages to that moment. Now messages were being transmitted thick and fast in plain language. Obviously there was a great deal of confusion on the ground and in the ships at Pearl Harbor. I found myself wistfully wishing I were on board one of the special attack submarines. They had front row seats. I later heard that they saw massive explosions, and a great pall of black smoke rise over the enemy base. They also heard depth charge explosions nearby, and feared for the five midget submarines launched hours earlier.

As near as I have been able to determine only one of our midgets managed to get inside Pearl Harbor. Two may have, however. I think that the first midget pilot, Lt. (j.g.) Masaharu Yokoyama, from *I-16* got inside safely, only to be sunk after firing his torpedoes at a destroyer tender and a destroyer. *USS Monaghan* sank her. The U. S. destroyer *Ward* definitely sank a midget submarine, which appears to have been Lt. Iwasa's. *Ward* sighted a midget trying to follow the tug Antares through the harbor entrance while Antares had a barge in tow. Yokoyama and Petty Officer Teiji Ueda were still inside the hull when it was used as fill material near the submarine base's bachelor officers' quarters, where a new dock was constructed a short time later.

Next to approach was Ens. Kazuo Sakamaki of *I-24,* who had trouble with his gyroscope on being launched. He ran aground on a reef off the harbor entrance, and was shelled by a destroyer. Through a stroke of good fortune he slipped off the reef, leaving the destroyer gunners convinced they had sunk him. Damage had been done to *I-24's* midget, though, and the crewmen were overcome by fumes from their batteries when sea water seeped inside the hull. They tried to make it back to the rendezvous, but had to abandon their craft off the north side of Oahu when their batteries gave out. Petty Officer Kiyoshi Inagaki drowned, and Sakamaki barely made it to shore where he passed out. He became the first Japanese fighting man to pass through San Francisco's Golden Gate a little later, but he did it with the marking "Prisoner of War No. 1" on the back of his shirt.

Iwasa's was almost surely the midget sunk by destroyer *Ward* outside Pearl Harbor. Thus, as Adm. Yamamoto had feared, a midget was detected before the hour set for attack. Yet, by the time the word got to Admiral Kimmel, commander of the U. S. Pacific Fleet, our aircraft were nearly all over their targets.

It is remotely possible that either Ens. Akira Hiroo *(I-20)* or Lt. (j.g.) Shigemo Haruno *(I-18)* got inside Pearl Harbor. They were the last two midgets away, and it is known that the Americans left their antisubmarine net open from well before the time of the attack until well after it was over. Perhaps one or both of them also got out. Official reports show that American warships did attack submarines close to Pearl Harbor after Fuchida's planes had gone back to their ships. And we had no large submarines near Pearl Harbor by that time. All five had retreated to the rendezvous point.

After the attack, the Nagumo task force ran northwestward as fast as it could, to escape possible enemy counterattack from the air. We in submarines grew tense. Our moment was supposed to come now. *I-15* surfaced after sunset on the war's first day, and kept a sharp lookout for ships from Pearl Harbor, but sighted none to the north of Oahu. So, at sunrise of the second day we submerged once again, rising once more when the sky was dark. The second day after the attack was a repetition of the day before. Until the evening.

I-6, under Cdr. Tsuso Inaba, sighted an aircraft carrier and two cruisers, heading northeast, USS *Enterprise* and her escort. Cdr. Inaba radioed his sighting to Vice Adm. Shimizu who had moved his 6th Fleet headquarters, the old cruiser *Katori*, to Kwajalein, in the Marshalls. Shimizu's reaction was prompt. "All submarines of SubRon 1," he messaged us, "except those of the Special Underwater Attack Force, will pursue and sink the *Enterprise*-class aircraft carrier."

On board *I-15*, we were jubilant. We were among those ordered to chase the carrier. After three days of no action, it looked as if we were getting into the war at last.

* * *

Chapter 3.

FROM SAN FRANCISCO TO CEYLON.

I-9, *I-17*, *I-19*, *I-21*, *I-23*, and *I-25* set out after the American aircraft carrier *Enterprise*, and our *I-15* came to the surface at once to join the chase. We worked up to 22 knots in pursuit, but never spotted anything. Some of the other submarines got into firing range of the *Enterprise*. Torpedoes were fired at her on two different days, one missing her by only 60 feet. This was a preview of what lay in store for other American carriers. Our submarines would do well in combat against them.

I-170, under Takashi Sano, was lost during the pursuit. An *Enterprise* plane, on patrol, swooped down swiftly and bombed the submarine on the morning of Dec. 10. Enough damage was done so that Cdr. Sano dared not submerge his boat, and another *Enterprise* plane found him on the surface trying to make repairs in the afternoon. Cdr. Sano, who'd been fortunate enough to survive the sinking of *I-63* nearly three years before, went down with his ship and crew.

To that point, the submarines in the 6th Fleet had nothing

to show for their eastern strike except the American merchantman *Cynthia Olson*. Cdr. Minoru Yokota, in *I-26*, sank this 2140-ton vessel about 750 miles northwest of Seattle on the day war began. Four days later another of our submarines got SS *Lahaina*, 5600 tons, between Oahu and San Francisco. *I-9* was victor in that encounter. *I-10* sank SS *Donnyvale*, 4473 tons, on Dec. 9, on her way north to the U.S. west coast.

On Dec. 14 the submarines that were chasing USS *Enterprise* were ordered to continue on to the west coast of the U.S. There the seven of us, plus *I-10* and *I-26*, were assigned patrol stations in order to attack enemy shipping. It was our job to cut off any supplies and reinforcements destined for Pearl Harbor, where enemy losses had been great. *I-15* took station west of the Farallon Islands, off San Francisco.

On December 17, through my binoculars I could see the glow cast upon the sky by the lights of San Francisco, and thought to myself, "They certainly don't act like there is a war going on, allowing such illumination to silhouette their shipping along the coast." Capt. Hiroshi Imazato, who commanded the first division of SubRon 1, was on the bridge also, chatting with Cdr. Ishikawa. "I've never been to America," he said, jokingly. "If we weren't at war, this would be an excellent chance to pass in through the Golden Gate and visit that famous city of San Francisco."

Our *I-15* was one of 11 boats in the Pearl Harbor force that carried an airplane, so I interrupted the conversation of my two seniors. "Sir," I said to Capt. Imazato, "if you wish, we could launch our aircraft. That would give you an excellent chance to do some sight-seeing." They both laughed and joked about it for quite a while, which shows how high our spirits were in those early days.

There were no light reflections in the sky the following night. Somehow the Americans had learned of our presence. We heard a number of patrol boats, and our radiomen listened in on many plain-language uncoded message exchanges. This made it easy for us to dodge the hunters. We were on station for 8 days, but made neither a sighting nor an attack during that time. Other submarines fared better. Cdr. Kozo Nishino's *I-17* claimed two cargo ship sinkings. Cdr. Kanji Matsumura's *I-21* also claimed a pair. Cdr. Genichi Shibata's *I-23* attacked a small patrol boat in full view of spectators on shore at Monterey, California. Cdr. Meiji Tagami's *I-25* chased a large merchantman right into the Columbia River, Oregon, where it ran aground. Besides these reported kills our submarines made hits on other ships which managed to limp away. One of our subs, off Long Beach, California, reported many people sunning beneath colorful beach umbrellas, as though they'd never heard of a war. This same submarine reported that its crewmen on deck could read print at night by the lights of automobile headlights on the shore. Such things made Japanese navy men contemptuous of Americans at the war's start.

A few days after we got on station, *I-15* and other submarines received a wireless from Vice Adm. Shimizu. We were to depart our patrol areas on Christmas Day and return to Kwajalein, where he had his headquarters. But first he had a special present he wanted delivered to America—all the rounds of 4.7" amunition we could pour out of our deck guns. All nine submarines were to shell the mainland, *I-15's* target being San Francisco. On December 24, just hours before *I-15* was to commence its bombardment, this order was countermanded by one from Tokyo, sent by Adm. Osami Nagano. I never learned the reason why. So it was "bows west" for *I-15* next day, without having hurt the enemy at all.

Nor had much been accomplished by our subs that remained in the Pearl Harbor area. On December 17 and 18 they sank two merchantmen, SS *Prusa* and SS *Manini*, *I-172* getting the first and *I-175* the second, but the great bag of warships envisioned by Admiral Shimizu never materialized. The submarines that launched midgets never recovered any of them, and had to be content with shelling Maui, Hawaii, and Johnson Island. Chief accomplishment in Hawaiian waters was brought off by *I-7*. At dawn on the 16th, she launched her Type 96 float plane and sent it over Pearl Harbor for reconnaissance. What the pilot and his observer saw confirmed the reports by Cdr. Fuchida's fliers nine days earlier. Five American battleships, including USS *Utah,* were sunk and many ships in the harbor had been damaged, besides the airplanes destroyed. The Pacific battle fleet of the U.S. was no more. At least for a good long while.

The reconnaissance aircraft landed alongside *I-7* and its crew swam to the submarine which dived at once, abandoning the aircraft. Information was more important, especially since it confirmed a great victory. Later, we were amused that American authorities held back the truth about the damage inflicted at Pearl Harbor for a very long time. It was not a secret in Japan. We had full details, including pictures, right from the start.

Unusual about *I-7's* great coup was the way her aircraft was launched. She was the first submarine of our Navy designed completely by our own people. Her aircraft catapult was mounted aft of her conning tower, and her plane launched over her stern. Whenever there was not enough wind to give the aircraft flying speed, *I-7* had to head into the wind, to "make" enough relative wind for the plane to take off. But she had to run *in reverse* to do this. So it was on December 16, 1941, nine days after an all-out attack by our 1st Air Fleet, that the defenses of Pearl Harbor supposedly thorough-alert by now, were penetrated again, this time by a slow-flying biplane, after it was launched from a backward-churning submarine!

Wake Island was attacked and captured while *I-15* was off San Francisco. Submarines played no role in this fighting, except to act as sentries for ships that shelled Wake and unloaded assault troops there. An American relief force, centered on the carrier *Saratoga,* approached the island from the east, but was summoned back when only a day's cruising from strike position. The official U.S. naval history of the war, which is replete with errors, criticizes the admiral responsible for this decision, but he may have made a wise one. The American antisubmarine technique at that time was very poor, though it would be refined to a great art later. Our RO-Class submarines, under Rear Adm. Shinzo Onishi, might have had an unpleasant surprise waiting for *Saratoga* and company. Twice in the war our submarines would put *Saratoga* out of action for long periods, with their torpedoes. Those early days of the war might have seen them sink her had she come much closer to Wake Island!

Two submarines scouting and covering for the force taking Wake Island collided in close maneuvers on Dec. 17. *RO-66* hit *RO-62,* commanded by Lt. Hideyuki Kurokawa, not far from Wake, but most of the latter's crew were saved before the submarine went down. And 14 days later *RO-60,* arriving at Kwajalein in very bad weather, ran aground with such force that she split her hull and had to be abandoned. All hands were saved, though, and lived to fight again. At the close of 1941, the 6th Fleet had lost three submarines—*I-170, RO-60,* and *RO-66.* These losses didn't seem damaging. At the time we had 29 additions to the 6th Fleet under construction.

RO-Class submarines operated against Howland and Baker Islands, and in the Solomons area. In the western ocean areas, our Army and Navy were meeting with success after success. They had taken Hong Kong on Dec. 25, and our troops were ashore in the Philippines and doing well. Roads on the Malay Peninsula were few and bad, but a bicycle with a man on it needs only about a foot-wide path. Our infantry carried bicycles that could be disassembled and folded into a small package, as Occupation troops who purchased them after the war found out. These carried Japan's land forces across the swampy, marshy areas Great Britain had counted upon to provide a barrier against any enemy marching on the Singapore bastion by land. Meanwhile at sea, Japanese submarines played a singular role in an event that had "battleship admirals" rubbing their eyes in disbelief when they read of it.

The 30 submarines sent eastward, and the 9 in the Mandated Islands, left 18 available for use in the southern areas, which were marked for Japan's main advance. All four boats in SubRon 6 were minelaying types, old and slow, and definitely not considered choice duty by submariners. They were *I-121*, *I-122*, *I-123*, and *I-124*, under Rear Adm. Chimaki Kono. They laid mines off Singapore just as the war began, and claimed the sinking of one merchantman in that area. Then they moved off to the Philippines, in support of our troops landing there.

The other 14 submarines in the south included 8 of SubRon 4, under Rear Adm. Etuzo Yoshitomi, and 6 of SubRon 5, under Rear Adm. Tadashige Daigo. All had the same triple mission: protect Japanese Army troops wherever landed; patrol waters off the Malay Peninsula; and attack enemy ships as they appeared. Two of these submarines, in SubRon 5, hurried the end of HMS *Repulse* and HMS *Prince of Wales*, the "striking force" sent to the Far East by Churchill, as part of an anti-Japanese agreement made between the U. S. and Great Britain many months before the war started. These battleships were to join up with American and Dutch forces, and crush any southward Japanese naval movement.

The striking force was weaker than had originally been intended. HMS *Indomitable*, a British aircraft carrier, was to have been part of it. But she ran aground at Kingston, Jamaica, on Nov. 3 and had to be put into drydock. So Rear Adm. Tom Philips of the Royal Navy had only two capital ships and no naval air power when he reached the Far East. He was heading for Singapore when the U. S. aircraft carrier arrived at Capetown, South Africa, as escort to 20,000 British troops. *The Ranger*, 2 cruisers, and 8 destroyers had accompanied 6 transports from Halifax, leaving there nearly a month *before* war began. America (supposedly at peace) provided safe conduct for troops of a nation at war, troops who could only be employed in war against Japan!

Philips took his two battleships into Singapore, left them

there, and flew at once to Manila for conferences with Adm. Thomas Hart, commander of the U. S. Asiatic Fleet. Philips was very worried about having no screening force except for a few escorts for his capital ships. But, as he was leaving Manila, Hart told him that four American destroyers were refueling at Balikpapan, Borneo. They were supposed to top off their tanks and head for Batavia, Java, for a period of rest and recreation, but had been putting off their departure under various pretexts. When they did leave, Hart told Philips, they would secretly steam north to join *Prince of Wales* and *Repulse*. Under the ruse of "joint maneuvers," a strongly escorted Striking Force would thus be formed, ready to challenge any Japanese naval movement southward. The scheme of the two flag officers did not work out. Philips was dead and his two great ships sunk before the American destroyers reached Singapore.

When "Tom Thumb," (as British sailors called him because of his diminutive stature) arrived back at Singapore, he learned that a British plane had sighted a large Japanese convoy steaming west across the Gulf of Siam, north of Singapore, heading for Thailand. This was our invasion force, which had rounded the southern tip of Indochina. Philips knew he'd have very little air cover to defend him from the planes we had stationed around Saigon, but he dared not wait. He couldn't allow an invasion landing to be successful. He slipped out of Singapore, ran east for a while in the hope of confusing our navy, then headed north. He hoped to catch our invasion fleet while it still stood off the beaches on the east coast of the peninsula, landing troops.

Philips' feint to the east did him little good. Within 24 hours of sailing, he was sighted by *I-156,* Cdr. Hakue Harada. At about 3 P.M. on Dec. 9, the two battleships appeared in Harada's periscope. He surfaced after they passed and radioed their position to our Indochina land-based planes. Somewhere in the coding, transmission, decoding, and transcribing, a mistake was made. The positions the air squadrons got was 07-00N, 105-00E. This almost caused our search planes to attack our Covering Force, which was trailing our own convoy, ready to attack anything that challenged it.

But another submarine captain, Lt. Cdr. Katsuo Ohashi, in *I-156,* sighted the two battleships about 13 hours later. By then Philips had given up hope of catching the convoy, which had unloaded its troops and departed. He was steaming south when Ohashi saw him, at too high a speed for a torpedo attack to be made. When this second sighting was reported, pilots took off at first light. Ten hours after Ohashi's sighting, the great behemoths were at the bottom of the sea. Our Navy planes had flown twice the distance any other country thought bombers could to sink them. American pilots would not make a strike as long-reaching as this for several years. Our training had paid off with Japan's winning control of all the waters around Malaya and the Philippines. And battleships were finished as the backbone of modern fleets. Though Great Britain and America built numbers of them during the war, and Japan completed *Yamato's* sister ship, *Musashi,* no battleship would accomplish anything of significance during the Pacific naval war. Submarines and aircraft would write the story.

I-15 arrived at Kwajalein on Jan. 15 from the American coast. Until then our contribution to the war effort had been exactly zero. Our crew was cheerful, though. In spite of a very rough first Pacific crossing that had wrecked some submarine-borne aircraft, the success of 1st Air Fleet's smash at Pearl Harbor buoyed us up during weeks that passed without any major accomplishments by 6th Fleet submarines. At a conference held on board *Katori* the day we arrived at Kwajalein, the total result of our efforts was summed up. My squadron was credited with 11 ships sunk, 2 damaged. SubRon 2 was credited with 4 sunk, 1 damaged. This last was the carrier *Saratoga,* into which *I-6* had put a torpedo on Jan. 10, about 500 miles southwest of Pearl Harbor. This ship (much feared because our aircraft had not found her present at Pearl Harbor on Dec. 7) was put out of action for five months. She missed the Battle of Midway.

SubRon 3 was credited with 2 ships sunk, against the loss of *I-170.* The total of 17 sinkings and 3 ships damaged, compared with German successes in the Atlantic, was not considered impressive. Vice Adm. Shimizu was much dismayed and others who were with him at the conference expressed the same disappointment. Yet, some who were present concentrated on discussing the poor antisubmarine tactics of the American navy and ridiculing poor American marksmanship. The conference decided that Japanese submarines should in the future be used mainly for the destruction of enemy supply ships. The previous strategy of sending us against warships was to be discarded. We would pay dearly for the change.

Crew rest was the order of the day for all submarines upon first arriving at Kwajalein. My check of *I-15* turned up a surprising fact. In eight weeks of cruising, we'd not had a single case of illness, injury, or a maintenance problem of more than minor importance. Though fresh water must be conserved on submarines, my records showed that I'd been able to allow our men showers every three days, and washing of underwear every five. The war would later change this, but at the moment morale was high. "Except for no drinking or recreation," said one crew member, "I prefer wartime cruising to peacetime." Everyone, thinking back on the long, difficult fleet exercises and the days-on-end weariness, had to agree with him. Hard training had cost us three submarines, since 1939, and there had been many cases of collisions and near-collisions as 6th Fleet boats slipped beneath escort screens during maneuvers, to "attack" our capital ships. Surface ships had also suffered collisions during the night practice drills the Imperial Navy concentrated on so much. Our aircraft losses were greater, in peacetime, than any other nation's due to intensive training that often saw pilots in the air as long as 12 hours per day. Now, with the war at last started, life seemed far less difficult than in those days.

Our lookouts were as alert as ever, for example, but less tense. They felt they knew their jobs, and could do them well. A ship spotted on the horizon *now* would not have a Fleet "umpire" on board it, but rather a ready gun crew. And an airplane sighted would no longer be a friendly one from Iwakuni or Atsugi, but one whose crew wanted to sink us.

Yasukuni Maru, a former liner making European runs, had been converted to a submarine tender. She was in company with *Katori* at Kwajalein, and crews of all submarines were treated to hot baths on board her. Pure hot water and soap can provide one of a man's most thrilling experiences, especially when he has been confined within a stuffy steel tube with 100 other sweaty, dirty, smelly human beings. Showers can never get a man as clean as our old-fashioned Japanese bath. We scrubbed ourselves immaculate first, using small buckets and soap, then rinsed ourselves off with hot water, using the same buckets. After that, we lowered ourselves into a deep *ofuro* with a long, drawn-out "Aaaaaaaaaah!" of pure contentment. While I lay there, letting the heat soak to the marrow of my bones, I thought of my wife and infant son in Japan.

My first-born son, Shuichi, came into the world on July 28, 1941, while *I-15* was still on maneuvers in the Mandated Islands, preparing for the day when we might have to defend those islands against an enemy. On arrival at Yokosuka, I had no chance to visit my family. My duties as executive officer were too many and important to allow me time away from the ship. It was a 30-hour train ride via the fastest express to Kagoshima, where they were. I had to settle for an evening of *sake* celebration at the officers' club with Minoru Yonehara,

Toshisada Tokutomi and Seihachi Toyomasu, fellow sub-mariners and lieutenants who had been my classmates at Eta-jima.

Later, when *I-15* went to Kure for a while, I strongly urged Hisako to come and visit me, although our son was only weeks old. We Oritas had three quick-passing days in a Kure hotel together, and now I had only pictures of my wife and son to re-mind me of home. It was bitter (just as it would be many other times during the war) to think as I lay in that tub that I had let nearly six years pass for Hisako and myself between our *Omiai* (first confrontation) and our marriage in 1939. Those extra half-dozen years would have given me hundreds more sweet memories to carry to war with me.

The baths were followed by a motion picture, and a dinner consisting of fresh foods. Both were pure delights to men who'd had only one another to look at and who had been eating out of tins since before taking station off Pearl Harbor. I have read that on board American submarines during the war the food was truly delicious, and that great pains were taken in selecting cooks, as well as menus, to make it so. In our submarines we had better than average food, but nothing like what the Americans had. During the third year of the war great emphasis was placed by 6th Fleet headquarters on our men getting special food. Before that, men sometimes suffered mild cases of beri beri on long cruises, in spite of vitamin injec-tions.

After a few days of rest, I started *I-15's* men on the task of readying our boat for her next sortie. The hull, weapons, and engines received a thorough going over. This is much harder to do at a mid-ocean atoll than at a home shipyard, where the skills and tools of civilian workers can be employed. No wonder Lt. Cdr. Yahachi Tanabe, after he had sunk the U. S. aircraft carrier *Yorktown* at Midway and was awarded a new submarine to command, asked especially for crewmen who had plenty of civilian mechanical experience to be assigned to his boat. He got them, and as a result survived in *I-176* what should have been certain death from the guns of American ships. I'll tell of that, later.

Repair and maintenance, including a new coat of black paint for *I-15's* hull, kept the crew busy when they were not on air raid watch. We expected enemy aircraft carriers to make some kind of thrust before long. When they came, we wanted to be ready. Tokyo was very worried about *Lexington, Yorktown, Saratoga,* and *Enterprise*. The submarine who sank one of them would receive great honors.

Before that happened, Jan. 17 arrived with it a flood of orders from Tokyo that caused a general shuffling of 6th Fleet officers. Many new submarines were scheduled for completion in 1942. All would need commanding officers. I was one of those selected to take the commanding officers' course at submarine school. This was a double thrill for me. It meant I would soon be commanding my own boat, something I'd been hoping for since my days as a lower classman at the Naval Academy. It also meant I would have some time with my family. Perhaps Shuichi would get to know his father this time. And I would have a chance to enjoy reading, walking, and seeing motion pictures with Hisako, three pastimes we both enjoyed very much. I also looked forward to my wife's fine meals.

My relief arrived at Kwajalein on Jan. 21. I spent two days turning over my post to him, then boarded *I-6* on Jan. 24 to leave for Japan. The return trip was pleasant, because her crew was so elated over their successful attack on the carrier *Saratoga*. That one blow had seriously weakened any move the Americans might make against our forces for a while. I also spent a lot of time conferring with *I-6*'s officers about our submarine operations to that date. We agreed that trying to approach enemy ports, the pre-war strategy, was practically hopeless with the enemy aroused and alert: the best thing to do was to attack merchantmen, without whose support warships in the Pacific could not operate for long. Mentioned frequently was the success Germany had been enjoying with these tactics for more than two years.

As soon as I got ashore in Yokosuka, I sent a hasty message to Hisako, asking her to join me at Kure with our baby. Then 16 of us headed south to submarine school. Before our classes started, we discussed over and over again what had been talked about at Kwajalein. Finally, we drafted our opinions as seconds-in-command into one statement and requested that the course we were going to study should give special attention to the following set of opinions.

"1. Our torpedoes are propelled by oxygen. They are very fast and give off no wake, but at shallow depth setting, especially at 6 or 7 feet, they often 'porpoise'. The enemy can see them and dodge, shifting at once to the counterattack, very dangerous to us. Also, our torpedoes have impact-type exploders, requiring a direct hit to detonate them. Torpedoes might be more effective if they had less speed, more shallow water stability, and a magnetic type exploder that would make them detonate beneath a ship if they passed under it.

"2. Torpedoes should be expended more liberally. At present the tendency is to fire only one or two if the target is a destroyer or cargo ship and to fire a full salvo only at a cruiser or larger vessel. This is foolish economy. It increases the enemy's chances of getting away. Also, though Intelligence has provided us much information about enemy warships, we possess very little about enemy merchant ships. This should be increased.

"3. Small ships are a submarine's worst enemy, being hard to hit and hardest to evade. When we reach the attack-practice portion of the course, small ships of high speed should be used for targets, also merchant ships when available. From our practice, we can develop proper tactics for use against these two types."

I-6 arrived at Yokosuka on Feb. 1, the same day an American task force under Rear Adm. William Halsey attacked the Marshall Islands. Fortunately for our submarines, Halsey's planes hit another part of Kwajalein atoll before hitting our base. That gave plenty of time for all submarines to "pull the plug" and drop to the lagoon's bottom. And, fortunately for Halsey, his carriers were a good distance from Kwajalein when his planes were launched. Otherwise they might have suffered the same fate as *Saratoga* or worse, because Halsey remained in one area for quite a long time. No submarines were damaged at Kwajalein, but our surface ships and the shops on shore suffered some. Admiral Shimizu was wounded, and eventually had to be relieved of command. Before that, he ordered all submarines present to find the enemy task force and sink it. They headed out on the surface at top speed, but none could catch up with Halsey's force. So most put about and returned to Kwajalein. *I-9* and *I-23* went to the Hawaii area. *I-17* went on to the west coast of the U. S. *I-25* came back, and shortly thereafter set out for the south seas. Her aircraft pilot, Warrant Flying Officer Nobuo Fujita, made flights over several enemy strong points, and brought back information that helped keep our high command informed of enemy warships' locations.

Submarines had not been idle since the first of the year. *I-24* had been patrolling off Hawaii. Our minelaying squadron was in place off northern Australia. The RO-types screened and scouted for aircraft carriers that smashed at Rabaul, on the island of New Britain, and for our ships that landed men there to take Rabaul easily on Jan. 23. The Rabaul capture put the total of successful Japanese amphibious operations since Dec. 7 past the 20-mark. *I-*

18 and *I-24* tried to shell Midway Island, but had to dive when enemy gunners returned fire.

Along the Malay Barrier, which the enemy was trying desperately to hold as the last barricade against any Japanese advance on Australia, our 6th Fleet boats were helping surface ships and aircraft against the enemy. *I-162, I-164, I-165* and *I-166* all reported sinking ships, off Sumatra, Java, Burma, Ceylon and India.

We lost three more submarines during January. Lt. Cdr. Shun Hasegawa and his crew in *I-160* fell victim to the British destroyer *Jupiter* in the Sunda Strait, on Jan. 17, while attacking enemy shipping heading to and from Singapore. *I-173*, the boat of Cdr. Akira Isobe, was sunk in mid-Pacific 10 days later. Her loss confirmed the complaints submarine captains had been making about Tokyo requiring too many wireless reports. *I-173* was geographically located and her intentions roughly determined, because of this. She had been patrolling off Hawaii and was on her way to Yokosuka. Powerful American radio direction finders plotted the sites of her transmissions by triangulation, and her course and speed were roughly calculated while she was responding to numerous requests for information. The American submarine *Gudgeon* was able to lie along her proposed path and sink *I-173* north of Midway.

The third submarine lost in January was *I-124*, a minelaying type, like the American submarines *Nautilus* and *Argonaut* of that era. *I-124* was off Singapore when the war began, secretly laying mines that we believe sank several merchant ships later. Then she moved to the Philippines, where she reported sinking one ship before sailing south to stand watch off northern Australia. Our land and sea forces were rolling very rapidly through the southern area, so much sought-after for its raw materials and other resources. Adm. Yamamoto very much wanted information about any proposed enemy movements to block our attacks on Rabaul and New Guinea. The carriers *Kaga, Akagi, Shokaku* and *Zuikaku* had enough air strength to handle any opposition to the invasions, but the *Nagumo* force needed to know of any surface opposition headed its way.

I-124 must have ventured too close to the enemy port of Darwin, Australia. Perhaps Capt. Keiyu Endo, her division commander, who was on board, had ordered her taken that far in. She was detected by the U.S. destroyer *Edsall* just outside Darwin, while the American destroyer was escorting a convoy into port. *Edsall* radioed a position report, but stayed with her charges until they were safely inside the anchorage. Then she put about to join three Australian corvettes that had answered her call. They were dropping depth charges when the American destroyer returned to the scene. She used her sound equipment to assist them, then made a depth charge attack herself. Lt. Cdr. Koichi Kishigami, his crew, and his division commander went down with their ship. This was an unusual sinking, in that it was later fully confirmed by Allied divers, who went down and actually stood on *I-124's* hull.

That made six submarines lost in a little more than six weeks. Fate allowed HMS *Jupiter* and USS *Edsall* no more chances at us. Both went to the bottom before the middle of March, along with nearly all the naval strength that the Allies sent into the Malay Barrier area. Meanwhile, *I-17* was getting ready to make coastal residents of America scream, "Where is our Navy?" In Tokyo orders were being passed from the red brick building of our Navy Ministry to Combined Fleet for a special operation. These orders, relayed to 6th Fleet headquarters and to land-based naval aircraft commands, would give Americans at Pearl Harbor something new to think and worry about. It would be called the "K-Operation."

* * *

Chapter 4

SHELLS ON SANTA BARBARA.
MORE BOMBS ON PEARL HARBOR.

Cdr. Kozo Nishino had command of *I-17* at the time Vice
Adm. Shimizu ordered all submarines at Kwajalein to chase
and sink the American task force. Nishino pursued almost as
far as Oahu, then continued to the U.S. west coast, where his
gun crew shelled an oil storage field at Elwood City, near
Santa Barbara, California.

The diary of Seaman Genji Hara, radio operator serving
with Nishino, has survived. Here are some excerpts from it.

"Feb. 21. *I-17* is once more operating off the coast of
America, but this time we are alone. Our movements have
been slow, and the sea ripples softly along the sides of our ship.
The vast spread of the Pacific seems like a watery waste to me.
Wireless reception from the 6th Fleet communications tower
on Kwajalein was very good today, but I could not hear much
of what *I-23* was sending. She is in the Hawaiian area, and
must be having trouble with her transmission equipment.
Around midnight I heard a lookout reporting a lighthouse off

to port, but by 0100 it was discovered to be a light from an enemy small craft. It could have been a fishing boat, but the captain thought it might be a patrol boat. We increased speed, and rapidly moved away from it.

"After getting off watch I slept a while, but was awakened at 0200 with the order 'Stand by to submerge!' The voice on the loudspeaker circuit said 'There may be an enemy patrol boat following us. All hands rig for depth charge attack!' Then *I-17* dipped silently beneath the surface, where we cut off all unnecessary machinery. The only noise I could hear came from the hum of our sound detection equipment.

"Nothing happened. After a while, we surfaced. I went back to the radio room, and found that some messages that had arrived earlier had been decoded. They listed the places that *I-17* (together with other submarines) were to bombard and others (like San Diego) we were to avoid. I felt a thrill, as though we would really carry out the task this time and not have it cancelled, as it had been in December.

"Feb. 24. After surfacing, Captain Nishino told the crew of his plans. 'We are now entering Santa Barbara Strait.' he said. 'We will lie submerged tomorrow, doing reconnaissance with our periscope. Then, tomorrow night, we will surface after dark and bombard the Elwood oil field, inside the Strait.'

"*We are really going to do it this time!* I told myself. As a substitute gunner in case a gun crew member was injured or killed, I had to check over our deck weapon. About 30 knots of wind was blowing over the deck while we did it and there were plenty of white caps on the waves. There was a dull half-moon, with a hazy halo about it. I looked up into the sky and located Great Bear and the Northern Star. Then I tried to estimate the direction of Japan from where I stood. In that moment I hoped that, if I died, the people back home would know that *I-17* had reached out 4000 miles to strike at America for them. I felt very warm and full of sentiment at that moment.

"Feb. 25. Today I was fascinated by sounds Seaman Nagashima was picking up on our sound equipment. 'Iruka!' he called out suddenly, and those of us in the room listened to the bleating noises similar to the 'crying *iruka* fish,' off Kyushu, near home. Then we settled down into silence, everyone probably thinking the same thing as I. We will bombard. . . . The enemy will return our fire. . . . We will run away to escape. . . . They will come after us. . . .

"Lunch was canned *inari-zushi* (vinegared rice wrapped in thin, fried bean curd). All hands waited anxiously for the order to battle-surface. Someone passing my station while coming down from the conning tower said, 'Land is in sight.' Then *I-17* changed course and, at a slow pace, began navigating blindly through Santa Barbara Strait, not even showing its periscope for fear of making a telltale spray. I tried to calm down by reading a book, but couldn't. I had finally decided to try to eat something, to distract my mind, when the word was passed 'All hands to battle stations!' It was then about 5:30 **P.M.**

"Ten minutes later Captain Nishino ordered 'Battle surface! Man the deck gun!' The gun captain had assembled his crew near the hatch earlier. They went on deck. Captain Nishino kept calling out, asking the distance to land and the submarine's depth, giving instructions about the targets. He ordered that shells be fired only at oil tanks.

"Only the gunners were on deck. The rest of us in our 'window-less barracks' could only listen and imagine what it was like above from the sounds and shocks that came through the hull.

"One . . . two . . . three . . . we could imagine the gunners loading each of those rounds; the trainer and the pointer trying to sight on the target. We had counted up to seventeen when the shooting suddenly stopped.

"Petty Officer Homma and I had the radio watch. We spun our receiver dials, trying to find some indication of American reaction. There was none. We heard no alarm or call for help. The California radio station programs continued as leisurely as before. Gunners dropped through the hatch and *I-17* began picking up speed. Two of the crew, Onodera and Nagata, came into the radio room. 'What did we hit?' I asked them. 'I don't know.' Onodera said. 'I only saw flashes. I had no time to confirm anything.'

"Nagara said it was beautiful and that he could see automobile headlights. The navigator came into the radio room then. 'We started shelling right after sunset.' he said. 'There was no reply until we started speeding away. Some enemy planes dropped flares, but they were far from our position.'

"The reaction set in then. 'We are the first to bombard America!' everyone began telling one another. 'Even if we didn't hit a thing, they know *I-17* has been here!' All of us felt like heroes."

It was a feeling *I-17*'s crew had earned. Newspapers in California carried panic headlines and stories about the shelling by a "Jap U-Boat." Demands were made on the American government to protect the coast with its navy. For 17 rounds of ammunition, Nishino's men cost the U.S. Navy many millions of dollars in time, money, ships and men, providing escort. Three years would pass before West Coast waters were considered safe from our attacks.

Less than two weeks after *I-17*'s bold feat of shelling the American coastline, a feat comparable to that of the great John Paul Jones' raiding of the English coastline generations before, our 6th Fleet submarines helped embarrass the U.S. Navy again. This action, titled "K-Operation," was planned in Tokyo during January, 1942, then passed to Adm. Yamamoto for execution. The Japanese Navy would attack Pearl Harbor *again*!

Two giant four-engined flying boats were to be used. These massive patrol planes could fly nearly across the Pacific Ocean non-stop, each bearing one ton of bombs. Not very much explosives, but if they could be dropped on the American base, it would shake the morale of the Americans. Or, so it was thought.

Some writers have said that a story in the *Saturday Evening Post* before the war, inspired the K-Operation. I don't know if this is true, but it was a most imaginative idea that required much planning and careful execution. Seven of our 6th Fleet's submarines were to take part, providing support for these two bombers.

The bombers would fly from Japan to Wotje (in the Marshalls) where submarine crewmen were training in the technique of refueling aircraft from their boats. On a designated day the planes would take off from the lagoon at Wotje, and fly to French Frigate Shoals, over 1600 miles away in the northwest portion of the Hawaiian Islands chain. One of our submarines, *I-9*, would take station halfway along this route, and provide a radio beacon to guide the bombers on their way.

French Frigate Shoals is a small outcropping, just barely rising above the sea, about 500 miles northwest of Oahu. It is far enough away from Pearl Harbor that the enemy neglected it, knowing it was too small for us to base aircraft there or to be used as an air base by them. It did have a navigable lagoon, though, and that's all that the K-Operation needed.

My old boat, *I-15*, together with *I-19* and *I-26*, had their aircraft removed, and the hangar space was used for storing a massive amount of aviation gasoline. These three boats were to head for French Frigate Shoals and wait for the two flying boats. The amphibians would be refueled to capacity, and take off again, swinging southeast to Pearl Harbor.

A long dock on the shore opposite the south side of Ford Island was to be the aiming point for the planes' bombs. Their arrival over Pearl Harbor was timed for after midnight, as the enemy's capability for night fighting was considered very poor. The bombers would make one pass, dropping their bombs and then head back for Wotje, non-stop. A fifth submarine, *I-25*, would be standing by south of Pearl Harbor for air-sea rescue, a use to which our subs were put long before the Americans thought of it. Another pair of submarines were to be deployed as radio beacons along the southern route home.

Cdr. Akiyoshi Fujii's *I-9* and Cdr. Genichi Shibata's *I-23* were given their K-Operation instructions by wireless on Feb. 14, so they would have time to take stations by March 1. Fujii acknowledged, and carried out his assignment. Shibata also acknowledged, on Feb. 14, but nothing was heard from him after that.

I assume that *I-23* was lost operationally some time later. Submarine crewmen get tired, and bored, and weary, and sleepy. The peak efficiency they reach after months of training falls off during weeks of hard patrolling, sometimes only just long enough for a vital valve to be left open or the wrong control wheel turned. It happened to American submarines during the war and it happened to ours. Boats disappeared without a trace, although no combat log of either Japan or America reported any attack on them.

The flying boats arrived in the Marshalls in mid-February. They made practice refuelings and short flights. *I-19*'s aircraft made a reconnaissance of Pearl Harbor on Feb. 23, the second such flight over the island fortress since Dec. 7, 1941. Then *I-19* made for French Frigate Shoals.

On March 3, 1942 the two planes took off on their historic flight at about 3:30 A.M. They landed at French Frigate Shoals 13 hours later. *I-15* and *I-19* were in the lagoon, waiting. Their crews gave the two aircraft a great drink of fuel and the amphibians were away again about 3 hours after that, arriving over Oahu about 1 A.M. They were detected by radar, just the planes originally attacking Pearl Harbor on Dec. 7 had been, but our planes once more got above the island without opposition!

Up to that point, all had gone off without a hitch. Then the weather took a hand, something that might not have happened had Kwajalein heard from *I-23*, which was supposed to be providing weather reports. Our pilots found a low overcast obscuring their target. Flying blind, each pilot tried to get his bearings from a landmark, and calculate where the long dock (called 1010 by the U.S. Navy) was. This didn't work, so the

51

pair dropped their bombs anyway—just to let the enemy know that Japanese planes had been overhead again.

Both arrived safely home, after a flight that covered 4000 miles and took 24 hours to complete. One load of bombs fell harmlessly into the sea. The other landed far from Pearl Harbor, to the east of downtown Honolulu. It caused consternation among the public, who blamed the American military for carelessness. The American military put the blame on one another, with Army pilots accusing Navy pilots of jettisoning bombs without watching where they went, and vice versa. It was not until bomb fragments were found and identified that the truth came out.

Our K-Operation has been criticized by writers as having no effect on the war. I think of it as indicating the kind of spirit that prevailed among Japanese leaders at the time: Hong Kong, Manila, Singapore and Java were in our hands, as were Wake, Guam, and portions of the Philippines. Our ships and planes were scoring one victory after another. Our high command felt very confident, and willing to try anything that would keep the enemy off-balance and worried.

I was starting the commanding officers' submarine course at Kure and enjoying the only home life I would know for a long time, when the Java Sea Battle was fought. A mixed force of British, Dutch, American and Australian ships under the Netherlands admiral Karel Doorman tried to stop our invasion convoy headed for Java. Our covering force nearly wiped out the Allied force, mainly through use of the above-water counterpart of the torpedo carried in our submarines. Named the Model 93, it had been first tested in 1933, and was kept completely secret from all foreigners. It would remain secret until 1945, although I understand that Americans obtained one during the middle of the war, without realizing its speed and power.

March and April were fairly good months for the Japanese submarine fleet. Our boats did well in the Indian Ocean and Java Sea, as well as on the east and west coasts of Australia. On March 16 the wounded and ailing Shimizu was relieved as Commander, 6th Fleet, by Vice Adm. Teruhisa Komatsu. In April it was declared formal policy to have our submarines operate chiefly against enemy merchantmen instead of against warships. This was pleasing news to us at submarine school. We thought the anti-merchant effort a much better use of submarines, and kept pointing to Germany as an example.

Our new plan to throw a blockade around Allied holdings in the Pacific-Indian Ocean areas might seem overly ambitious, and one look at a chart of that part of the world might at first prove dismaying. But a closer look would show the enemy held only a few worthwhile ports in early 1942, mostly in Australia and India. Covering the Cape of Good Hope and the exits from the Suez Canal sufficiently should cut the flow of goods from the west. And we were to have the help of some German submarines in doing that.

American supplies could land at only a few places in New Zealand, New Caledonia and Australia when coming from the east. With Truk and Rabaul as bases, our submarines could easily be deployed across shipping routes. Besides our submarine effort, plans were being made to move into bases in the southeastern Solomons. From there, sea- and land-based aircraft could keep an eye on the southern seas, assisting us.

For these purposes, submarines began returning to Japan for refit, and overhaul. *I-25* got back to Yokosuka after having sent Warrant Officer Fujita's plane over a number of enemy anchorages. SubRons 4, 5 and 6 were ordered back from southwestern waters, and some of its boats were earmarked for withdrawal from active combat service. They were to be assigned as training boats in the Inland Sea for men who would man the new submarines to be commissioned.

While I was at Kure, trying with fellow students to work out the best methods possible of employing the submarines we would all command, our southern forces rolled steadily onward. On March 15, Gen. Douglas MacArthur told his unit commanders: "Help is on the way from the United States. Thousands of troops and hundreds of planes are being dispatched. The exact time of arrival of reinforcements is unknown, as they will have to fight their way through Japanese attempts against them. It is imperative that our troops hold until reinforcements arrive."

The general and his men would see no ships or troops. Except for a trickle of supplies and ammunition brought to Corregidor by submarine (the same vehicle MacArthur later used for his escape to Australia) no help got through to the beleaguered enemy. The Imperial Navy had unchallenged control of all waters where it operated in March and April, and the Imperial Army was rapidly securing control of all land masses. Tulagi and Guadalcanal were seized in May, a few weeks after Nagumo's planes made the first attack an aircraft carrier ever made on another. His far-ranging sea eagles buried HMS *Hermes* under a hail of steel in minutes, just as they had the British cruisers *Dorsetshire* and *Cornwall*.

By the time spring came to Japan—that soft season when

cherry blossoms *(sakura)* bloom first in the south then creep northward and spread a pink-and-white blanket over my beloved homeland—the Combined Fleet was ready to rest on its oars for a while. Nearly all warships were home or headed home for refit, the carriers to obtain new planes and pilots to replace losses, the rest to get an overhaul in preparation for our next move. No one knew just what it would be, not even the members of our high command. They were arguing hotly about it, and would for weeks before a decision was reached. Then a man in the United States, whose name has been forgotten by most Americans and is unknown to nearly all Japanese, got an idea. He was Capt. Francis S. Low, USN. Another man would take the lead in carrying it out. He is much better known to Americans and Japanese. His name is James Doolittle.

* * *

Chapter 5.

VICTORY VIA MIDWAY?

Once the first great flush of victory had passed, Japan's military leaders had to decide what to do next. So far, everything had gone just about as planned. Although we had, in the first four months of war, lost some planes and airmen that would not be easily replaced, we still had a mighty aircraft carrier force completely intact. Our battleships had not a scratch on them, chiefly because most of them rode serenely at anchor off Kure while our other warships carried Japan's war effort one-third of the distance around the world.

New submarines, destroyers and aircraft carriers were coming off the ways, too, but at nothing like the rate our leaders knew America could produce them. So, Japan could not afford to sit still, waiting for the enemy to gain strength and assault us. Already his aircraft carriers had begun nibbling at our outposts.

No nation ever won a war of expansion by pausing for long breaths between victories. Japan would have to consolidate her holdings and seek out and destroy any force that might be used against them.

There were several schools of thought among the men responsible for Japan's strategy. One group wanted to push westward into India and, perhaps, link up with a German-Italian thrust across Africa and southeastern Europe. Another group wanted to keep pushing straight southward and seize Australia, the most logical base for a land offensive against the areas we had taken. This second group wanted to deny a great training ground to the Americans, who could build military, naval, supply and air bases in Australia.

The third group—the one that finally got its way—was centered about Adm. Yamamoto. Very much mindful of the five battleships sunk by our naval air forces at Pearl Harbor and the two sunk off Malaya, these men had been keeping a close eye on American carrier operations. These planners had an abundance of proof of what naval aircraft could accomplish, and felt that Japan's holdings could not be protected unless the American aircraft carriers were destroyed before they were joined by two or three times their number from busy American shipyards. It had not gone unnoticed in Tokyo that America had been gearing its industry to war for more than two years. Her effort to assist Great Britain had helped all sectors of American industry recover from a national depression. Much of America's unemployed found jobs in its expanding defense works, including shipbuilding. In spite of what many writers have said on the subject, the U. S. was very much ready for war, at least industrially, on Dec. 7, 1941. Then our attack on Pearl Harbor unified what had been a divided national spirit. The citizenry was welded into a common effort to seek revenge.

Japan could only win this war by working herself into such a position of strength that a negotiated peace would appear to be a better alternative to Americans than a bloody fight for many years in the Pacific. We needed another mighty victory like Pearl Harbor. What was left of U. S. naval power had to be destroyed in one decisive battle. Adm. Yamamoto and those who agreed with him decided that a thrust to the east ought to be made. Target would be Midway Island, less than 1500 miles from Pearl Harbor.

If Midway fell into Japanese hands, the U. S. would be delayed for years in mounting a Pacific offensive. Hawaii itself might fall. The oceanic war would then become a stalemate, with Japanese naval power blocking any move westward. So, a move on Midway was bound to make the American Navy come out and fight. In that case, Yamamoto was sure, it would be utterly defeated.

The internal struggle that took place among our war planners when Midway was suggested as next objective has been adequately covered by other writers, so I will not till plowed ground. Suffice it to say that the I-Operation, as it was called, finally won approval. Opposition still continued, though, while details were being discussed. Officers who were responsible for fuel supplies, replacement aircraft, provisions, supplies, and ammunition for the 5000 troops needed to take and hold this island, kept producing statistics to show that this thrust to the east would strain Japan's resources to the limit and beyond it.

They might have had their way, had not Capt. Francis Low suggested to Adm. Ernest King that an attack on Japan proper might do wonders for American morale, while at the same time pushing us off-balance. King agreed and a plan was drawn up to use an aircraft carrier for this purpose. In order to drop as many bombs on Japan as possible, the U. S. decided to experiment with some of its medium bombers, hoping that they could be flown from aircraft carriers. They called upon a former stunt pilot, Lt. Col. James Doolittle, to lead this effort. He did, to a success. A force of North American B-25 "Mitchell" bombers (named for a man who, interestingly enough, had predicted a war between Japan and the United States years before) suddenly appeared in our skies on April 18, 1942.

This dramatic attack, coupled with Adm. Yamamoto's frequent earlier warnings about American aircraft carriers, turned the tide of argument as effectively as his threat to resign had done it a year before. It must be remembered that Yamamoto had been opposed to any war with America. He knew the power of America too well. He had confided to Prince Konoye that he could not guarantee any hope for success in a war, after the first six months or year.

So he advocated the surprise attack in hope of winning a major advantage with one stroke. He could lead a formidable force of surface ships, plus 20 submarines in such an effort. Against the meager strength pitted against him, these should prove overwhelming. And at Midway, he did have overwhelming odds on his side. Japanese aircraft carriers outnumbered American ones 8-3; battleships 11-0; cruisers 18-8; and destroyers 65-15. American submarine scouting strength was 15.

The Combined Fleet sortie was to be the greatest array of

seapower ever seen upon the ocean up to that time. Altogether more than 200 ships would gather from all parts of the empire to move eastward, and submarines would also be striking to the north, south, and west. The Japanese Navy planned to strike not only at Midway, but also Australia, the Aleutians, and Diego Suarez (Madagascar) off the east coast of Africa.

Our submarines were to have an important part in the struggle for Midway. First of all, they were to help repeat the K-Operation of early March. Two "Emily" flying boats would be used, as before, but they would not carry bombs this time. Their mission was to be strictly reconnaissance. They would again take off from Wotje, in the Marshalls, and land at French Frigate Shoals. There they would refuel from minelaying submarines *I-121* and *I-123*, which had their mine storage areas remodeled so they could each carry 50-ton loads of aviation gasoline and oil. They would have on board teams of mechanics, to service the monster flying boats at the rendezvous. Lt. Cdr. Yasuo Fujimori had *I-121*, and Lt. Cdr. Toshitake Ueno had *I-123*. The third submarine in their division was *I-122*. Lt. Cdr. Sadatoshi Norita would patrol the small islets in the Hawaiian Chain between French Frigate Shoals and Midway in her. All three boats were under the command of Capt. Takeharu Miyazaki.

Rear Adm. Chimaki Kono had SubRon 3, composed of five submarines. Two of these, Lt. Cdr. Yahachi Tanabe's *I-168*, and Lt. Cdr. Katsuji Watanabe's *I-169*, were to patrol off Midway, reporting any enemy activity there. Lt. Cdr. Rokuro Kawasaki's *I-171*, Lt. Cdr. Toshi Kusaka's *I-174*, and Lt. Cdr. Kameo Uno's *I-175* would work to provide radio beacon and rescue service for the second K-Operation.

If all went well, a pair of flying boats would be over Pearl Harbor once more. They would gather information on ships present. This would be relayed to Adm. Yamamoto, so he could use it in his plan to smash Midway with his air strength, then take it with troops. He fully expected that the American fleet would sortie from Pearl Harbor once this had happened, knowing it could not let Japan have this key base. Yamamoto then expected to send his refueled, re-armed and rested airmen against the American ships, while at the same time he closed with his battleships and cruisers to clean up whatever was left. Once that happened, ships would be able to ply back and forth through our defense network as safely as though they were sailing the Inland Sea. Nothing would be left to fight them, except a few submarines that could only operate out of Pearl Harbor, cutting radically their operation time in any combat area to a very low level. Naval planners who stood with Yamamoto even foresaw a move against Oahu itself before the end of 1942. Success there would truly make the Pacific Ocean a "Japanese lake!"

Two other forces of submarines, meanwhile, were to strike in the south and the west. Rear Adm. Noboru Ishizaki, in his flagship *I-10*, commanded by Cdr. Yatsuchika Katahara, was to have *I-16*, *I-18*, *I-20* and the new submarine *I-30* with him in the Indian Ocean. They were to make a reconnaissance of the African coastline, and they were also to make an air reconnaissance of Diego Suarez, a former French base that British forces had taken over. They were also to launch a midget submarine attack at Diego Suarez at the end of May.

Far to the east of Ishizaki's group were five more boats, *I-21*, *I-22*, *I-24*, *I-27* and *I-29*. The last two were brand-new boats. It was their task to make a similar air reconnaissance of Sydney, Australia, and also carry out a midget submarine attack. Our high command believed that these two assaults would help unsettle the enemy and keep him relatively in the dark as to the Combined Fleet's true intentions. The attack on Midway would be brought off in such a manner as would jar American forces into immediate retaliatory action, which, of course, Adm. Yamamoto wanted to see happen.

There was another diversionary operation also worked into the Midway plan. A strong northern force was to seize Attu and Kiska, in the Aleutian Islands. Scouting there for it were Cdr. Meiji Tagami, in *I-25*, and Cdr. Minoru Yokota, in *I-26*.

I-9, *I-15*, *I-17* and *I-19* were scheduled for the Aleutians, too. The first three were to send off planes for reconnaissance flights, then move on to the south, leaving only *I-19* in the north as a sentry on patrol. The trio would then form one of three sentry lines, deployed so as to provide warning of any American force approaching from the U. S. mainland.

These three sentry lines were actually *the real core* of the entire Midway operation. Added to the K-Operation, their task was to provide advance information of any U. S. naval movement, so that Yamamoto's ships could deal with it. All three lines were to be in place five days before X-Day, which was set for June 5, Japan time.

I-9, *I-15* and *I-17* were to station themselves on a north-south line far to the northeast of Midway, some 1000 miles off the American west coast. They would watch for anything coming down from the north, or from the northwest coast of the U. S.

I-168 and *I-169* were to scout off Midway Island, and then move southeastward. They would take positions with *I-171, I-174* and *I-175* after these submarines had carried out their portions of the K-Operation. The Hawaiian chain of islands falls away in a generally southeastern direction from Midway, and ships approaching Midway from Oahu would have to come alongside one side or the other of the chain. The five submarines of SubRon 3 would be somewhat south of French Frigate Shoals, lined up north-to-south. It would be their task to report, intercept and attack any forces coming up the southern side of the island chain.

The third patrol was to consist of eight submarines under SubRon 5 commander Rear Adm. Tadashige Daigo. They were to station themselves about 900 miles due east of Midway, in position across the path any force had to take when proceeding from Oahu to Midway along the northern side of the island chain. They held the key role in the plans for the Midway battle.

To the uneducated eye, viewing a chart of the mid-Pacific, the deployment of submarines in the Midway campaign probably seems excellent. Diversions as much as 5000 miles away might help throw the enemy off the scent. Then, using the poor weather of the north Pacific to advantage, our aircraft carriers would race in from the north undetected (as they did at Pearl Harbor) and numb Midway's garrison into helplessness with one mighty blow. After that, our invasion force would come from the west, taking the island without trouble once its air defense was wiped out. At the same time, behind the carriers to the north of Midway, a massive battleship-cruiser group would start moving down to back up the aircraft carriers that had never yet encountered difficulty in carrying out assigned missions. When the remnant of the American Fleet hiding at Oahu came out to counter attack, it would be sent to the bottom by our planes, cruisers, and battleships.

There was only one way the American navy could thwart this grand plan—by keeping its naval air strength intact and hidden until some kind of opportunity came to strike hard and fast. Besides a great deal of skill, the American navy would also need a great deal of luck, to prevail against the overwhelming odds.

To the professional eye (particularly that of a submariner) it appeared far different. Cdr. Shojiro Iura, a member of the Naval General Staff, was an adviser on submarine affairs. Here is what he told me about the planning for Midway:

"Shortly after I assumed my post on the Naval General Staff in March, 1942, one of Admiral Yamamoto's staff officers, Captain Yasuji Watanabe, arrived in Tokyo with a rough plan for the attack on Midway. It had been worked out in table-top maneuvers on board the new superbattleship *Yamato,* at Kure, and approved by Admiral Yamamoto. Captain Watanabe was relaying an urgent request from the commander-in-chief that the plan be given full approval by the Naval General Staff as quickly as possible."

Capt. Sadatoshi Tomioka, in the General Staff's operations section, was responsible for carrying out plans once they were approved. He opposed the operation. His stand reflected the prevailing opinion among the General Staff at that time, which was that the Americans should be lured into one decisive battle but not in the vicinity of Midway. Most members preferred an attack on the Fijis and Samoa, which were along the U.S.-to-Australia supply route. The American fleet could tolerate an attack less there than on Midway, they felt. It would have to counterattack. The difference was that in the Fijis-Samoa area the Americans would be very far from any reinforcement or assistance. The Japanese preponderance in naval strength would count for even more in such a case. These people felt that *the most favorable point of attack* should be the first consideration, because Midway (or any other base, like New Caledonia) could be taken with ease once the American fleet was wiped out. Primary objective, they said, was elimination of the enemy fleet at minimum cost to our own. This could be more easily done the further the Americans were from their major base, Pearl Harbor.

Iura also told me how Capt. Kameto Kuroshima, operations staff officer for Yamamoto, argued with Capt. Tomioka. "The Midway plan must be approved!" Kuroshima insisted and cited the danger Japan faced from aircraft carriers if she did not eliminate them.

"No!" said Tomioka, his anger also rising. "Even if we are successful, look at the great difficulty we would have keeping Midway supplied!" Japan's merchant fleet, though large, still was barely sufficient to support operations already going on in the south. The bulk of it was employed in transporting oil, rubber, tin, tungsten and other strategic materials back to our industrial complex. Very few ships could be spared from the task of strengthening our defense through homeland construction of war instruments to provide follow-up support of a Midway operation, Tomioka noted.

Capt. Tomioka and Capt. Watanabe were already in total agreement on the major point, that the American fleet *must* be lured into battle. After heavy argument, reluctant approval was given to go ahead with general planning for the attack on Midway. Not long after that, a detailed operations plan was drafted by Yamamoto's staff and sent to Tokyo for final approval. Once this was given, the final preparations would begin.

At this point Rear Adm. Shigeru Fukudome, Tomioka's senior in the Operations Section, had to give approval. Cdr. Iura read the detailed plan as soon as it arrived, and was on hand to advise Admiral Fukudome. He noted that SubRon 5 was included, and this was the focal point of his objections to the Midway plan. "I cannot agree or recommend the use of that squadron in the task it has been given!" Iura told Fukudome. "Those submarines are too old and too slow for that mission!"

SubRon 5 was under Rear Adm. Tadashige Daigo, and was at that moment in Japan undergoing overhaul and repair. Most of these obsolescent boats were supposed to go into the reserve fleet on training duty. Every one was at least a dozen years old. None could dive safely past 200 feet.

"The main core of the American fleet in Hawaii," said Cdr. Iura, "will be composed of aircraft carriers. The old submarines of SubRon 5 cannot cope with air attacks and patrols. They cannot carry out reconnaissance against such a foe, nor can they attack aircraft with any hope of success. I realize, of course, that every available warship must be committed to this operation. But I think the Combined Fleet staff officers are taking too much for granted when they station such a worn-out group of submarines in the path the Americans are most likely to use!"

Iura's arguments did not prevail. The I-Operation detailed plan was approved unchanged so far as use of submarines was concerned. Iura would later have the satisfaction of being able to say, "I told you so." But it would be poor satisfaction.

Yamamoto's plan to move against Midway, lure out the American fleet, and destroy it was given the green light. All submarine commanders began making preparations to carry out their tasks, unaware that U. S. intelligence experts had broken the Japanese naval code. The Americans had a vast amount of information about our intentions. From this they built a mosaic of our plans for Adm. Chester Nimitz in his hilltop headquarters above Pearl Harbor.

Yet, even if the Americans had not broken our code, I am not surprised that they learned of our intentions. Or at least that they knew Midway would be the next point of attack. Our security was awful. The talk at Kure, where I was about halfway through the course for submarine commanders, was all about Midway. It was on everyone's lips.

"Next time we meet," one submarine crew member would call out to a friend on the one moored abreast of his, "we will meet at Midway!"

"If we live, that is!" his friend would answer.

"Of course we will be alive!" the first sailor would shout back across the few feet of water. "We don't want to die before we have taken Hawaii, do we?"

First of the submarines to leave home waters were those sent on scouting and midget attack missions. They departed early in May, the other submarines streaming out into the Pacific's broad blue waters for two weeks after that. One boat was almost sunk by USS *Silversides* just after leaving port, but the American submarine's commander missed his target.

Capt. Hanku Sasaki, who had directed the midget submarine attack against Pearl Harbor five months before, led submarines south along the coast of Australia. On May 29 a plane from *I-21* flew off its catapult and over the city of Sydney without running into any opposition. When pilot and crewman got back aboard they reported three capital ships and numerous smaller warcraft present in Sydney harbor. Sasaki decided he would launch a midget submarine attack within 48 hours, using the three midget subs he had on hand. Lt. Keiu, who had secretly scouted the entrance to Pearl Harbor while supposedly a tourist on board the merchant ship *Taiyo Maru* just before the war, was pilot of *I-22's* midget. His crewman was Petty Officer Takeshi Omori. *I-22* was Sasaki's flagship as before, with Cdr. Kiyotake Ageta still its skipper.

I-24's midget pilot was Lt. (j.g.) Katsuhisa Ban, his crewman Petty Officer Mamoru Ashibe. Cdr. Hiroshi Hanabusa still had the boat, but he had lost Lt. Mochitsura Hashimoto, who was with me at the Kure school.

I-27, completed at Sasebo three months before setting out on this mission, was captained by Cdr. Iwao Yoshimura. His midget pilot was Lt. Kenshi Chuman, with Petty Officer Masao Takenaka as crewman. Capt. Sasaki maneuvered all boats into position on May 31 and, about 4:30 P.M., began sending off his midgets. Launching point was about 7 miles off Sydney Harbor. Pilots were ordered to penetrate the anchorage, wait on the bottom until dark, then come up to periscope depth and make their attacks. Each had two torpedoes.

A postwar check showed that one of our midgets did not penetrate the harbor. It either suffered some kind of malfunction, or became entangled in anti submarine nets. It was never seen or heard from after leaving its mother ship. The other two got into the harbor, having made their way up a difficult winding channel. They were detected on the way in by sound equipment the Australians were using for just such kind of protection. It was nearly 11 P.M. when one of these two midgets was sighted from USS *Chicago*, a cruiser. About two hours later, *Chicago's* lookouts saw a torpedo heading their way. It missed the cruiser, a destroyer, and a Dutch submarine, but hit a hotel ship, HMAS *Kuttabul,* sinking it and killing some men on board it. A second torpedo was found run up on the shore next day. That pilot had bad luck, his torpedo missing the cruiser ahead of its bow. The big ship was missed both fore and aft!

There are varying foreign versions of what happened to our midgets at Sydney. None can be correct, because all state that *four* midget submarines were launched. They agree that two got inside Sydney harbor, because both were found on the bottom by Allied divers. One had not yet fired its torpedoes. Capt. Sasaki's young men had missed their chance to get both USS *Chicago* and HMAS *Canberra.*

Capt. Sasaki waited off Sydney for two days, hoping to pick up his pilots and their crewmen, giving up only when the midgets' endurance time had expired. "The Battle of Sydney" ended with Cdr. Hanabusa's gun crew loosing several rounds at the Australian city, which was immediately blacked out. *I-24* then dived quickly and fled.

While Capt. Sasaki was leading his five submarines down the east coast of Australia, Rear Adm. Ishizaki (in *I-8*) was off the east coast of Africa. *I-10's* aircraft was sent over Diego Suarez on May 30, and the admiral ordered a midget attack made the next night. *I-18's* midget could not be sent off because of a breakdown of its engine, due no doubt to the fact that this sub had been cruising for about a month before the day of attack came. So, only two midgets could be sent into Diego Suarez where a battleship of the *Queen Elizabeth* class, several cruisers, and many smaller vessels lay at anchor. Cdr. Kaoru Yamada launched Ens. Katsusuke Iwase from *I-16,* with Petty Officer Kozo Takada as crewman. Cdr. Takashi Yamada sent Lt. Saburo Akeida away from *I-20,* with Petty Officer Masami Takemoto. Akeida had been waiting four years for this chance. He had been a pioneer midget pilot with Lt. Naoji Iwasa in 1938, when the weapon had proved itself well enough to gain approval for mass production. Akieda had also played an important role in training in the *koryu* (the Inland Sea). These young lads, the cream of young Japanese manhood, thought very highly of themselves and their weapon. They were not organized as a *tokko* corps; were never meant to be suicide pilots. Still, they had a streak of fatalism in them, as testimonials left behind them show. Off Pearl Harbor, Lt. Iwasa had written the words *"shi sei"* (utmost loyalty) with brush and ink on rice paper as a memento for *I-22*'s crewmen. He and many other midget submariners never truly expected to return alive from missions, though some did during the Solomons campaign. All faced danger cheerfully and fearlessly.

The attack on Diego Suarez was very successful. The battleship HMS *Warspite* was hit, and badly damaged. She retreated quickly to Durban (South Africa) and posed no threat to our Indian Ocean forces for quite a while. An enemy tanker was also sunk. A reconnaissance flight over Diego Suarez from one of the submarines after the attack found the battleship missing from her mooring place and at first our high command concluded that she had been sunk. The truth was learned later, through careful monitoring of enemy broadcasts. From these same broadcasts it was learned that two Japanese men, possibly Akieda and Takemoto, had gotten ashore after the battle, and tried to attack the shore garrison. They continued to charge after being ordered to surrender and were killed. The submarines waited in vain for midgets to return.

Lt. Cdr. Ueno took the fuel-laden *I-123* out, and slipped right up to the edge of French Frigate Shoals from Kwajalein without any trouble, arriving outside the reef on May 26. But, when he peered through his periscope, he received a terrible shock. There, in the lagoon, was an American ship! It was identified as a small seaplane tender. Certainly no flying boats could land at French Frigate Shoals now! Nor could *I-123* try to torpedo this barrier to the K-Operation, either. Even one radio message, gotten away before the enemy sank, might reveal the plan. Captain Ueno decided that the thing to do was to wait and watch. That is what he did, for most of five days. Then, with time running out and the enemy showing no sign of moving, he finally sent off a wireless message to Vice Adm. Komatsu, in his flagship *Katori* at Kwajalein. "The enemy's watch is intense," it read: "There appears to be no chance of carrying out the K-Operation." This word, relayed to Adm. Yamamoto, caused cancellation of the planned air reconnaissance of Pearl Harbor. The Midway battle would have to start with no information about what ships the enemy had at Pearl Harbor, the most important base from which a strike against our forces could be dispatched.

The first thing that could go wrong with our Midway operation had now gone wrong. Other things were to follow. Cdr.

Shojiro Iura, representing our submarine fleet at Tokyo, had shown great foresight by protesting the use of SubRon 5 boats, all obsolescent, in the Midway operation. He predicted that they would not be able to do the jobs given them. He proved to be very, very correct.

These eight old boats, under Rear Adm. Tadashige Daigo, who used *Rio de Janeiro Maru* at Kwajalein for his flagship, had done some good work in the early operations to our south. *I-156* had pinpointed the position of HMS *Prince of Wales* and HMS *Repulse* for the *Mihoro, Genzan* and *Kanoya* naval air corps, which lost no time finding them and blasting them into extinction. All boats had later operated extensively with the fleet in those waters, for a period longer than should have reasonably been expected of them, before returning to Japan for overhaul. It takes far more effort to put an older warship back into battle condition than it does a new one. The submarines of SubRon 5 proved no exception to this axiom. Work on them took so long that they did not get clear of Japanese waters until well past their scheduled date. Then, after stopping at Kwajalein to refuel, they still had 2000 miles to go before reaching the posts assigned them on the patrol line. Much of this distance had to be traveled underwater, at slow speeds, to avoid detection by the long-range Catalina patrol bombers operating out of Midway! This wasted even more time.

Entirely too much credit for the American victory at Midway—and it was truly a great naval victory, won by brave and daring men—has been given to the fact that the Americans had broken our code and could read our messages almost as fast as our radio operators could. All that did was tell the Americans *where* we were going to attack and let them know how overwhelming was the force being sent against them.

Adm. Nimitz deduced the *place of attack* by a simple ruse. Thinking it might be Midway, he told the commander of that island to send him a message, *in plain language,* telling him it was having trouble desalting water. We had been calling Midway "Island F" in our messages, and when his intelligence men decoded our message saying that Island F was experiencing a breakdown in its water supply, Nimitz had final confirmation of our destination.

He still, however, had a much greater problem than merely knowing where we were going. How was he to defeat a force of more than 100 surface warships, when he could muster only a little more than two dozen to send against them? One of his ships, USS *Yorktown,* got into battle only because hordes of naval shipyard workers at Pearl Harbor (many of them the sons or grandsons of men born in Japan) swarmed over the big aircraft carrier and did a hurry-up job that let her go off to battle in spite of severe damage suffered a few weeks before at Coral Sea.

Knowing we were going to attack Midway, and having a pretty good idea of when, Adm. Nimitz planned to station all of his available surface forces at sea off our left flank. They would be given orders to make an all-out attack on our aircraft carriers, as soon as these were identified and located. Like Yamamoto, Nimitz greatly feared his enemy's naval air power. So he pinned all of his hopes on sinking as many of our aircraft carriers as he could. He positioned his striking force well to the northeast of Midway, where they were to hide and wait for the time of greatest opportunity.

Nimitz knew he was sending his ships and men on an almost-suicide mission. Should they encounter our surface fleet, they wouldn't have a chance. All of his hopes rested on two things. His very-long range patrol planes based on Midway had to locate our aircraft carriers, while his own carriers stayed out of range of the shorter-range planes we could send searching for them from our carriers. Then, his carriers might be able to race in and attack ours with their aircraft.

They got their chance chiefly because of the way SubRon 5 and other boats of the 6th Fleet were employed in the Midway campaign. Had our submarines been used properly and effectively, the history of the Pacific naval war might have been written quite differently.

Chapter 6

DEFEAT AT MIDWAY

The submarines that were heading for the Midway operation began leaving Japan on May 10, 1942. They kept streaming out of Tokyo Bay and from Bungo Strait, the water passage separating the islands of Honsho, Kyushu and Shikoku
from one another, for two weeks after that.

SubRon 5, the vital "sentry line" group of submarines so
important in the battle because it was supposed to provide us
any knowledge of the enemy nearing our aircraft carriers, was
in two divisions. Capt. Ryojiro Ono had four boats. These
were *I-156* under Lt. Cdr. Katsuo Ohashi, *I-157* under Lt.
Sakae Nakajima, *I-158* under Cdr. Sochichi Kitamura, and *I-
159* under Lt. Cdr. Tamori Yoshimatsu.

Advance notice of the poor fortune SubRon 5 would experience was given on May 17, just after some of the submarines had cleared Bungo Strait. Lt. Cdr. Yoshi Niina had
barely brought his boat around toward the east after exiting
the passage, and was cruising serenely on the surface, well with-

in range of protective air bases, when the USS *Triton*, which had been crusing in waters south of Kyushu, spied it. With one torpedo, *Triton* sent *I-164* to the bottom. The American submarine did not stop to pick up any of the survivors.

We suffered another submarine loss that day, but it was a boat playing no part in the Midway operation. She was *I-28*, only three months off the shipways, and had left Truk on April 30 to participate in the Coral Sea battle. On May 11, the battle over, *I-28* was ordered back to Truk. On May 16 she reported by wireless that she was 250 miles north of Rabaul, and having engine trouble. The American submarine *Tautog* surprised her next day. Cdr. Yasuo Yajima went down with his submarine and crew. If, as American sources claim, *Tautog* had also sunk *I-23* three weeks before off Oahu, she was indeed proving herself to be a powerful enemy.

On May 27 (the Japanese Navy Day because it is the anniversary of Adm. Heihachiro Togo's great victory over the Russian fleet at Tsushima in 1905) the bulk of our surface forces departed Japanese waters. The Northern Force, under Vice Adm. Moshiro Hosogaya, headed for the Aleutians. Hosogaya had under him a carrier striking force, invasion troops for Attu and Kiska, and the submarines of Rear Adm. Yamazaki. The Midway Invasion Force moved out from the Marianas, under Vice Adm. Nobutake Kondo. He also had auxiliary ships with him, and his force of 15 troop transports was protected by the world's greatest torpedo tactician, Rear Adm. Raizo Tanaka. Tanaka would become "chief engineer" of what the Americans called the Tokyo Express in the Solomons a few months later. They would nickname him "Tenacious" Tanaka because of his aggressive spirit, and he was also called "the Japanese Arleigh Burke." Some students of naval warfare like to ponder Tanaka and Burke in the same way American boxing fans speculate about Jack Dempsey and Joe Louis, both former world's heavyweight boxing champions. They try to imagine what it would be like if those men met each other in a match while each was at the peak of his prowess. The torpedo tactics of both Tanaka and Burke are studied by destroyermen, for the battles of Cape St. George and Tassafaronga during the struggle for the Solomons. Tanaka had been transferred to a shore station in Burma by the time Burke got into the Pacific theater of war. It would have been interesting had these two great fighters met in sea combat, but it is perhaps fortunate they never did. One or both might have died facing each other.

The Carrier Striking Force that was to immobilize Midway

Island, and soften it up for invasion, was centered around *Kaga, Akagi, Hiryu* and *Soryu,* under Vice Adm. Chuichi Nagumo. He had led these four flat-tops, plus *Shokaku* and *Zuikaku,* against Pearl Harbor in December. But *Shokaku* had been heavily damaged in the Coral Sea battle two weeks earlier and *Zuikaku* had lost aircraft and men that could not be replaced in time to let her join Nagumo's forces. Another of the earlier objections by Naval General Staff members to the Midway plan—that replacement of aircraft and airmen was a critical problem—had been proven.

Still, Adm. Yamamoto, steaming to sea with the Main Body in the tradition of a sea leader accompanying his ships, was full of confidence. The force around his flagship *Yamato* included two other battleships, a light aircraft carrier, a light cruiser, and nine destroyers. He also had with him *Chiyoda* and *Nisshin,* still listed as seaplane carriers but actually having on board 24 midget submarines. After Midway was taken, these were to be put ashore to help defend the island.

The plan for use of submarines extended well past the battle of Midway. Once 6th Fleet had been committed to it, planners started work on what would follow this great victory. The policy set down after our poor showing at Pearl Harbor, that submarines would operate chiefly against merchant vessels rather than against warships, was adjusted to follow up on the Midway operation.

A victory in mid-Pacific would leave the great might of our Combined Fleet barring the way across an ocean bereft of American naval power. Few ships would be able to supply Australia or fight against us. The air base to be built on Guadalcanal, in the southeastern Solomons, would help our ships keep watch on the U.S.-Australia route. So would a seaplane base to be established at Tulagi, just north of Guadalcanal. Air and surface operations would meet no opposition if the high command later wanted to take New Caledonia, Fiji, Samoa, the New Hebrides or any other place.

Strength in the central Pacific would free our submarines for other operations in other areas. We intended to use nearly all we had in the Indian Ocean. Our best submarines would be employed in one massive blockade. So submarine commanders operating in the Midway, U. S. West Coast, and Aleutians areas were ordered to put about after Midway was taken and to take up stations off Australia and in the Indian Ocean. We had an excellent base at Penang, Sumatra, from which the Indian Ocean submarines could operate in two groups. One of these would shut off the exit areas from the

Suez Canal, through which ships were coming in an effort to build up Allied strength in India. In concert with German submarines, these and another group of Japanese submarines would block supplies moving to Australia and India via the Cape of Good Hope.

You can see from the above how much depended on success at Midway. But this dream would never be realized, chiefly because use of our submarines in the Midway operation was so poor. Perhaps Combined Fleet had a low opinion of submarines, which had not sunk many enemy ships in the war's first months.

I shall only summarize the main action of the battle for Midway here. Nagumo's carriers moved in and made their attack on the island. American planes there (forewarned by patrol planes) took to the air before Nagumos's air strike arrived and landed after it left. Then the American land-based planes took off again, this time to strike at our aircraft carriers. Our ships' gunners and combat air patrol shot nearly every one of these attackers out of the sky.

Nagumo's air officers, meanwhile, had advised him that another air strike on Midway was necessary. At that time he had a force of torpedo planes in reserve on board *Kaga* and *Akagi*, plus an air strike force ready on *Hiryu* and *Soryu*. He quickly re-armed all returning planes, so that they could join in a massive air strike against an enemy sea force. He could have completely destroyed the American carrier force, which had not yet been found by his ship-based patrol craft.

But, when he came under attack from Midway aircraft, Nagumo decided to hit the island a second time, to destroy this threat from land. He ordered the torpedo planes to be struck below decks, so they could re-arm with bombs for this purpose. (Note: We had planes that could serve double duty, as torpedo or level bombers; the Americans did not). Nagumo's force was in this vulnerable condition, with his cover of fighter planes down near the surface beating off attackers from Midway and with torpedoes and bombs lying loose around the hangar decks of *Kaga* and *Akagi*, when enemy dive bombers suddenly appeared overhead. In a very short time, three of his four carriers were practically destroyed, with the fourth getting a fatal blow not long afterwards. By the next day at noon, *Kaga*, *Akagi*, *Hiryu* and *Soryu* were at the bottom of the sea. The only real damage done to the Americans in exchange for this horrendous loss was two bomb hits and two torpedo hits on the U. S. aircraft carrier *Yorktown*.

Adm. Yamamoto, with his heavy ships, raced rapidly toward Midway, hoping to catch the American carriers during the night and sink them; but he turned back after some hours on this course. The American carriers, on the other hand, steamed westward for a while, then wisely retreated to the east. Our invasion force had to be turned around, too, now that it had no air cover. Yamamoto eventually had to turn his entire fleet around and head back for Japan.

Just as Adm. Nimitz hoped, the flanking force of American aircraft carriers had been able to get into position northeast of Midway, and wait. The American aircraft carriers were able to reach their hiding position safely, and remain undetected there, *because the sentry line of SubRon 5 arrived on station too late!*

Japanese submarines enjoyed only one bright moment at Midway, and that came two days after the main battle was over. When three of our carriers were put out of action within minutes, the fourth one was a little to the north, and escaped that first blow. She was *Hiryu,* which managed to get off two small strikes against the American task force. *Hiryu*'s pilots bored in and crippled the *Yorktown,* suffering the loss of two-thirds of the their number in the attack. Those that got back reported one American carrier hit and burning.

At that time Lt. Cdr. Yahachi Tanabe was off Midway, within visual range of the island. He had been watching it for four days (through his periscope by day, and with binoculars at night). His *I-168* sent off the early reports of heavy activity by American patrol bombers based on Midway. It also had a front row seat for our air attack on the island.

Early on June 5, when Yamamoto was still speeding in with his Main Body, Tanabe was ordered to shell Midway, and was told he would be joined by our four heavy cruisers racing in from the west. Tanabe was spotted as soon as he surfaced and had to dive quickly. Later that morning, after scout planes from Nagumo's force again sighted *Yorktown,* they reported her as being dead in the water, about 150 miles northeast of Midway. A message was sent out at once: *"I-168* will locate and sink the American carrier."

Tanabe set off at once, cruising submerged until the sun had set. "Then," he said, "we ran on the surface for a while, but not at top speed because I was afraid we might miss the enemy in the blackness. It was 5:30 in the morning when one of my lookouts sighted the enemy carrier. She was a big shape on the horizon about 12 miles away."

I-168's crew leaped to their battle stations. "Stand by to dive!" shouted Tanabe. "Come right to new course, zero-four-five! Dive!" After he was inside his submarine's hull he ordered, "Level off at 90 feet! Slow to 6 knots!"

Six nerve-stretching hours followed, while *I-168*, slowed almost to a creep, worked her way into attack position. She eased off on her engines until her screws were barely making 3 knots. Every 30 minutes Tanabe brought *I-168* up to periscope depth so he could take a quick look at the situation. His periscope was never up for more than 5 seconds, but he was able to get a clear impression of what was happening. One ship, which he thought to be a destroyer, had the aircraft carrier in tow. He could see three more destroyers, so he assumed that there were at least two more on the carrier's other side, patrolling against submarines. The destroyers were about one mile out from the carrier, which convinced Tanabe that if he got off a shot at the carrier they would surely sink his boat in the counterattack.

Still, he pressed on. That aircraft carrier was too important a prize to let escape. He changed course a few degrees to the right from time to time, having noticed that the *Yorktown* was making some headway under her tow and moving east.

I-168's sound man told his captain that the American destroyers were operating their sound equipment. But, a little after 11 A.M., their "pinging" could no longer be heard. This puzzled Tanabe, but he kept his voice light as he told his crew, "The Americans seem to have interrupted their war for lunch!" and a crew member answered, "We shall give them some torpedoes for dessert!" The next time Tanabe put up his periscope for a quick sweep, he found himself inside the destroyer screen. Two destroyers were abaft his beam; one about 1000 yards to starboard, the other an equal distance to port. He was now heading straight for the carrier's center and should have given the order, "Make ready to fire!" Instead, he stunned his crew by calling out, "Down periscope! Right twenty degrees rudder!"

Tanabe's men must have thought he'd gone mad, but they obeyed his orders even before he began an explanation for his actions. *I-168*'s captain had been so intent on getting safely past the American escort ships that he had actually let himself get too close to the *Yorktown!* Now he was afraid that the run of his torpedoes would be too short to arm them, since it took several hundred yards to do that. What he had to do was make a complete circle, and get back on his original track. But he wanted to end up further away from the carrier when his circle was completed, so he eased off the rudder as *I-168* started to come around. The submarine made a wide circle, taking about an hour to do so, while her crew, in bare feet or thin cotton slippers, kept near-total silence.

I-168's periscope did not again appear above the surface until she was almost back on her original approach course. While he waited, Tanabe outlined a special plan to his torpedo officer. *I-168* at that time did not mount the giant Model 95 torpedoes with their 890-lb warheads. Tanabe's boat was armed with Model 89's, whose warheads carried only 649 pounds of explosive. He had an idea, as he put it, "for making 95's out of my 89's."

The usual spread for torpedoes was 2 or 3 degrees between their paths. Should *I-168* fire full salvo from her four forward tubes, the total spread would be 9 degrees. "But I wanted to concentrate my punch in the carrier's center," he said, "rather than spread it out along her hull. So I planned to fire my torpedoes in pairs, with a 2-degree spread for each pair. Furthermore, I planned to fire Tubes 1 and 2 first, then send torpedoes from Tubes 3 and 4 right behind them, in their wakes. If all went well, those four torpedoes would hit very close together and do maximum possible damage to the enemy ship."

By 1 P.M. of June 6, Tanabe was squared away on his original track, but the American destroyers appeared to have no knowledge of his presence. I have since read that a thick blanket of oil, seeping from the damaged flat-top, may have affected performance of enemy sound equipment, rendering it practically useless. Ready to fire, Tanabe began to plan his escape after the attack. The wakes of his torpedoes, which were not of the oxygen-propelled type and therefore could be easily seen, would reveal his position. Men on board the carrier would know at once where they came from, though it would do them little good by that time. He called out "Fire!" and the torpedoes raced out ahead of him while he kept his periscope above the water to observe their results.

Nearly a full minute passed before the first torpedo struck. "A hit!" Tanabe shouted, and someone else in the conning tower responded with *"Banzai!"* Others called out, "We did it! We did it!" as they heard more explosions follow the first one.

"Go ahead at full speed!" ordered Tanabe. "Dive to 200 feet!" The submarine lurched forward and downward, and Tanabe soon called out, "Slow to 3 knots!" He planned to get squarely beneath the carrier if possible, then make a turn toward her stern and escape under cover of explosions above him. He had seen a fifth destroyer nestled alongside the carrier, and felt that no depth charges would be fired for fear

74

of killing any men who might land in the water.

Once below the *Yorktown*, Tanabe swung his rudder left and began creeping past her stern. The American destroyers were on him at once. Three appeared to be attacking him; one holding his position on its sound equipment while the other two made depth charge runs. These ships should have killed *I-168*, but Yahachi Tanabe led a charmed life. Each time his sound man reported an enemy ship making its run, Lt. Cdr. Tanabe would swing his boat around to a course opposite that of his attacker. Most of the time this resulted in the Americans over-running him, all depth charges dropping into the water well aft of *I-168*'s stern.

The enemy was clever enough not to stay with one tactic for too long. Two hours passed without much more damage done to *I-168* than a good shaking up. Then one destroyer dropped a pattern of depth charges short. They exploded very near *I-168*'s bow.

"All lights went out at once," says Tanabe, "and a few seconds later my forward battery room was reporting water leaks." These could cause chlorine gas to form, killing the crew of 104 (for whom Tanabe had only 10 gas masks on board). Lt. Gunichi Mochizuki, the electrical officer, took the masks and a few crewmen and went into the battery room. His party disconnected the flooded batteries, eliminating this danger. Then word of another danger was passed from the forward torpedo room. "The outer and inner doors of Torpedo Tube No. 1 had been sprung by the blasts," he says, "and water was coming into the boat. Unless it could be stopped, *I-168* would become bow-heavy, sink below her safe operating depth, and be crushed by sea pressure along with all of us in her."

Crewmen finally sealed off the damaged torpedo tube with wedges, dowels, and whatever else they could lay their hands upon. The immediate danger was averted. "But we were still down by the bow because of the water we had taken aboard," says Tanabe, "so I used a tactic other submarines were to use throughout the war. I sent forward all crewmen who could be spared. Each one of them picked up a sack of rice or a box of provisions and carried it aft, going back again for another."

That tactic helped Tanabe get his boat back on a fairly even keel by the time electrical power was restored.

By then *I-168* had been cruising submerged for nearly 12 hours. Her batteries and air supply were low, because of the maneuvering done while dodging depth charges. She would soon have to surface to recharge batteries and to replenish her air tanks. From 3:30 in the afternoon the depth charges had been coming down less and less often and in smaller groups. Tanabe decided that the Americans were hoarding what depth charges they had left. Actually, a few more all-out attacks might have caused *I-168* to broach out of control, an easy target for gunfire. The same depth charge that had sprung her torpedo tube doors and caused flooding of battery cells had also made her surge nearly 100 feet toward the surface, temporarily helpless.

Tanabe had 5 pistols and 10 rifles in his small arms locker. He issued these, and ordered his deck gun crew to stand by near the conning tower, so they could get on deck quickly. Sunset was not far off. If he could avoid the enemy ships for a little while longer, he hoped to surface after dark, run a while to recharge his batteries and air, then make another dive. He still had plenty of torpedoes, with five tubes left for firing them, and intended to make a fight of it. In the dark, he felt, his submarine might have an advantage, even though outnumbered.

A long lull occurred in the enemy's fire. Tanabe decided his chance had come, his soundman having reported only very weak propeller sounds. "Surface!" he ordered, and began running west at 14 knots, the best speed *I-168* could make while taking in air and recharging her batteries. Far to the east, beyond the horizon, he was sure an enemy aircraft carrier was sinking. He had seen his torpedoes strike into her and explode. Not as far to the east, however, were the three destroyers. They were about six miles astern of him, heading away from him at a good speed. Two came about in pursuit and a race against time began. With their superior speed, the destroyers were sure to overtake Tanabe before long. He had to stay free long enough to let his men get *I-168* ready for a dive.

"Make smoke!" he ordered, and a great, billowing black cloud soon streamed over his stern. He used it for cover. It helped for a little while and the first shells from the destroyers landed nowhere near him. The Americans had started shooting at a range of four miles, seemed too excited to shoot straight at first (perhaps because they wanted revenge so badly) but they soon became more accurate. Before long, Tanabe's boat was straddled by a salvo of shells. It was merely a matter of time until an alert gunnery officer "walked" shots back and forth across him for a direct hit. That would mean the end of *I-168*.

"I can remember the moment of that straddle most vividly,"

says Tanabe, "Men on deck began darting quick looks at me, their faces taut and pale. They were anxious to get back inside the hull and for *I-168* to dive. Only their long training and discipline kept them at their posts, just as it kept me at mine. I could also detect a note of strain in the voices of the men below, as they called up reports. Those men, intent on dials and gauges, knew we had to stay on the surface long enough to give our boat a fighting chance. But they also wanted to get beneath the surface, away from enemy guns. I held off as long as I dared, then shouted down, "Have you enough air and power for short-time operations?"

"Yes!" came the rapid answer.

"Then stand by to dive!" Tanabe yelled, ordering his gun crew and lookouts below. He followed them down the hatch and tried another ruse to fool the trailing destroyermen. He ordered the rudder put full over, reversed his course while still on the surface, and dived while heading straight at his pursuers. Because of the black smoke, they couldn't see what he was doing. As Tanabe hoped, the destroyers ran right over him and *I-168*'s crewmen enjoyed a few moments free of fear. The destroyers located him again after a while, but fired only a few more depth charges before breaking off their attack.

The enemy faded off Tanabe's sound equipment to the east. He assumed that they had been summoned back to the carrier, possibly to help pick up survivors. In any case, his ship was spared. By carefully husbanding his fuel supplies, Tanabe was able to make it back to Kure via a northern route, heading first for Hokkaido, veering south for Yokosuka, then to Kure. He deliberately passed up the shorter trip to Truk, in case the enemy were still searching for him.

A great crowd awaited *I-168* at Kure. Tanabe was hailed as a national hero. He was immediately given command of a new submarine, *I-176,* together with the privilege of hand-picking the crew for it. His experiences in *I-168* made him pick men with lots of factory machine experience as civilians. The wise choices he made were to save his life and his new submarine later.

The battle for Midway was over. Japan had lost four of its first-line aircraft carriers, a heavy cruiser, 300 aircraft with most of their airmen, and 2000 sailors. This proved to be the turning point of the war, even though the Americans also suffered very severe losses in planes and pilots, plus a carrier and a destroyer. America could never have made its assault on Guadalcanal two months later, had it not known that Japan's carrier airpower had been sorely weakened in the June battle.

When the Combined Fleet returned to Japan, the crews of its ships were restricted to their vessels for weeks. Even flag officers like Rear Adm. Raiso Tanaka had to remain on board, for fear that word of the awful defeat might leak out. The wounded were taken from their ships at night and secluded in hospitals with no visitors allowed. Publicly, the high command put a bold face on things, releasing the following communique:

"IMPERIAL GENERAL HEADQUARTERS, June 10 (3:30 P.M.) Imperial Navy units operating in the eastern Pacific repeatedly raided Dutch Harbor and enemy key points in the Aleutians on June 4 and 5.
"On June 5 they vigorously attacked Midway Island in the center of the Pacific, inflicting heavy losses on the American fleet and air units in that area.
"In effective cooperation with the Imperial Army units, the Navy has captured key points on the Aleutian Islands since June 7. The battle in that sector is still going on.
"The results ascertained to date are as follows:
1. In Midway area. One American aircraft carrier of the *Enterprise* class and one American aircraft carrier of the *Hornet* class were sunk. Approximately 120 enemy planes were shot down in air battles. Military key points were blown up.
2. In Dutch Harbor area. Fourteen enemy planes shot down or destroyed on the ground. One large transport was sunk. Two groups of petroleum and a larger hangar were caused to burst into flames.
3. Losses to the Imperial Navy were one aircraft carrier. Another aircraft carrier and a cruiser were badly damaged, and 35 planes have yet to return to their bases."

The truth was not very long in getting out. Men could not be held on board their ships forever, and in a few weeks word spread through the Fleet of our terrible losses. The news spread among the citizenry after that, but not much happened. Top officials could show that Japanese garrisons were almost everywhere. The great victory in the Philippines (over an army of 100,000 men) was still fresh in all minds, Corregidor having surrendered in May. And the public still believed the communiqué issued after the Battle of the Coral Sea. It had listed two American aircraft carriers, one American battleship, and one destroyer as having been sunk. It also claimed heavy damage to a British battleship, an Australian heavy cruiser, and an American heavy cruiser of unidentified class. It reported that

89 enemy planes had been shot down, while admitting only the loss of a small Japanese aircraft carrier.

But, so far as the Japanese public was concerned, all seemed to be going well. They continued to endure the hardship of rationing, just as they had been doing for the previous three years, well before the war started. They did not know that all the damage 125 Japanese warships had been able to do in the Pacific, outside of a few bombings, was sink the aircraft carrier *Yorktown,* destroyer *Hammann,* and two merchant ships, SS *Coldbrook,* 5104 tons, and SS *Coast Trader,* 3286 tons. I give Cdr. Minoru Yokota and *I-26* credit for this last vessel, sent to the bottom off the U. S. West Coast.

I will now indulge in what the Americans call "Monday morning quarterbacking." After the Battle of Midway, the staff of Adm. Yamamoto got along much better with members of the Naval General Staff, chiefly because the defeat made Combined Fleet staff men a lot less arrogant. But Midway should have been a victory. Over 200 Japanese ships were employed in this effort. Some have written that American intelligence efforts really won the battle. This is not true. Others have put the blame on Adm. Yamamoto, saying he should have kept his vast naval strength together, crushing the Americans with it when they met. Yamamoto is blameless. He did what was right. He kept his Main Body in position where it could move to back up either his northern or southern forces (Aleutians or Midway) if either were attacked.

American carrier admirals, who have the advantage of speaking from victories they won only when they finally outnumbered the remaining Japanese carriers and had learned many lessons from men other than themselves, say that Yamamoto should have put his Main Body among his carriers, so it could provide antiaircraft protection for them. Had this been done, they say, Nagumo's ships would not have suffered so much harm in just one dive-bombing attack. It is true that these men employed their battleships in company with their carriers, but I suggest that it might have been more because they *had to,* rather than that they *wanted* to. In the first years of the war, the Americans had to make do with what they had. It is to their credit that they refined the carrier-battleship task force into a mighty weapon. Again, however, one should look at the list of ships America could use in front-line battle during 1942-43, before deciding whether battleships-with-carriers was an invented or a necessary development of naval warfare.

Nagumo has been attacked for his indecisiveness. Of this

charge he certainly was guilty. A look at the Pearl Harbor and other attacks he led, provides evidence to support this verdict. On Dec. 7, 1941, Nagumo sent half of his air strength in, and kept the other half ready for a repeat attack. This second half was also ready to attack enemy aircraft carriers, should they appear. And, while the second half was over Pearl Harbor, the first half was on flight decks, arming and refueling for a strike against any naval force sighted.

Four months later, when the Nagumo force hit Colombo, Ceylon, the same tactic was used. One wave went in, while another stood by. The first wave was enroute to target when scouts reported the presence of British capital ships. Without hesitation Nagumo sent off his second wave against these new targets. It sank the british cruisers *Cornwall* and *Dorsetshire.*

A few days after that, Nagumo attacked British shipping in the harbor of Trincomalee, Ceylon. Again he had a second wave ready, and again a scout reported the presence of a second force, this one including an aircraft carrier. And again, without any hesitation, Nagumo launched his second wave against a second target. Those planes sent the carrier HMS *Hermes* and HMS *Vampire,* a destroyer, to the bottom.

The general impression has been that American fliers were the first to sink a carrier from a carrier, and that the Battle of the Coral Sea was the first time a battle was fought without the opposing ships coming within sight of each other. This impression is, of course, wrong. HMS *Hermes,* a light carrier, was sunk by Japanese flyers a full month before the Coral Sea battle, in the first such engagement.

Now then, since he had twice done so earlier, why did not Nagumo send off his ready aircraft against the American ships in the Midway battle when they were first sighted? *And,* there is a much more important question to be asked than why Yamamoto spread his strength so widely, and why Nagumo hesitated. Neither question would have to be asked, had the enemy been located earlier. So I ask, *why were submarines not used properly in the first place, since they held the actual key to success at Midway?*

For the attack on Pearl Harbor, a total of 14 submarines were used in a screen. I was executive officer in one of them, *I-15,* cruising in line abreast with 10 other submarines, 300 miles ahead of Nagumo. Three other submarines were just 50 miles ahead of him. Had this simple tactic been repeated during the approach to Midway, with the line of submarines swinging to the eastward on Nagumo's flank, surely some submarines would have sighted the American carriers. Cdr. Iura was cor-

Seated with the *kaiten* pilots of *I-36* in foreground is Vice-Admiral Daigo, unjustly executed for being a war criminal.

Kaiten pilots of *I-36* of the *Todoroki* Group, were a Japanese last-ditch *tokko*, or suicide attempt to slow allied invasions.

Early in the war, Nobuo Fujita flew a biplane over Oregon and dropped fire bombs and was the only man to bomb the United States.

In the student hall of the Naval Academy at Etajima, the first floor was reserved for study halls and the second for sleeping.

The long-distance swimming exercises practiced at Etajima were to later save lives when men were stranded in the open sea.

Modern physical education programs were stressed at Etajima Academy.

Traditional naval skills like rowing were highly stressed for the development of skilled Japanese sailors.

Ancient martial arts like *kendo* were emphasized to maintain pride in Japanese culture and traditions.

Forward-thinking men like Nariakira Shimazu (1825-1858) felt that to survive in a modern world, Japan would have to become a modern nation with a well-armed navy.

Takamori Saigo was one of the men who helped throw out the feudal regime of the *shogun* and establish the emperor as supreme ruler of Japan.

This midget sub, or *koryu*, attempted to penetrate Pearl Harbor but sank outside the harbor entrance.

Once its *kaiten* were mounted on a sub, it could submerge and search for a target ship to attack.

This post-war photo shows the catapult ramp from which the *Seiran* aircraft were launched from the deck of the *I-400*.

The *Seiran* were single-engine monoplanes whose seaplane floats could be jettisoned for a *kamikaze* attack on enemy ships.

Hiroshi Kuroki and Sekio Nishina were co-inventors of the *kaiten* weapons that preceded the *kamikaze* effort.

Submarine N. 6 sank during testing by T. Sakuma. It was raised to become a monument to submariners.

Midget subs launched from the decks of fast-moving destroyers were to be a surprise to the U.S. Navy.

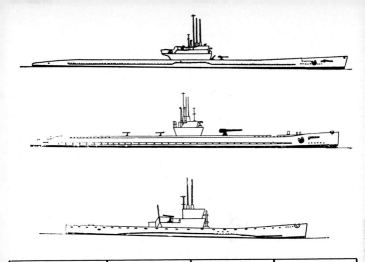

Transport Sub		I-351	I-361	Ha-101
Disp.	Surface	3511	1779	429
	Sub	4290	2215	493
Dimension		111x10x6.1	73.5x8.9x4.8	44.5x6.1x4.0
Sp (S.H.P.)	Surface	15.8 (3700)	13.0 (1850)	10 (400)
	Sub	6.3 (1200)	6.5 (1300)	5 (150)
Armament		8cmAA x 4 25^m/mMG x 7 Tube 4 (aft) Torpedo 5	14cm x 1 25^m/mMG x 2	(Single screw) 25^m/m x 1
Radius	Surface	14-13000	10-15000	10-3000
	Sub	3-100	3-120	2.5-46
Max. Depth		90	75	100
Same type		2	12	12
		Gasoline 500T. torpedo, bomb.		

The Japanese navy used three basic types of transport subs to supply their troops when conventional means were considered impossible.

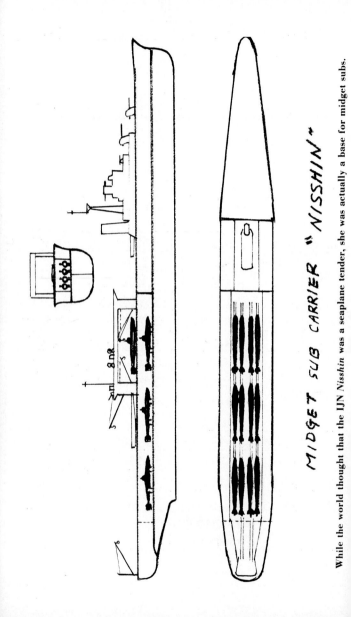

MIDGET SUB CARRIER "NISSHIN"

While the world thought that the IJN *Nisshin* was a seaplane tender, she was actually a base for midget subs.

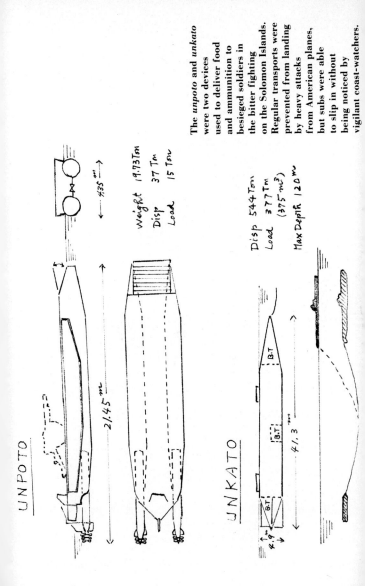

UNPOTO

← 4.35 m →

Weight 19.73 Tm
Disp 37 Tm
Load 15 Tm

UNKATO

Disp 544 Tm
Load 377 Tm (375 m³)

Max Depth 120 m

← 41.3 m →

B.T

B.T

B.T

4.9 m

The *unpoto* and *unkato* were two devices used to deliver food and ammunition to besieged soldiers in the bitter fighting on the Solomon Islands. Regular transports were prevented from landing by heavy attacks from American planes, but subs were able to slip in without being noticed by vigilant coast-watchers.

Carrier-based Japanese planes dropped their bombs at Pearl Harbor, and the 1,500-ton destroyer *Shaw* was turned into a twisted mass of wreckage

rect, of course, in his low estimate of SubRon 5's ability. Tokyo planners should have listened to him. A moderate change in plans could have sent newer and more powerful submarines out far earlier to form that sentry line between Pearl Harbor and Midway. They would have discovered the Americans lurking on Nagumo's flank, would have alerted Nagumo and probably sunk some of them, too.

Because it wasn't done at Midway, what Adm. Yamamoto feared *did* happen. The enemy came in from the flank, catching our forces by surprise and Japan lost the bulk of a naval air strength which, to that point, had been responsible for nearly all of its victories. The master plan to close off more than half of the world's waters to the enemy was wrecked. And it all happened purely because those planning the Midway assault did not give enough attention to establishing early contact with the counterattacking force. Again and again, this lesson of poor employment of submarines at Midway would later be brought home to us. American submarines, on many occasions, reported movements of our forces early, and struck at them as they passed (using the basic strategy we ourselves had been practicing for in the pre-war years). One-third of all Japanese warships sunk went down before the torpedoes of submarines under Vice Adm. Charles A. Lockwood, commander of U. S. underwater forces in the Pacific. Apparently he and his staff had far less trouble convincing their seniors how submarines should best be employed in war. Except for heavy accent on how many of our merchant ships they sank in the war, the full role of American submarines against us has never been properly explained: They won the Pacific naval war for America!

Some of the Japanese submarines with the Aleutians force went on to the west coast of America after the Midway battle. *I-26* shelled a Canadian telegraph station at Estewan Point, Vancouver, on June 20. On the next day *I-25* shelled Fort Stevens, Oregon, with Cdr. Tagami shrewdly taking his boat in and out through a fleet of fishing boats. This made detection and pursuit of him very difficult for the enemy.

The midget-carrying submarines off Sydney continued to operate in those waters and reported several sinkings. On June 7-8, *I-21* bombarded the city of Newcastle, Australia. It was the other group of midget carriers, however, that sent in the best news. After severely damaging a British battleship and sinking a tanker at Diego Suarez, they moved north and covered the Suez Canal exits. *I-10* especially enjoyed great success. All told, these submarines sank more than 20 enemy ships in the two months following the Midway battle.

I graduated from submarine commanders' school at the end of June, with orders to take over command of *RO-101*, a brand-new medium-sized submarine. Just before I finished the course, our class received some startling news. We did not fully realize it at the time, but it was the true turning point of the war for Japan's submarine power, just as Midway was the true turning point for our naval airpower. *I-1, I-2, I-3, I-4, I-5, I-6,* and *I-7* had been dispatched from home waters to support the thrust into the Aleutians. On June 21, while patrolling in a very thick fog which made visibility almost zero, *I-5*'s deck watch suddenly found themselves showered by enemy shells, some of which came dangerously close to hitting their submarine. *I-5*'s captain ordered a crash dive at once, and the sub just barely escaped annihilation. This was the first indication that the Americans had *radar* in their ships, and could use it to control gunfire. Radar was to prove a big factor in the defeat of my country, and the most ironic thing about it is that the Americans, for all their reputation for inventiveness, *got the heart of their radar from Japan!*

Radar was not in any kind of sense an American invention or development, since the Americans got their first assistance with radar from the British, who were reluctant at first to share this secret with their proposed allies. Dr. Hidenobu Yagi, of Japan, developed the "Yagi antenna," whose principle was the heart of most radar sets used during World War II and later. He developed it long before World War II started, but no one in Japan attributed any military significance to Yagi's invention, thus proving the biblical saying that a prophet is not without honor, except in his own country. The Japanese scientist accomplished this, mind you, nearly *10 years* before the Pacific war started!

During the early thirties Dr. Yagi visited the United States, where he delivered papers on his antenna before various scientific bodies. These papers were printed in American journals. Later, enemy scientists turned his writings to their advantage to help them in refining this electronic phenomenon. Japan, on the other hand, made no great effort to produce radar. More than two years of conflict passed before a dependable radar set appeared on board any of our warships.

So, as June, 1942, ended, the general news coming to us at Kure was not good, except for the accomplishments of the Indian Ocean submarines. Nevertheless, I was optimistic. I had enjoyed a few months of Hisako's excellent cooking and warm companionship, together with the gurgling company of my fine son Shuichi. And before long I would board my first submarine command, something I had been looking forward to since my days at Etajima.

Chapter 7.

MY FIRST COMMAND.
GUADALCANAL ASSAULTED.

I had been looking forward to the day I took command of *RO-101* to supervise her completion for more than a dozen years. I had high hopes for what I might accomplish with her because I was a "Kagoshima boy." All my life I had been very aware of this. I still am. The place of my birth is where the Imperial Japanese Navy was also born.

In June, 1853, an American squadron under Commodore Matthew Perry docked at Uraga-machi, on Tokyo Bay. In September of that year, a Russian force of ships moored at Nagasaki. Japan, after nearly 240 years of self-imposed isolation, had her doors wrenched open to the world against her will. In my home city of Kagoshima at that time lived the *daimyo* Nariakira Shimazu, the noble whose family had ruled the southern section of Japan's southernmost main island for generations, using *samurai* warriors to control it. Of all our people, Lord Shimazu knew most about foreigners. Kagoshima City is in the prefecture (state) of Kagoshima, which has a long coastline, and includes many small islands. Our people were hardy seafarers, who therefore had some previous contact with the outside world.

Lord Shimazu at once realized that Japan would be ravaged by foreigners unless she built adequate defenses, a prediction shortly proved true by the infliction on us of unfair, one-sided treaties and the bilking of us out of our gold supplies. *Jokamachi* (castle towns), like Kagoshima had been for nearly 700 years, might be all right for maintaining internal security, but they meant little against a sea invasion by foreigners. Shimazu at once requested permission of *Shogun* Hideyoshi Tokugawa's regime to build a warship for coastal defense. Receiving it, he launched a warship the next year, mounting cannon. These were tended by *samurai* artillerymen from among his retainers.

He helped overthrow the *shogun* regime and restore the Emperor to his throne, but Lord Shimazu also later became involved in a civil war over attitudes toward foreigners, his ships fighting a naval battle with those of the new government. Nevertheless he holds a dear place in the hearts of Kagoshima people for his effort to bring them swiftly out of the medieval and into the modern age. He opened many schools so young people could get an education. The brighter students he sent to Tokyo (and some to Europe) for higher learning. He wanted to bring knowledge of Western civilization to our home. Because of Shimazu, a preponderance of modern Japan's educated men came 'from Kagoshima, although it was the poorest section, materially, of Japan. These men played important roles during the last part of the 19th century.

A part of Kagoshima City near where Shimazu's castle was located is called Kajiya-cho. It is a very small area, even smaller than one square block of New York City, but the *samurai* spirit has always been strong there. This tiny place had an impact on Japan all out of proportion to its physical size. Among the famous men born in Kajiya-cho was Takamori Saigo, Japan's first modern general. He played a leading role in the Restoration, which culminated in 1868 with the *shogun* overthrown and young Emperor Meiji ascending the throne to power. Prior to that, for centuries our Emperors had been figureheads, the real power being exercised by *shogun* (foreigner-defeating warriors) who were charged with the defense of Japan. Another famous Kajiya-cho man was Iwao Oyama, who helped mold a modern army out of Japan's peasant class when the *samurai* were disbanded. He was senior officer in the Imperial Japanese Army during the Russo-

Japanese War. A third was Toshimichi Okubo, faithful servant of the Meiji government and contributor to the first parliamentary system of rule in Japan. A fourth was Tamesada Kuroki, general in the war with Russia. A fifth was Gombei Yamamoto, who became Navy Minister during the war with Russia and was twice Prime Minister, as well as attaining the Navy rank of Admiral.

And there was still another man who came from this tight cluster of homes in Kajiya-cho. Still idolized in Japan, he was Heihachiro Togo, who defeated one force of Russian ships then completely destroyed or captured a second force sent more than halfway around the world to defeat him. His flagship at the Battle of Tsushima Strait, IJN *Mikasa,* was restored in Yokosuka as a national shrine during the fifties. An American who greatly admired Togo was Fleet Adm. Chester W. Nimitz, USN, who lent his great name in an effort to remind our people of their great naval traditions through IJN *Mikasa.* Nimitz compared Togo's flagship with HMS *Victory* and with USS *Constitution,* the "Old Ironsides" of which America is so proud.

I was born on March 20, 1910. Throughout my boyhood and young manhood I strove to be as much like Admiral Togo as possible, especially in physical accomplishment and stamina. So, I think, did every other Kagoshima boy. Togo's father was a *samurai,* who gave his son an extremely spartan example to emulate. The younger *samurai* excelled not only in studies, but in fencing, swimming, *sumo* wrestling, hiking and mountain climbing. When he was only 17, he helped fight off a British force that shelled Kagoshima in reprisal for the killing of two Englishmen near Yokohama. Togo enlisted in Shimazu's navy at 19 and fought in two naval battles not long afterward. When he was 26, the national government sent him to England, where he studied the ways of a modern fleet. His victory over the Russians on May 27, 1905, at Tsushima Strait (northwest of Kyushu) electrified the world, especially the Japanese people. Suddenly Japan, in less than 40 years, had leaped forward 400 years! In 1867 her warriors wore suits of armor and fought with swords. In 1905 they crouched over telescopic gunsights in steel turrets, mounted in ships so superior that British newspapers complained that Britsh shipyards built better ships for foreigners than for the Royal Navy. The victory also affected other Asians deeply, for this was the first victory over white men in that part of the world.

All this was a great source of pride to the stern, tough people of Togo's home town. It affected every activity of my youth.

Each day, after grammar school classes, I went with my schoolmates (all boys) to a club. There, in an effort to be like Admiral Togo, I studied, debated, and learned from older persons about our traditions, while competing with other in fencing, *judo,* and *sumo.* The *samurai* spirit was high in us as we voluntarily performed close-order drill. We talked much about how a Japanese should be brave, be courteous and be simple in his living habits.

Once a year the Imperial Combined Fleet would come to Kagoshima and anchor in the broad bay. Swarms of people would go out to visit it. When I was 11 years old the mighty battleship *Mutsu* was its flagship and I was much impressed with the shining brasswork, the gleaming steel decks, and the immaculate messing and berthing spaces. It was a great thrill for a young boy to see those officers and sailors move briskly about their duties. I visited the very peak of the forecastle (the tip of the battleship's bow) and laid my hand on the gilded chrysanthemum carried there, the symbol of Imperial Japan. At that moment I made myself a promise. "Some day, Zenji," I told myself, "you are going to serve in the Imperial Navy! You will be a crew member of this mighty ship and you will again lay your hand on this glorious symbol."

I was still a student in grammer school when some war booty German submarines were exhibited at Kagoshima. My teacher visited one and actually made a dive in it. He told us many stories about that adventure and of what the German submarines had accomplished before their nation was defeated. This and the visit to *Mutsu* made me feel strongly that I wanted a Navy career.

Two other boys in my class were similarly influenced, Taro Ebihara, son of a retired rear admiral, and Shigeshi Kuriyama, son of a pharmacist. Cdr. Ebihara died on board a destroyer in the fighting for the Solomons. Lt. Cdr. Kuriyama gave his life while skippering *RO-33,* just about the time I put *RO-101* in commission.

I moved up to Kagoshima's Middle School in 1922, a step that made my parents very proud. It was located in Kajiya-cho, near Shimazu's castle. Only top students could enter this school, which had a reputation for scholarship going back 50 years to the Restoration period. Discipline was tight, the course difficult, and the athletic program very strenuous. I did pretty well in my studies, but actually excelled in sports. Included in the curriculum (which was much influenced by the *samurai* spirit universal among Kagoshima people) was military training, supervised by a pair of retired Army officers.

Under them was a major who inspired all of us, though he was very tough. He maintained high standards, demanded high performance, and talked often about the importance of both. The Washington Naval Disarmament Treaty of 1922 had caused Japan, like other nations, to make a radical reduction in the student bodies of its military and naval academies. "That is why now is the best possible time," this man would say to us many times, "for you to enter the military life. Before many years pass, men from the two academies will be the leaders of Japan's military forces. And those forces will again be much larger than they are now."

Many years later I would command a submarine rushing to this man's aid at Okinawa. There, American marines and Army troops would learn what a strong and disciplined fighter he was, and pay for this lesson in rivers of blood. His name was Mitsuru Ushijima, his rank then Lieutenant-General.

Because the Kagoshima district was so poor, few boys could get higher educations. So it was everyone's dream to win admission to the military or naval academy. Few from Kagoshima got into the military academy, which got the bulk of its cadets from Yamaguchi prefecture (an area strongly inclined toward Army life) but many were successful from near my home (an area with a long sea tradition) at getting into the naval academy. In January, 1928, I took the entrance examination for Etajima, Japan's Annapolis. Over 4000 boys throughout Japan, all holding high academic standing, competed for the 130 appointments. Unlike the U. S., where most appointments are obtained through political influence, our academy was open to every boy in the land. Requirements were: a good character, attested to by several prominent citizens; a high level of physical fitness; and a high academic standing. No one who wore glasses was considered at all, nor were men who had more than a couple of teeth missing. There was but one exception to the rules: members of the Royal Family could enter, provided they passed the physical examination. They did not have to take the other tests. And some members of the Royal Family *did* matriculate at Etajima, including Prince Takamatsu, brother of the Emperor.

The physical examination was most meticulous, the written one very severe. There were tests on eight different academic subjects, and the entire proceedings took a week. Then we all went home, nervous and irritable. All 4000 candidates must have been impossible to live with during the next two months while they waited for the results. In spite of the tension, I enjoyed basking in the new attention given me locally. About 150 boys from Kagoshima took the examination that year, which in itself was a great honor. I found myself thinking that at least I had been allowed to take it, which would be some consolation should I fail to gain entrance.

Then, in March of 1929, seventeen other boys and myself received word that we had been selected. My back was very stiff with pride on April 4, 1929, as I entered Etajima, my new blue uniform as yet unwrinkled, a short sword at my side. I was in the 59th Class. While Annapolis men are marked by the *year* in which they are graduated, Japanese men used the graduating class *number*. My class was to be the 59th to complete the course, and I would ever after be a "59th man."

On my first Sunday at Etajima, an instructor marched all 130 of us to the top of Mt. Furutaka, which rose 1000 feet behind the academy. As we stood on its crest and looked north, we could see Hiroshima. To the east was the great naval arsenal at Kure, black plumes of smoke rising from its shops. Below us lay the academy compound, and on the water between our island school and the mainland lay countless moored ships. I can still recall my main thought on that day— how the scene before me seemed divided between the artificial and the natural—the man-made ships and the lovely pine trees, sea and grass.

Then I buckled down to months of arduous schooling. Our day began at 5:30 A.M. and ended at 10 P.M., with little time spared for leisure. Our subjects included the Japanese language, mathematics, electronics, machinery engineering, astronomy, oceanology, and others. In addition, we had the special naval subjects of gunnery, torpedoes, navigation, communications, and engineering. The English language was a required subject for every midshipman, and we also had to study one other foreign language as well. I chose French.

There were three classes (the 57th, 58th, and 59th) in the academy when I started there, having about 120-130 midshipmen in each. We were organized both horizontally and vertically. The 59th, for example, was split into four divisions. I lived, ate, slept, and studied with mine. There were, of course, 12 such in the Academy, giving horizontal organization within our own graduating groups. Vertical organization was accomplished by dividing each class into 12 sections, a section of one class, (say the 59th) being combined with sections of the 57th and 58th for all extra-academic activities. Thus a man in Class 59, Division 1, Section 1 went to class with Division 1 men, but when it came time for athletics he participated with Section 1 men of the upper classes. This gave good

105

balance and made sports highly competitive. It also helped men to become acquainted with those senior to them at an early date, rather than be segregated from them for 3½ years, then have to meet them for the first time on active duty.

Meals were simple. So were accommodations. We had one general sleeping room and one general study room for every 30 cadets or so. All midshipmen ate in one general mess hall, which had much room to spare because classes had been so reduced in number. Our only really free times were Saturday afternoons and from 8 A.M. to 5 P.M. on Sundays. The two half-hours we had free during the rest of the week were usually given over to some extra, needed study. We could leave the compound on Sundays and go into the town of Etajima, but there was no kind of diversion there at all; no stores, no teahouses, or restaurants where a midshipman might want to shop or relax. What we did have there, were clubs. The welfare and morale department of the Academy arranged that the use of one was obtained for 30 midshipmen. We could lie around on *tatami* mats, play records, take naps, or stuff ourselves with *sukiyaki*.

It seems strange, looking back over the decades, that I ever could stand such a Spartan life. Later, when I learned of it, I marveled at how Annapolis men could have girl friends, and dates, and dances, and sometimes a weekend of fun and pleasure. A three-week winter holiday and a four-week summer holiday was all the time we had off away from the Academy. And even then, one's behavior had to be most circumspect. A Japanese officer was socially-acceptable anywhere, a most unusual thing in class-stratified Japan. It was a great honor to be one, or even training to be one. So, one's manners and conduct had to be above reproach at all times. Our family backgrounds (even before taking the competitive entrance examination) had been checked by the police. Becoming involved in some form of forbidden behavior, even while on vacation, could mean immediate expulsion and disgrace.

This was a very rare happening, however. Maintaining high standards of conduct was a challenge, as were other things at Etajima, like the annual boat race and annual swimming race. It gave me pride to see 360 young bodies pulling at oars for all they were worth. And at Miyajima, where we had our annual 10-day camp-out just before summer vacation, the men who were not good swimmers would spend practically all of each day in the water so they could build enough stamina and skill to complete the 10,000-meter swimming race that ended the stay. Of the men who failed to graduate from Etajima, only a handful flunked scholastically. Most failures came from breakdowns in health because of our rigorous physical training.

A great deal of our leisure discussion at Etajima, naturally, centered about sea life. At the start of my summer vacation in 1931, I decided to stop off at the Kure Naval Arsenal to see some of the "real Navy." Midshipman Zenshin Toyama went along with me. We were welcomed gracefully and given a tour of the submarine school.

In one corner of the grounds Toyama and I saw an old-style submarine, on rests. It was Submarine No. 6, recovered from Hiroshima Bay after sinking there on April 14, 1910. Beside it, encased in glass, was the final will of Lt. Tsutomi Sakuma, captain of the tiny submersible, written while he was waiting to die. For 20 years he had been the inspiration of Japan's small but growing submarine fleet.

Japan first thought of getting submarines for its navy at the same time as America did. On March 14, 1900, when Mr. John Holland demonstrated his underseas boat for Adm. George Dewey and other notables, a naval member of the Japanese embassy's staff was present. He was much impressed, and at once recommended to Tokyo that Japan purchase some of these boats. On April 11, 1904, the U.S. accepted USS *Holland* (SS-1), and 15 months later the first Japanese submarine performed excellently on its first sea trials, amazing the Americans who came along to provide technical assistance. They had not expected our men to master the submarine so quickly.

Our government bought five of Mr. Holland's boats, plus the plans for two improved models. At that time Japan had 7 fine foreign-built battleships and 15 fine foreign-built cruisers in its navy, plus 5 cruisers built at home. We were making our own armor plate at Kure by then and moving rapidly ahead in seapower. Great Britain had already noticed this and seized the chance in 1902 to effect a treaty with Japan. This action, taken only 35 years after Japan's fighting men gave up wearing helmets and armor like the knights of the Crusades, signified her formal entrance into the society of modern nations. Because of the alliance with Japan, Great Britain needed to keep only a small naval force in the Far East and could concentrate her main naval strength in the Mediterranean where Germany was threatening. How right Britain was in this move was shown on May 27, 1905, when Ādm. Togo eliminated the only other naval power that threatened Britain's interests in Asia, Russia.

Submarines seemed ideally suited for defense of our island kingdom. Between 1905 and 1914 Japan bought them from Great Britain, France, Italy and Germany, finally basing her home-built submarines on the last, which were then the world's best. During that period and for years afterward, Japan was truly the only sea power in the Orient. True, Pres. Theodore Roosevelt sent his "Great White Fleet" around the world in a show of strength in 1907-08, but this impressed no one but the American newspapers. While the White Fleet cruised, Great Britain completed construction of HMS *Dreadnaught*, which made Roosevelt's ships obsolete before they got home. Also, Japan's naval strategists noted something important about Roosevelt's force. Every bit of support for its 16 battleships had to be supplied by foreign ports and foreign ships. The "Great White Fleet" could not carry enough of its own fuel to fight a war with Japan. The White Fleet, in fact, because it could not even steam from Hawaii to Japan and back without refueling, dictated Japanese naval strategy for the next 30 years. This was based on defeat of an *approaching* enemy by catching him with his fuel depleted, far from his support bases. Our defense strategy meant *defense*, not *attack*, which accents how novel and daring it was for us to attack Pearl Harbor.

On April 14, 1910 (the year in which I was born) Lt. Sakuma took Submarine No. 6 (our submarines had numbers only until 1923) out on special trials. He was experimenting with a forerunner of the famous *schnorkel*, just as Mr. Holland had. Sakuma wanted to be able to operate submerged while his gasoline-powered engine "breathed" air from the surface. But his boat took a sudden dip, and water flooded in through his crude air intake. Before it could be closed, Submarine No. 6 was so weighted down with water that it sank. When it was finally raised and the dead bodies taken from it, this memorial written by Lt. Sakuma, was found.

"It is regrettable that because of carelessness on the part of the captain of the ship (Sakuma himself—Orita), His Imperial Majesty's ship was sunk and the crew members are about to die. All hands remained at their stations and worked calmly as death approached them.

"We are not afraid to die doing our duty, but we do fear that this accident may make Japan hesitate to continue further efforts to advance the development of submarines. Do not misunderstand, we beg you. Please continue the effort.

108

"The cause of sinking was that, while navigating submerged and using the intake pipe, we went too deep and water came in through the pipe. We tried to close the valve in a hurry, but it jammed. Water filled the after compartments and we bagan sinking with the stern down at an angle of 25 degrees. Time: 10:40 A.M.

"After sinking, the boat came to rest with the bow up at an angle of about 13 degrees. Batteries were covered with water and all lights went out. We began blowing the main ballast tank as soon as the submarine started down, but have been using the hand pump since the electricity failed. Not much result! The time is now 11:45 and I am writing this in the conning tower.

"As submariners we must be very careful, but at the same time we must be bold if the submarine is to make progress. I have always reminded my men not to be over-cautious. Some may laugh at today's failure, but I still think my warnings were correct.

"Submarines must have the best possible crews. I am satisfied with the crew I had. All worked well, and stood to their stations.

"And now, I make my public will. I humbly address myself to His Majesty. Please take good care of the families my crew members leave behind. That is the only thought that concerns me at this moment. Time is 12:30.

"It is now very difficult to breathe. I am affected by gasoline fumes. Time is 12:40.

Signed,
Tsutomu Sakuma"

Toyama and I were very much moved by this memorial. A lot had been learned about submarines since Sakuma's death and we both knew that a very simple safety device on his breathing tube would have eliminated the cause of his death. Still, his will exemplified what we admired most in Imperial Navy officers: courage, concern for subordinates, devotion to the Emperor, and calmness in the face of death. These were the marks of a true *samurai*. At that moment we both decided that we wanted to be submarine men. We both eventually got our wish.

While I studied at Etajima, the naval might of Japan grew. In 1928 the first *Nachi*-class cruiser was laid down, a ship superior to many of her foreign counterparts. In that same year Japan completed the first of the *Fubuki*-class destroyers, of which she built 24 in the next five years. These displaced

1980 tons and could make the exceptional speed of 37 knots. At launching they were the world's largest, fastest, and most powerful destroyers, with three triple torpedo tubes for firing nine "tin fish," plus six spare torpedoes, as their main armament. In 1930, the London Naval Conference was held. Our country was given parity with Great Britain and the U.S. in cruisers. Japan laid down *Mogami* and *Mikuma* as light cruisers, bearing 15 six-inch guns each. This move made America and England hurry ahead with construction of light cruisers to offset these. The foreigners had no idea that the *Mogami* class would be pulled into shipyards years later, and fitted with the eight-inch, longer-ranged gun batteries for which they had *originally* been designed!

In 1931, two things happened that were of great importance to me. Japan began scrapping her old submarines (the old ones had to be scrapped so we could stay within the Treaty submarine strength of 52,700 tons). And I graduated from Etajima.

Nine submarines were laid down in 1931, as part of what was called The First Replenishment Plan. Six were of the fleet type (*I-68* to *I-73*, later given numbers *100* higher). One was a cruiser type, *I-6*. And two others were what we called "Medium Type 2." They were *RO-33* and *RO-34*. The larger submarines were intended to have a surface speed of 24 knots, in conformance with the strategic doctrine of having them engage an enemy far at sea.

My 59th Class graduated from Etajima on Nov. 16, 1931, two months after the Mukden railway incident in Manchuria. This incident involved Japan in a war with China that did not end for 14 years. It only ended when we were defeated by the Americans. About the time I began my first training cruise in the old cruiser *Asama* (a veteran of the Tsushima battle) American Secretary of War Stimson announced a non-recognition policy toward the state of Manchukuo, which Japan had set up. My country was defended in her action by the Hearst press in America, which pointed out to Mr. Stimson the similarities between Japan's acquisition of Manchukuo, and the way the U.S. had seized Texas from Mexico.

Throughout the thirties, men of our Foreign Office often succeeded in enraging American diplomats by using terms of historic significance whenever speaking. Once was in December, 1934, when Japan said she wanted naval parity with the U.S. and Great Britain "for prestige and manifest destiny." Mr. Cordell Hull turned livid at this, although men who held his very office 100 years earlier had often used the phrase to justify America's movement westward into the great prairie areas belonging to others. And Mr. Hull also became very upset when Japan declared a "Monroe Doctrine for Asia," objecting to Western domination of China and asserting that she (Japan) was assuming sole responsibility for keeping peace in the Orient. Our Foreign Minister Matsuoka pricked American consciences, too, by stating, "Japan is expanding. And what country in its expansion period had ever failed to be trying to its neighbors? Ask the American Indian, or the Mexican, how excruciatingly trying the young United States was once upon a time!"

I am neither a politician, nor a diplomat. I cite things like those above to show how the great naval powers succeeded only in alienating one another more and more, during the 10 years preceding the Pacific war. Japan felt that she deserved a place in the Asia sun, because of the great strides she had made since 1868. Isoroku Yamamoto, our great admiral, put our country's position neatly at one of the disarmament conferences when, as a Captain and a delegate, he objected to the 5-5-3 ratio, under which Japan was to have only 60% of the capital ships allowed each to England and the U.S. At one of the evening dinners given after day-long discussions, Yamamoto toyed with his fork and said "Although I am smaller, I am not asked to eat only two-thirds as much."

Among Japan's immediate observations after Commodore Perry forced open a door she'd kept shut nearly 250 years, was that the Western countries profited greatly from the weak ones they entered. She did not intend to let it happen to her. During the thirties, she also felt that Great Britain, America, and Holland were trying to close her in again, shutting her off from the modern age and all of its opportunities. In all dealings during the thirties, neither side would concede the least thing to the other. Instead, each concentrated more on inflaming the minds of its citizens than on making peaceful overtures and compromises. This eventually led the way to the awful Pacific war, for which all countries involved must accept a share of the blame.

Such thoughts were certainly not in my mind when I stepped aboard *Asama*. Since 1902, when Japan and Great Britain signed a mutual defense treaty, America had been for strategic planning purposes our "most logical enemy." And, since Japan felt England had betrayed her at the 1922 Naval Disarmament Conference, Britain was from that time considered an ally of America, rather than of Japan. My task in those days was simple, requiring no deep philosophical thinking. As a "passed Midshipman," my job was to prepare myself to be commissioned an Ensign, an officer prepared to defend his country against an enemy coming from the east.

I looked forward eagerly to my first tour at sea. It proved to be disappointing. Shipboard life was not bad, but because of the fighting in Manchuria we were looked upon with cold eyes when we made port in Korea, Dairen, Port Arthur, Tsingtao, and Shanghai. People on the continent had no love for my country.

My second training cruise was a little better, although British authorities would allow no Japanese sailors to go ashore at Singapore. They didn't want us to get a glimpse of the great new base they were building there. At Manila we exchanged formal greetings with American army and navy men, but at Hong Kong the Chinese population raised such fierce opposition that the British refused us shore leave at that Crown Colony.

The South Seas, however, extended its traditional hospitality. We sailed completely around the continent of Australia, making stops at Fremantle, Adelaide, Melbourne, Sidney, and Hobart, in Tasmania. Our training fleet, under Vice. Adm. Nobujiro Imamura, also visited Wellington, New Zealand. Official welcomes were stiff and formal, but private ones were something else again. Our first contact with a white nation made a favorable impression on us, chiefly because Rotary Club members in each port went far out of their ways to show us a warm welcome.

We visited Truk, Saipan, and the Fijis on our northward trip home. A very curious thing happened in Suva, the Fijis' capital. Besides the British Governor-General and the Mayor (who declared a holiday in honor of our visit) the native Papuan chief visited our flagship. My classmate, Midshipman Minoru Yonehara, was assigned to escort the chief's eldest daughter around the *Asama*. This lovely girl spoke excellent English but Yonehara's was somewhat halting, because we had very little chance to practice our school-learned language, except on one another.

The young lady became so absorbed in conversation with my friend, who stood six feet tall (remarkable for a Japanese in those days) and whose skin was almost as brown as her own, that she tripped over a projection in the main deck. It cut an ugly gash in her bare foot. *"Hotokesama"* Yonehara (the nickname we gave the contemplative midshipman because of his Buddha-like characteristics) showed his gentlemanly breeding and training at once. He whipped out his

112

handkerchief, bound the young lady's foot, and picked her up in his arms. He dashed for sickbay, where the doctor treated the wound. Then the visitors left the ship.

On the very next day the chief's servant appeared on board, his face very serious, and asked to see Capt. Kasuya, CO of *Asama*. He told our commanding officer that his master had been very impressed with the gallant and knightly conduct of Yonehara. The chief very much wanted the midshipman as a bridegroom for his eldest daughter.

Capt. Kasuya could not believe his ears. At first he thought it was simply the chief's method of expressing his appreciation of Yonehara's behavior. He interpreted the statement merely as a very sincere compliment. As the conversation continued, though, he realized the messenger was fully serious.

What to do? Capt. Kasuya at once consulted with Vice Adm. Imamura. And with Imamura's staff. All agreed that this was indeed an unprecedented happening in the Imperial Navy. For one thing, Japanese naval officers were not allowed to marry foreigners. They weren't even allowed to marry *Japanese* without the permission of the Navy Minister. But the naval officers surely could not offend their host by telling them that. All they could do was keep talking graciously, hoping some way out could be found. The servant went on to say that his master desired Midshipman Yonehara to leave the ship, marry his daughter, and succeed to the rule of the Fijians. Aha! Yonehara was called, and answered this for himself. He extended his regrets, but stated he could not leave his ship and the Navy because he had given his solemn oath to defend his native land by service at sea. He could not break his oath to his homeland, could he?

The chief understood this kind of talk. He appreciated Yonehara's love of country. On our sailing day, the same servant reappeared. With him he had a beautifully woven mat. "It is the gift of my master," he said. "Only a man fit to rule in Fiji may sit on it." After that we no longer called Yonehara *"Hotokesama."* We called him *"Waka Shucho"* (Young Tribemaster).

One officer had been in favor of Yonehara's staying at Suva. He foresaw war with the whites one day and felt that a Japanese man holding influential position at Suva could be of great help and a source of valuable information in the future. Perhaps Yonehara might have been happy at Suva, too. In true Japanese tradition, he was later to lose his life near the scene of this incident.

We returned to Japan in July. The following month I was

113

transferred to the heavy cruiser *Haguro,* a proud ship. Duty in the battleship *Mutsu* followed that, during which tour I was able to keep that boyhood promise to myself by touching her Imperial crest, and was commissioned as an Ensign. I then spent a year in destroyer *Kaki* before getting orders to submarine school, where I trained in *RO-27,* an 800-ton boat. I was to have duty in five more submarines, a cruiser, and a destroyer before getting my own command. But I was well prepared for it by then, having served as navigator in *I-7* and *I-152,* and as executive officer-torpedo officer in *RO-33, I-160,* and *I-15.* Now, in 1942, I had my own ship, a fine new boat of 601 tons displacement, the submarine *RO-101.*

The *RO-100* class of submarines consisted of 18 boats. All had been built as part of the Imperial Navy's 4th Replenishment Plan, originated in 1939 and revised in 1940. It included one sub of the *I-9* class, fourteen of the *I-15* class, ten of a new *I-176* class, nine of the *RO-35* class, and nine of our class. Our construction group was labelled "submarine, small," and numbered from 100 so as not to confuse them with the fast-production *RO-35* class, which were a third again our size at 1000 tons. The *RO-100* class was to perform good service for Japan, although all would be lost during the war.

Anxious to get her finished, I took over *RO-101* while she was still under construction. Her length was 200 feet, her range 5260 miles at 12 knots. All four tubes were in the bow, and she carried a load of 8 torpedoes. Top surface speed was 14.2 knots, underwater speed 8 knots. We had no deck gun, only a pair of 25mm machine guns forward of the bridge. *RO-101*'s underwater endurance was 60 hours at 3 knots and she could dive safely only to 250 feet. Though small, she was a good boat for short range operations. I knew we'd see combat in her not long after she was finished. The *RO-100* class was designed for defense of the Mandated Islands. After Midway, it became more and more certain that fighting would move to that area. We had a base set up at Truk and another at Rabaul. I would be heading for one of them as soon as our shakedown training was finished.

I was still overseeing details of *RO-101*'s final construction when men in Washington, D.C., came to a decision that would make "Solomons" a fiery chapter in the world's history. Based on a report that an American aircraft had sighted airfield construction at Guadalcanal Island, the U. S. Joint Chiefs of Staff ordered the island's seizure before the airfield could be completed and used against U. S. forces.

The 8th Fleet of Japan, called the "Outer South Seas

Defense Fleet," was activated at Rabaul, on New Britain Island, not long afterward. It was under Vice Adm. Gunichi Mikawa, who had led the battleship-cruiser portion of the force that had attacked Pearl Harbor. Soft-spoken, intelligent, and courteous, Mikawa was held in high esteem. To back him up, and to oversee submarine operations against Australia, the 6th Fleet's headquarters was moved from Kwajalein to Truk.

In the Aleutians, *I-1* through *I-7* of SubRon 2 had moved up to relieve the boats that had gone there with the assault force in May. At home, a 5th Replenishment Plan had been altered somewhat. (We called ship construction plans Replenishment Plans under the grand strategy of replacing our entire fleet with more modern vessels we hoped could cope with those of U. S. and Great Britain). A new plan had been put forward, to construct mammoth plane-carrying submarines with the ability to cruise *completely around the world.*

Each of these would be able to cruise from Japan, down around the Cape of Good Hope, and into the Atlantic with ease. They could then take stations off places like New York and Washington, D.C., and launch air strikes at the enemy's chief city and his capital. A total of 18 such submarines (largest ever built until America in 1958 launched the large nuclear submarine *Triton*) were authorized. They were the *I-400* class, again numbered so as not to be confused with any others.

Besides this long-range plan (submarines had to be built for it, first), a similar mission to bomb the U. S., but much sooner, was approved. In the first week of August, the American marines landed on Guadalcanal. In its third week Cdr. Meiji Tagami left Yokosuka with *I-25*. On board was Warrant Flying Officer Nobuo Fujita, the only man ever to bomb the United States.

* * *

Chapter 8.

AMERICA IN THE SOLOMONS;
FUJITA OVER OREGON.

After the Midway operation, Japanese submarines were re-called, and deployed to other areas than the eastern Pacific. SubRon 2, as I said, went to the Aleutians. Most of the sub-marines not in home waters were operating off Australia, in the Bay of Bengal, off Suez, and in the Indian Ocean. We had nothing near the Solomons-Bismarcks area except *RO-33* and *RO-34*. On Guadalcanal, work was moving ahead rapidly with the airstrip. Nearly 2600 men were laboring there, with 400 riflemen forming the garrison to protect them against sudden raids. The airfield, which could accommodate 60 aircraft, was to be ready by the end of August. At that time the 26th Air Flotilla was to move in and begin operating from the field. But plans went awry.

Early in the morning of August 7, 1942, an American amphibious force crept around the western end of Guadalcanal under cover of poor weather and awakened our troops there and at Tulagi (an island to the north) with a salvo of gunfire. Vastly outnumbered, our men retreated into the jungle. The Americans put 10,000 marines ashore before night-fall, *25 times the number* of fighting men we had on that doomed island. Our 25th Air Flotilla (then based at Rabaul and awaiting relief) flew a strike down the 650-mile long "Slot," the route between New Britain and Guadalcanal. Warned by Australian coastwatchers, American carrier planes were waiting for them. Our fighter planes gave good account of themselves, but our ambushed bombers suffered severe losses while doing little damage to the enemy's ships.

Admiral Mikawa, who had the 8th Fleet, was at this time in Rabaul, with some of his cruisers away at Kavieng, New Ireland. So little indication did we have of a possible enemy attack on the Solomons, that these cruisers (the bulwark of any defense against such a move) were refueling at Kavieng for a trip westward to Manus, in the Admiralty Islands. Mikawa hastily summoned the cruisers to join him, sent messages to all available submarines to move into stations around Guadalcanal, and set out to do what damage he could do to the enemy fleet. He left St. George's Channel in the afternoon of August 7, with cruisers *Kako, Furutaka, Kinugasa, Aoba, Chokai, Yubari,* and *Tenryu,* plus the destroyer *Yunagi.* In spite of being spotted almost at once (and at least twice enroute) he bored into Sealark Channel in the early hours of Aug. 9 and began shooting. Mikawa's sailors sank three American cruisers, USS *Quincy,* USS *Vincennes,* USS *Astoria,* and the Australian cruiser *Canberra.* They also damaged a fifth cruiser. He intended to race on past these guardians and demolish the transports moored off the Guadalcanal and Tulagi beaches after that, but in the melee his ships became scattered.

Fearing that re-assembling them, attacking the enemy's amphibious force, then retreating past Savo Island would take too long, Mikawa then broke off his attack. He headed back for Rabaul, trying to get out of carrier aircraft range before dawn. He couldn't know, of course, that the American carrier admiral had pulled his flat-tops out of the area so hurriedly that he would later suffer censure (undeserved) for it. So, due to a combination of poor performance, poor communications, poor deployment, and poor preparations by the enemy, coupled with the excellent marksmanship and high state of training of the 8th Fleet, we inflicted on a superior U. S. force the worst defeat the American Navy had suffered in 125 years. Japan's name for this victorious engagement was The First Battle of The Eastern Solomons. Americans called it Savo

Island.

On Aug. 17 the Americans put two of their mine-laying submarines to unusual use. A force of 222 marines under Lt. Col. Carlson went ashore from the USS *Nautilus* and USS *Argonaut* at Makin Island, in the Gilberts. This raid was intended to divert our attention from the Allied operations in the Solomons, but of course it did not. Anyone who owned a chart of the Pacific Ocean could tell what the Americans intended to do—island-hop up the Solomons and Bismarcks island chains toward Japan. In fact Gen. Howland M. Smith, USMC, called the Makin Island raid a blunder in a book he later wrote. All it accomplished, he said, was to make Japan worried about her island holdings in the Gilberts, with the result that she fortified them heavily, which cost the lives of many marines in November of 1943.

Our submarines began moving into the Solomons area, to help with its defense. *RO-33* and *RO-34* took stations, as did *I-121*, *I-122*, and *I-123*. These were buttressed by *I-9*, *I-15*, *I-17*, *I-19*, and *I-26*. The new submarines *I-31* and *I-33* also went into the Solomons, and *I-11*, *I-174* and *I-175* moved up from the east coast of Australia. The majority of these boats concentrated southeast of Guadalcanal, where they could report and intercept any Allied ships bringing reinforcements to the island. *I-9* tried to attack USS *Enterprise*, but was sighted by three destroyers and was herself attacked. She got away. *I-17* was also attacked and suffered some damage, but she also escaped destruction.

By mid-August, the Americans had their situation well defined. They had to stay on Guadalcanal Island, keep and complete the airfield that was 90% finished when they landed, then use it to provide air support when they later moved further up the chain. It had a second value, too. So long as they kept it, we could not use it for harassing their south seas shipping from the air. The problem of the Japanese army and navy, of course, was to dislodge these marines and take back the island. About 1000 Japanese troops were quickly put ashore, the high command thinking that this number, together with the troops already there, were sufficient to do the job of driving the marines into the sea. They were wrong. Marines outnumbered our forces very heavily at that time, and very nearly wiped out the entire reinforcing group within 48 hours of its arrival.

Adm. Yamamoto then decided to send in a larger force, while at the same time sweeping the surrounding seas of any enemy naval strength. On Truk he had 5000 troops (intended earlier for landing at Midway). He put about 1500 of these in ships and sent them south toward Guadalcanal. To make sure they got there without interference he dispatched a total of 3 battleships, 3 aircraft carriers, 12 cruisers and 25 destroyers to screen and defend them, as well as to sink any American ships that might try to interfere.

The carriers were under Vice Adm. Nagumo. He split one of them, *Ryujo,* off from the force, sending her out as a decoy. While she drew American carrier aircraft to her, planes from *Zuikaku* and *Shokaku* would be free to attack the American flat-tops. Our battleships and cruisers were to dash in and bombard Henderson Field (the name Americans had given our airstrip) wrecking it and the planes stationed there. This would preclude any land-based counterattack. Our land-based planes at Rabaul would also attack Henderson Field, after which our transports would go in and land troops.

Our submarines gave early warning of the enemy, having sighted a striking force south of Guadalcanal, but our attempt to reinforce the island was turned back, with loss of carrier *Ryujo* and destroyer *Mutsuki.* We also lost *RO-33, I-123* and *RO-61* within a few days, though *I-123* was the only loss directly in the Guadalcanal area. She was scouting when, on Aug. 28, the old American destroyer *Gamble,* which had been converted into a minelayer, sighted her shortly after 8 A.M. The location was Indispensable Strait, a body of water separating the eastern end of Guadalcanal and Malaita. *Gamble* kept attacking with depth charges until noon. Lt. Cdr. Makoto Nakai and all hands in *I-123* were lost.

During the final week of August, what Americans came to call "The Tokyo Express" began steaming out of Rabaul. Made up of groups of Japanese destroyers, it usually left in the afternoon, running along the north side of the island chain that day and most of the next. Then, on the second night out of port, it would make a high-speed run in to the western end of Guadalcanal. It would land troops in the middle of the night, and speed away northwestward to get out of range of American aircraft by daylight. Several thousand men were put ashore on Guadalcanal by this method between Aug. 29 and Sept. 7.

While this was going on, Cdr. Meiji Tagami's *I-25* was cruising to a point off the Oregon coast, not far north of the California-Oregon border. On the morning of Sept. 9 Tagami's aircraft pilot, Warrant Flying Officer Nobuo Fujita, was sitting on his bunk, cleaning his pistol in an effort to while away waiting time. Fujita was to do something no one had ever done before or has done since—bomb the United States.

Fujita had been conscripted into the Navy from his home village in 1932, when our military forces began an extensive expansion program. He had been a pilot for about nine years when the war started, with 3500 hours in his flight log, much of it in combat over China. In 1935 he had been a test pilot with Lt. Minoru Genda, helping check out experimental aircraft that later became our first line planes. Fujita was promoted to warrant officer grade and ordered to duty on board *I-23* in September, 1941. He was transferred to *I-25* a short time later and began intensive drills. During these he was catapulted from *I-25* at night, and sent out to locate "enemy forces" composed of our own warships. He would approach these from the down-moon side and radio their positions to his mother ship. He flew a Type 96 biplane with floats.

This aircraft was a development perhaps peculiar to Japan, our Navy having considered the idea of mounting aircraft on submarines as early as 1922. The following year a Heinkel U-1 was purchased from Germany and experiments began. Two years later, in 1925, we had a plane of our own, developed from the German one. It was test-flown, using the mine-laying submarine *I-121* as its sea base. Our plane was called *"Yoko, Type 1"* and was of unusual construction in that it was a biplane with no struts between its wings. *Yoko* could make 70 knots with its 80 hp engine and its endurance was about two hours air time.

From this plane was later developed the Type 91 small seaplane. It was the one flown from *I-5* in 1936 during Fleet maneuvers, though no catapult was used, the plane being lowered into the water for takeoff. In that same year the Type 96 float plane was accepted by the Navy Ministry, after testing by Lt.(j.g.) Kunihiro, who later became a general officer in Japan's Air Self-Defense Force. From that year on, it was the only type aircraft flown from our submarines. It was called *"Geta,"* because its floats so resembled Japanese footwear.

For storage purposes, the Type 96 submarine scout plane could be disassembled into 12 separate parts: wings, fuselage, tail, floats, etc., and quickly assembled again. It was stored in two hangars in *I-7* Class boats, or in a single hanger on *I-9* and *I-15* classes. I was attached to *I-7* as communications officer during her construction and witnessed many takeoffs and recoveries of this type plane.

Fujita's crewman was Petty Officer Shoji Okuda. Together they made a number of daring flights in the first nine months of the war, although they were cheated of a chance to fly over

Pearl Harbor. *I-25*'s station on Dec. 7, 1941, was about 100 miles north by east of Pearl Harbor , and both men had hoped to be launched. But, while enroute to their assigned station the men of *I-25* heard a thumping noise from the deck hangar as the boat plowed through rough seas. Fujita cursed when the noise was investigated that night (when I-25 surfaced to charge batteries). The plane had not been properly secured in the hangar and was damaged beyond possible use.

After successfully dodging four bombs dropped by planes of the USS *Enterprise* after the Pearl Harbor attack, *I-25* went on to the U. S. west coast. Once, just after surfacing, she received a wireless report concerning some American transports, but these were too far away to pursue; whereupon Fujita got an idea. He discussed it with his executive officer, Lt. Tatsuo Tsukudo.

Up until that time, submarine-borne planes carried no heavy armament. "If our planes were armed with bombs," Fujita told Tsukudo, "I could search far ahead of the submarine. I could not only locate enemy ships for *I-25*, but also join in attacks to sink them." Tsukudo was entranced with the idea and the two went on to discuss how submarine-launched planes might attack the Panama Canal locks, blocking reinforcement from the Atlantic of America's Pacific Fleet. Or, they could hit american aircraft factories on the west coast of the U. S. Tsukudo finally suggested that Fujita put his ideas into writing and forward them up the chain of command.

A simple, modest man, Fujita was too shy to take such action. The subject was dropped while *I-25* patrolled in the eastern Pacific, where she sank the SS *Emidio* on Dec. 19. But they did talk it over on the way back to Kwajalein. And when Tsukudo left the ship for submarine commanders' school in January, he had Fujita's written suggestion in his pocket.

I-25 then went into the southern seas for six weeks, during which Fujita made six flights over enemy territory without mishap, although he almost missed finding the submarine on one return flight. Cdr. Tagami helped him on that occasion by exploding a yellow smoke bomb. Fujita; far to the north of his submarine, saw this and landed safely beside her a few minutes later.

During February and March the float plane, with Fujita and Okuda in it, made reconnaissances of Sydney and Melbourne, Australia; Hobart, Tasmania; and Auckland and Wellington, New Zealand, piercing the Allied defenses without problem. In late March they flew over Suva, in the Fijis, and had an amusing experience. On the way in, their plane was

121

sighted, and a blinker light challenged them.

"What should I do, Sir?" said Okuda through the voice tube.

"Send something back to him!" said Fujita. He didn't dare take immediate flight, for fear enemy pursuit planes would chase after him.

"What shall I send?" asked Okuda, his blinker lamp at the ready.

Fujita got impatient as well as worried. "Send him *anything!*" he shouted.

That's what Okuda did. Holding his blinker lamp over the side of the plane, he sent *"dot-dot, dot-dash-dot, dot-dash-dot-dash,"* the Japanese code signal for "anything."

I-25 refueled at Truk and headed for Yokosuka, arriving there on April 5. On May 11 it put to sea again, heading for the Aleutians, where Fujita made a reconnaissance flight over Kodiak Harbor on May 27, coming back with a report of 4 submarines, 3 destroyers, and some fishing boats moored there. Cdr. Tagami's boat was back at Yokosuka again on July 10.

On July 27 Fujita was mystified by a special wireless signal shown him by his commanding officer. "WARRANT OFFICER FUJITA IS ORDERED TO REPORT TO IMPERIAL NAVAL HEADQUARTERS AT ONCE." it read. The puzzled flyer got into his best clean set of whites, and caught a train to Tokyo (one hour's ride away) with instructions to report to Cdr. Shojiro Iura. He entered the old red brick building, found Iura's office, walked in and came to attention. "I am Warrant Flying Officer Fujita, Sir," he said, "chief flying officer of *I-25.*" At that moment another door opened and a man walked in, wearing the uniform and insignia of a commander. Fujita recognized him at once as Prince Takamatsu, younger brother of the Emperor and an Etajima graduate. This so flustered the ex-farm boy that all he could think of to do was to sound off with his name and rank again.

Prince Takamatsu quickly put him at ease, and the three men joined another at a table where some American charts were spread out. They had been captured at Wake Island, and were of the U. S. west coast. One of the officers ran his finger north, along the coast of California and into Oregon. "We plan for you to bomb forest areas for us, Fujita," he said, "right about here."

Fujita was stunned, until things were explained to him: A member of Japan's diplomatic corps who had served in Seattle had written Capt. Sadatoshi Tomioka, in the Operations Section. He suggested that the American mainland might be bombed. Somewhere that letter had crossed paths with Fujita's letter, because Fujita, *I-25,* and Cdr. Tagami were mentioned by name in the final operational plan.

On Aug. 15, the same day *I-26* left Yokosuka for the Solomons and fame, Cdr. Tagami again took *I-25* out of that port also. He headed east, Fujita's plane on board, newly-fitted with bomb racks. On Sept. 9, 1942, *I-25* was in sight of Cape Blanco lighthouse on the coast of Oregon and could see its beam. This surprised *I-25's* crew, because the war had been on for more than nine months. They could not understand why the American high command allowed such beacons to be lighted, serving as guides for an enemy. Fujita was summoned to the conning tower and Cdr. Tagami asked him to look through the periscope. Straight ahead lay the Oregon coastline, its inland mountains wreathed in haze and the white face of Cape Blanco just discernible through the early morning darkness. Fujita agreed that the seas had flattened enough to make launching operations feasible and went below to make final preparations. He put on his flight suit and went through a ceremony peculiar to the Japanese Navy.

The Imperial Army, when possible, cremated its dead and sent their ashes to the homeland, for delivery to relatives. But Navy men usually died in such ways that their bodies could not be recovered for cremation, so we followed a special custom. Fujita packed all of his belongings into one large box. In a smaller one he placed his will, a few strands of his hair, and some fingernail cuttings. If he died on his air mission, and *I-25* returned safely to Japan, these "remains" would be placed in a special box of paulownia wood and presented to his family. That lightweight box would be honored in a small household niche, or *butsudon,* at his home for a long time, though the remains would be removed to the Fujita family grave after a while.

These things done, Fujita went on deck and watched seven special technicians get his plane ready. First the hangar deck doors were swung open. Then men hauled on a line attached to the plane's fuselage. They tugged it forward until it rested on a small dolly that ran along rails to *I-25's* catapult. This was a swift, silent operation, with no one speaking while wings, stabilizers, rudder and pontoons were unclamped from the hangar's inside walls and put in place. Men had to be both careful and speedy. No time could be wasted, because *I-25* was most helpless at launching time. An enemy plane could destroy her easily. Once his plane was ready, Fujita got in, started his engine, checked meters and gauges, then got out and reported to the captain.

"All is ready, Sir." he told Tagami. The captain answered with "Very well. Good luck, Fujita."

A few minutes later *I-25*'s executive officer waved a flashlight in a circle, and the catapult was fired. Fujita and Okuda were away, enroute to accomplish what no foreigner had done in America since 1814 (when the British burned its capital). They would invade, attack, and escape!

The sun, which had begun climbing as Fujita's plane did, filled the eastern sky with a red-gold brightness as he increased his altitude by 350 feet per minute. The *Geta*'s 300 hp engine could only pull him along at 90 knots and Fujita feared detection because it meant almost certain death. He flew about 50 miles inland and ordered Okuda to release the first bomb. "Okuda freed the one under my left wing," Fujita said when interviewed by Mr. Harrington, "and the remaining bomb's weight almost pulled us into a right-hand diving turn. I corrected this at once, and looked below. Our bomb hit and burst, splashing a brilliant white light over the earthscape. *Good!* I thought. I had been moored near *Chitose* at Yokosuka on April 18 when one of Doolittle's bombers hit her, killing some men. Now I was returning the enemy's attack."

Fujita had been worried about the bombs. Each weighed 154 pounds, and was armed by a wind-spun propeller as it fell. And each carried 512 tiny fire bombs in its thin casing. I-25 had taken six such bombs aboard at Yokosuka, so that three missions could be flown. The bombs were designed to scatter the incendiary capsules upon impact, making a circle of fire 200 yards in diameter, with each tiny bomb burning at 2000 degrees. Planners in Tokyo felt that this was certain to cause tremendous forest fires and gave Fujita specific orders to drop them in unsettled areas only, distant from inhabitants, so they would have a good start before fire fighters got to them. It was hoped that large fires would spread panic in Oregon and other forested areas. Public opinion might be aroused and a demand raised to pull back American ships from mid-Pacific operations to guard the shoreline against repeat attacks.

I-25's pilot flew eastward for another 10 minutes and ordered the second bomb let go. Then he dived for the ground, leveling out at 100 feet and racing for the ocean, hoping to get back out to sea undetected. As Fujita passed over Cape Blanco he saw two American merchant ships, both heading north, a few miles separating them. Diving until the wavetops almost brushed his pontoons, he passed midway between the two, hoping neither would recognize his plane as Japanese. His procedure called for him to return to *I-25* along a bearing opposite to that along which he had left her, but when he found himself far south of the submarine he had to go back and approach her again, alternately swooping and climbing as a recognition signal. He was alongside the boat before long and reported the two merchant vessels to Tagami after he told him his mission had been successful.

Crewmen were still disassembling Fujita's plane for stowage as *I-25* built up speed to 18 knots for a pursuit of the two merchant ships. But the plane had barely been stowed away when out of nowhere dived an American plane. It dropped two bombs (which fortunately missed) and Tagami crash-dived his sub to 250 feet, shutting off engines after arriving at that level. Throughout the day his crew could hear the detonations of depth charges, all of them far away.

After sunset, Tagami surfaced and ran north at high speed to clear the search area. Several days later he picked up a wireless report from Tokyo. It told of intercepting a San Francisco broadcast describing how an airplane, presumably Japanese, had dropped incendiary bombs upon Oregon forest areas, causing some casualties and much damage to the woodland.

I-25 sank SS *Commercial Trader*, 2606 tons, on Sept. 16, about 40 miles from Galera Pt. Lighthouse (British Columbia) and Tagami made other attacks, not all of them as successful, before turning south. He planned to have Fujita make his second flight over California's redwood forest, east of Cape Mendocino. But the seas there were found too rough for flight operations so, on Sept. 29, at night, *I-25* was back near Cape Blanco. Cdr. Tagami hoped to fool the Americans by striking twice in the same general area, but making the second attempt at night.

Lt. Kasuo Fukumoto, executive officer, once more waved his red-lensed flashlight in circles. Once more Fujita was catapulted eastward. The moon was in the northwest, over his left shoulder, as he raced in over the coast, dropped two more fire bombs and sped back out to sea. He missed *I-25* on his return trip, so he went back to Cape Blanco lighthouse to reestablish his bearings and tried again. This time he remembered to compensate for the same error in his simple compass that made him miss his mother ship off Australia months before. Keeping to the southward of where *I-25* was supposed to be, Fujita finally picked her up in the moonlight's path, by sighting an oil slick she was trailing.

Tagami took time to congratulate Fujita, before ordering the oil leak found and repaired. Then he continued to cruise off America, hoping to find shipping targets and a suitable place for a third bombing attack on the mainland. On Oct. 5 he sank the 7038-ton tanker SS *Larry Doheny*, between Seattle and San Francisco. He hit another ship next day, but it limped safely into port. On Oct. 10 he sank SS *Camden*, 6653 tons, off Seattle. This left him with but a single torpedo remaining. At that point he told Fujita that the Americans would be too alert for another air attack to be successful, and turned *I-25*'s bow west. He fired his final torpedo at a pair of submarines the next day.

They were on the surface, about 500 miles west of Seattle, moving side by side. The range was very short, less than a half-mile, and Tagami reported a sure kill on his return to Japan. The U.S., right up until long after the war was over, denied losing a submarine on that date in that area. Even the famous American submariner and author, Capt. Edward Beach, concluded that Tagami was mistaken. Beach wrote that it must have been USS *Grunion*, lost on July 30, 1942, that Tagami must have sunk, during *I-25*'s second of the three patrols she made along America's coast.

Time proved Tagami correct, though it took 19 years doing so. In 1962 it was finally revealed that there had been a submarine sunk by *I-25*, on that date and at that place. But it was not American. It was *Russian*! Perhaps Russia did not want to admit that her submarines were visiting a country with which Japan was at war while Japan and Russia had a non-aggression pact. The submarines *L-15* and *L-16*, nonetheless, were enroute from Vladivostok to San Francisco, according to the final account, when there was a monstrous explosion and *L-16* disappeared. *That* was the submarine sunk by Tagami's *I-25*.

Chapter 9

THREE WEEKS THAT COULD HAVE
MEANT VICTORY

We had 13 submarines deployed in the Solomons by Aug. 24, 1942, when what the Americans call the Battle of the Eastern Solomons began. It marked the first of our major attempts to get the enemy off Guadalcanal. Before we gave up, we would lose 25,000 good men and two dozen ships. In the early days, we gained an important tactical victory. And, in the weeks that followed, we could have had a vital strategic one.

On Aug. 9, at Savo Island, Admiral Mikawa bloodied the enemy's nose. He sank the American cruisers *Quincy, Vincennes* and *Astoria*, and the Australian cruiser *Canberra*, while also damaging three other warships before he retreated. Foreign writers made much of his leaving the scene at his moment of great victory. But only one, Richard Newcomb, has spelled out in detail how poorly the Americans and Australians fought that night. In spite of having great superiority in forces, plus radar, and the advantage of having located Mikawa's ships only hours after they left Simpson Harbor, Rabaul, the enemy took a terrible beating. Nearly 1100 of them lost their lives, while Mikawa's losses were one-twentieth of that number. Mr. Newcomb rightly titled Savo Island a "debacle."

After smashing the enemy group of ships located south of Savo Island, Mikawa ordered a turn made to engage the force north of it. While executing this turn, his ships became divided into two columns. This error helped in one respect, because the second enemy force was trapped between these two columns and Mikawa's men actually had two more enemy ships under fire before their captains could be gotten out of bed! But the division also caused his ships to be scattered. At 2:15 A.M. he was ready to go in, unopposed, against the transports off Tulagi; but didn't dare. It would take an hour to get his ships gathered back into column formation and another two hours to reach Tulagi and polish off the transports. That would see him still in Sealark Channel after 5 A.M. He knew that carrier-type aircraft had defended against the air strike from Rabaul two days before, and feared losing all of his ships to an attack by them. Though he was criticized by the high command at once (and by foreign writers later) Mikawa was right in withdrawing. How was he to know that American carriers had already fled the area?

Mikawa's victory put fear into the enemy. The transports that had brought U.S. marines to Guadalcanal also made a hurried departure. The amphibious crafts' commander felt they were defenseless after Mikawa's sinking of four heavy cruisers that were supposed to protect them, so he sent them away while they were only half-unloaded. This left some 20,000 Americans on Guadalcanal with ammunition for five days of battle, but food enough for only three! For the next three weeks the only enemy ships that dared poke their bows through Indispensable Strait or Sealark Channel were high-speed destroyers converted to transports. Meanwhile, the American marines learned to eat Japanese food, having found stores of rice and canned food we had stockpiled on the island.

Nine of our submarines were south and southeast of Guadalcanal by Aug. 24, to act as sentries and interceptors. They sighted and reported the enemy force of three carriers, plus a battleship with cruisers and destroyers, moving up to stop the Japanese southward thrust from Truk. Our subs made no kills, though. In fact, *I-17* and *I-19* barely escaped destruction during this battle.

The decoy carrier *Ryujo* served her purpose. She was sunk, but not until she had drawn the bulk of the enemy's carrier planes to her. *Zuikaku* and *Shokaku* were able to launch their strikes without trouble. Japanese aircraft hit the battleship *North Carolina,* and also caused heavy damage to USS *Enterprise.* The carrier had to retreat to a southern base and was out of action for two months. One American flat-top was temporarily scratched. Added to *Lexington* (sunk at Coral Sea) and *Yorktown* (sunk at Midway) that made three enemy carriers that could not be employed against us. We knew that the carrier *Ranger* was in the Atlantic and we had information that the carrier *Wasp* was on her way to the Solomons. That left only two American carriers opposing the Imperial Navy, of the seven that started the war against us. They were *Hornet* and *Saratoga.*

Our forces were still making moves to the south and west of the Solomons, although not major ones. Troops moved into the Gilberts, New Guinea, and Ocean Island. In the Solomons, two submarine commanders were cruising, looking for a chance to hurt the enemy. Both got their opportunity.

Cdr. Minoru Yokota had won himself honors on the very first day of the war, sinking SS *Cynthia Olson* off the coast of America, after scouting the Aleutians. Yokota took *I-26* out of Yokosuka on the same day *I-25* had headed out to bomb America. He arrived in the Solomons shortly thereafter, his patrol station southeast of Guadalcanal. On the morning of Aug. 31 he raised his periscope, and saw before his eyes a submariner's dream. There on the surface were a carrier and a battleship, escorted by cruisers and destroyers. Shortly before 8 A.M. Yokota worked into an excellent position, having run right up to the edge of the destroyer screen. He launched a full spread of six torpedoes at the aircraft carrier.

I-26 was spotted by the U.S. destroyer *MacDonough* almost at once and had the terrifying experience of feeling the enemy's bottom scrape her superstructure as it passed over her. Depth charges were dropped, but they failed to explode as *I-26* dived. Some American had forgotten to set the charges! *I-26* was still plunging downward when crewmen heard two giant explosions. The enemy American carrier had been hit.

Then followed nearly 12 hours of dodging . . . creeping . . . stopping . . . maintaining silence . . . then trying to creep away again. Yokota reported the American antisubmarine tactics as being very poor (which may later have given some of our submarine captains too much confidence; a number of them were sunk while emulating Yokota's action and trying to penetrate screens of large U.S. task forces). Meanwhile USS *Saratoga,* already hit once in the war by *I-6* in January, again had to move out of the combat theater. She stayed out of it until the end of November.

In the jungles of Guadalcanal at this time, battles were raging between the American marines and our troops, who never reached sufficient strength in numbers to achieve anything. Our commanders had not yet realized that it would take at least a full army division to make any headway against the enemy's vast numerical superiority. They were feeding in troops a few hundred at a time. And the U.S. Marines killed many off as soon as they landed.

Neither side at that point (Sept. 1) had the right composition of forces. On shore our troops could fight only a holding battle, until enough reinforcements arrived to make possible a mass attack on Henderson Field. This crude airstrip was the key to the overall campaign. Whoever could hold and exploit it would control both the island chain and the surrounding seas. All the American strength at that time was daylight strength. U.S. carrier aircraft could cover the waters around Guadalcanal and perhaps 100 miles up The Slot and protect the ships and troops below them, but only while the sun was shining. American pilots did not have the skill necessary for night carrier operations. So the seas belonged to Japan during the hours of darkness. Our ships, loitering at the extreme of American carrier plane range, would start a high speed run-in as soon as the sun set to discharge loads of troops, ammunition, and supplies. They might also lob a few shells into the Henderson Field area to damage enemy planes and further fatigue enemy troops. All that the Americans could do at night was dig in and wait for the morning.

I-19 and *I-31* made shore bombardment runs on an enemy seaplane anchorage during this period. On Sept. 6, 1942, *I-11* (in an effort to repeat *I-26*'s feat) crept up on a screen surrounding USS *Hornet*. Cdr. Tsuneo Shichiji fired torpedoes at her. A hit appeared positive until an alert enemy pilot spotted the oxygen-driven, wakeless torpedo and dropped his load of bombs in its path. Their explosions caused enough turbulence to make the torpedo run erratically. It missed!

The top Japanese submarine commander of World War II was Cdr. Takaichi Kinashi of *I-19*. He was in command of the obsolescent *I-162* when the war began, operating off Malaya and in the Indian Ocean. When he got back to Japan he had 6 enemy ships to his credit, totalling about 40,000 tons. Then he had some bad luck, getting to station off Midway (like the other boats of SubRon 5) too late to sight any enemy. He might still have made some kills, but Adm. Yamamoto had not thought to summon that patrol line of submarines westward until it was too late. By then, Spruance and his ships were hauling out at high speed and SubRon 5 entered waters empty of possible targets.

In July, 1942, Kinashi took command of *I-19*. In August he was ordered to help stem the enemy's offensive in the Solomons. On Sept. 15, singlehanded, he amost sank the enemy's best hopes.

On that afternoon, Kinashi swung his periscope around for a quick look, and beheld a vision even more pleasing than that seen by Yokota, in *I-26*, two weeks earlier. Although he could not see all of them at once, a total of 23 enemy warships were within range of his Model 95 torpedoes. Nearest to him was the carrier *Wasp*, escorted by cruisers and destroyers. Beyond her was the carrier *Hornet*, with a similar screen that also included the battleship *North Carolina*. Cdr. Kinashi took his submarine in to close range and fired a full spread of six torpedoes.

Nearly three tons of high explosive raced toward the enemy at more than 30 knots. Three of them crashed into the *Wasp*'s starboard side. So great was their striking force that the explosions flung aircraft upward from *Wasp*'s flight deck. She was mortally wounded. In five hours, despite the best efforts of brave men who tried to save her, *Wasp* was at the bottom of the Pacific.

Three torpedoes hit, and three missed. This trio raced on past the carrier, to wreak still more havoc. They cleared the *Wasp* group, headed for the *Hornet* group, to score the war's biggest bag for one torpedo salvo. They missed two destroyers; then one of them roared into the side of battleship *North Carolina*. Another smashed into destroyer *O'Brien*. Five out of six torpedoes had scored and three warships had gaping wounds!

North Carolina was a new ship. Unlike the ancient battleships moored at Pearl Harbor on the war's first day, she could not be greatly damaged by one torpedo because of her up-to-date design and compartmentation. Still, she had to fall back to the rear out of action for two months. As for *O'Brien*, the torpedo from *I-19* did not spell her end for 60 more days. Retiring from the Solomons at the same time the *North Carolina* did, *O'Brien* was given temporary repairs and sent home to America for permanent ones. She never made it. Kinashi's Model 95 had fractured and twisted her back. The rolling Pacific eventually snapped it. *O'Brien* sank between New Caledonia and California!

One air strike and two submarine attacks had very nearly

wrecked what part of the American fleet could be used against us. Now they had only one left in the Pacific that could fight, USS *Hornet*. And only one battleship, USS *Washington*. This sister ship to *North Carolina* was rushed around from the Atlantic, where she had been patrolling in defense against the German battleship *Tirpitz*.

Against this single carrier in mid-September, our navy could range eight. While *Hornet* could put about 75 planes into the air against us, *Zuikaku, Shokaku, Zuiho, Taiyo, Junyo, Hiyo, Unyo* and *Shoho* could launch more than 360, all told. Against *Washington* we could pit *Musashi* and *Yamato*, mightiest battleships ever built, plus eight other battleships far superior to the obsolescent ones America was keeping well to the rear. Mid-September of 1942 was the period of golden opportunity for the Combined Fleet. Yamamoto and his staff failed to capitalize on it. The fabled tiger that had gone out more than 1000 *ri* to hunt, confident that he could return safely, had had his claws broken at Midway. He was more cautious now.

We still had such superiority in forces that it seems almost unbelievable now that the chance to race down on Guadalcanal with overpowering strength was not seized. A swift and overwhelming blow could have been struck at Guadalcanal at any time between Sept. 15 and Oct. 1. There would have been absolutely no way for the Americans to counter it.

The much-publicized B-17 Flying Fortress couldn't help. It had proved completely ineffective against our navy, in spite of the fact that Army pilots flew back to Honolulu and took credit for the victory at Midway while the battle was still going on. As of September, 1942, B-17's had yet to make their first hit on one of our warships. American surface ships had been defeated by ours wherever met. And the U. S. carrier striking force (the weapon we feared most) had been whittled down to one ship.

I attribute Japan's failure to capitalize on the August-September events and the favorable situation they created to a number of things. For one, the defeat at Midway had made members of the Naval General Staff cautious. Two, they were less vulnerable to being stampeded by Adm. Yamamoto's staff members, who had lost some of their earlier arrogance and daring. It might have been very difficult for anyone to get a massive strike on Guadalcanal moving quickly. Also, our Army commanders were slow to take the landing on Guadalcanal seriously. They were concentrating on capturing all of New Guinea in order to secure the Empire's southwest flank. In other theaters of war, hundreds of thousands of victorious Japanese troops sat idle (opposition to them having been eliminated) while the reinforcement of Guadalcanal by Americans increased slowly from a trickle to a slow flow.

The Solomons campaign would remind admirals and generals of ancient principles of war they were ignoring—mass and movement. From August through the end of 1942, Japan sent 36,000 men to Guadalcanal. Nearly 15,000 died in ships enroute, while unloading from ships, or in battle. Another 9000 perished from wounds, starvation, sickness or disease, and about 1000 were captured. In February, 1943, ships took off about 13,000 ragged, exhausted, starving skeletons, most shivering with malaria.

We did not learn the full details until long after the war was over, but in September, 1942, we had America nearly beaten in the Pacific. President Franklin Roosevelt at that time was actually considering whether or not to move his marines off Guadalcanal before they were slaughtered. He actually held a secret conference of his closest advisors, to get their sentiments on how the American public would receive news of such a defeatist evacuation. Mr. Roosevelt was lucky. He put off making an immediate decision, and in the end did not have to make a decision at all. Our high command solved his problem by *not* doing what Mr. Roosevelt feared most we would do— bringing down upon Guadalcanal all the force Japan could exert. Instead, it committed forces piecemeal to the American marines' meat-grinding attacks, and made a major movement only when it was too late.

Only one Japanese flag officer, the long-faced, lean Rear Admiral Raizo Tanaka, put his finger on things as they really were. In one of his reports this king among destroyermen wrote, "Gradual reinforcement of landing forces by small units is subjecting all of the troops involved to the danger of being destroyed bit by bit. Every effort must be made to use large units, all at once!"

For this and other expressions of disgust with higher-ups, Rear Adm. Tanaka was beached. One of the most effective fighting men in our history was yanked out of the Solomons campaign and sent to Burma, where he spent the rest of the war in command of a naval base. Hero of Java Sea and Tassafaronga, plus many successful runs of the Tokyo Express, Tanaka was forced to spend the rest of the war well behind the lines, out of action!

Early in October, *I-26* left Rabaul for a patrol in the Solomons, where she acted as a floating fuel station for some of our flying boats. Crews of these slow-flying, long-range monsters did an excellent job of keeping an eye on American ship movements, but almost always at the cost of their own lives. It seemed that no sooner did one of these planes report an enemy than up would come a speedy fighter and shoot it down. A Japanese flying boat did not have much chance against the enemy, unless there were thick cloud banks handy. A number of enemy pilots fattened their kill scores on these ponderous amphibians.

Just before *I-26* left Rabaul, Lt. Gen. Masai Maruyama landed on Guadalcanal with 10,000 men of the 2nd Army Division. These men came from Java, with a stop at Shortland Island base, about halfway down The Slot from Rabaul. The Army had at last become concerned about the Solomons, sending off troops a month-and-a-half after the Americans landed there.

Little use existed for these troops in Java after their swift victory there. The native population had cooperated excellently. One of the main reasons the Dutch evacuated the island so quickly was the great native hatred for them. No Dutchman dared retreat to the hills for guerrila fighting, for fear natives would betray him to the Japanese. Javanese willingly loaded hundreds of ships with materials destined for Japan.

Two submarines were lost in October. First was *I-30*, Cdr. Endo's boat, which had gone to Germany. She made it back safely as far as Singapore, but hit a mine when leaving there for Japan on Oct. 13. Cdr. Endo and 86 members of his crew were saved, plus a considerable amount of secret devices, machine tools and other cargo. The other sub, lost near the end of the month, was *I-172*, commanded by Lt. Cdr. Takeshi Ota. American sources list this, the 14th submarine we lost, as having gone down both on Nov. 10 and Dec. 16. Both dates are wrong. *I-172* left Rabaul for patrol on Oct. 12. She was last heard from on Oct. 28, and I believe she was lost operationally.

We lost a number of submarines operationally during the war, usually from accident rather than enemy action. As the war wore on, American anti-submarine patrols grew very intense. A submarine dared not surface for long, chiefly because of the enemy's excellent radar. Some of our submarines were trapped in patrolled enemy areas, or had to dive to escape attack. In either case, they had to remain submerged for very long periods. Then, with crewmen exhausted from long stays underwater with their air becoming foul, an error would occur for which all would pay with their lives. Also, an enemy ship or plane might drop depth charges and have no time for further attack. It would leave that area without knowing how seriously the submarine might have been damaged. Later that damage would worsen, and she would sink. I am also sure that certain enemy units have been erroneously credited with sinkings of Japanese submarines and other ships and planes caused the deaths of submarines for which they did not get credit. I know of several cases like the first and was involved in one of them myself. USS *Taylor,* a destroyer, was credited by the U.S. with sinking *I-25* in the Solomons on July 12, 1943, at 08-00S, 157-19E. That is not correct. The Taylor attacked *my* submarine that day, and not *I-25.* I escaped (an experience of which I will tell later). As for *I-25,* she was not sunk until six weeks later, and in an area far south of where USS *Taylor* was cruising.

RO-65 was the 15th submarine to be lost in the war. Under Lt. Shoichi Egi, she sank accidentally in Kiska Harbor, Aleutians, on Nov. 4. All hands were lost. Even had they been able to use the Momssen lungs (which few commanders kept on board after the war began) I think the icy water would have killed them before they could have been picked up. The 16th submarine lost was my old boat, *I-15,* of which Cdr. Nobuo Ishikawa was still captain. Ishikawa had nearly hit USS *Washington* with a torpedo on Oct. 27, three weeks after leaving Rabaul, but it exploded prematurely without completing its run. This sometimes happened with both the Model 95 and the Model 93. The last time *I-15* was heard from was on Nov. 3. She was sunk one week later.

On Nov. 10 the USS *Southard,* an ancient four-stack destroyer converted to a minesweeper, was heading for Guadalcanal with a load of ammunition and food. At 2:30 A.M., one of her lookouts sighted a submarine on the surface. This leads me to believe that *I-15* must have been just arriving at the surface after a submerged run and had not yet gotten her lookouts to their posts. I doubt whether any American ship during the war, using visual means only, ever sighted a Japanese man-of-war before being sighted herself. We had the world's best-trained and equipped lookouts, most of whom received some kind of reward from their captains when they made a sighting that led to a victory. Our lookouts employed powerful binoculars in their work, too (Japanese lookouts during the battle of Savo Island helped Vice Adm. Mikawa slip between two American sentry destroyers, both of which were equipped with radar).

The destroyer-minesweeper-transport opened fire. *I-15*

dived. A ten-hour search-and-attack period followed, during which many depth charges were dropped. The last barrage of these hit their target, causing *I-15* to pop to the surface like a wounded whale. American gunners finished her off.

There were two sea battles in October. Americans call the first one the Battle of Cape Esperance. It took place off the western end of Guadalcanal when an American force of 4 cruisers and 5 destroyers tried to stop Rear Adm. Aritomo Goto from reinforcing the island. We lost cruiser *Furutaka* and destroyer *Fubuki* in this clash (while sinking the U. S. destroyer *Duncan*) but our transports got through. Goto died but his men, despite the advantage given the Americans by radar, did well. They damaged the destroyer *Farenholt,* put the cruiser *Salt Lake City* out of action for six months, and hurt the cruiser *Boise* so badly she was out of action for more than a year. *Boise* had to go all the way to the east coast of the U. S., where over-eager newsmen gave her a reputation all out of proportion to what she deserved; she had seen so little combat.

Between the Battle of Cape Esperance and the battle that occurred two weeks later, Lt. Cdr. Yahachi Tanabe added to his reputation. On Oct. 20, while on patrol north of the New Hebrides in *I-176,* he sighted an enemy task force. Tanabe closed in and let fly a salvo of torpedoes; then reported by radio that he had sunk an American battleship of the *Texas* class. Actually he had hit the heavy cruiser *Chester,* knocking her out of the war for more than a year.

The next October battle took place on the 26th and 27th, with only one of our submarines scoring a success. This battle stemmed from another major attempt to recapture Guadalcanal. The thousands of men we had by then put on the island were to make an all-out attack and seize Henderson Field. At the same time a task force sent down from Truk by Adm. Yamamoto was to sink any sea resistance offered. This attempt was unsuccessful because it was made after our great opportunity had passed. It was launched after the enemy had passed his critical period and recovered. Our warships outnumbered his almost 2-1, but he had restored an aircraft carrier to duty. That and another damaged two of our aircraft carriers very badly. But our planes hurt USS *Hornet* so badly that she had to be sunk by her friends to avoid capture; and USS *Enterprise* was again damaged.

Once more we had left the Americans with only one carrier operating in the Solomons area, but our golden chance had gone. From then on, time worked against us. America repaired her ships faster than we could ours and added new ones to the front lines at a phenomenal rate. Japan in this battle also lost all possible chance of restoring air power balance. She never after came near regaining the air advantage. Our surface ships had to operate in the Solomons with practically no sky cover. *I-21*, trying to pierce the USS *Enterprise* screen, succeeded only in torpedoing USS *Porter*, a destroyer the Americans later sank.

During the second week in November there was another great sea battle in the Solomons. Again it centered around a land attack on Henderson Field, followed by a sea attack. Again we failed, both ashore and at sea. The Americans lost 2 cruisers and 7 destroyers in this three-day battle. Japan lost 2 battleships, 1 cruiser, and 3 destroyers. Our forces had to fall back on land and at sea.

On Nov. 13, our Cdr. Minoru Yokota helped build the reputation of *I-26* still more. He was southeast of Guadalcanal and sighted five enemy ships, all headed south. They were the cruisers *Juneau* and *San Francisco*, with destroyers *Sterett*, *O'Bannon*, and *Fletcher*. All but *Fletcher* had been damaged in battle, and were heading for repair facilities in the New Hebrides, chief base from which the enemy operated against Guadalcanal. *I-26* was picked up on sonar and attacked, but Yokota still pressed in. Shortly before 11 A.M. he fired a full spread of torpedoes. These missed *San Francisco* but got *Juneau*, which blew up and sank almost immediately, taking nearly 700 men with her.

An American motion picture made about five brothers who died in this action shows it occurring at night. Actually it happened in broad daylight, under conditions very favorable to the enemy surface ships.

What the Americans call the Naval Battle of Guadalcanal ended on Nov. 15. Japan was to make no more major sea attacks on "Death Island." That day marked the actual turning point of the Pacific naval war (not the battle of Midway). By the time our high command made up their minds to do something, Henderson Field was completed by the Americans and operating effectively, a launching point for attacks on our ships and a safe haven for American carrier aircraft that were damaged or had lost their way. From Nov. 15, 1942, Japan was purely on the defensive.

Only Japanese submarines tried to interfere with American supply movements to Guadalcanal after Nov. 15. Three of them, *I-16*, *I-20* and *I-24*, were assigned to launch midget submarine attacks on the enemy transports, which moored off Lunga Point to discharge their cargoes. Commanders Kaoru

Yamada, Takashi Yamada, and Hiroshi Hanabusa had these three submarines. They sent a number of midget submersibles against enemy ships after creeping through heavy destroyer and PT-boat screens. They claimed a total of 7 sinkings in these operations, and three midget pilots were lost: Lt. (jg) Yasuaki Mukai, Lt. (jg) Hiroshi Sato, and Lt. (jg) Tomio Tsuji. Lost with them were Petty Officers Kyuguro Sano, Shinsaku Iguma, and Tamaki Tsubokura. I have, however, been able to confirm only one success for them, the American cargo ship *Alchiba*. She was hit on Nov. 18, but the enemy saved her by beaching her. She was later repaired.

By mid-November we had over 15,000 troops on Guadalcanal. They had to be sustained, if another all-out try to re-take the island was to be made. But our destroyers and transports had suffered so many losses supplying these men that on Nov. 16, in Tokyo, a major new decision was made. Since the enemy had control of the air (which gave them control of the sea's surface), *submarines* would supply our troops on Guadalcanal!

Submarines were to load up at Buin, on the island of Bougainville (outside the range of enemy planes at Guadalcanal) at the rate of one boat per day. They would then proceed to Makino Point, at the western end of Guadalcanal, and unload ammunition, medicines, and provisions. One submarine could carry two days' provisions for our forces. A meeting was held on board 6th Fleet flagship *Katori,* at Truk, to discuss this new order. Submariners opposed it vigorously. "How can submarines carry out their foremost mission—attack—" they asked, "when we are forced into this stupid kind of work?" The arguments waged hot and long, for quite a while before Admiral Komatsu raised his hand and called for silence.

"Word from Tokyo," he said, "is that our Army troops under Lieutenant-General Harukichi Hyakutake are starving on Guadalcanal. They used the last of their rations several days ago. More than one hundred men are dying from hunger daily. Many of the rest are eating grass. Very few men are fit for fighting. What are we to do, let our countrymen starve to death in the jungle? We must help them, no matter what sacrifices must be made in doing so!"

That ended the discussion. All present were aware of the value of Guadalcanal. Each skipper realized that the supply job, though it would radically reduce the overall effectiveness of our submarine force, had to be done. There was no more complaining. What submarines were available were ordered into Rabaul and placed under command of Rear Adm. Hisao Mito. Then began the *"mogura"* operation, so named because it operated like moles do, slowly and out of sight. *I-176,* under Lt. Cdr. Yahachi Tanabe, made the first successful transport run to Kaminpo Point.

I was to learn much of these operations, personally. My *RO-101* completed shakedown training in December, and I received orders to proceed to Rabaul.

* * *

Chapter 10.

"*MOGURA*" OPERATIONS.

Three more submarines were lost before my *RO-101* got into the southern seas. *I-22* was caught by an American PT-boat near New Guinea on Nov. 12. Cdr. Chinao Narizawa, her new captain, was lost with all of his crew. And on Dec. 9 we suffered the first casualty suffered by the "Underwater Tokyo Express." She was *I-3*, under Cdr. Ichiro Togami. She departed Shortland Island, east of Bougainville, on Dec. 7 with a load of provisions and medicines, and also carrying a *daihatsu* (landing craft) lashed to her deck, the after gun being removed to make room for it. She was attacked by an American torpedo boat off Cape Esperance two nights later and sunk. All hands were lost.

The third casualty was *I-4*, under Lt. Cdr. Toshitake Ueno. When high officials decided to supply Guadalcanal via submarine they also included New Guinea, where the same problem (heavy enemy air coverage) had to be overcome. Also, it was not very far from Rabaul to where our forces on New

Guinea were fighting.

Ueno took *I-4* out of Simpson Harbor on Dec. 19 and headed for Buna. He was supposed to make contact and delivery on Dec. 21 but could not, because enemy troops landed the previous month had driven ours away from Buna. Ueno decided to head back for his base, and was very nearly home when he was sighted by the American submarine *Seadragon* on Dec. 24.

The Yankee boat was able to make two big reports when she returned from her war patrol, the sinking of an I-boat and the successful performance of an underwater appendectomy. The latter took place in *Seadragon's* wardroom one week before she fired four torpedoes at Ueno's boat, sinking it. I later read that the patient was already back at his regular battle station when this happened (which shows what caliber of men serve in submarines).

The year 1942 ended with more bad news for Japan. On Dec. 31 the new U. S. aircraft carrier *Essex,* first of many to be built by the Americans during the war, was commissioned. Carriers would prove to be the deadly enemies of our submarines in the war's final year.

A total of 1592 Allied and neutral merchant ships went to the bottom of the ocean in 1942. Nearly three-fourths of these were sunk in the Atlantic and Mediterranean Oceans. Of those sent down in the Pacific and Indian Oceans, our submarines accounted for only a small portion. Our 19 submarine losses since Pearl Harbor were not compensated for by great accomplishments. And 1943 did not promise to be a banner year, chiefly because so much of our submarine force was tied to supply operations.

Around the end of 1942, because of the war's changing pattern, Japan's top strategists realized that the "decisive battle" concept of warfare was giving way to an island-by-island struggle. This gave birth to the *I-351* Class of submarines, and later to the *I-361* Class. Both were designed strictly for transport operations. *I-351* was designed to carry materials necessary for use at midget submarine bases which the Naval General Staff planned to scatter throughout our network of island defenses, so this type submarine could also serve as a secret submarine base herself. A lot of discussion was held concerning the *I-351* Class, of which three were planned. Only two were laid down, but they were finished as seaplane-tending submarines to do the kind of work *I-26* and *I-124* had done in the Guadalcanal fight. Each boat was 364 feet long and displaced 3531 tons. They could make 15.8 knots on the surface and 6.3 knots submerged. Range was 13,000 miles at 14 knots and they had a special capacity of 365 tons of gasoline over and above the submarine's fuel load. This was to be carried in special tanks set outside the inner hull, amidships.

I-351 could carry 15 aircraft torpedoes, plus 30 of our 550-lb. bombs, or she could carry 60 of the bombs if no aircraft torpedoes were loaded aboard. She could also carry an extra 1½ tons of provisions and 11 tons of fresh water as cargo, and cruise for periods up to 60 days. Her crew would be 77 men, plus 13 passengers as relief crews for the flying boats tended. By use of special fittings, *I-351* and *I-352* could each refuel three seaplanes at the same time.

Armament of the *I-351* Class was four bow tubes. She could load these before sailing and carry four spare torpedoes if her other ammunition cargo was reduced. When finally completed, *I-351* had no large deck guns, but mounted 7 machine-guns. These were two twin 20mm on the conning tower and a triple 20mm on deck forward. This pair of submarines were called *"sen-ho"* (replenishment submarine) type.

The decision to make plans for these specially designed transport submarines came just after the Battle of Tassafaronga, on Nov. 30, 1942. Rear Adm. Raizo Tanaka, with 8 destroyers, met an American force of 5 cruisers and 6 destroyers while making a supply run to Guadalcanal. Although the Americans surprised him by picking him up on radar and opening fire before he was aware of their presence, Tanaka fought a great fight. IJN *Takanami* went down, but so did the U.S. heavy cruiser *Northampton*. Tanaka's intrepid destroyermen then used American gun flashes as points of aim and blew the bows off the heavy cruisers *Minneapolis* and *New Orleans*. This second vessel may have been the world's only warship to collide with *herself!* Her bow, separated from the ship, came about and crashed into the Chief Petty Officers' quarters, at the ship's stern.

Tanaka's men also wounded another heavy cruiser, USS *Pensacola*. This trio of warships saw no further combat for more than a year. A fifth cruiser, USS *Honolulu,* escaped harm only because she turned behind the other American ships and was screened.

Tanaka retreated because he didn't have enough torpedoes on board his ships to make a second engagement feasible. Superiors leaped at this seeming reluctance to wage battle as an excuse to relieve this quick-to-laugh critic, who had put his finger on the situation's center point right after arriving in the Solomons. He had almost immediately suggested Japanese evacuation of Guadalcanal rather than its reinforcement. He advocated withdrawing up the Slot, then digging in and preparing bases for a counterattack, using air cover from airfields that would be closer to the point of combat than Rabaul. When this suggestion was shunted aside, Tanaka recommended massive (as opposed to piecemeal) reinforcement of the island. His second piece of advice was taken too late, and his first was taken only after he was relieved and transferred to the rear area!

Historians all state that the *first six months* of 1943 were a combat "lull." I and other Japanese submariners can tell them quite differently.

On Jan. 14 I took *RO-101* out through Tokyo Bay on her way to Rabaul. I arrived at Rabaul on Jan. 27, hoping to accomplish great things. I made none of the Guadalcanal runs, as it turned out, being assigned to patrol missions instead. But 16 other submarines were assigned to that type of work. Torpedoes were loaded into their tubes, but all spare parts were put ashore, together with most of the topside armaments. Rations for each submarine's crew were reduced to the minimum, so boats would have more room for rations for the 20,000 starving soldiers. One large-size submarine could carry enough food to last the Guadalcanal garrison for two days, and Rear Adm. Mito made a run himself in *I-8* to see how the operation worked. By February of 1943 a total of 28 successful runs, delivering about 1500 tons of supplies and ammunition, were made. Our submarines were attacked on seven different occasions and two were sunk. One, *I-3*, I have already told about. The other was *I-1*.

Lt. Cdr. Eichi Sakamoto took *I-1* out of Rabaul on Jan. 24, and put into Buin to pick up supplies. Then he moved down to Guadalcanal, arriving off Kaminpo point on Jan. 29, having traveled most of the way submerged. This grandfather of our modern submarines was nearly 16 years old when she surfaced that night about 9 P.M. and prepared to off-load cargo. Unknown to Sakamoto, his boat had already been picked up on radar by the Australian corvette, HMAS *Kiwi*. *I-1*'s after gun had been removed to make room for a landing craft to move cargo to shore. So, on finding herself under fire she could only man her forward deck gun. Its crew was wiped out instantly. Sakamoto himself was mortally wounded by fire from this small but deadly enemy, which kept pouring out shells from her deck and machine guns. Even rifle fire was exchanged during the battle and, during one of the three times *I-1* was rammed by *HMAS Kiwi*, her navigator tried to board the

Australian ship and fight it out hand-to-hand with his sword. A sister ship of *Kiwi,* the HMAS *Moa,* joined the battle after a while, and also rammed *I-1.* With 30 men dead, the executive officer, Lt. Sadayoshi Koreeda, tried to beach the submarine. He ran his submarine up on the beach and with the remnants of his crew (50 men) joined our forces in Guadalcanal's jungle.

The U.S. Navy claimed that it captured many secret documents from the beached *I-1,* but this is open to question, because Lt. Koreeda told me he burned them on shore.

My first patrol in *RO-101* was made on orders from Rear Adm. Kaku Harada. Harada sent three submarines out to stations east of Port Moresby, with orders to stop any enemy attempt to interfere with the planned withdrawal from Guadalcanal. *RO-100* and *RO-103* went out when I did. *I-18,* already in the Coral Sea for this purpose, was lost carrying out her mission.

In the first week of February, Japanese destroyers made 60 runs to Guadalcanal, bringing off an evacuation which for daring and success compares favorably with the English at Dunkirk and the American at Hungnam, Korea. It had one more thing in common with the American evacuation during the Korean War, too, because when American marines in 1950 said "Retreat, hell! We're advancing in another direction!" they were copying a phrase from their former enemies, the Japanese, who had coined it seven years earlier. Altogether, 13,030 of our men were taken off Guadalcanal, 832 of them Navy men, without a bit of opposition, in what our high command called a *"tenshin"* (turned advance).

American records list our *RO-102* as being sunk on Feb. 11, 1943. They are wrong. It was *I-18,* under Cdr. Tomiichi Muraoka, lost in the Coral Sea on that date, the 2604th anniversary of our Emperor Jimmu's accession to the throne of Japan. (Our belief is that Japan became a nation when that happened, and our calendar is based on it. I, like thousands of other men in 1939, had chosen Feb. 11 for my wedding day, feeling that no other day could possibly be more auspicious for a marriage than Japan's 2600th anniversary).

Cdr. Muraoka's boat *(I-18)* was the victim of a combined air-sea attack. She was sighted by a scout plane from the American light cruiser *Helena.* It dropped a bomb, then a smoke pot to mark the sub's location for destroyer *Fletcher,* which hurried to the scene, picked up *I-18* on her sonar equipment, and laid down a barrage of depth charges. A short time later the men in *Fletcher's* gun houses heard an explosion so great that they thought their ship had either blown out its own bottom with shallow-set charges or had been hit by a torpedo. Actually, it was the death of *I-18*.

RO-100 was *almost* sunk. She was 30 miles south of Port Moresby on Feb. 14, when Lt. Kanemi Sakamoto sighted an enemy transport. He began maneuvering to attack and became so engrossed in trying to make a kill that he neglected to observe the submariner's routine precaution, frequent sweeps of the entire seascape with his periscope. As a result, an American destroyer escort was able to approach him almost unnoticed. Sakamoto saw this onrushing ship at the last moment and dived. The DE dropped over a dozen depth charges. They smashed *RO-100's* periscope, and caused other damage. Sakamoto, unable to continue on patrol, had to make for Rabaul.

I was almost trapped, too. I got word on Feb. 16 of what happened to *RO-100,* and arbitrarily maintained radio silence for four days to avoid detection. On Feb. 22 my navigator, Lt. Shigeshi Kondo, sighted a single-stack ship of about 4000 tons displacement. She was obviously an old ship and appeared to be an easy victim. Still, something about her bothered me when I took over the periscope from Kondo. Her Plimsoll line was well above the ocean's surface and I could clearly make out the difference between her above-water and below-water paints.

"That ship is very nearly empty," I told Kondo, "and if she is empty it is because she is returning from a supply trip to Port Moresby. In that case, she would be heading east. But—she is heading west! I don't like it. Let us wait a while before attacking."

So we waited. The enemy ship continued on her eastward course for some time, then turned to the north. I waited some more. After a while she changed course again—to the west!

"Aha!" I cried out. "A Q-ship!"

During World War 1 the British, whom the Japanese helped in escorting ships through the Mediterranean (in exchange for which Britain backed her demand for a mandate to the German islands north of the Equator) had disguised and equipped old merchants ships with masked gun batteries and depth charge racks. These vessels proved to be deadly lures for the German U-Boats, many of whose captains paid with their lives for taking the bait. I decided that I would not join those dead German submarine captains. I kept *RO-101* submerged (instead of surfacing to close in rapidly) and used my periscope sparingly. We had sighted the enemy ship about 3 P.M. I decided I would stay down until well after dark, surface very late at night to recharge batteries, then submerge to prepare for a dawn attack.

My plan didn't work. At sunset the enemy vessel suddenly picked up speed, and ran away in the direction of Port Moresby. I searched for it the next two days without success, and returned to Rabaul on Feb. 28. *RO-103* came in two days later. Her skipper, Lt. Hidenori Fujita, had had no luck either.

When our submarines began their transport work to Guadalcanal Gen. MacArthur's offensive in New Guinea intensified. It became very difficult for Japanese surface ships to get in past MacArthur's air umbrella, so submarines were ordered to lend a hand there. Before I came on the scene, 9 submarines had made a total of 20 trips from Rabaul to New Guinea. After my *RO-101* joined the operation, 75 more trips were made, through September of 1943. Total supplies put ashore on New Guinea by submarines from December, 1942, to September, 1943, was about 3500 tons. These operations, strangely enough, cost us only one submarine, *I-4* (although *I-176* did suffer heavy damage during an attack).

In replenishing New Guinea, Japanese submarines employed two ingenious devices. They were called *"unkato"* (stores carrier tube) and *"unpoto"* (cannon carrier). The *unpoto* was introduced first. It consisted of two hollow cylinders, placed side-by-side with a platform built over the top of them. Overall length of this device was 71 feet, overall width 13 feet. On top of the platform an artillery piece was lashed into place and tied down securely, along with cases of shells for the gun. Slung under the platform were the after parts (the power plants) and fuel flasks of two torpedoes. An *unpoto* weighed 20 tons and displaced 37 tons after cargo was loaded.

One of our submarines would strap a loaded *unpoto* to its after deck at Rabaul, after loading its other cargo, then head for a New Guinea rendezvous. There the submarine would rise to just below the surface, its deck just a bit awash. Crewmen would climb out, unlash the *unpoto,* then return to the submarine's hull leaving only the cannon carrier's operator above the water. The submarine would then lower itself only enough to let the *unpoto* float free, after which the operator would start the torpedoes' power plants, which could drive the mechanized raft about 2 miles at 6 knots. The operator would run it right up on the shore at a selected spot, then let down a special ramp at the *unpoto's* bow. Soldiers would hasten on board, carry away the ammunition, and roll the artillery piece into the jungle.

The *unpoto* was already working successfully when the

"*unkato*" was introduced. This was truly a remarkable experiment. The *unkato* was a cylinder 136 feet long, with cone-shaped ends. It was 16 feet in diameter. Both of the cones were ballast tanks, and there was a third ballast tank in the *unkato's* center. These three compartments were separate from the long cargo space, which had a capacity of 377 tons of food, ammunition and medicines. With a strong hull structure that permitted submerging to depth of 400 feet, the *unkato* was adjusted after loading so that it had slightly negative buoyancy, then it would be towed out into the middle of Simpson harbor and secured by a long tow line to the stern of a submarine. Once the submarine cleared Rabaul, it would cruise along the northern coast of New Britain to the point where its submerged run was to begin. When the submarine dived, the *unkato* would submerge with it. On arrival off New Guinea, the submarine would surface and release the *unkato,* which was then towed to the beach by men from the shore.

I-21 was operating off Sydney when I arrived in Rabaul. During January and February she was credited with a total of 6 ships. *I-10* was in the south, also, her plane making reconnaissances over Noumea, Torres Island, and Auckland, to report on enemy ship groupings. The Japanese Army, meanwhile, had gotten into the submarine business, too. It had decided it needed an underwater fleet to supply outlying posts. Gen. Hideki Tojo was in on this plan, which he ordered kept secret from the Imperial Navy. "If the Navy learns of Army plans to build submarines," he said, "it will surely oppose them. So don't tell the Navy. Construct all submarines in secrecy."

Later on, when the Navy learned of this work, it cooperated in the building of them; lent technicians and provided advice. However, we had nothing to do with the actual operation. These special submarines were called "*maru yu*" (circle transport), the first word meant nothing. It was merely a security device. About 50 were built, but only 3 got into service, making supply and transport runs to the Philippines in late 1944. The rest were still undergoing shakedown and operational training when the war ended. Because so many records were burned in 1945, I have been able to learn nothing about these submarines except that they displaced 270 tons, had no torpedo tubes or torpedoes, carried a single 13mm machine gun on deck for armament, and were an awful waste. Our Navy's submarine fleet could have used the skills and materials that went into building these useless craft. Especially when the year 1944 saw most of our submarine fleet wiped out.

It was early in 1943, also, that Germany made a special proposal to Japan. U-Boats were then sinking Allied ships faster than they could be replaced and Hitler offered to give Japan, at no charge, two of his newest and best submarines. We were to study these, then turn out copies in large numbers for a massive assault on enemy supply lines on our side of the world. Agreement was reached, and *U-511* left Lorient, France, in May, 1943, with a German crew. She refueled from *I-10* in the Indian Ocean enroute and made port finally at Kure during August. That German submarine was studied very carefully, then given to the submarine school for use as a trainer, being re-numbered *RO-500.* I will tell of the submarines that were developed from it, later.

My next two sorties from Rabaul were special ones, not regular patrols. I got orders for the first one in the officers' quarters at Rabaul, halfway up the hill from Simpson Harbor. With me were the captains of *RO-100* and *RO-103,* Lts. Sakamoto and Fujita. I was a Lieutenant-Commander, having been promoted on my graduation from submarine commanders' school. The date was March 3.

"Today is *Hina Matsuri."* Sakamoto was saying. He was referring to Japan's annual doll festival, its "girls' day" (celebrated by everyone although it is supposed to be a special day just for females). "Let's have a *sake* party tonight!" Fujita and I had just agreed that this was a fine idea when a sedan from submarine headquarters raced up and screeched to a halt. Its driver jumped out and came to attention. "Captains Orita and Fujita are wanted at headquarters right away!" he blurted out.

We got into the car and headed for the dock where the flagship, IJN *Jingei,* was moored. There Cdr. Miyoshi Horinouchi, chief staff officer to Rear Adm. Harada, explained things while the admiral looked on. "The convoy that left here for Lae two days ago has been under heavy enemy air attack since yesterday. We have suffered very great losses in the Bismarck Sea area. Many soldiers and sailors have been cast into the sea and no surface ships can get near enough to rescue them." Horinouchi was referring to 8 transports and 8 destroyers that had put out from Rabaul to make a mass reinforcement of New Guinea.

The novel technique of "skip bombing" was employed against our ships in this action, and it worked excellently. Instead of dropping their bombs from high altitude, enemy bombers approached very low and half-dropped, half-flung their bombs at the sides of our ships, almost as though they were launching torpedoes. Even when a bomb missed, it exploded upon impact with the water and had the effect of a mine going off nearby. As a result, all 8 transports, plus 4 of the destroyers, were sunk.

"The enemy's watch is very close," said Horinouchi, "so we plan to use submarines to make rescues. Orita, you will get *RO-101* ready for sea at once. Fujita, you will get *RO-103* ready and stand by to go out later."

I had my boat running out of Rabaul by dawn of the next day. Being watchful for enemy aircraft made our progress cautious and slow, so we did not arrive in the disaster area until the evening of March 6. The best chart of the area we had on board *RO-101* was more than 50 years old. We had constantly to remain alert for uncharted reefs.

It was dawn of March 7 when one of my lookouts finally sighted the first lifeboat. We approached, and found some survivors in it. They waved feebly and tried to thank us, but did not have the strength. We later located 2 more boatloads. All were severely sunburned, and none had eaten for four days. When they managed to croak out a word it was *"Omizu!"* (Water!). Once they received some they began weeping, and crying out, "The flag of our regiment is missing. You must search for it!"

This was insanity. I could not take time out to search for a flag, even though I knew how much it meant to them. In the Japanese Army it was a tradition that any unit losing its regimental standard died with that loss. The unit's name was stricken from Army records. It was bad fortune, and survivors naturally lost face and felt accursed. Though it pained me, I had to ignore their pleas. I ordered *RO-101* to submerge, and stay below until after sunset. The 47 men we had picked up really cramped us. I wirelessed Rabaul that I had a full load and was returning. *RO-103* left Rabaul then, to continue the search.

Fujita's submarine got into trouble on the evening on March 9, running up on an uncharted reef. *RO-103* wirelessed Rabaul for help and I was ordered out to tow her free. Fujita was able to free *RO-103* before I arrived by jettisoning all the food that could be spared and casting his torpedoes over the side. An American destroyer was sighted to the south on the afternoon of March 10, prompting Fujita to throw all classified documents into the sea, lest they be captured. When the enemy ship steamed away, apparently without having spotted him, Fujita dumped more excess weight and was able to float free by morning of March 11.

149

I heard the full and horrible story of the Bismarck Sea later, after a boatload of 13 men, carrying with them the standard of the 115th Regiment, was cast up on New Britain. Private First Class Shotaro Tamura, official flag bearer for Col. Torashi Endo's regiment, told its story.

"On March 2," he said, "we were met in the sea of Dampier Strait by enemy bombers. They were waiting for us. The attack that day was not very severe. I saw flames rise from only one transport before it sank.

"Enemy reconnaissance planes kept following us after that. They dropped flares throughout the night, exposing every ship as if in daylight. No one got any sleep.

"At about 8 A.M. on March 3, we saw countless bombers coming at us from the direction of New Guinea. They were so thick that they looked like a flat black cloud, spreading wide on both sides. The wings of the planes seemed almost to touch one another."

Tamura and his comrades aided the ship's gunners by opening up at the enemy planes with rifles, machine guns, and even pistols. It did no good. The first wave of planes on that second day did mortal damage.

"A second wave came in about two hours later," said Tamura, "I could see many Curtiss, Bell and Lockheed fighters in it. The convoy was just about destroyed by then, so these planes concentrated on the survivors. They came in to strafe again and again, their guns like a great rake collecting leaves. We leaped from the lifeboats each time they approached, clambering back on board after we thought they had gone. Fighter groups kept coming at us every 30 minutes or so. Colonel Endo was killed in a lifeboat, the victim of seven fighter planes. He was standing, telling us what to do, when bullets tore into him. Eight more of my comrades were killed that way, while still in lifeboats. Lt. Kondo, of my company, was also killed in this manner.

"About 7 A.M. the next morning (March 4) we were strafed again. No one was killed, but several men were wounded. About 1 P.M. we sighted Japanese planes overhead and cheered. They didn't stay long, though, and at 2 P.M. more enemy planes appeared and strafed us. That time we saw them early and suffered no casualties because we all leaped into the water in time."

There were 39 other men in the lifeboat with Tomura. Each one had a day's rice ration with him. There were also 16 *katsuoboshi,* a sort of salami-shaped stick of dried bonito fish. With rice, it could sustain a man pretty well for a short period.

The men also found 20 sacks of hard biscuits in the boat, plus two small kegs of water. This, together with what each man carried in his water canteen, was the total of their food and water supply for 31 days. Of the 40 men in that lifeboat who were alive on March 4, only 13 staggered ashore on a beach near the western end of New Britain in April. Of nearly 7000 men, more than 3000 had been killed. Most of these were slaughtered by low-flying enemy planes after they had safely abandoned ship, or by American PT boats that came out of New Guinea bases "to mop up" as American historian Morison puts it in his official history of the U. S. Navy in World War II.

In 1948 I was called and interrogated by Occupation authorities in the Ichioka case, which involved some Japanese submariners who had maltreated or machine-gunned ship survivors in the Indian Ocean. These men were tried and convicted of violating the rules of war. Since I had never operated in the Indian Ocean, and since nothing of that kind occurred in the Pacific, I was released after about six hours of questioning. On that occasion, and sometimes since, I have thought of the comparison between events in the Indian Ocean and what took place in the Bismarck sea slaughter. I suppose "war atrocities" are committed only by the losing side.

We suffered no submarine losses at all during the month of March, 1943, although we very nearly lost *I-176,* the boat of Lt. Cdr. Tanabe, the hero of Midway. He had made the first (and other) successful supply run to Guadalcanal, and was making one to New Guinea when death reached out for him again. I have the story from Asakichi Araki, who later commanded Japan's first post-war division of submarines in our Maritime Self-Defense Force. In 1943 he was a Lieutenant and the executive officer of *I-176,* which was standing about 400 yards off Lae on March 19. She had a cargo of food and ammunition, and was taking advantage of evening twilight to unload them.

"The sea off Lae was still as a mirror," says Araki, "and I could see the reflection of the setting sun in the western sky. The dark mountains of New Guinea were silhouetted against it. We were surfaced and waiting for some *daihatsu* that had just put out from shore, to come alongside. Captain Tanabe and I were on the bridge of the conning tower. On the main deck our crewmen were wearing white *hachimaki* (bandanas of determination) about their foreheads. Two of the landing craft moored on each side of us and our men began carrying bags of supplies from the hatches to these four craft. *I-176* crewmen were experienced in this effort now and their precise, labor-saving moves reminded me of the works of a clock.

"Each grain of rice meant added life to the soldiers and Navy men at Lae. They were half-starved, and the *daihatsu* working parties gave a ragged cheer as their landing craft came close to us. For their part, our sailors were moved deeply by the sight of these brave men. They added small gifts to the cargo, each one welcomed by the Lae garrison, even if it were only a torn and creased newspaper.

"It became quite dark as the loading proceeded. The job was about half-done when, suddenly, I saw red rockets rise above the beach and burst. This was the danger signal. 'Emergency dive!' shouted Captain Tanabe, but it was too late. Three medium bombers swooped over a nearby hill, machine guns twinkling in their noses. They came in low, and dropped a cluster of bombs. I dropped through the hatch into the con-ning tower just as *I-176* took a great lurch to port, slamming me against a bulkhead. When the submarine remained in a listing position, I automatically shouted 'Blow the port main tank!' I was sure our boat had been holed, and wanted to lighten her so she would roll back to an even keel. If she didn't, she might capsize.

"Reports of many leaks in the submarine began coming to the conning tower. I ordered them repaired. The next moment I looked up, and saw Captain Tanabe trying to make his way down the ladder from the open bridge. 'I'm shot,' he said feebly, 'Take command, Araki.' Our signals petty officer helped me get Captain Tanabe through the hatch, then closed it. As he did so, I could hear water sloshing about the open bridge. *I-176* was already diving. A few moments more, and Tanabe would have been left up there to drown.

"Later on I learned from men on shore that they'd seen a high pillar of fire rise from our stern, where a bomb had struck. *I-176* had listed to one side and disappeared almost at once, making them think we had been sunk. Days after that we learned from foreign news reports that enemy aircraft claimed to have sunk a destroyer at Lae that night. It was a good thing those planes *thought* they sank us in that first pass. Had they made another, they would have been sure to do the job.

"We found that Captain Tanabe had a bullet lodged near his heart. I had command. What to do now? Surface? The enemy might be waiting. Remain submerged? Impossible!—I could hear air hissing from leaks all over the boat. We were taking on too much water. We would keep going right to the bottom unless something were done.

"Captain Tanabe was gotten to his berth, where I told him I intended to beach the submarine and try to make repairs. He could only nod, he was so weak. He knew the tide rise was enough so that if I put *I-176* on the shore now she could be floated off when the tide was full.

"I left his side and returned to the conning tower, where the water reached to my knees. I ordered the periscope raised to its maximum height, and peered through it. Scanning the shoreline, I made out the mouth of a river. That was where I could beach our boat! I called out, 'Right full rudder! All engines ahead full!' We had our main air pumps working, expelling air from the ballast tanks, and our depth gauge showed 60 feet. I received reports from time to time that the water leaks were being stopped. That was good news. 'Slow to standard speed!' I ordered; then 'Stop engines!'

"I-176 still had some way on and was coasting toward the shore. Just as I felt her hull scrape, I ordered all engines backed full a few seconds, then stopped them. Everything fell silent. A look at the depth gauge showed me that *I-176* should be at least partly above water now, so I ordered the conning tower hatch cracked. To my relief no water came in, so I climbed up to the open bridge. I looked around. All of the hull, except for the extreme forward section and part of the conning tower, was still under water and the bow was elevated at a slight angle. I ordered more water blown out of the main tanks. Soon most of the main deck was above water. Then I ordered crew members out on deck to find the rest of the leaks and plug them. Some checked the upper hull, while others got into the water and felt along the sides of the submarine with their bare hands. I had to order the deck grating torn up to get at holes in our main deck.

"The chief engineering officer didn't think *I-176* could make it back to Rabaul. He didn't like the list we still had on, and neither did I. Inside a submarine a sharp list has a deep psychological effect on crewmen, making them fearful of a capsizing. I masked my feelings, and told the chief engineering officer in a voice loud enough to carry well, that we would repair *I-176* or die trying. I think my words gave me more courage than they gave to others, but the crew worked hard as I moved among them, urging them to hurry and get the job done before midnight. We had to get off during that tide, or sit in the open, an easy target, all the next morning.

"Things seemed to be going well after a while, so I went below to see the captain. 'If repairs can be finished in time, sir,' I said, 'I will haul off, make a test dive, and start back to

Rabaul.'

"In a soft voice, he said that he didn't like that idea. 'It might be better,' he said, 'to lie here on the bottom in shallow water for a while and make sure that all is well.' I appreciated his advice, wondering why I had not thought of that myself. Perhaps my mind had been preoccupied with getting *I-176* out of the danger area. Patience, I realized, would serve me better in the long run.

"Repair work was still going on, when the four *daihatsu* that had been searching for possible survivors came upon us. They were sure that *I-176* had been destroyed, and was somewhere on the bottom. I told them to get the food, guns and ammunition off the ship. This they did, lightening us considerably. The officer in charge of these craft wished us well as he backed off into the darkness, his boat bearing away the bodies of two crewmen who had been killed in the bombing-strafing attack, plus the wounded Signals Petty Officer Nomura.

"I had suggested to the captain that it might be well if he went ashore, too, so he could get medical treatment at Lae. He declined, preferring to remain with his ship. The tide was high by then, and our air flasks were full, our batteries fully charged, so I tried backing *I-176* off the shore. She wouldn't move. The hull had settled. Suction kept us fast to the shore!

"At that point I ordered all hands who were not needed at cruising stations to assemble on deck. As I ordered the engines backed, they ran from one side of *I-176* to the other, shifting their weight. They laughed and shouted like children playing a game. After a while *I-176* rolled a bit with them; then a bit more. All of a sudden, she shook herself free of the earth's grip and floated. We were free! Crewmen ran to the base of the conning tower, and grinning and shouting congratulations to me.

"I returned their grins, then ordered all hands below except the bridge watch. We moved out a short distance, submerged, and rested on the bottom at 135 feet. I let all crew members who were not needed to check leaks get some sleep and, after I made several turns through the boat to check the water-tight integrity myself, turned into my bunk. When I awoke, it was nearly sunset. All holes in the submarine had been plugged with dowels and rags, thanks to the ingenuity and skills of Captain Tanabe's hand-picked crew. Some holes were five inches in diameter, but I felt sure they would withstand pressure.

"Slowly we came to the surface. All was well. The repairs held. I swung *I-176* about, and we steamed smoothly out of

Lae Harbor at a respectable 18 knots."

I-176 got back to Rabaul on March 22. Tanabe received preliminary medical care there and was sent home to recuperate. There he was honored by a personal audience with the Emperor. The rest of us submarine captains prepared to take part in another mass attempt to smash the enemy power in the Solomons-Bismarcks theater. My portion would include my first war patrol in the Solomons.

* * *

Chapter 11

THE SOLOMONS, BISMARCKS,
AND THE ALEUTIANS

Two days after Tanabe's *I-176* got back to Rabaul, I left
there for a station southeast of Guadalcanal. *RO-101*'s mission
was to make weather reports, provide air-sea rescue, and to
attack enemy shipping. Our departure was made seven days
before X-Day (April 1), the date Adm. Yamamoto had set for
an all-out air attack on enemy holdings in the Solomons. For
this he had put about 175 of his carrier planes on Rabaul, to
supplement about 200 already there. Most of the planes staged
right through Rabaul, moving on to other airfields we had by
then established closer to Henderson Field.

Reinforcements began moving out of Rabaul by sea on
April 1 protected by a great overhead blanket of Zero fighters.
Air fights continued in the Solomons for the next six days,
climaxed by a heavy air assault on Guadalcanal. Then Adm.
Yamamoto turned on New Guinea, sending all available
planes against Buna, Port Moresby, and Milne Bay. On Apr.
16, satisfied with the results reported by our fliers, Adm.

Yamamoto ended this operation. He believed that nearly 30 enemy ships had been sunk and 180 enemy aircraft destroyed. Outside of making weather reports twice daily, *RO-101* did nothing on this patrol, having sighted no enemy vessels we could attack. On Apr. 5, I received a wireless order from Rabaul to head for waters off Cape Esperance, where some of our bomber crewmen were down and adrift. As we approached the position given, we found it thick with PT boats.

American PT boats turned out to be the unconquerable enemy of Japanese submarines. They were very small, which made them hard to see, either at sea or against a shore line. It did no good to fire torpedoes at them, as the Model 95's passed well beneath them. And they had radar. While they could hide under the smallest cover cast by an overshadowing cloud or in a cove, they could still see us at a great distance with their electronic eyes. They could dart in and attack with machine guns, torpedoes or depth charges, then race away at high speed before a submarine could do anything. When a Japanese submarine spotted one of these torpedo boats, the only thing it could do was dive and run away. That's what I had to do. I got back to Rabaul on Apr. 11.

Two days after I left Rabaul on patrol, there was an old-fashioned sea battle in the Aleutians area. One of our escorted convoys, trying to reinforce Attu, had to turn back while its protecting escorts engaged an enemy interception force. It was cruisers and destroyers fighting against their counterparts, in a fog, without help from submarines or aircraft on either side. Our ships managed to damage an American cruiser and a destroyer. The battle broke off when both sides began to run short of ammunition.

Japanese submarines operating in the Pacific enjoyed moderate success from April through June. *I-17*, *I-19* and *I-25* were in the Fijis-Samoa area, while *I-26*, *I-174*, *I-177*, *I-178*, and *I-180* were off the Australian coast. These eight submarines claimed a total of nine sinkings during this period. I have been able to verify only five; SS *Phoebe A. Hearst*, SS *Willian K. Vanderbilt*, SS *Lydia M. Child*, SS *Chief Ouray*, and SS *Robert T. Lincoln*. All were in the 7000-ton range.

RO-34, under Lt. Rikichi Tomita, left Rabaul the day after Yamamoto's operation began, with orders to take station down The Slot, providing weather information and scouting intelligence. She was the first Japanese submarine, so far as I know, to fall victim to radar. Lt. Tomita had his submarine on the surface in the evening of Apr. 6, recharging batteries, when the USS *Strong* picked her up on its search set. Another destroyer, USS *O'Bannon*, used its radar-directed gun mounts to open up an attack with gunfire, then finished off *RO-34* with depth charges. Thus perished the 21st of our submarines to be lost in the war.

We lost our Combined Fleet commander-in-chief in April, too. After securing his massive air operation, Adm. Yamamoto decided to make an inspection swing through the islands. The Americans, through code-cracking, learned of this, and set an ambush of 16 Lockheed P-38 fighter planes. Yamamoto perished in the wreckage of his shot-down aircraft. His chief of staff, Vice Adm. Matome Ugaki, survived the crash of the plane accompanying Yamamoto's. This happened on April 18. Three days later, Adm. Mineichi Koga was named Yamamoto's successor as commander-in-chief.

Late in April, our *I-29*, with Cdr. Takaichi Kinashi commanding, rendezvoused with a German submarine in the southern Indian Ocean. Kinashi picked up Mr. Chandra Bose, and took him to Penang, Sumatra. Bose was the center of anti-British feeling and strength in India. He and his associates were *almost* successful in their efforts to help Japan take India. The spirit that Bose rallied endured through and past the war's end was instrumental in winning India's independence.

About this time, an American cruiser-destroyer force shelled our base on Attu, in the Aleutians. This was interpreted as meaning that the enemy planned to make a move in that area, so a number of submarines were pulled north, to reinforce those already there. *I-31*, *I-34* and *I-35* had been making patrols in the Aleutians since the previous September. They were joined in April by *I-2*, *I-5*, *I-6* and *I-7*, under command of Capt. Tomejiro Tamaki. Nine more submarines were also ordered to that area—another excellent example of how Japan's submarine strength was diluted and diverted during the war. More than two-thirds of the submarines Japan could send to sea were engaged either in defensive or supply missions. Our contact with the oncoming enemy (except for the Indian Ocean area) was meager. This pillar-to-post method of doing things eventually eradicated what once ranked with the world's best in submarine forces.

My fifth sortie from Rabaul began on Apr. 30. I was to patrol off Milne Bay, at the eastern end of New Guinea, along the enemy's Australia-to-New Guinea supply route. He had made a quick amphibious move around the island's tip, and put troops ashore for a drive westward against our men on New Guinea's north coast. *RO-102*, under Lt. Shoji Kanemoto, had been added to my submarine squadron. It followed *RO-101* out on May 2.

I reached my patrol area on May 3. Kanemoto had orders to take station 50 miles due south of me. On May 10, we were ordered to exchange patrol areas. I acknowledged, but *RO-102* did not. She was never heard from again. I think she was either lost operationally, or fell victim to one of the many patrol aircraft flying out of New Guinea and Australia. In any case, the official U.S. Navy Chronology of World War II listed her loss incorrectly. Last word from *RO-102* came on May 9, so she could not have been sunk on Feb. 11, as the chronology states.

The Americans assaulted Attu on May 11, with 11,000 troops and a heavy covering force that included battleships. This was the first use of America's old pre-war battleships against Japan. Until then, they had been kept well out of the combat areas since their poor compartmentation made them easy victims for our giant torpedoes. Nearly 20 destroyers screened the three old battlewagons. Nevertheless two of our boats penetrated the escort screen and fired at USS *Pennsylvania*. *I-31* made an attack the day after the assault on Attu began. Her torpedoes missed, after which she underwent a severe attack by a patrol bomber and two destroyers. She escaped, due to the skill of her commanding officer. *I-35* missed *Pennsylvania* in a torpedo attack three days after that, but she was also able to elude the sea greyhound that counterattacked.

When the Americans landed on Attu, more submarines were sent north. They were *I-9, I-21, I-24, I-155, I-157, I-159, I-169, RO-104* and *RO-105*, all under command of Rear Adm. Takeo Konda. He used *Heian Maru* for his flagship, and operated out of Paramushiro, in the Kuriles chain northeast of Japan's Hokkaido. Three submarines had to be withdrawn from this effort before long, *I-2, I-155* and *I-157*. The first and third ran upon shoals, suffering damage to their bottoms, while *I-155* had to go home for repairs after being badly buffeted in a severe storm. At a meeting on board *Heian Maru*, the other captains were cautioned about operations near the Arctic. Cdr. Tatsuo Irie, skipper of *I-34*, and the senior submarine captain present, said, "While you are operating up here, don't delude yourself into thinking that fog will hide you. The enemy is equipped with a weapon he calls 'radar.' You can never tell from which direction a shell or torpedo might come at you, in spite of the fact that a heavy fog may be surrounding your boat. Also, keep in mind that the ocean currents up here are treacherous and unpredictable. One can quite easily drift far away from his estimated position without knowing it. Use every chance you get to make a star or sun sight. Keep rechecking your position at every opportunity. Nothing can put you so much at a disadvantage up here as not knowing exactly where you are at all times."

Irie, who was known to many for the deep love he held for his wife, closed the conference on a humorous note. "Don't leave your periscope up long enough for seals and otters to nibble at it." he said. "Catch a few of them instead, and bring the furs home for your *okusan*."

On the night of May 26-27, 1943, the submarine *I-7* sailed into Attu and took off 60 wounded men, while also unloading food and ammunition. Two days later, the fighting on that island ended. Over 2300 Japanese were killed and about 30 taken prisoner. During the battle, they killed or wounded some 1800 Americans. On May 29, we lost another submarine thousands of miles south of Attu. She was Cdr. Hidejiro Utsuki's boat, *I-178*, on patrol in the south Pacific. The American sub-chaser *SC-699*, a small craft, sank her.

From May 12 to June 23, submarines made a total of 13 runs to Kiska and Attu. They took in 125 tons of ammunition, and 100 tons of food, while bringing out 820 men. After no more was heard from Attu, it was decided to remove all of our troops from Kiska, which was cut off by the capture of the more westerly island. Our troops on Kiska were in a pincer, and there could be no chance of victory. Four submarines were lost in the Kiska evacuation operation, trying to help the 6000 Army and Navy men marooned on that island.

I-24 was the first. Under Cdr. Hiroshi Hanabusa (who had figured in nearly all of our midget submarine attacks, at Pearl Harbor and other places) she failed to report after June 7. She may have hit a rock pinnacle, or perished in a storm, or simply suffered an accident. The Americans claimed no submarine sinking in the month of June for which we could not account, so *I-24* must have been lost operationally.

I-9, under Cdr. Akiyoshi Fujii, who'd had command of her since the war began, was sunk on June 11. The American patrol craft *PC-487* picked her up on its sound equipment and raced in, dropping four depth charges as *I-9* dived to escape. Fujii's boat was hurt badly. It broached, rolling helplessly on the surface, and the small American ship made a high speed run, ramming *I-9*. Then *PC-487* backed off, opened up with gunfire, and followed with another ramming. It was a brilliantly executed kill. *I-9* went down with all hands, without ever striking back at this smaller but alert enemy.

Lt. Cdr. Kikuo Inouye's *I-31* was less than a year old when he very nearly sank USS *Pennsylvania* on May 12. Later

Inouye left Paramushiro, to make an evacuation run to Kiska. He was picked up on the radar of the American destroyer *Frazier* on June 13. Inouye tried to escape, but the *Frazier* opened up first with gunfire, then depth charges. When *I-31* got beneath the surface, a second depth charge barrage came down on her, then a third. This last brought her end in a great gush of fuel oil bubbling up.

Three days after that, *I-157* ran aground at Kiska. Her crewmen jettisoned everything possible, including all of her torpedoes, half of her batteries, and most of her fuel. She was able to get off and into deeper water, but lacked power to run for very long should she have to dive. She had to retreat all the way to Kure on the surface.

The fourth submarine lost in attempting to assist men on Kiska was Lt. Cdr. Katsuhiko Nagai's *I-7*. She fell victim to the American destroyer *Monaghan* (the same ship that sank one of our midget submarines within Pearl Harbor on Dec. 7, 1941). A few hours after midnight on the morning of June 22, the submarine on which I had once served was picked up by *Monaghan's* radar at long range. The enemy ship closed in to about one mile, still using her radar, and opened fire with deck guns. Nagai, on the bridge of his boat, was killed in the first barrage. So was Capt. Tomejiro Tamaki, commander of the submarine division to which *I-7* belonged. He had been using her as his flagship. Lt. Yoshio Hanabusa, the executive officer, took over. He swung the bow about and made best speed into Vega Harbor, Kiska. He got there safely, and ran up on shore, where his crew was able to make partial repairs and get the submarine off again that night. Hanabusa decided to use darkness as a cover, and attempt an escape. He worked *I-7* up to her top speed, and raced out of Vega Harbor, only to find enemy patrol craft waiting for him. They crowded him into shoal waters and *I-7* was again hung up. She had to be abandoned, although most of her crew survived. The quick-witted executive officer, furthermore, had completed an important mission.

The admiral, at Paramushiro, had been making plans with officers of the Kiska garrison (who had been taken off the island earlier via submarine) to get the rest of the island's forces away safely. One of those staff officers had been sent back to the island on board *I-7*, so he could brief its defenders on when and how Vice Adm. Hosogaya would come for them. He had a list of the "one-word" code signals to be used. These were drafted so as to avoid heavy radio traffic, which the enemy could intercept and interpret as meaning something important was about to happen. Lt. Hanabusa had put that officer ashore on the island.

On learning of *I-7's* loss, Vice Adm. Hosogaya, in charge of all northern naval forces, ordered that no more submarines be used in the Kiska evacuation. But, because of *I-7* and her crew, nearly 5200 other Japanese men were saved.

They were saved on July 28, when Rear Adm. Masatomi Kimura arrived off Kiska. His two cruisers and six destroyers slipped through the fog like phantoms. They loaded up the waiting 5200 troops in less than 60 minutes, and disappeared like ghosts in the gray mist. This was the second completely successful evacuation of an island brought off by Japan in less than six months (the first being Guadalcanal). The enemy arrived off Kiska about three weeks later with 100 ships and 35,000 troops. After a ferocious bombardment of Kiska, American troops stormed ashore. They managed to shoot one another in the darkness for a while, and ended up capturing some pet dogs our troops had left behind. As one American later put it, "We dropped about 100,000 surrender leaflets on the island, but those dogs couldn't read."

The American military and naval phonetic alphabet in World War II used "Dog" for vocalizing the letter "D." The Americans also used "D" to denote the days of their various landings and invasions. Japanese sailors and soldiers, a long time later, would still be able to get laughs out of comrades by mentioning Kiska's "D-for-Dog Day."

While the northern submarines were making runs to Kiska, I was on patrol in the Solomons. I left Rabaul June 8, the same day our battleship *Mutsu* was lost in the Inland Sea. Although her accidental sinking had nothing at all to do with submarines, I tell of it because I believe the anecdote will reveal for the first time one of the secret weapons that Japan had.

Skipper of *Mutsu* when she sunk was Capt. Teruhiko Miyoshi. With 1120 of his men, he perished when she suddenly blew up just south of Kure. Senior surviving officer was the navigator, Cdr. Hideya Okihara. All he remembered was walking on deck toward the bridge, then suddenly finding himself in the sea a good distance away clutching a small piece of timber.

The reason for this monstrous explosion in home waters was kept secret. I learned the cause of the disaster a long time later from Vice Adm. Mitsumi Shimizu. Shimizu had command of the 1st Fleet when *Mutsu* blew up, and was on board his flagship, IJN *Nagato,* anchored not far away, when it happened. "The smoke from the explosion was a very bright white," he told me, "the color characteristic of our Mark 3 bomb. I said so at the investigation that followed. It was my opinion that Mark 3 explosions had caused the ship to blow up. The blast was tremendous!"

Our Mark 3 bomb was an ultra-secret weapon as closely guarded as the American atomic bomb. Each one weighed a ton and was constructed like a high-caliber battleship projectile. Each contained inside its casing ammunition equivalent to about 300 artillery shells. *Mutsu's* magazines were filled with Mark 3's. A full salvo of these, fired from *Mutsu's* main turrets, would detonate at a height of 100,000 feet and rain down like thousands of artillery shells on an enemy ship formation. One salvo was considered enough to destroy an entire enemy task force. But the chance to prove this died with the men who died in *Mutsu*. Officials decided that the Mark 3 was too dangerous to be carried around in quantity. *Mutsu* still lies off Kure, all but 272 bodies recovered from her. Only 250 men survived the explosion.

In mid-1943, officials at Rabaul were convinced (because of heavy enemy radio traffic, and other intelligence) that the Americans were planning an assault near the center of the Solomons chain. The enemy had already seized Russell Island, northwest of Guadalcanal, and fitted it out with a radar station to warn Henderson Field of our aircraft whenever they approached. My assignment was to patrol south of Vangunu Island (which is near Russell) and to watch for the enemy. If I saw any ships, my warning to Rabaul would bring down planes from there, Buka, Bougainville, Vila, Munda, and Ballale (a small island southeast of Bougainville).

By July 18 I had sighted no ships at all. This worried me. Such inactivity could be the calm before a great storm. Still, *RO-101* continued on our mission, although half our cruising capability had been used up. We stayed submerged by day, and surfaced only after dark. About midnight of June 23 my navigator, Lt. (jg) Shigeshi Kondo, who had the bridge watch, heard the high sound of a Packard engine. We dived at once and listened to American PT boats pass above us, heading west. I decided they were running toward Bougainville to make a reconnaissance, so I radioed this information to Rabaul a few minutes later. For the next seven days we saw nothing, except that on the night darkness of July 25 we noticed fiery bullet trails on the horizon. I took this to be an exchange between some PT boats and some of our aircraft. By July 30 our food supplies were running low, so I began edging westward, trying to get the most possible patrol work out of *RO-101's* cruising endurance. Unknown to me, the Americans had already landed at Segi Point, New Georgia, nine days earlier.

About 90 minutes before sunrise on June 30, while cruising west, we again heard Packard engines, well astern of us. I dived. A short time later my sound room picked up propeller sounds, I took a chance on using my night periscope, and saw landing craft all around me. It took about 30 minutes for all of them to pass, and meantime I ordered a coded message made up. Without surfacing, I put up our radio antenna and beamed out "Group of enemy landing craft sighted, heading west, at 5:45 A.M.," adding our position at the time.

It was too near daylight for us to try to make a surface run after this quarry. I kept *RO-101* submerged, cruising westward at 4 knots as the propeller sounds diminished in the distance. I kept our radio antenna up for a long while, though, thinking that Admiral Harada would have some orders for my boat in spite of its being near the end of its cruising endurance. Just before noon we intercepted a wireless from the Munda garrison. "Enemy landing forces are in sight." was followed by "Enemy troops are landing with amphibious tanks in the lead. We are exchanging fire with them."

I kept heading west. At 4 P.M. an order came from Rabaul. *"RO-107* will approach Munda beach through Branche Channel," it read. *"RO-101* will do the same from the area west of Rendova. Both will attack enemy forces off the beachhead. *RO-100, RO-103* and *RO-106* will leave Rabaul at once and head for Munda."

I ordered our torpedoes checked over and readied for loading, then swung north. By dawn I was at a point about 30 miles from the concentration of enemy vessels. Almost immediately, I saw two PT boats about 500 to 1000 yards from us, almost as though they were escorting us to the beachhead. I ran along as silently as I could, but lost them in about an hour. Then more PT boats appeared in my scope. These did not appear to have noticed us, but stayed in one area persistently. *RO-101* had to go deep and we could not approach the Munda beach area.

At 2 P.M. on July 2, I tried again, and got to about 20 miles from our targets. But *RO-101's* battery charge was now below half-strength, which did not leave me enough power to conduct underwater attack operations. I decided to retreat, recharge my batteries and try to attack the following day. The enemy appeared to have thrown rings of interceptors out to protect his landing force from submarine attack. I slipped under the PT boats, and surfaced well out to sea that night for a battery charging. Then I tried to slip back in again. Early in the morning of July 2 my lookouts cried out, "Destroyers! Destroyers!" and again I dived. The enemy vessels proved to be PT boats, not destroyers, when I put my periscope up for a quick look around. They moved about us as though they might have picked us up on their radar sets.

I used up all of that day getting away from the PT boats, but they prevented my approaching on the next day, too. Then I received orders to head for Rabaul. When I arrived in Simpson Harbor, we had only two days' provisions left on board. *RO-107* did not return at all.

During the Occupation, when I was interrogated by American officers, I learned that the American destroyer *Radford* was credited with sinking my *RO-101*, on July 1. Americans records were not correct on that score. *RO-107*, commanded by Lt. Shoichi Egi (who had survived the accidental sinking of *RO-65* the previous November) was the submarine USS *Radford* sank. The destroyer used radar to entrap her, just as radar would trap so many more of our submarines in the night's darkness. *Radford's* captain made a simple, classic attack. He kept his radar on *RO-107* while he moved into one-mile range. Then he flipped open his searchlight shutters and opened fire at the same time. He repeated his salvo twice, and *RO-107* was dead!

I learned after the war that the American Navy leased the plush Royal Hawaiian Hotel at Waikiki Beach for its submariners, allowing them to have a full and relaxed rest between war patrols. Japanese submariners enjoyed nothing like that kind of comfort. Four days after reaching Rabaul we were on our way out again with orders to intercept and attack an enemy force. It had been sighted heading for Kula Gulf, a body of water between New Georgia and Kolombangara (the next island northwest in the Solomons chain). Because of intense enemy air patrols, I was forced to keep at 3 to 4 knots speed underwater, during daylight, and 10 to 12 knots on the surface during some parts of the night. I got to Kula Gulf on July 11, long after one of our destroyer reinforcement groups had sunk the U.S. cruiser *Helena* in a night battle. That scramble cost us a pair of destroyers in exchange for the American cruiser, but 1200 troops got ashore on Kolombangara.

Early on the morning of July 12, I myself became one of the incorrect listings in American histories. The USS *Taylor* is credited with sinking *I-25* on that date. She sank nothing. But she did hurt *RO-101* badly. It happened just before 5 P.M., while we were on the surface to recharge batteries and replenish air supplies. My executive officer, Lt. Hiromi Tokugawa, had charge of the lookouts and I was below. We had no idea *Taylor* had us on her radar set and was closing in for a kill.

Without any warning, a sudden barrage of shells exploded on and around the starboard side of *RO-101*. I ran from my cabin to the conning tower, shouting "Full speed ahead! Emergency dive! Emergency dive!"

When I stepped into the tower, two lookouts were dropping through the hatch, blood dripping from their wounded hands. "Probable destroyer, Captain!" they called to me, adding "The executive officer is wounded!"

Tokugawa kept saying "Forget about me, Sir. Dive the ship!" but Seaman Yoshio Nakahara and I pulled Tokugawa's plump body through the hatch just as *RO-101* began her plunge. Three other men had also been wounded, but we got the hatch closed before water covered the bridge. Shells were still exploding along side us as we slipped beneath the waves. As we passed the 100-foot mark, the destroyer roared past overhead. A depth charge came down, followed by 10 more. Each time one went off we suffered damage to some piece of equipment or another but, strangely, *RO-101* kept to an even keel. Also, strangely, the enemy dropped no more depth charges after those eleven. I read later that USS *Taylor* turned away almost at once, and rejoined the convoy she was escorting. Her captain must have been satisfied that he had finished us off.

I wanted to level off at 230 feet (the safe depth level of that class of submarine being 250 feet). But, without the services of the wounded Tokugawa, who doubled as my diving officer, adjustments to the ballast tanks went roughly. *RO-101* kept plunging downward. I watched in horror as the depth gauge needle passed 250 feet, then 300, then 350. Finally it went past the last figure on the dial — 395 feet! If the drop could not be stopped, *RO-101*'s hull would cave in under the sea pressure! "Blow the main tank for ten seconds!" I shouted, but a long 30 seconds passed before I heard the sweet hiss of air into the ballast space pushing out water and making *RO-101* lighter. Had the enemy remained on the scene of attack a few minutes longer, he would have sighted rising bubbles, indicating that we were still alive.

RO-101's fall slower gently to a stop, like an elevator. Then she started upward. I hurriedly ordered the blowing stopped, lest we broach and become an easy target. The trim had to be adjusted several times, due to lack of Lt. Tokugawa's services, before the boat could be steadied at 200 feet. I finally caught my breath then, and thanked heaven. Had the American shown just a bit more persistence and determination, he would have had a kill. Instead, RO-101 enjoyed three more months of life.

A check of damage revealed that our periscope was smashed. That cut our operations short. I put about, and headed back for Rabaul.

Lt. Tokugawa died before morning, leaving us the problem of disposing of his body. One seaman suggested that we place it in a torpedo tube, which is what we did, sealing the tube against odors.

On arrival at Rabaul, we counted a total of 127 dents in *RO-101*'s hull where shells from USS *Taylor* had struck. She must have been using high-capacity type, rather than armor-piercing ammunition, else I would not be alive today. The gunnery of that American ship was excellent.

RO-101 was out of action awaiting installation of a new periscope that had to come from Truk for the rest of July. During my period of enforced idleness, Japan lost three more submarines.

Back home, in the Inland Sea, Lt. Cdr. Hiroshi Yuasa was conducting shakedown training in *I-179*. His ship suffered an accident and sank on July 14. *I-179* remained on the bottom until *1956*, when it was salvaged. Examination of it at that time revealed an open hatch near the bow. A careless crewman had neglected to close it and the bow filled with water, sinking the ship.

I-168 was next. Yahachi's old boat, killer of USS *Yorktown* at Midway, left Truk for a patrol on July 25. She was sunk in a submarine-versus-submarine battle on July 27, by USS *Scamp*. Apparently, both submarines fired torpedoes at each other, but *I-168*'s missed. Americans erroneously listed this sinking as that of *I-24*, which actually had already been lost far to the north in the Aleutians eight weeks earlier.

The third submarine lost was *RO-103*. Under Lt. Rikinosuke Ichihara, it left Rabaul, on patrol duty July 11. She was last heard from on July 28, when Ichihara reported "Sighted enemy ships on three occasions between July 15 and July 24, but had no chance to attack."

I do not think that this boat was lost operationally, but rather by either enemy aircraft or PT boats, which sometimes attacked a submarine contact but didn't get credit for a kill because they couldn't provide physical evidence that the submarine was sunk. Enemy patrols were so heavy in the Solomons at that time that it seems to me very likely that one of them made a hit on *RO-103*. Or perhaps the submarine struck a mine, after which Ichihara's boat crawled away to die.

Lt. Kazumichi Tanabe was flown out of Japan, to take the place of my slain Lt. Tokugawa. We also received three fresh and bright young seamen from the Rabaul base to replace those injured by USS *Taylor*'s gunfire. Our new periscope was installed, and we were combat-ready by August 3. I then conducted three days of drills and refresher training and found morale very high. The men of *RO-101* had been through the shattering experience of being both shelled and depth-charged, and survived. They were full of fighting spirit and eager for revenge. We put to sea again on Aug. 7, this time headed for waters south of Vella Lavella Island.

* * *

Chapter 12

THE SOLOMONS AND NEW GUINEA

The Battle of Vella Gulf was fought the night of Aug. 6.
Four Japanese destroyers (carrying 900 Army troops for rein-
forcement of Kolombangara) were intercepted by six
American destroyers. We lost three ships and 1500 men.
About 300 men made it to shore from the sunken ships.

The Americans' campaign had gone well for them in spite of
losses in the year between their landing on Guadalcanal and
my setting out from Rabaul on Aug. 7, on my eighth
Solomons mission. Although the going had been slow and the
fighting hard, the Americans progressed without a setback up-
wards along the stinking, disease-ridden chain of islands. They
had covered half of the distance from Henderson Field to
Simpson Harbor. And, on New Guinea, in the long campaign
written of as "the toughest fighting in the world," our troops
had been driven back from within sight of Port Moresby (their
chief objective on the island's south side) and had to retreat
northward over the Owen Stanley Mountains under ghastly

conditions. Now they were being pushed westward, along New Guinea's northern shore.

RO-101 was on station by Aug. 10, but as a sentry we were, for the most part, ineffective. We were often attacked by planes at night, when I had to surface to recharge batteries. Apparently the enemy was spotting us on airborne radar, then shutting down his engines to dip in and make a silent, glide-bombing attack. We rarely heard these aircraft until almost too late. And, once the bombers came, PT boats usually showed up within the next 30 minutes.

After a while, knowing that the enemy was always avidly seeking us during the late hours of darkness, I got an idea that served *RO-101* well. Enemy patrols, I had observed, were lightest during the morning and evening twilight periods. And those times gave my lookouts some light by which to see any bombers approach. Instead of the standard tactic, submerged daytime cruising followed by night time surface operations, I cruised submerged all day long and surfaced during evening twilight, while the sun's glow was still in the sky but visibility was poor. Once my batteries got a full charge, down I would go again and remain underwater all night, surfacing just before the sun rose. Then we'd recharge and go down again.

My tactic was successful, but it limited *RO-101's* ability to patrol any significant-size area because of our low underwater speed. And the pesky PT boats seemed always to be about. We had to stay down to avoid detection, PT boats made my submarine totally worthless on that patrol.

By Aug. 15, 1943, I had moved north to Gizo Strait (south of Vella Gulf). We knew that U.S. interceptor forces were watching in that area for Japanese attempts at reinforcing our garrisons in various parts of the Solomons and I hoped to pick off a few enemy ships. About 1 A.M. on the morning of Aug. 18, I saw some gun flashes through my periscope. To the north, surface ships were exchanging gunfire. I thought that our ships must be clashing with American ones and ordered my crew to battle stations, submerged. "Load all tubes!" I called out, and made ready to join in the battle as soon as I could determine friend from enemy. One hour later, while I was still making an underwater approach to the scene of the battle, my sound operator picked up an echo on his equipment. "Possible destroyer!" he called out. "Running at high speed!"

"Stand by all tubes!" I ordered, "Target is a destroyer! Set torpedo running depth at two meters!" All lights in the conning tower had long since been dimmed, so I could avoid night blindness. I swung the periscope about until it was on the bearing the sound operator had given me. There was a faint moon and the horizon was clear. But I could make out no ship.

"Target approaching." was the next word I received. "Degree of intensity is four!"

Five was the lowest reading our sound equipment registered and one was its highest. The first report had been five. After this second report, I began to make out a dark image on the horizon. Then I discerned another. Two ships were heading in our direction, both coming directly at *RO-101*. Their head-on approach made the silhouettes very slim and I could not identify them by type. I tried to judge their speed from the bow wave each was making and called out, "Target speed is 26 knots! There are two ships in sight!"

The targets then began veering off, a bit to my right but still making good speed. I was sure our presence was not suspected, because no ship could use its sonar while moving that fast. Their own propellers drowned out everything. Now I could make out their flat, flush decks. They were American destroyers. The nearest one was not more than 500 yards away from me and crossing rapidly. I realized that I had no chance at all to hit him with a torpedo and swung my periscope over to the second ship. Then I began calling out ranges and bearings.

"Bearing mark!" I cried out, and Lt. Kondo answered "Set!" I was ready to give the order to fire when the great wake of the first ship rolled toward me, obscuring my view. I cursed mightily, but could not let the chance pass without an attempt to strike at the enemy. In seconds that second ship would escape.

"Fire!" I ordered, even though I could not see my target, and four torpedoes leaped, one after another, from their tubes. The angle between the destroyer's bow and the line of sight between my boat and him was forty degrees, right. Range was 600 yards. My torpedoes would have to make a run of less than a half-mile. A submarine could not possibly have a better setup for a torpedo attack. But my torpedoes were wasted. All four missed the enemy ship, astern.

He must have been making at least 30 knots, instead of the 26 knots I had estimated. I was ashamed of making such an error in judgment. Nothing humiliated a submarine commander before his crew more than wasting torpedoes in such a manner. The only high moments in the lives of men who lived for weeks in Japan's iron whales were when they heard their torpedoes crashing into an enemy's hull. We heard one explosion a long time afterward, but not from the direction in which I had fired. I ordered the periscope up again and looked north through Gizo Strait. A ship was aflame there. Was it one of ours, or one of theirs?

From postwar readings, I have determined that the burning ship was the Japanese destroyer *Isokaze*. She had been hit by American ships in Vella Gulf. The ships that my torpedoes missed were two victorious American destroyers, which were withdrawing after the battle. They were seeking out the small craft that had been escorted by four of our destroyers under Rear Adm. Matsuharu Ijuin. As a Lieutenant-Commander, he was my swimming instructor and also was my instructor in Torpedoes during my years at Etajima. He pushed us very hard in both things, since he was also the supervisor for the annual 10-mile swimming race. Had I hit one of those destroyers, I might have saved some of the men Ijuin had been prevented from saving, because those American ships (after driving off Ijuin's force) ran rampart among our landing barges loaded with reinforcements. Many men died.

I was called back to Rabaul on Aug. 24 and arrived there on Aug. 26. A cabled set of orders was waiting for me. I was to depart *RO-101* and take command of *I-177*. I felt sad at leaving the crew that I had trained from before *RO-101*'s completion, but that is the way it is in a war. As a man gets more experience, he moves into positions calling for greater skills, greater responsibilities, and greater challenges.

While I had been out on this patrol, Japan lost four more submarines. The war in the Pacific was truly developing into a hellish one for our 6th Fleet. Submarines in the Indian Ocean had things a lot easier than we did in the Pacific. *I-10* and *I-27* both reported sinkings in August. We at Rabaul envied them, because they were doing what we felt all our submarines should be doing, attacking enemy supply lines. We were accomplishing very little in our theater of war and were paying too heavy a price to spot and stop the Americans as they advanced.

I-17, which had shelled the American west coast in February, 1942, left Truk on July 25, to make air reconnaissances of Espiritu Sancto (in the New Hebrides) and of Noumea, New Caledonia. She had a new captain, Cdr. Hakue Harada. As commanding officer of *I-165* in Malay water at the war's start, Harada had been the first to sight HMS *Prince of Wales* and HMS *Repulse,* thus launching the great search that saw our aircraft send these two battleships to the bottom.

On the morning of Aug. 19, 1943, Harada was about 40

miles off Noumea, preparing to launch *I-17*'s plane when an American land-based aircraft sighted his submarine in this helpless state. It attacked at once, and a number of men were caught on deck. The New Zealand corvette HMAS *Zui* came up and joined in the attack. *I-17* was sunk.

Next to be lost was *I-182*, commanded by my Etajima classmate, Lt. Cdr. Minoru Yonehara. The "young tribemaster" left Truk for the New Hebrides area, and was not heard from after Aug. 28. His was truly a tragedy in the great Japanese tradition. American sources state that *I-182* was sunk by USS *Trout* in the Philippines on Sept. 10. This claim is ridiculous! Yonehara's boat was nowhere near that area..He and his crew were off the New Hebrides, which are not very far (as Pacific Ocean distances go) from the Fijis. *I-182* was lost in the same part of the Pacific where the native princess lost her heart to its captain years before. I think that the American destroyer *Wadsworth* (although it did not receive official credit for a sinking) sent I-182 down about the first of September.

I have also read that Americans claim to have sunk *I-178* on Aug. 25, 1943. They did not! That submarine had already been lost three months before. The boat that they sank that day, off the New Hebrides, was *RO-35*, Lt. Cdr. Masateru Manabe. She went to that area from Truk and, on Aug. 25, radioed that she had a convoy of six transports in sight. She was not heard from again. The American destroyer *Patterson* picked up *RO-35* that night on its radar. *Patterson* moved in, and *RO-35* dived. But sonar, tenacity and depth charges enabled *Patterson* to sink *RO-35* before midnight.

The last time anyone heard from *I-25* and Lt. Cdr. Masaru Kobiga was on Aug. 24, when he reported that his aircraft's reconnaissance of Espiritu Sancto was successful. Kobiga, who had left Truk late in July, sent a report on the ships that were present in the enemy anchorage and was never heard from again. I think that his boat, like *I-182*, was attacked and sunk by an enemy ship (or perhaps even an enemy plane) which never received credit for a kill because it could not provide evidence of a sinking. Warrant Officer Nobuo Fujita, who had made so many flights from *I-25*, including his fire-bombings of America, was not lost. After his attacks on Oregon he made only one more flight over enemy territory, at Noumea. Then he was transferred from submarine duty to a flight instructor post at Kasumikaura, not far from Tokyo, where he spent the rest of the war training pilots for our naval air force.

These four submarines were the price we paid for sinking

only two enemy ships, which went down in the New Hebrides. *I-17* reported downing one before she was lost. *I-19* claimed another upon her safe return to Truk.

I-19 had hit the American lumber carrier, SS *Absaroka,* with torpedoes on Christmas Eve, 1941, off San Pedro. Eighteen years later a Mr. Robert Bell claimed to have found the hull of a submarine on the ocean floor nearby and Fort MacArthur records showed that a Japanese submarine identified as *I-19* had been sunk there in 1941. This is, of course, not true. All of the nine submarines that went to the U.S. west coast early in the war returned safely.

I-11 had some luck in southern waters. She sank three ships in one day off Australia. These were SS *Coast Farmer,* SS *G. S. Livanos,* and SS *William Dawes.* She got them on July 21. On Aug. 30, while returning from patrol, she sank SS *Star of Oregon.*

I spent a few days turning over command of *RO-101* to my successor, Lt. Masataka Fujisawa. We went out and made a few dives, too, so that he could become familiar with the little oddities each individual ship has which give it the personal character that crewmen come to know and have affection for. On Sept. 4, 1943, I left *RO-101*, somewhat heavy of heart. This feeling had to disappear almost at once, for in a few minutes I was on board and in command of *I-177*, moored only 300 yards away. I relieved Cdr. Hajime Nakagawa. For the previous four weeks, he had been making supply runs from Rabaul to New Guinea.

The attempt to reinforce and keep the Guadalcanal and New Guinea garrisons supplied was made in four different ways. First, of course, were the large-scale attempts made with transports that were escorted by cruisers, destroyers, and sometimes battleships and aircraft carriers. We lost too many of the large type ships in the first fierce fighting around Guadalcanal to continue this method. The Imperial Army then brought its own sea forces into play.

The Army would assemble a convoy of 10-20 small cargo carriers and landing craft, each carrying 10-20 tons of food and ammunition, at Shortland Island, off the southeast tip of Bougainville. From this staging point, about halfway down The Slot from Rabaul to Henderson Field, they would steam for the combat area. Their pilots knew nothing of the area's geography and the smallest craft mounted but a single machine gun each.

Moving only by night, they hid in coves and inlets during the day. Their average pace was a sluggish 6 knots. It took these vessels more than a week to cover the 300 miles to Guadalcanal and American PT boat squadrons often attacked them enroute. Dozens were sunk, but surviving craft pressed toward their destination with vigor and determination. Because they swarmed down in groups like ants, this means of supplying Guadalcanal was called the *"Ari"* (Ant) system.

But, no matter how hard these "ants" worked, what they got through to the hard-pressed garrison on the "death island" was like a cup of water poured on the desert—not enough to sustain life. So, Adm. Yamamoto made the difficult decision to employ destroyers for supply runs. A group of destroyers would form up at Shortland, usually loaded with troops and hundreds of drums of supplies lashed to the decks. Many of these drums contained gasoline and one enemy hit could make a funeral pyre of a ship. The destroyers would race out in the morning and make their way at 30 knots to the western end of Guadalcanal, covering the final miles during darkness. Because the destroyers could carry large payloads of troops and supplies, the method was moderately successful. They did not fear the PT boat attacks, because they could fight back hard when attacked. The Americans found this to be true at Tassafaronga on Nov. 30, 1942, the night when Rear Adm. Raizo Tanaka mauled three American cruisers and sank a fourth, although his ships were outnumbered, outgunned, and had their decks crowded with drums of supplies.

The Americans nicknamed this "The Tokyo Express." We Japanese called it the *"Nezumi"* (Rat) system. With their radar, the American destroyers were like cats in the dark, ready to pounce, and the "rats" had to elude them. Our best weapons were speed and elusiveness, which is what rodents use to escape death.

American aircraft, however, with their radar, could detect the "rats" at a great distance, then swoop in like eagles to attack them. On dark nights they had additional help in their bombing runs, being guided to their targets by the phosphorescent wake every ship makes in the Solomons' waters. So, whenever lookouts heard the roar of aircraft engines, a ship's captain would slow his vessel radically to leave very little wake, then change course sharply so the glowing path left behind would not serve as an arrow pointer for the bombardiers. If aircraft, in spite of this, still found our ships, at a given signal all searchlights (which had been aimed at the attacking plane) were turned on simultaneously. This sudden glare would blind the enemy pilot. Antiaircraft and machine guns then were often able to shoot him down, or drive him off.

The Americans countered by using the glide-bombing tactic, which I had to endure many times myself. Upon locating one of us, the enemy planes would shut off their engines and drop silently down. Having no radar, our destroyers found it especially difficult to cope with this attack, so they were rarely used for transport operations after Nov. 30, 1942.

That is when the *"Mogura"* (Mole) system was put into operation. At about the same time, for the same reasons (shortage of surface ships plus intensified enemy air operations) the *mogura* method was used in supplying New Guinea, too. Most of our operating submarines were used for this work, leaving very few for offensive operations against our enemies.

Usually one or two, at the most three, submarines were sent to waters east of Australia at a time. They could do very little to stop the massive flow of supplies that was coming out of the United States to equip forces gathering on the southern continent. It was easier for the Americans to supply Australia all the way from the United States, than it was for us to supply our southern holdings from Japan, which was a much shorter distance away. And enemy submarines inflicted upon Japan many more times damage than our submarines inflicted upon the enemy.

Nevertheless, *I-10* sank SS *Samuel Gompers* off the east coast of Australia on Jan. 29, 1943, and *I-21* got SS *Star King* on Feb. 9 in that same area; but throughout the first half of 1943 our sinkings of enemy ships were very few. On Apr. 27 SS *Lydia Child* went down off Brisbane before the torpedoes of *I-178*. *I-19* sank two ships on a cruise into the southern seas, SS *Phoebe A. Hearst* (near the Fijis on Apr. 20) and SS *William Vanderbilt* (east of New Caledonia on May 16). *I-174* got two ships on the same day, south of Guadalcanal, sinking SS *Chief Ouray* and SS *Robert Lincoln* on June 22.

The day before I assumed command of *I-177*, we lost still another submarine in the New Hebrides area, *I-20*, under Lt. Cdr. Hitoshi Otsuka. On Aug. 30 a report came in from Otsuka that he had sighted a force containing one battleship and one aircraft carrier. No more was ever heard from him. On Sept. 3 the American destroyer *Ellet,* notified that a submarine had been spotted in her area, picked up *I-20* on radar. She closed in and blinked "AA . . . AA . . . AA . . ." (the call signal for challenge). When she received no answer, she illuminated the seascape with her searchlights and saw a submarine diving. Depth charges soon killed *I-20*, which was our 37th submarine lost in the war.

Upon taking command of *I-177*, I joined the New Guinea

supply effort. At the outset I was in fine health. I had a stocky body frame, which I kept fit through exercise and healthy through good food. After my tour of duty in *RO-101*, during which I ate well, slept well, and was usually fairly relaxed, I was hale and hearty. Whenever in port at Rabaul I had played tennis to keep fit, and gone fishing to relax. Also, whenever possible, I had a one-hour nap in the afternoon, drank a little beer now and then, and took advantage of being on shore to take soothing hot showers often. That peak condition, I believe, sustained me during my tour of duty as commanding officer of *I-177*. I was able to carry on longer than most.

I made a total of 14 transport runs to New Guinea from Rabaul in *I-177*, the second highest number made by any I-boat captain. I set out on the first one on Sept. 10. *RO-101* also left Simpson Harbor that day. She was ordered into the southeast Solomons, but not one word was heard from her after her departure. After the war, I learned that my former boat had been sunk almost as soon as she got on station. Lt. Cdr. Fujisawa met up with a small convoy on Sept. 15, and launched an attack. His torpedoes missed, and one of the convoy escorts, USS *Saufley*, tracked him down. The destroyer attacked with depth charges, finally hitting close enough to make *RO-101*, blasted upward by explosions, broach. *Saufley*, joined by a Catalina patrol bomber, opened up with gunfire while the aircraft dropped depth charges. *RO-101* was sunk quickly.

Before departing Rabaul, I was briefed on the New Guinea situation by Cdr. Miyoshi Horinouchi, chief of staff to Rear Adm. Harada. "On the fourth of the month," he said, "the enemy landed troops at a point north of our garrison at Lae. Our garrison of about 7000 men is now surrounded."

Horinouchi told me that Lt. Gen. Hatazo Adachi, commander of the 18th Army Corps, was in charge of all Japanese troops on New Guinea. His chief subordinate was Lt. Gen. Hidemitsu Nakano, who had the 51st Division. His chief Navy subordinate was Rear Adm. Kunizo Mori, commander of the 7th Base Corps, an organization like the SeaBees of America. Men of our Base Corps would set up a base and operate it, also helping to defend it if it were attacked. Japanese sailors also were formed into amphibious attack units, too, like the American marines, getting training in machine guns, artillery and tank warfare for this purpose. Such men defended Tarawa and other island bases.

"Because of their current poor tactical situation," said Horinouchi, "the Lae garrison is going to execute a withdrawal. Beginning on the 11th, they will start moving out. All troops should be away from there by the 16th. They will cross the mountains and regroup at Gali, on New Guinea's north shore. The mountain range is over 14,000 feet high where they will cross it, and they will require three weeks to make the trip. To sustain them during this maneuver, they will need the food we are going to put on board *I-177*. It's up to you, Orita, to get through.''

My Etajima classmate, Mochitsura Hashimoto, had been through submarine commanders' school with me in 1942. After graduation, he was assigned to the old boat *RO-31* for eight months. He was the man who carried out the experiments that developed the containers used by our submarines in supplying Guadalcanal and New Guinea. Hashimoto was aghast at seeing the first contrivance he was asked to test. It was a sort of fragile torpedo. "A rubber bag was filled with rice," he said, "and was then put into a long wooden cylinder that had a hard veneer all over it. The idea was to fire these containers like torpedoes at Guadalcanal, so that men could retrieve them from the beach while the submarine lay offshore, still submerged. But, when we used a normal charge of high pressure air to fire them they burst, with rice going everywhere. The idea just wouldn't work. Which surprised no one because it was so ridiculous."

Another idea did work. Balloons and rubber bags were partially filled with various supplies, then inflated with air while lying on *RO-31*'s main deck. Then they were lashed into place. A submarine could release these and dive out from under them, leaving them to float on the surface, so small craft from shore could recover them. This useful idea, coupled with one of using partially filled steel drums, was used by us in the south.

Our plan was avoid full-moon periods whenever possible, and arrive at our destination after dark. There, barges and lighters from shore would take off the supplies we carried, although in an emergency we could simply roll the steel drums over the side. They, like the rubber bags, would float.

It took two days to load *I-177* properly. We loaded 40-50 tons of supplies inside of the submarine and 20-30 tons on deck in rubber bags and drums. Sometimes we worked under fire. The Americans were making daily raids on Rabaul after Oct. 20, 1943.

A humorous thing about these air attacks Mr. Harrington told me is that, during the war, writers always described us Japanese as being very predictable. Oddly, we found the

Americans very predictable in attacking Rabaul. The raids usually were made between 10 A.M. and 2 P.M. So, we would start our loading early in the morning, knock off work in time for the air raid, then submerge to the bottom of the harbor to have our lunch. We would come up after 2 P.M., when the air raid was over, and continue to load. At 120 feet, the only effect *I-177* felt was a gentle rocking when a bomb exploded in the water.

During the time I was operating out of Rabaul, I can remember only one submarine being damaged in an air raid. It happened in the late morning of Oct. 12, 1943. I had just completed a transport run to New Guinea, and was making my report to Rear. Adm. Harada on board his flagship, IJN *Jingei*, an ancient cruiser. About 50 Japanese warships, including submarines, were at anchor when a large group of B-17's and B-24's came over. They seemed to be directing their chief effort at our submarines, because no bombs fell near *Jingei* or the destroyers that were present. I watched the bombing with Admiral Harada and some of his staff, and became very worried about my boat. All submarines out in the harbor quickly dived, but bombs were falling so close to them that we could not really tell whether they were diving or sinking. Seven boats were present: *I-36, I-38, I-176, I-177, I-180, RO-105*, and *RO-108*. All but *I-180* were moored in deep water. She was alongside a pier, undergoing repairs.

From where we were, it looked like *I-180* took a direct hit. We soon received "no damage" reports from the other boats. I was relieved to hear this, but the word from *I-180* after the attack was over was sad. "Bomb hit, just forward of the bridge," it read. "Superstructure destroyed. Executive officer, Lt. Toshio Higuchi, killed. Three seamen of bridge watch seriously wounded."

Soon after the raid, the other six boats surfaced. I hastened to my ship. There I congratulated my executive officer, Lt. Yoshinosuke Kudo, and my crew, for their alertness in diving the boat.

A supply run to New Guinea usually required seven days for the round trip. We left Simpson Harbor, and swung around to run along the north side of New Britain, traveling submerged after the first day's run. Boats were scheduled to arrive at destination during the third night out. After unloading, a submarine would race away at top speed in the darkness, cross the sea underwater in daylight, and return to Rabaul the same way she had left.

I cleared the harbor, and was running along the north side

of New Britain, worried that the rough seas might carry away some of my on-deck cargo the men on New Guinea so sorely needed, when I received a wireless report from Rabaul. It said the enemy was making landings at Finschafen, north of Cape Cretin, somewhat to the east of Lae. "*I-177* will intercept." read the new orders.

When I announced this change of plans to my crew, all hands at once shouted "*Iko!*" (Let's go!). They were sick and tired of the dull transport duty they had been carrying out before I took over command. Here was a chance to fight! We had all four forward and both after tubes loaded with torpedoes and the men were eager for battle. We stole cautiously through Dampier Strait underwater and arrived off Finschafen on the evening of Sept. 13. Not one destroyer or any other enemy vessel was to be seen. I made a wide scouting sweep of the area, then headed for Lae.

We arrived at the rendezvous point about 90 minutes after sunset on Sept. 14. The last of our forces were clearing out, and Lae was about to fall to the enemy. I could see fire at several places along the shore. Someone shouted across the water to me, "It is too dangerous to discharge your cargo right now! Enemy artillery can reach you!" I put *I-177* about and sailed away for a while. Enemy shells fell in our wake not long afterward, prompting me to dive the boat. About 20 minutes later we surfaced, returned to the rendezvous and began unloading. My crew quickly turned to, moving out the interior cargo via three hatches. We were almost finished with the job when my sound watch reported propeller noises some three miles distant. I quickly cleared the main deck and dived *I-177* again, going all the way to our maximum safe depth of 330 feet.

The sound watch reported four destroyers coming at us. I ordered the boat rigged for depth charge attack. But nothing happened. No depth charges were dropped upon us and that somewhat disrupted my plans. I felt we'd been trapped and intended to come to periscope depth, there to fight it out, rather than simply taking blow after blow until my ship was destroyed. As time went by I realized that although he might have picked us up on his radar earlier the enemy did not now have us on his sonar. Temperature of the water was 80 degrees on the surface, which probably saved my boat, crew and me. In the tropics, water can develop into strata at various levels. This caused sound inpulses to bend, giving false indications or none at all on the sonar equipment used in World War II.

After a while, I took *I-177* up to periscope depth. The

destroyers had departed, so I moved to the surface and built up speed for the run out of that area. Mine was the last supply trip that Japanese submarines made into Lae and I was back at Rabaul on Sept. 17, completing safely my first round trip to New Guinea. Added to runs made by submarines between March and September, 1943, the total cargo carried was more than 4000 tons of food, ammunition, medicine and other supplies.

On the same day I took command of *I-177*, a special order went out from Vice Adm. Komatsu to Cdr. Tsuso Inaba, who had *I-36*. Equipped with the scout aircraft nicknamed *"Geta"* because its pontoons resembled Japanese wooden clogs, *I-36* was then at Yokosuka, undergoing refit. Adm. Koga had deduced from intelligence reports that the Americans were gathering in great strength at Pearl Harbor, so he made a special request of the 6th Fleet commander. Admiral Komatsu's message to Inaba said "You will make an air reconnaissance of Pearl Harbor base and report on enemy strength there."

On the following day, *I-8* arrived at Brest, France, the second Japanese submarine sent to Europe. She had left Penang, Sumatra, in July and was destined to be the only one of five Japanese submarines sent to Europe that made the round trip safely. The other four were lost enroute.

Captain of *I-8* was Cdr. Shinji Uchino, like myself a Kagoshima man. He had graduated from Etajima 10 years before I did and, so far as I am concerned, he was the master submariner of Japan. He was skipper of *RO-27*, the first submarine I went aboard. He gave me my first acquaintance with submarines at that time. In 1940, when I was an officer student at submarine school and again when I took the commanding officers' course in 1942, Uchino instructed me in submarine attack methods. In 1944, when I took command of *I-47* and was assigned to SubRon 11 while undergoing shakedown training, Uchino was its chief staff officer. Again he taught me combat tactics. In 1945, when I took over the attack section of the submarine school at Kure, he was senior instructor there.

Throughout my submarine career I always seemed, somehow, to be under Uchino's wing. By nature I was a plodding man and absorbed things somewhat slowly. I was often criticized by others as too slow to be a good submarine man, but Uchino always stood by me. He was not talkative, more like a scholar than a military man. But he was sympathetic and patient with others as well as me. Because of this kind man (who developed the method of torpedo fire control adopted by

181

the Imperial Navy) I became a passable submarine captain. To this great man I owe the fact that I was one of the few Japanese submarine captains to survive the war.

RO-500, the first of two German submarine gifts to be taken into the Japanese Navy, was officially received on Sept. 16. Uchino, in *I-8*, had taken to France the crew for manning the second, *RO-501*.

I had hardly gotten *I-177* back from its run to Lae when I was ordered out again, this time to Finschafen, an emergency landing point for submarine-borne supplies. *I-174* and *I-176* had just made trips there successfully. Now it was our turn.

The entrance to the bay was about 200 yards wide and its area about two square miles. If there was no interference from enemy surface patrols, a submarine could move in easily, unload and turn around for the run out. It was almost ideal for our purposes.

I headed there on Sept. 21, 1943. On the way out of Simpson Harbor, we met *I-176*, now commanded by Lt. Cdr. Kisaburo Yamaguchi. He hailed us, and sent me a signal. "PT boats are constantly patrolling near Finschafen Bay," it read. "It would be best if you tried to make your run right into the bay while still submerged rather than entering on the surface. Don't forget that a red light on the point means danger and a green light means that all is well. Good luck."

On the second night out from Rabaul, I received a wireless that enemy troops had landed just north of Finschafen the night before, but no change was made in my original orders. At sunset of Sept. 23 I arrived at a point about one mile from the mouth of Finschafen Bay. I took a good look around through the periscope, but saw no PT boats. Nothing was picked up by the sound watch, either.

I held a flashlight to the periscope and pointed the periscope toward the shore so that men there could see it. A green light flashed in response. "All ahead full!" I ordered, and kept *I-177* submerged until we were well inside the bay. Then I slowed down and surfaced, moving in to within 100 yards, then 50 yards, of the shore. Almost at once boats were alongside us and unloading began in the darkness. It was finished in 30 minutes. Soft calls of *"Arigato . . . arigato . . ."* (thank you) floated across the water's surface. When the green light flashed from the mouth of the bay, I swung *I-177* about and worked up speed to 20 knots as we dashed out of there. We encountered no trouble on the way back to Rabaul, and arrived there on Sept. 26.

The month of September 1943 was a fair one in the Indian

Ocean for Japanese submarines, but a poor one in the Pacific. We had eight boats to the west, working with German U-boats. They sank half-a-dozen ships, although the U-boats did better. In October our Indian Ocean boats began withdrawing to Penang for refit, so no sinkings were made between Africa and Australia by the 6th Fleet. Nor did our Pacific Ocean boats get any.

Besides my two September trips to New Guinea, I made four in October, three in November, and four in December, plus one in January. Six other submarines engaged in that effort during that period; *I-6, I-16, I-36, I-38, I-174,* and *I-176.* Cdr. Eitaro Ankyu, of *I-38,* made the most trips (16 while I was second with my 14. It was Ankyu who towed an *unkato* loaded with supplies and ammunition from Rabaul to Salamaua in June, 1943. Cdr. Tsuso Inaba had tried to tow one all the way from Kure to Kiska with *I-36,* but trouble developed with his towing equipment and the mission was unsuccessful.

All of my trips followed pretty much the same pattern. The six torpedo tubes were loaded, in case we met the enemy, but the extra torpedoes were removed from the hull to save weight. Our deck gun had already been removed, of course, leaving us but a single machine gun for defense on the bridge. All shells for the deck gun left the ship with it (further decreasing our weight) and we made further reductions by removing all spare parts possible and cutting down on provisions for the crew. We carried only enough food for seven days. Even our ballast tank water loads were kept to a minimum, to allow more cargo to be loaded under the close supervision of my new executive officer, Lt. Tadashi Obori, and Chief Petty Officer Yukio Oka, my chief of the boat. They gave all orders to the crew, and carefully directed the loading, stowage, trim and balance. Submarines heading for New Guinea often encountered enemy air attacks along the way, so the loading had to be done in such a manner as would still permit us to dive swiftly when necessary.

Rice and wheat usually made up the bulk of our loads. These were poured into rubber sacks (44 pounds to the bag) and sealed so just enough air was left in each sack to give it some buoyancy. The bags were stacked on deck, covered with nets, and lashed down securely. What couldn't be put on deck went below. As for the rest of our cargo, a typical load consisted of canned food, canned biscuit, salt, soy bean sauce, *miso* (bean paste), and *umeboshi* (dried plums). Many Japanese then believed that one could survice indefinitely on a diet of rice and *umeboshi.* Also included was *katsuoboshi,* the sticks of dried bonito fish I mentioned earlier. And, of course, we tried to load plenty of cigarettes.

Cothing supplies included boots, "*jika-tabi*" (split-toed sandals with rubber soles), and "*kaya*" (mosquito nets). Munitions included small field guns, rifles, machine guns, bazookas, hand grenades, and small arms ammunition. We also took along portable radio transmitters and receivers. Quinine, for fever, made up the largest part of our medical supplies. Miscellaneous equipment included bicycles and small carts that could be towed behind the bicycles, flashlights, candles, and matches. And I must not forget to mention what men on New Guinea often considered more important than anything else—mail from home.

By the middle of October, the American drive through the Solomons and Bismarcks had really begun to gain momentum. They had driven us out of Kolombangara and Vella Lavella, and were gaining in strength on New Georgia. They were also massing for a move against Bougainville, an island that would put even their fighter aircraft within range of Rabaul. Nearly 350 enemy planes from New Guinea and Australia struck at Rabaul on Oct. 12. From then on attacks were almost constant.

On Oct. 15, construction of the final ship in the *I-176* class was completed. She was *I-185*. On Oct. 18 the Army's retreat from Lae, New Guinea, over the mountains to Gali, on the north shore, was completed. Of the 7000 men who started out, over 1000 perished along the way. The Army could assemble only 4600 men of the 21st and 51st Divisions at the rendezvous, the Navy 1300. Lt. Gen. Adachi requested that submarines come to Sio and Gali after that, so from Oct. 18 that was our destination. Sick and wounded were brought aboard from one side of a submarine while supplies were off-loaded into *daihatsu* on the other. I would put all hands who were not actually on watch, to work unloading and they could usually finish the job in about 30 minutes. My men would form chains, and they resembled a series of well-oiled pistons as I watched them from *I-177*'s bridge. While 50 passed supplies over the side and took the helpless and sick on board, another 10 would undo the lashings that held down our deck cargo. When our hull was emptied of cargo and the sick men safely below, I would button up the boat and let *I-177* slowly submerge. The bags of rice and wheat would then float free, and the *daihatsu* working parties would still be picking them out of the water as *I-177* cleared the area.

I-36, under special orders from Adm. Koga, tried to send her plane in over Oahu on Sept. 21. The attempt was unsuccessful. Cdr. Inaba tried again on Oct. 8, with no luck. The hills of the Hawaiian chain were studded with radar sets by that time. Patrol ships also carried them, as did patrol aircraft. Inaba's reconnaissance pilot's problem was three-fold. First he had to avoid aircraft and get in past them close enough for his plane to make the round trip. Then he had to avoid ships which ranged far out from Pearl Harbor on surface patrol. After that this pilot, in a very slow plane, had to avoid radar and high-speed interceptor planes which could shoot him down in one fast pass.

Inaba's aircraft pilot and his crewman finally solved the problem. "The submarine cannot get in close enough so that an island will shield us from enemy radar during launching, Captain," they told him and suggested that he launch them from far out at sea. They pointed out that a low-flying aircraft might be able to "slip under" the enemy's radar beams, provided that the shore defenses had not been alerted to a submarine's presence. Inaba, then 300 miles south of Oahu, pointed out to the men that at that range they would not have enough fuel to get back to I-36. The pair simply shrugged.

On Oct. 19 the plane was launched, and a shiver went down American spines when it got through. Its sighting caused a lot of excitement. The pilot reported seeing 4 aircraft carriers, 4 battleships, 5 cruisers, and 17 destroyers moored at Pearl Harbor. He was never heard from after that. I think he dived his plane into the sea rather then wait for pursuers to catch up with him. His information got to Adm. Koga, and was followed by more from I-36 the next day. Cdr. Inaba reported a large convoy south of the Hawaiian Islands, heading west. Almost immediately I-19, I-35, I-169 and I-175 were ordered out to intercept.

It was in October, after having carefully studied the German submarine we had given the designation RO-500, the high command ordered construction of 23 special submarines. These were a revolutionary type of boat, designed expressly for very high *underwater* speed, which was considered the best defense against enemy antisubmarine vessels (whose sonar could not work effectively if their propellers were turning over rapidly, as during a pursuit). The subs were to be named the *I-201* Class and would have a speed that no other nation's submarines would ever match for years. With a length-to-beam ratio of 12-1, the *I-201* subs would make 19 knots underwater for one hour. They were to be completely streamlined, with disappearing forward and after machine guns dropping down into the deck when not needed for use. The first of these submarines was completed in February, 1945, just after I returned from a second mission using the most fantastic weapons of World War II. These were our "*kaiten*," our "human torpedoes."

* * * *

Chapter 13.

BOUGAINVILLE; THE GILBERTS;
MY LAST RUN TO NEW GUINEA.

The enemy wanted to establish an air base on Bougainville. From there, his land-based fighters would be able to provide protective escort for the bombers attacking Rabaul. This was part of a general plan to encircle our key base in that area, cut it off and render it useless. Then the enemy would sweep around and past Rabaul toward other objectives. On Nov. 1, 1943, Bougainville was invaded at Cape Torokina, on its southern shore, with thousands of enemy troops moving into an area that was only lightly defended by our garrison. The enemy then dug in only 225 miles from Rabaul. He had to be driven away!

This landing caught Admiral Koga, commander-in-chief of the Combined Fleet, somewhat off balance. He had just put almost all of his carrier-based planes ashore at Rabaul for a massive strike he intended to make against enemy ships in New Guinea waters. The bulk of his surface fleet was off Truk, so he sent down the ships from Rabaul to attack the enemy beachhead. This resulted in the Battle of Empress Augusta Bay, which pitched 4 Japanese cruisers and 6 destroyers against an American force of 4 cruisers and 8 destroyers. It was a fight that might have been even had it not been for radar. In this battle the American destroyers fired their torpedoes, then swerved out of the path of Japanese gunfire. The American cruisers, under Rear Adm. Merrill, stood off and poured out many salvoes of 6-inch shells, changing course every few minutes so as to avoid any torpedoes fired at them. One of our cruisers was sunk, as was a destroyer. Four others of our ships suffered damage. The counter-strike was turned back without getting anywhere near the enemy transports off Cape Torokina.

The cruiser sunk was IJN *Sendai*, flagship of Rear Adm. Matsuji Ijuin's Destroyer Squadron 1. Ijuin survived the sinking, but was not rescued at once. With the battle going against them the rest of his ships had no choice but to retreat hastily. But Ijuin's great interest in physical fitness paid off for him. IJN *Sendai* went down early in the morning of Nov. 2. In the forenoon of Nov. 3, after swimming for nearly 30 hours, Ijuin was taken aboard Lt. Kenji Matsuda's *RO-104*, which had been sent out from Rabaul to search for him. Had the situation not been so grim, there might have been humor in it. As an instructor at Etajima, Ijuin had been very hard on Matsuda during swimming classes!

I-29 left Penang for Germany about this time. She was the third Japanese submarine to head for Atlantic waters. Her commander was our underwater ace, Cdr. Takaichi Kinashi, who had been scoring again in the Indian Ocean. Unfortunately, this mission was to be Kinashi's last. It would end in his death.

November 3 was the day Adm. Koga sent Vice Adm. Takeo Kurita down from Truk with 8 cruisers and 6 destroyers. Kurita was to stop off at Rabaul for fuel, then race into Empress Augusta Bay of which Cape Tokokina formed one arm. There, Kurita hoped he would find and smash the enemy's ships. When the enemy first landed on Bougainville our air strength at Rabaul was nearly 400 planes. This force was to support Kurita by providing air cover. Kurita's force was smashed while still in Simpson Harbor. Two American aircraft carriers sent nearly 100 planes over Rabaul on Nov. 5 to hit Kurita, having sighted his ships while they were on their way down from Truk.

Mr. Harrington learned from an American admiral who, as a Commander, led some of the fighter planes in that attack, that American pilots had orders to "cripple as many ships as possible" (rather than concentrate on sinking just a few) so our ships could not get out to hit the beachhead at Bougainville. This the Americans truly accomplished. They put four of our cruisers and one destroyer out of action. Two undamaged cruisers had to escort the damaged ones back to Truk. The loss of half his forces and most of his firepower eliminated any chance for Kurita to make a surface strike. Two days later, using destroyers, our navy put 500 men ashore near Cape Torokina in a counter-landing, but this force was wiped out in a few days. Nothing could stop the Americans' march westward.

By this time Tokyo had reports from Tarawa Atoll (in the Gilberts) that the enemy was making air attacks on it. Rear Adm. Keiji Shibasaki, in command of Tarawa, had been building defenses there to anchor our island network of defenses. He had close to 5000 men with him and concentrated his efforts on Betio, an island at the atoll's southern end. Shibasaki expected that any attack made on him by ships would be driven off by long-range bombers from New Britain and New Ireland, plus the heavy guns of Kurita's cruisers. But Kurita's strength was sapped in just one aerial attack and the Bismarcks air strength was shattered by American air attacks in early November. Shibasaki had to fight it out alone!

On Nov. 11 the fourth submarine attached to Europe, *I-34*, left Singapore under Cdr. Tatsuo Irie. He was to stop at Penang enroute, then proceed to the Atlantic with a cargo of tin, tungsten, quinine and rubber for our German allies. All of it went to the bottom of the sea. Irie (the man so enamored of his wife) died with all hands two days out of Singapore, ambushed by the British submarine HMS *Taurus* in Malacca Strait.

Mr. Harrington interviewed one of two enlisted men who, with an officer, were the only Japanese to survive Betio, where the heavy fighting on Tarawa Atoll took place. Petty Officer Tadao Oonuki later became a taxicab dispatcher. In early 1943 he was a truck driver with the Mihoro Air Group at Rabaul, and was returned to Yokosuka when the group was disbanded for lack of replacements. Oonuki answered a call for volunteers to perform "hazardous duty in the south," and soon found himself on Betio early in July. There he was driver of a Type 97 light tank.

"Life on Betio was good." said Oonuki. "We had plenty to eat, drink and smoke, which was more than other outpost garrisons could say. Our *sake* ration was 1½ quarts a month and there were enough non-drinkers and non-smokers that a man could always exchange enough sweets to put himself in a smoky cloud (or alcoholic haze) when he was off duty. Our recreation consisted chiefly of swimming and fishing. We all stayed very healthy because of Betio's malaria-free climate."

Betio's tank was one of those assigned to protect Admiral Shibasaki's command post bunker, which looked out over the atoll's lagoon. Betio was heavily defended, because after the raid on Makin Island, in August, 1942, high officials decided to fortify our Gilberts holdings heavily.

Besides a thick palisade of logs and sand running along the water's edge inside the lagoon, Betio had many pillboxes built of logs reinforced by steel casings and sand. "Most of the defenses were completed by the time I arrived at Betio," Oonuki said, "but we spent the next four months improving them." Physical fitness has always been a fetish with many Japanese, and Oonuki told Mr. Harrington that many men improved their physiques by building bunkers stronger in their free time; adding extra layers of logs to them, and heaping up more sand on their roofs. Admiral Shibasaki said "A million men could not take this island in a hundred years!" when the defenses were completed.

American long-range bombers attacked Betio sporadically for months. Carrier planes hit it on Nov. 18 and 19. Since we had no surface fleet to send south, only submarines were sent to repel attackers. Six out of nine boats ordered into the Gilberts were lost there before Dec. 1. The counterattack on Tarawa should be studied by future submariners as a horrible example of how *not* to use underseas ships.

American marines landed on Betio against heavy opposition on Nov. 20. They paid a high price for the island, but wiped out nearly all of its garrison and took control of the place in three days. On Nov. 19, while carrier planes were still attacking, Vice Adm. Takagi (from his flagship *Katori* at Truk) issued the first of many confusing orders. Lt. Cdr. Zenshin Toyama was patrolling in *I-169* between Hawaii and the Marshall Islands, and was just about at the end of cruising endurance, but Takagi ordered him into the Makin area since that island was also being attacked. With *I-19*, *I-40* and *RO-38*, this boat was later ordered to form an intercept line north of Makin Island. All told, Takagi set up five sentry lines in five different areas, all to be formed in a period of 11 days. His staff tried frantically to deploy submarines rapidly, to meet a changing tactical situation hundreds of miles away; ordering boats to change positions frequently, to cruise on the surface sometimes, and submerged at others. They filled the air with messages, which may have caused the loss of some submarines, and disgusted the captains (including myself) of the remainder. Surely the enemy intercepted some of these, and must have either decoded (or at least evaluated) some.

I-19, under Lt. Cdr. Shigeo Kobayashi, left Truk for the Hawaii area on Nov. 3. On the 17th of that month its plane made a reconnaissance of Pearl Harbor, returning safely to the ship. Kobayashi was then ordered to proceed to the Gilberts.

Cdr. Katsuji Watanabe had *I-40*, a new ship that had arrived at Truk on Nov. 19 just after completing its shakedown training. Watanabe was a brave and experienced man, who had successfully freed his stuck ship, *I-169*, from antisubmarine nets in the Hawaii Islands on Dec. 9, 1941. He was ordered south, and left Truk on Nov. 22.

RO-38, under Lt. Cdr. Shunji Nomura, was another new submarine. He headed out of Truk on Nov. 19, on his first mission as a submarine captain.

As the situation developed, Takagi began sending out his series of "sentry line" orders. The first, for the submarines already mentioned to form a line north of Makin, went out on Nov. 26. The following day an order went out for the submarines to form two new sentry lines, one east and one west of Makin: *I-19*, *I-169* and *RO-38* to the east; *I-40*, by *I-39*, and *I-174*, to the west.

Two days later Admiral Takagi ordered *I-21* and *I-174* to remain in the Makin area. *I-21* had come up to help from her patrol area in the Fijis. The other five submarines were to move south to positions east of Tarawa and form a line running southwest-to-northwest. Then, a day later, Takagi ordered *I-69* back to the Makin area and the other four boats to move even further southeast. On Dec. 3, when all submarines were ordered to report, only three responded.

To get a clear picture of what happened in the Gilberts, let us follow all nine submarines, one after another. *I-35*, left Truk on Oct. 11 for a patrol east of the Gilberts. Lt. Cdr. Yamamoto, its captain, was on mission for more than five weeks when he was ordered to head for Tarawa. The 6th Fleet flagship next heard from him on Nov. 22. "Yesterday," his message read, *"I-35* pierced the enemy screen and got within sight of Tarawa. Sighted large enemy task force and tried to approach it, but was intercepted by aircraft and had to dive." This was the last word heard from him. On that same afternoon Yamamoto again tried to get in and sink some of the enemy ships, but was detected by sonarmen of the U.S. destroyer *Meade*. Assisted by USS *Frazier*, this ship blasted *I-35* with depth charges, forcing her to the surface where gunfire finished her off. Only two of the crew survived to be taken prisoner.

I-19 (the killer of USS *Wasp* and wounder of USS *North Carolina* and the ill-fated USS *O'Brien*) headed for Tarawa after recovering its plane off Oahu. The gentle, smiling Kobayashi messaged Takagi's headquarters on Nov. 22: "I expect to arrive within 30 miles of Tarawa in another 48 hours." Then no more was heard from him. The U. S. destroyer *Radford* picked up *I-19* on radar in the darkness on Nov. 25. She closed in and dropped depth charges. Down to the bottom went the crew of *I-19* and Kobayashi, the scholarly leader who was generally credited with playing an important role in evolving the Model 95 torpedo used in our submarines. (The great Model 93 had a diameter of 24 inches. Kobayashi helped modify it to 21 inches, so it would fit our tubes, while retaining its great speed and striking power.)

Besides these two, we lost four other submarines in the Gilberts, which Japanese usually consider part of the Marshalls campaign. The fighting there took place because the Americans had to secure their flank from attack before striking at the Marshalls themselves. I cannot account for the exact date of each submarine's loss, or the conditions under which they were sunk. However, it is certain they went down before the very intense antisubmarine effort of the enemy escort ships and aircraft in the Tarawa-Makin area. The Americans had developed their antisubmarine tactics by that time to a degree our 6th Fleet staff members did not appreciate. *I-21* was not heard from after Nov. 27. Cdr. Hiroshi Inada had taken his boat out from Truk on Sept. 25, for a patrol in the Fijis. He sank SS *Cape San Juan* on Nov. 11. Ordered to Tarawa, he headed there although his crew was weary and his submarine near the end of its cruising endurance. On Nov. 27 the boat was 30 miles southwest of Tarawa and Inada reported on ships sighted, but that was the last heard from him. It is hard to say, also, what happened to Shunji Nomura's *RO-38*. A surviving headquarters map, discovered after the war, shows him to have reached the positions assigned him by Admiral Takagi in messages sent on Nov. 25, 26, 27 and 29. But he did not answer a general order to report sent out on Dec. 3.

Lt. Cdr. Makio Tanaka left Truk in *I-39* on Nov. 21 with orders to take a lone position 60 miles southwest of Tarawa. He reached it on Nov. 25 and radioed that he had attacked enemy vessels. But no more was heard from him, either. As for the sixth submarine lost, *I-40* arrived in position at the first

192

sentry line on Nov. 26 and the same surviving map shows that it moved to all positions ordered as Takagi's messages poured out. It also did not answer the Dec. 3 general call to report.

Two American claims for submarines sunk in the Gilberts are wrong. USS *Griswold* claims to have sunk *I-39* in the Solomons on Dec. 23, 1943. We lost no submarines at all during that month. And *I-21* was certainly not the submarine sunk by destroyers *Charrette* and *Fair* in the Marshalls on Feb. 5, 1944. A fresh review of attacks made on our submarines by enemy ships and planes in the Gilberts during November, 1943, would probably give correct credit to whichever units did sink *I-31, I-39, I-40* and *RO-38*. I am convinced that all were at the bottom of the sea by Dec. 2.

The story of the three submarines that did make it safely back to port is an interesting one. Toyama's *I-169* was east of the Marshalls when ordered south. Toyama put into Kwajalein to refuel from *I-32*, and dug into the submarine's food supplies deeply, as well. Extremely intense American air and surface antisubmarine patrols kept Toyama almost constantly submerged, but he was able to receive radio messages and make his station changes when ordered. Destroyer activities kept *I-169* well away from its intended targets. He missed the one chance that came his way through no fault of his own. Forced under on Dec. 1 by an enemy plane, Toyama picked up a convoy on his sound equipment. It was so well escorted, though, that he could not come up and attack it. Toyama arrived back at Truk on Dec. 9, with nothing but an exhausted crew to show for his efforts.

I-174 was the boat of Lt. Cdr. Nobukiyo Nambu. He was relieved of transport duty between Rabaul and New Guinea and arrived at Truk on Nov. 16, en route to Japan for general overhaul and repair. Takagi ordered him south, however, and after making hasty repairs Nambu departed Truk on Nov. 24. He arrived west of Makin on Nov. 29, but saw no enemy ships that day or the next. Nambu then recieved a report of an enemy convoy 200 miles east of Makin, so he maneuvered to ambush it. "On December 1," he said, "I was not more than 3 miles off Makin, waiting for that convoy, but no enemy ships appeared. In the meantime, other submarines were dashing back and forth between the various stations assigned to them by 6th Fleet. First an order would say 'move.' Then it would be changed to 'move, navigating on the surface.' Still later it would become 'wait, remaining on the surface.' These orders ignored completely the strong and weak features of a submarine. I'm positive that most of our submarines that were lost went down during this hectic and confused period."

On Dec. 3, Nambu was ordered to head for a point 250 miles southeast of Abemama, an islet southeast of Tarawa Atoll. There he was to intercept ships the enemy was expected to send to the island they had just taken from us. "The next night," he said, "we were cruising on the surface. There was no moon, but the sky was clear, with the stars bright. All of a sudden one of my lookouts shouted 'Destroyer! Destroyer! Coming up fast, astern!' "

Nambu dived his boat. Depth charges exploded all around *I-174* while she passed the 100-foot mark. All lights went out and all power was lost. "We kept from plunging all the way to the bottom" Nambu said, "only by blowing water from the ballast tanks, but each time we did that a stream of bubbles gave the enemy another aiming point and down would come another string of depth charges. Eventually we sprung leaks in both the main engine room and in the electric motor room. All pumps stopped with the power failure, of course, so I ordered a bucket brigade to be formed."

Crewmen used buckets, tin cans and whatever else they could get their hands on to bail water out of the power room because if it reached the electric motors *I-174* would lose all movements completely. Carefully, water was scooped up and dumped into the engine room. The level was reduced to just below the electric motors and kept there.

As the attacks continued, *I-174's* supply of pressured air was slowly used up. Finally, with barely enough left to blow tanks and surface, Nambu decided to fight it out. His crew and he tightened *hachimaki* around their heads and blew ballast. Fortunately for them, no destroyer was in sight when they surfaced. In less than two minutes, however, an enemy plane was overhead and they had to dive *I-174* once more.

"We were in a more serious condition than ever, then." said Nambu. "I was not sure we could bring the boat up one more time. As a last resort we used the pressurized air for accelerating the diesel engines, and tapped what air there was left in the torpedoes. This helped to stabilize the boat and, after three more hours, we broke surface again. *I-174* was no longer in condition to fight, so I cabled Truk that we were returning."

The one bright spot in the Gilberts operations was the accomplishment of Lt. Cdr. Sunao Tabata's *I-175*. Summoned from patrol northeast of the Marshalls, *I-175* was off the north side of Makin on Nov. 23. When Tabata spotted four enemy destroyers. This prevented his maneuvering freely. On Nov. 24, however, he got an aircraft carrier in his periscope, and fired several torpedoes. USS *Liscome Bay* blew up at once and sank within 30 minutes, taking nearly 650 men with her including the admiral commanding the carrier group. *I-175* was counter-attacked at once and suffered great damage. She headed north and finally eluded her pursuers by running for the protection of air bases at Kwajalein. She circled north and limped safely back to Truk. Tabata's crew was just as exhausted as the men under Nambu and Toyama, but at least they had something to show for their hard work.

In exchange for the six submarines we lost in the Gilberts campaign, the Americans lost two. IJN *Yamagumo*, a destroyer, sank USS *Sculpin*. I'll tell later how USS *Corvina* was sunk. Both boats had been detailed to scout around Truk and to report any ships leaving there for the southern area.

All this while, the dull and deadly work of getting supplies from Rabaul to outposts went on. We lost another of our submarines on Nov. 25, the same day Radford got *I-19*. She was *RO-100*, commanded by Lt. Cdr. Hisao Ogane, who left Rabaul on Nov. 23 for Buin, at the southeast corner of Bougainville. Ogane got safely past enemy air and surface patrols, only to hit an enemy mine just short of his destination and sink. Also, on that same day, a battle was fought that brought Captain Arleigh A. Burke, USN, fame. It made him, one might say, the "American Raizo Tanaka." This was the sea battle off Cape St. George, New Ireland.

Off the northwest tip of Bougainville, separated from it by a narrow strip of water, is Buka, the airstrip nearest to Rabaul. The Americans had bombed and shelled it frequently, so we decided to put more troops ashore there in case of an amphibious attack and to take off plane-less airmen who could be of more use elsewhere. Five destroyers under Capt. Kiyoto Kagawa were given the job.

The trip out from Rabaul was uneventful. Troops were landed and airmen picked up but, on the way back, Kagawa ran into five American destroyers under command of Burke. Using radar to establish range and bearing, Burke fired torpedoes (keeping his guns silent so flashes would not betray his position). Two of our destroyers were hit and sunk. A third was caught and sunk in a pursuit. None of Burke's "Little Beavers" were hurt.

I was sleeping soundly in the officers' quarters on a hill above Simpson Harbor when the battle began. I needed rest badly (having completed a transport run shortly before) but a jangling telephone awakened me. On the other end was chief staff officer Horinouchi, who rapidly explained that three of our destroyers had been sunk and that it was important to rescue as many of the airmen passengers as I could (Japan was truly in short supply of experienced fliers by that time). "How soon can you get underway?" I was asked. "I'll be out of the harbor in an hour!" I replied.

"Good!" Horinouchi exclaimed. I don't remember what else he may have said. My mind was filled with how daring the Americans must be, attacking our large, 35-knot destroyers right on our doorstep.

I dressed rapidly, and had *I-177* moving out within an hour as I had promised, racing down St. George's Channel at 22 knots. As I swung east around the cape I made a decision. A submerged run would be wise, but I couldn't delay. I kept *I-177* on the surface, trusting to my crew's skill to avoid an ambush. By noon we had survived four different attacks by patrol bombers, their depth charges exploding in *I-177's* wake as we dived. From noon on, I ran submerged. At 3 P.M., having been told by my navigator that we should be about three miles from where the survivors were, I raised the periscope. At once I could see two men in the water, so I surfaced right in the middle of a group of survivors. Setting a doubled watch for enemy aircraft, we started taking men aboard. Most were semiconscious from shock and exhaustion and all were thickly coated with fuel oil. Luck was with us. We hauled men out of the sea for three hours without seeing enemy planes. At 6 P.M. I asked the executive officer how many we had on board.

"There are 227 so far, Captain," he answered. "I've got them behind the main engine, in the pump room, in the storerooms, in all passageways, and even under the mess tables."

With my crew, this brought *I-177's* human load to more than 300. No more could be safely brought aboard and still permit me to work the ship. We couldn't do much once darkness fell. I had no radar. Enemy night searchers would be aloft. It was heart-breaking to halt the rescue effort while there were still men in the water, but I couldn't risk 300 lives just to save a few more.

"Clear the deck!" I called out, and men engaged in rescue work scurried inside the hull. I let my navigator have the conn, but remained on the bridge as *I-177* worked up speed.

A few minutes after we started moving west, two great water columns spouted up, one on either side of *I-177*. Bombs! Seconds later an enemy plane passed over us so close that I could see his exhaust smoke in the twilight. My navigator shouted "Clear the bridge!" and I dropped down the hatch to get out of his way. He followed the lookouts and myself down, shouting "Dive! Dive!" *I-177* was under the waves before the plane, which had glided silently in on us, could make another pass. We got back to Rabaul without further incident and put our passengers ashore.

I took supplies to Sio, New Guinea, four times in December and brought back men sick beyond the ability of doctors and facilities on that island to help them. They were dirty, starving with every rib showing starkly. All resistance to disease was gone. The merest insect bite would suppurate. All gave off a stomach-turning stench. Many came down with malarial seizures, and groaned awfully. We fed them "*kayu*" (the rice gruel used throughout Japan for nursing the ill) and it sometimes gave them a bit of strength. Still, on each trip, two or three men would die before we reached Rabaul.

Only a man who fought on New Guinea can really tell how awful an ordeal the campaign was—for both sides. Men so sick they could hardly stand, staggered out to do battle on the ground and in the air for both sides. Thousands of Japanese died of starvation on that black island. Thousands more—plus thousands of Americans, Australians and New Zealanders—succumbed to disease. And even more thousands who survived the war have never recovered their health.

I-8 arrived safely in Europe on Dec. 1. All hands were treated royally by the Germans. Cdr. Uchino and his men had lots of happy stories to tell when they got home.

On that same day the Japanese Imperial General Headquarters released a communique about the Gilberts battle. It claimed that our planes had sunk two enemy aircraft carriers, and one warship of an unidentified type. That brought the total of carriers we had supposedly sank in the Gilberts to *eight*! In November, the Imperial General Headquarters claimed to have sunk the following ships in battles for Bougainville: 4 battleships; 5 aircraft carriers, 12 cruisers, 9 destroyers, 6 transports, 1 warship of unidentified type, and over 40 landing craft.

As can be seen, the true picture of the Pacific war was not getting through to the average Japanese citizen. The British credit Japanese submarines with sinking nine of their ships in November-December in the Indian Ocean. And not more than three Americans ships fell victim to our boats in that area in that same period. In the Pacific our score was zero except for a submarine, a small aircraft carrier, and a cargo ship!

The enemy's assault on New Britain itself began on Dec. 15, with a landing at Arawe, about 200 miles west of Rabaul.

Eleven days later U.S. marines landed at Cape Gloucester, on the northern side of New Britain (near Damper Strait). We had an airfield there that the enemy wanted.

On Dec. 18 the first submarine of our new *I-52* Class was completed at Kure. All told, 46 of these were planned, but only 3 were laid down and completed; *I-52*, *I-53* and *I-56*. These were almost sisters to the *I-15* Class but carried no aircraft. They also had a second 140mm deck gun, although both guns were removed from *I-53* when she later became a *kaiten* carrier. *I-52* Class boats were 359 feet long and displaced 2563 tons. They made 17.7 knots on the surface, 6.5 submerged. Range was 21,000 miles at 16 knots, underwater endurance 105 hours at 3 knots. Besides six bow tubes and a load of 19 torpedoes, they had a 25mm twin machine gun mounted at the conning tower after end.

We lost 27 submarines during 1943. In that year the enemy lost only 26 merchant ships in the Pacific and 82 in the Indian Ocean. In the Atlantic and Mediterranean he lost 489 ships, which points up how much the change of our Japanese submarines into transports had hurt our offensive effort.

This was a criminal shame. Our men were as competent as American and German submariners and their morale was as high. Officers could not even get into submarine duty until they were Lieutenant, Junior Grade. After two years of a familiarization duty, they were ordered ashore to service schools in torpedoes, navigation, cummunications, diesel engines or electricity lasting six months. After that, they took four months of special training. It consisted chiefly of making dives, and learning the skills and techniques necessary for diving a submarine. Then they became department heads in gunnery, torpedoes or communication, sometimes serving concurrently as executive officer. After three to five years in submarines, they might be ordered to the submarine commanders' course. That's where the final weeding-out took place. Men showing lack of aptitude or physical defects were flunked. It took a good man to rise to command of a Japanese submarine. I must admit I needed a lot of help to make the grade myself.

Enlisted men came strictly from service schools having courses related to submarines, like torpedo, gunnery, or engines. Only those with fine physiques and especially good hearing were chosen. As with American submariners, men had to be psychologically fitted to live for long periods in confined spaces, and they trained for six months in submarine school before assignment to an active boat.

The pay *was* an attraction. All men received an extra 30%.

And, even in peacetime, time spent in submarines was counted double in calculating retirement allowances. There was never a lack of volunteers and a great spirit of fellowship developed from our having to be interdependent. We considered ourselves a breed apart from the rest of the Navy—another reason why we resented not being employed more effectively.

On Dec. 30, 1943, I made the report on my Sio mission to Rear Adm. Noboru Owada, who had relieved Admiral Harada as ComSubRon 7. Owada wanted me to take supplies into Buin, Bougainville, where none had been sent since *RO-100* hit 2 mines and sank (five weeks before). "You know I am not exaggerating, Orita," he told me, "when I say that the lives of men there depend on successful completion of this mission."

I did not doubt that. We had more than 20,000 men on Bougainville. They had been using up their supplies rapidly in the two months since the enemy had landed there. Unless they recieved some assistance, they would suffer the same fate as so many on Guadalcanal: malnutrition followed by death. I began preparations the following day, knowing it would not be an easy mission. Both straits leading into Buin had been heavily sown with American mines and PT boats kept a close watch. I doubted that even a mouse could slip into Buin but I was determined to try. My work was interrupted for Distant Emperor Worship on New Year's Day (and that ceremony itself was interrupted by an air raid) but I got *I-177* to the harbor's bottom and out of danger swiftly.

On the night of Jan. 2, I was summoned to SubRon 7 headquarters. From there I accompanied Admiral Owada to the operations room in the headquarters of Vice Adm. Jinichi Kusaka, commander-in-chief of the southeast area fleet. His chief of staff, Rear Adm. Ryonosuke Kusaka, told me that my mission had been changed. "Our forces at Sio are surrounded, Orita," he said. "The enemy landed troops at Saidor today. Road communication between Sio and Madang is cut off."

The enemy had been steadily pushing our troops westward, out of Buna, Lae, Salamaua and Finschafen, and were pressing against Sio. Our next strong point was Madang, about 110 miles further west. But the enemy had made a landing *between* those two places, at Saidor. This movement trapped the headquarters of the 18th Army and the 18th Naval Base Force at Saidor, where Lt. Gen. Hatazo Adachi and Rear Adm. Kunizo Mori were based.

"General Adachi has ordered a general withdrawal toward Madang," the chief of staff told me, "but estimates that it will take as much as two months to circle around through the jungle past the enemy. During that time he would be out of touch and could not direct land operations. So we have decided to use a submarine to move the General quickly from Sio to Madang."

This seemed to me like a good idea. If the enemy could leap-frog, so could we. I left Rabaul the following day.

Traveling most of the way submerged, I did not reach Sio until sunset of Jan. 8. Again I held a flashlight against my periscope's eyepiece so it could be seen from the shore; and my men were very swift in transferring cargo to the *daihatsu* that soon came out to us. Then a boat started from the shore, carrying General Adachi and Admiral Mori. It was less than halfway to us when a lookout shouted "PT boats!" My signals petty officer quickly blinked a message to the shore that I would return the following night. Crewmen secured what cargo was still on board. I dived *I-177*.

I came back the next night at sunset, as promised, but found PT boats hovering near my rendezvous point. I kept the boat submerged, but ran up the radio antenna and sent a message. "We will return tomorrow night," I messaged, "but before sunset. We will then try to take passengers aboard. Please stand by to repel enemy torpedo boats if they try to interfere." Then I moved out to sea.

On the following night (Jan. 10) I brought *I-177* off Sio while it was still light. If the PT boats followed their usual custom of coming in after sunset, I hoped to be gone before they arrived. I also went in much closer to the shore than before. As soon as my periscope showed above the surface, three *daihatsu* took stations around me, machine guns mounted and manned. Then, when I was sure that my passengers had left the shore, I surfaced the boat and crewmen ran to our 25mm machine gun. Two PT boats showed up right after that, but ran into a barrage from my machine gunners and the *daihatsu* men. They returned the fire, but it made them cautious and they hove to more than a half-mile away.

Gunfire rattled as I took aboard General Adachi, Admiral Mori, 10 of their staff members, and 25 bags of headquarters equipment and records. The *daihatsu* and PT boats were still exchanging fire as I backed *I-177* off, put her about, and dived. The next day I put my passengers ashore at Madang safely, and returned to Rabaul without further incident.

When I left for Sio, two other submarines left Truk, heading for Rabaul to help us in the transport effort. Lt. Cdr. Mitsuma Itakura (with whom I was later to work closely in the *kaiten* effort) had *I-41*. An Etajima classmate of mine, Lt. Cdr. Takeo Shimada, had *I-171*. Itakura made a successful run to some of our troops in western New Guinea who were trapped and needed supplies, then left Rabaul on Jan. 31 to do what I had been scheduled to do a month earlier. He headed for Buin. Displaying great skill, Itakura took *I-41* through mine fields and enemy patrols to land his cargo. Then he made his way out again, returning to Rabaul on Feb. 7.

Shimada did not have such luck. He was heading for Buka (at the other end of Bougainville from Buin) when he ran into a force of enemy destroyers on Feb. 1. These had on board a party of raiders who were heading for Green Island (not far from Cape St. George). Their mission was to determine whether that island was suitable for building an airstrip before the enemy would decide to take it. *I-171* was picked up by the electronic fingers of USS *Fullam*, and pointed out to the destroyers *Guest* and *Hudson*. They sank Shimada's ship.

Two other submarines were lost in 1944 before Shimada's boat went down, The first was *I-181*, commanded by Lt. Cdr. Kiyoshi Taoka. He left Rabaul on Jan. 13, heading for Gali, New Guinea (about 40 miles west of Sio), to land supplies there for the troops retreating toward Madang to rendezvous with General Adachi. *I-181* was scheduled to meet the troops on Jan. 16, but never arrived. A radio message from New Guinea said that PT boats or destroyers must have sunk the submarine in Vitiaz Passage, the strip of water off northern New Guinea.

The other submarine lost was *RO-37*, commanded by Lt. Cdr. Sakuma Sato. It had left Truk on Jan. 3 for a patrol of the New Hebrides. Sato met the American fleet tanker, USS *Cache*, on Jan. 23, and put a torpedo into her. She got off a distress call. Sato continued on his way, unaware that a nearby U.S. destroyer, *Buchanan*, had intercepted the call and was rushing to aid the stricken ship. Their paths crossed before *RO-37* had traveled another 30 miles, and *Buchanan*'s radar picked her up. *RO-37* was sunk by a depth charge barrage.

I was relieved of transport duty on Jan. 13, 1944. *I-177* by then had been operating almost continually for six months. Her crew, hull, weapons and engines were all about ready to collapse. My own health had been going steadily downhill, too, like all my men, although I had been fortunate in not contacting malaria. The sub needed overhaul badly, but enemy air raids on Rabaul had destroyed most of the shops, tools and equipment needed. So I left Rabaul for Truk on Jan. 14.

When I first arrived in Simpson Harbor (a year before) it

had been filled with ships, nearly 200 of them, and I had difficulty maneuvering through them to moor. On the day I left there were no vessels present other than the scorched hulks of three transports that had burned after being beached. There were still 100,000 men on New Britain. I felt sorry for these orphans of the South Pacific, surrounded and cut off. There was little hope for them.

The situation for our 6th Fleet was not much better at Truk. The Gilberts operation had cost six submarines, and captains of the three surviving ones had complained bitterly. "I am positive," Lt. Cdr. Nobukiyo Nambu reported, "that *all* the submarines lost went down without even getting a chance to attack the enemy." He claimed that radar had picked up all of them (including his own *I-174*) before they got within striking range. Nambu also pointed out that *I-169* and *I-175* should never have been sent at all, because their crews had already been out for some time and were tired. "As for *RO-38*," he said, "she was fresh from home waters, with an inexperienced crew that still needed lots of training." Lt. Cdr. Tabata, who had sunk *Liscome Bay*, and Lt. Cdr. Toyama, of *I-169*, agreed with Nambu.

"The enemy had his interceptors spread and waiting for us," they said, "and we made his task easy by putting so many boats into one small area. He had no trouble finding us. Wherever he looked, we were underfoot. And 6th Fleet headquarters required reports from us too often, again making for easy discovery through radio detection. And the orders to cruise on the surface, or wait on the surface, were ridiculous!"

I was in just as bad a temper when, dressed in my whites, I boarded flagship *Katori*. Vice Adm. Takagi, chief of staff Rear Adm. Hisao Mito, and operations staff chief Capt. Chosaburo Takahashi wanted to hear about our transport operations. I minced no words.

"As all here know," I began, "using submarines for transport is throwing away the reason for their construction. Presently, however, it appears that we have no choice. Still, the work is not as easy as headquarters planners seem to think. It takes too much out of the crews, both physically and mentally." Then I went on to give detailed reports on the 14 missions I had carried out, adding that my men wanted to fight, not pass boxes of cargo.

"I understand the problems very well, Orita," said Admiral Takagi, "and you may rest assured that I shall have attack submarines attacking as soon as the special transport submarines now under construction begin coming off the ways.

Thank you for your efforts. I hope you and your men will get a good rest while here at Truk refitting." With that he started to rise from his chair, closing the meeting.

But I was not passing up the only chance to say what I felt. I had an obligation to speak for all my friends who had given their lives in submarines. "Admiral," I said, "I have other things I would like to add."

Takagi, a polite man, begged my pardon, resumed his seat, and bade me continue. I did.

"My year down here has taught me many things." I said, "For one thing, submarines are of no use for counterattacks against enemy beachheads. Those places are too well screened. We do not have the underwater speed for getting in past them, or for escaping after detection. Submarines should be interposed between the enemy's beachhead and his supply sources, thus giving indirect support to our troops on land by reducing the amount of men and equipment that can be used against them.

"Then there is the matter of sentry lines. The wolf pack system makes it easier for the enemy to detect us. And where he detects one, he can detect the others even more easily. Thus, all are endangered by one. We must face the fact that submarines are designed not to give the enemy one great blow, but a number of small ones. Submarines should be deployed widely and independently. Their achievements cannot be measured over short periods but over great lengths of time.

"Third, our chief weapon for detecting the enemy at present is 120mm binoculars. Top priority must be given to equipping submarines with radar and electronic countermeasure devices.

"Lastly, there is the matter of surface mobility. Planning officers have too much faith in our high surface speed. This advantage is now gone because of radar. Nor is poor weather an advantage for us. In *RO-101* I realized that even darkness is no longer our friend. I charged batteries twice a day, using the dim twilight, *in RO-101* and also in *I-177*. The fact that they both survived many missions is proof that it is a good tactic."

Capt. Takahashi thanked me for my report, saying that his assistants would certainly take my ideas into consideration. Then Rear Adm. Mito spoke up. "What Lieutenant-Commander Orita says may be correct when weighed against new principles and developments in antisubmarine warfare," he said, "but operational control cannot always be tethered to principles. Sometimes we have to send our submarines out when there is not even a fifty-fifty chance of their returning."

Mito's bland disregard of all I had said angered me, and I

lost my temper. "All submariners are willing to give their lives at sea!" I said, pounding the table. "What we expect of you and your staff is that you keep that fifty percent chance in mind! Otherwise, we will lose all of our boats! It will be mass suicide for submarine captains!"

Mito didn't like this tone in a junior's voice. "Are you dissatisfied with the way the staff does things, Orita?" he asked, angrily. "Are you criticizing us?"

"It is not a matter of dissatisfaction, or of criticism!" I shouted back at him. "I am merely expressing my honest and ardent hopes, based on my experience in the combat areas!"

Vice Adm. Takagi broke in then. "Orita speaks from experience," he said, "and his views are valuable. There is no doubt of that. But, in my opinion, they reflect a negative attitude. No matter what the difference may be between our capability and that of the enemy, we still must carry out our orders, mustn't we? This has always been the battle spirit of Japanese submarine men, has it not?"

I wanted to say more. I wanted to tell Takagi that his words were immediate evidence of his own underestimating the enemy. The man with the longer sword usually wins a duel, no matter how great the "battle spirit" of his opponent. But I held my tongue. The admiral had his problems. Even though he was as worried about the proper use of submarines as I, he had to display confidence and optimism at all times. As the top man in our submarine command, he had to radiate calm and never doubt. I felt sorry for him.

The conference ended and a luncheon was served, but the situation was awkward. No one at the table said very much. And (an unusual thing for Japanese officers gathered around any kind of table) no one laughed.

* * *

Chapter 14.

THE MARSHALLS.

I stayed at Truk only a short while, having convinced Admiral Takagi that repairs on *I-177* could not be accomplished there. This Carolines base was by no means the "impregnable Pacific fortress" so many persons still believe it was. So, even during the war, little was available at Truk in the way of major repair facilities. It could not install the radar and anti-radar equipment I believed *I-177* should have before returning to combat. So, late in the month, I left Truk for Sasebo, on Kyushu, the southernmost of Japan's main islands.

The Americans by that time were directing their main attack toward the Marshall Islands, east of Truk. Although it was to be changed later the enemy overall strategy in early 1944 was to set up air bases in China, in striking range of Japan's industries. And, eventually to launch an invasion of our homeland from bases along the China coast.

A double-pronged attack had been decided upon. MacArthur was to proceed north from his base in Australia by way of New Guinea and The Philippines. Nimitz's ships would at the same time fight their way west through the Marshalls. Later, they would join their forces in China. They thought that our Navy would be spread thin during all of this and our high command kept uncertain as to where the next blow might fall. Tarawa, Makin, Abemama and other bases in the Gilberts were taken to eliminate counterattacks against the invasion of the Marshalls and to protect the Marshalls once they were taken. The Marshalls themselves could also provide protection to MacArthur's right flank as he pushed north. So after steadily bombing these mid-Pacific bases for nearly two months, the Americans invaded the Marshalls on Jan. 31, 1944.

Our Combined Fleet was helpless to stop them. Adm. Mineichi Koga sat at Truk in *Yamato* and fretted. He had carefully hoarded his striking forces, keeping them nearly intact for most of a year, hoping to win a decisive sea victory in one great engagement. But the enemy was too strong. The successor to Adm. Isoroku Yamamoto now found him to be correct. In 1941, Yamamoto had said: "For six months or a year I can run wild. After that, I don't know."

Koga (like Yamamoto) had put carrier planes ashore to hit New Guinea and Bougainville. He lost most of these, leaving his aircraft carriers almost without striking power. I have already told of his cruiser losses. The best Koga could do for the Marshalls outposts was to send about three dozen fighter planes there for air defense. It would be insanity to sortie into the Marshalls himself, for the enemy force numbered more than 300 war ships, with still more on the way out from America. Koga prepared to pull the Combined Fleet out of Truk, for once the Marshalls fell, Truk would not longer be a safe haven. So again it was left to the submarines to counterattack.

Lt. Cdr. Rikuta Tategami took *RO-39* out of Truk on Jan. 20, for a patrol east of the Marshalls. By the time he got to his station, heavy air attacks were being made on our holdings. Tategami, ordered to take station northeast of Wotje Atoll, was nearing there when the destroyer *Walker* picked him up in the darkness on Feb. 2. *RO-39* got off an emergency message to Truk as the destroyer illuminated the seascape with searchlights; then she dived. She was finished off by depth charges.

I-175 was next. She had sunk USS *Liscome Bay* off Makin, and Lt. Cdr. Tabata no doubt hoped to repeat his feat when he headed east from Truk on Jan. 27.

Tabata became the first submarine captain to fall victim to

another new American weapon—the hedgehog. The battleship New Jersey's radar picked up *I-175* on Feb. 5. The destroyers *Charrette* and *Fair* went out from the screen, located *I-175*, and sank her. American accounts erroneously list this sinking as *I-21*, lost two months earlier.

The hedgehog weapon would sink more of our submarines before the war ended. It was developed by the British, who let the Americans copy it. On American destroyers, a hedgehog battery carried 24 explosive charges on a mount and could fire all of them at once in a high-arcing barrage, like two dozen mortar shells. They made a circular pattern in front of the firing ship and would not explode unless they hit something under the water. Anyone of them, however, could punch a hole in the hull of a submarine—a large, deadly hole!

No country has a monopoly on brainpower, as the hedgehog and other weapons show. The British were first to use radar in war, but the Americans developed it to a high degree, using a principle discovered by a Japanese. American submarine torpedoes in the first two years of the war were terrible. Many ran erratically, many hundreds did not explode after striking a target, and still others exploded prematurely. When American submarines finally began enjoying success— and it was they who really did bring Japan to her knees, by cutting off imports of war materials and food—they did it with a torpedo copied from the Germans! We Japanese built excellent submarines, but they were developed mainly from what we learned from purchased German, French, and Italian submersibles. And we bought our first submarine, of course, from the U.S.

As for the Germans (who perfected submarine warfare in two wars) they captured their *schnorkel* from the Dutch, who invented it. And as for underwater demolition, practiced against our island bases in the last years of the war, the Italians mastered this art long before the Americans employed it.

The third submarine we lost in the Marshalls was *RO-40*, sunk on Feb. 15. Lt. Cdr. Yasuo Kido's boat was detected by the destroyer *Phelps* near a convoy off Kwajalein. *Phelps*, destroyer *MacDonough*, and minesweeper *Sage* all attacked *RO-40*, sinking her. The fourth victim was *I-11*. Cdr. Juichi Izu had taken her out of Truk on Dec. 21, 1943, and was patrolling between the Ellice Islands and Samoa when ordered to take station east of the Marshalls. The best evidence available suggests that the U.S. destroyer *Nicholas* picked up *I-11* on radar, then sank her, on Feb. 17.

A fifth submarine, intended for deployment in the

Marshalls, was sunk before she could get there: *I-43,* under Cdr. Shinobu Endo. He had taken *I-30* all the way to Europe and back safely before losing her to a mine off Singapore. Endo survived that sinking to take command of this new boat in the *I-40* Class. He went to Truk from Yokosuka and was then sent on a mission to Saipan, in the Marianas. Later, Takagi summoned this boat back to Truk on Feb. 14. The next day, enroute, she was sunk by the U.S. submarine *Aspro,* east of the Marianas.

During the first three months of 1944, our submarines in the Indian Ocean sank 6 American and 10 British ships. German U-boats sank still others. *I-26* sank SS *Robert Hoke* just before 1943 ended and got SS *Albert Gallatin* on Jan. 2, after which she sank SS *H.D. Collier* and SS *City of Adelaide* during the month of March. Other boats did not do as well, because enemy merchant ships were getting increased escort. Allied warships were being transferred from the Atlantic to assist them.

During February, we lost two more submarines in the southwest area. *RO-110* was sent to Penang, to strengthen our effort in that area. Lt. Cdr. Kazuo Ebato took his boat out of that base on Feb. 2, for a patrol off the east coast of India. Nine days later he attacked a convoy and damaged one ship, but the Indian Navy gunboat HMIS *Jumna* quickly detected him. Assisted by the Australian minesweepers HMAS *Launceston* and HMAS *Ipswich*, she sank *RO-110* about 200 miles northeast of Madras in the Bay of Bengal.

The very next day we lost another submarine in the Indian Ocean. This was *I-27*, the ship of Cdr. Toshiaki Fukumura. He was *I-27*'s third skipper and his boat was one of our best. During 24 months of war service it had accounted for 13 enemy ships in the Indian Ocean, with a total tonnage of 78,000 tons.

Fukumura got 9 of these—an excellent example of what the Japanese 6th Fleet might have accomplished had the Battle of Midway been won by us and all our other submarines loosed for attack operations in the west. Australia and India would have been cut off by sea. Years might have passed before any kind of major offensive could have been mounted against Japan, if at all!

I-27 left Penang on Feb. 4, and scouted around the Maldive Islands, southwest of India's tip. The British used them for a fleet anchorage and for staging convoys. *I-27* came across a convoy headed from Kalindini to Columbo and sank the transport *Khedive Ismail* on Feb. 12 with over 1000 troops on board. Within hours, however, the British destroyers *Petard* and *Paladin* sank our submarine, the 53rd lost in the war.

My *I-177* left Truk and was one day away from Sasebo when we received word of a heavy attack on the Marshalls by U.S. carrier planes. That was the Jan. 18 assault, which was followed by daily hammerings and the Jan. 31 invasion I've told about. I arrived in Japan on Jan. 30, and arranged with Sasebo officials for work on my boat. It was started by the time I boarded a train for Tokyo with Lt. Cdr. Kosaburo Yamaguchi, then captain of *I-176*. Mitsuma Itakura had taken temporary command of *I-176* when Yahachi Tanabe was wounded then turned it over to Yamaguchi, who had two unusual experiences in that sub. He brought back an American depth charge "alive"—and he became the only Japanese submarine commander to sink an American sub!

The first happened in October, 1943. Yamaguchi had unloaded supplies at New Guinea and was heading back for Rabaul when his lookouts spotted a pair of PT boats. *I-176* dived and Yamaguchi heard the torpedo boats roar past overhead, but he was puzzled when no depth charges exploded. Another surprise was in store for him when he surfaced a while later. There, on the deck of the open bridge, lay a depth charge! A yellowish powder was smeared on the deck and on the side of his conning tower. Yamaguchi took the depth charge back to Rabaul and ordnancemen there examined it. They told him that some over-eager American sailor had dropped the depth charge in such a hurry that he neglected to arm it. It was still set on "safe." A killer bulls-eye had been scored, but the target was intact. A miracle!

I-176 was relieved of transport duty the following month and ordered to Truk. On Nov. 16, when just a few hours from Truk's southern entrance, one of Yamaguchi's lookouts reported a black object on the horizon. Yamaguchi dived, and approached it, identifying the target as a surfaced submarine. He knew that no Japanese submarine should be in that location, so he fired three torpedoes at three-second intervals. Two explosions followed in 45 seconds and no submarine was seen after that. *I-176* had sunk the American submarine *Corvina*. As sometimes happened with submarines, the hunter had become the hunted and was himself slain!

Upon arrival in Tokyo, Yamaguchi and I spoke with Vice Adm. Shigeaki Yamazaki, who had become submarine advisor to the Naval General Staff. We told of our experiences in the south, pointed out new hazards and developments in antisubmarine warfare, and made recommendations. I was as vehement as I had been during my table-pounding session on board *Katori* and talked at great length, so I was surprised when Admiral Yamazaki said, gently, "You are right, Orita. We will give those matters our highest priority. I hope that, before long, you submarine captains will have everything you want." Yamazaki, I must add, was a long-time submarine man. Admiral Takagi had no submarine experience at all.

After more consultations with staff members in Tokyo Yamaguchi and I caught a train back to Sasebo on Feb. 9. En route I grew faint, then very feverish. Yamaguchi became quite worried. When the train arrived at Kure, I told him to go on to Sasebo and report my illness. I went home, staggered off the train, and hurried to my house. My wife, Hisako, was overjoyed to see me, but her delight turned to terror as she became aware of my condition. My fever ran higher and I began to have severe pains in the chest, so Hisako telephoned the Kure submarine base. I was unconscious by the time the ambulance came for me and I stayed that way for several days. The doctors told me that I had pneumonia brought on by fatigue, change of climate, and travel without rest.

I had fallen victim to an occupational disease of the Imperial Navy in the Pacific war—plain and simple exhaustion. It knocked down hundreds of officers and thousands of men who operated continually over long periods without respite. Officers often lost both their ability to fight and to make decisions calmly. Upon first taking *RO-101* to Rabaul I had been in excellent health, and stayed healthy while in her. After shifting to *I-177*, though, I went down hill physically, as did nearly every other man involved in the submarine transport effort. It was hard work physically, and the constant tension wore down one's nervous system. There was little rest between trips. Whatever spare time we had, was spent keeping the ship in shape. Still, I was lucky. I did not get malaria, as did so many men on New Guinea and New Britain. And I got all the way home before collapsing!

I recovered consciousness just about the time a great American task force hit Truk. Nine aircraft carriers sent in clouds of planes, which sank or disabled over 40 of our ships moored there. Adm. Koga had left Truk with his major warships only a few days before, or the damage might have been heavier. As it was, we lost IJN *Katori*, and submarine tenders *Heian Maru* and *Rio de Janeiro Maru*, plus two dozen auxiliary and merchant ships. Their sinking greatly affected Japan's capacity to move war materials about.

My classmate Mochitsura Hashimoto was on patrol out of Truk at the time and was summoned back to help defend the atoll. He didn't have enough fuel left on board to make a pursuit, so he headed for Truk to get some. Air attacks were so heavy that he dared not surface. He lay submerged off Truk for four days. And then, when the skies were clear of enemy planes, he had trouble getting *RO-44* in through the maze of sunken ships. By the time Hashimoto topped off his fuel tanks, the enemy task force was far away. Pursuit was fruitless.

At Rabaul, Mitsumi Itakura was ordered to make a second run to Buin in *I-41*, when *I-171* was lost enroute to Buka. Itakura left port on Feb. 12, scheduled to arrive at Buin on Feb. 16. Patrols were so thick that he didn't get in until Feb. 20. He then took 98 airmen to Truk from Rabaul. Their planes had been lost on the ground in the massive American attack.

While Itakura was making this second trip into Buin, something was happening in Tokyo that would affect him directly. The design for a prototype *kaiten* had been approved. After nearly 20 months of fruitless proposals through the chain of command, Lt. (jg) Kuroki and Ens. Nishina finally used a device often employed throughout Japanese history to show evidence of purest sincerity. They submitted a petition *written in their blood!* This got the desired attention and permission to build a few *kaiten*.

Our Model 93 torpedo used by surface warships was called "Long Lance," because of its great range. Its warhead was nearly 1000 pounds and it could make up to 49 knots, making it 50% more powerful and 50% faster than American torpedoes. It also had a range of 20 miles, equal to that of a battleship's guns. Kuroki and Nishina wanted to take a Model 93, cut it in two, then insert a passenger compartment with controls and a periscope at the center. Tokyo allowed them to go ahead, with the provision that a means of escape was provided the pilot of this human torpedo. At first the *kaiten* was not intended to be a *tokko* (suicide) weapon. The finished product ended up much thicker than the Model 93's original 24-inch diameter. Its length was extended from 30 to 54 feet and its warhead increased to 3000 pounds. It could make 40 knots.

I received excellent care at the Kure naval hospital and was soon out of danger. On Feb. 22, lying abed in my white hospital gown, I relinquished command of *I-177*. The doctors said I needed plenty of rest and I could not retain command if I were to be hospitalized a long time. I remained in the hospital about six weeks and was very nervous all of that time because I suffered from horrible dreams almost nightly.

All of the nightmares centered about the southern submarine operations. In one I would relive a depth charge attack.

My submarine would be knocked about severely, then have to go deep. We would sit there while destroyers dropped more and more depth charges upon us. Then the oxygen supply would run out and members of my crew would go mad. In another nightmare an enemy destroyer kept running up on my sub until his bow filled my entire periscope. Then there would be a grinding crash, as his sharp bow sliced into our hull. And a third nightmare was as bad as the others. It had *I-177* running blindly through uncharted waters while I stood in her conning tower awaiting that awful moment when an uncharted pinnacle would rip her open and sink her. When I woke from these dreams I would be stiff and cold as a corpse and soaked in sweat.

By the end of March I was well enough to leave the hospital. I spent 10 days at Beppu, a famous resort on the east coast of Kyushu. There, as so many tourists do, I buried myself in the hot volcanic sands of the beach and felt new strength flowing into me, as I relaxed and let my cares drift away.

Soon I became anxious to return to duty. The job of a submarine captain is to captain a submarine. Other men I knew had had their health broken completely. They never fully recovered. I had. And I wanted to return to sea.

Back at Rabaul, our forces were digging in. Practically every above-ground facility had been destroyed in the bombings. Submarine headquarters had been moved ashore, into caves. Then it was decided that command of submarine operations would no longer be based on New Britain. Itakura took Admiral Owada and the staff of SubRon 7 to Truk in *I-41*, arriving there March 25. After that, transport submarines operated out of Truk for a while.

The enemy had little trouble securing the Marshalls, and American air bases there made Truk a dangerous place to be. Our surface ships departed, and troops moved in to build defenses and make Truk difficult for the enemy to take. Some of Koga's battle fleet went to Japan, some to Palau. Vice Adm. Takagi was not to be at Truk much longer, either. Our high command did not even try to put a bold face on the Marshalls defeat. Its published communiqués claimed the sinking of 2 cruisers, 3 destroyers, and 13 transports as a result of American attacks on our southern holdings. And one communiqué admitted that our Kwajalein garrison was vanquished, while telling that "civilians there joined our troops on one last, glorious attack."

Things grew worse on New Guinea. The enemy had all the naval support he needed and our forces had none. They kept getting pushed back. Americans and Australians continued to make landings on New Guinea's north coast, capping their campaign with the seizure of Biak (northwest of it) in mid-year. General Adachi and his staff were cut off from Japan altogether.

(On Sept. 10, 1947, General Adachi slit open his stomach in *seppuku* at Rabaul, where he'd been kept prisoner for two years after the war ended. His final will, addressed to Gen. Hitoshi Imamura, his wartime superior, expressed his sorrow. "I lost 100,000 good men in three years on New Guinea," he wrote, "I had to demand of them work, marching and fighting beyond their strength. In spite of such cruel demands they obeyed my orders without question, and never faltered. My heart broke as I watched their feeble strength ebb away, and my men die." Adachi closed by saying that he had not committed *seppuku* earlier because of obligation to the Emperor, who had ordered surrender. He had stayed alive so he could see to the welfare of the men under him who survived. When at last they were released from POW camp, Adachi felt free to join the souls of others who had died fighting for Japan.)

On Feb. 5, 1944, the Americans made their first air strike on the Mariana Islands. Four days later, U.S. Army troops landed in the Admiralty Islands and hastened to seize the fine anchorage on Manus Island. On that same day *I-46*, first of three boats in her class, was completed at Sasebo. And Lt. Cdr. Hashimoto, making a supply run to Mili Atoll in the Marshalls, got an excellent target in his periscope about that time. Troops had withdrawn to Mili from Majuro, and *RO-44* was taking food to them. On the way back, Hashimoto put up *RO-44*'s periscope and sighted two large aircraft carriers, then a battleship, While he was maneuvering into position to attack them, six American destroyers came over the horizon in line abreast, as though sweeping for submarines. *RO-44* had to hide. When Hashimoto came up again, the big warships had picked up speed and were moving away too fast for him to catch them.

We lost two submarines in March. *I-32* left Truk on the 15th for a supply run to Mili, but Lt. Cdr. Masayuki Inamoto's orders were changed enroute. He was told to intercept an enemy task force. Inamoto found the task force and reported its position on March 23. The next day the enemy task force found Inamoto and reported sinking his submarine. *I-32* had shown up on the radar screen of the destroyer escort *Manlove*. She and *PC-1135* sank the 60th submarine Japan lost in the war.

I-42 was sunk on the same day that *I-32* sighted her enemies. Cdr. Tsunayoshi Ogawa left Truk with supplies for Palau on March 15, arriving at Palau on the 19th. He was on his way back when surprised and sunk by the American submarine *Tunny*. The enemy boat must have had an easy time of it. Every torpedo had been removed from *I-42*, even those in her tubes. And her deck gun had been left behind as well, to lighten her for carrying cargo.

Late in March, a horrible thing happened in the Indian Ocean. *I-8*, then under Cdr. Tatsunoke Ariizumi, torpedoed two ships, the Dutch merchant *Tsijalak*, and the American Liberty ship SS *Richard Hovey*. Many survivors of both ships were then killed by *I-8's* crew. Some lived through this experience, and gave postwar testimony at war crimes trials.

Japan, on the last day of March, again lost a Combined Fleet Commander. Adm. Koga boarded a flying boat at Palau and headed for Davao, in the Philippines. He was to confer on plans for an intended operation, but never reached the conference site. Koga's plane was lost over the ocean in a storm. Adm. Soemu Toyoda (who would later personally decorate me) took over as our top naval officer.

Also, on March 31, the first of three boats in the *I-54* Class was completed at Yokosuka. These were *I-54*, *I-56* and *I-58*, the third of which would later sink the U.S. heavy cruiser *Indianapolis*. All were 356 feet long, displaced 2607 tons, made 17.7 knots on the surface and 6.5 submerged. Range was 21,000 miles at 16 knots. Plans called for 21 boats of this class, all to carry aircraft, but only these three were built. *I-56* and *I-58* became *kaiten* carriers, their 140mm deck gun being omitted for this purpose. The boats could dive to 330 feet and had a maximum underwater endurance of 105 hours at 3 knots. They were similar to the *I-15* Class, but had lighter engines and 6 bow tubes with a load of 18 torpedoes. Their successors would have had 8 bow tubes, displace 2800 tons, make 22.4 knots, mount an aircraft, and be able to sow 8 mines.

By this time our submarines were taking supplies to Rabaul, from where supplies had flowed such a short time before. Lt. Cdr. Itakura again made a successful run to Buin, volunteering for it after Truk received a desperate message. He had his choice of returning to Japan to report for "a special mission" or making the Buin run. He chose to help our marooned comrades, and brought back 73 evacuees.

Other lives were not so charmed as Itakura's. On Apr. 4 the enemy raided Truk, and all submarines present dropped to the lagoon's bottom. *I-169* did not come up after the raid. She had flooded a compartment during her emergency plunge and some of her crew were lost. Among those surviving was her captain, Lt. Cdr. Shigeo Shinobara. An attempt was made to raise *I-169*, but the lift cables parted when she was just a bit clear of the lagoon's floor and she had to be abandoned.

Another unlucky group was the crew of *I-2*, headed by Itakura's classmate, Lt. Cdr. Kazuo Yamaguchi. *I-2* made it from Truk to Rabaul with supplies, arriving there on Apr. 2, but she was sunk on the way back, north of New Ireland, by the American destroyer *Saufley*, on Apr. 7 (the same ship that sunk my former command, *RO-101*).

We lost three other submarines in April, too. They were *I-174*, *I-180*, and *I-183*. Lt. Cdr. Katsuto Suzuki took *I-174* out of Kure on Apr. 3, heading for Palau. Seven days later he received orders to head east and patrol off Truk. I believe his boat was sunk by American submarine *Seahorse*, near the Marianas. American sources say this submarine was *RO-45*. Not true. *RO-45* was sunk just outside Truk later.

Lost in the Aleutians during April was *I-180*. Equipped with a rebuilt conning tower, she went there under Lt. Cdr. Hidenori Fujita, who had operated with me as the skipper of *RO-103* a year before. Fujita left Ominato, in northern Japan, on Mar. 20, to keep a watch on the enemy in the north. The destroyer *Gilmore* picked him up on radar and sank him with depth charges on Apr. 26.

I-183 was the boat of my classmate, Lt. Cdr. Takuo Saheki. I was saddened, after the war, to learn the manner of his death, because he had such a strong fighting spirit. Possessed of a long face and a receding hairline that made it seem even longer, Saheki had been a top student, both at the Naval Academy and had a reputation from his teens as an expert in "*kendo*," the Japanese stick fencing. On Apr. 28 the balding Saheki cleared Bungo Strait (the strip of water between Kyushu and Shikoku) and ran into another submarine captain as courageous as himself. *I-183's* silhouette was sighted by USS *Pogy*, which was then engaged in helping to blockade Japan. *Pogy* fired torpedoes in the darkness and *I-183* went down almost in sight of the homeland.

I was well enough by Apr. 18 to be given command of *I-47*, a new boat that was still under construction. Happily, two of my Etajima classmates were given command of her sister ships. Kosaburo Yamaguchi got *I-46*, and Zenshin Toyama, with whom I had been so moved at the Sakuma memorial when we were still Midshipmen, got *I-48*. These were improved *I-16* types, 360 feet long, with surface speed of 23.4 knots. They carried 20 torpedoes for the 8 bow tubes and could dive to 330 feet. *I-47* and *I-48* never did receive the 140mm deck gun intended to be mounted aft. It was eliminated to make room for *kaiten*.

Upon taking over a submarine still on the building ways, a Japanese captain was simultaneously appointed her chief equipment officer. That way, he could oversee the final details of her construction. What I had requested of Tokyo headquarters was electronic equipment, a *schnorkel* (which the Germans had promised to provide us), and improvements to eliminate all possible interior noises from the submarine. This last item would end much grumbling among I-boat captains. Our submarines were just too noisy! I am sure it caused the sinkings of more than a few. The only request, however, that was fulfilled before *I-47* slid into the water, was installation of Mark 22 surface search radar, whose antenna stuck up awkwardly from the bridge's forward end. There was no time to make the other improvements.

I was not very happy with *I-47* at first. Her high surface speed meant nothing to me. I was certain I would be spending most of my time underwater and that's where I really needed speed. And *I-47's* heavy displacement was sure to make maneuvering difficult. I would have happily settled for a smaller boat with greater speed underwater.

At first my crew also left much to be desired. Out of 98 men, only 15 had seen combat. So I pushed all hands very hard, insisting that each learned as much as possible about every part of the submarine. If *I-47* were to survive the growing odds against her, she'd need a crew that knew every section in her tubing, every rivet in her hull!

I did my best to make sure my crew received good food, which was harder to do in a shipyard than at sea. Japanese submariners, like American ones, ate very well at sea. A typical menu consisted of boiled rice (sometimes fresh, sometimes tinned), *"umeboshi"* (pickled plums), *"takuan"* (pickled horse radish), and *"nori"* (dried seaweed). These were on the mess tables in plenty at all three meals. *"Miso-shiro"* was always served for breakfast. This is a soup much favored by Japanese. It contains dried onions, fresh spinach, and added vitamin extracts.

Lunch and dinner were a little more elaborate. For about the first 10 days at sea we enjoyed fresh meat and vegetables. We ate broiled fish, beefsteak, pork cutlets and *"tempura"* (shellfish or vegetables, dipped in batter and fried). When fresh food supplies were exhausted, we would have tinned vegetables, fruit, fish, beef, pork, chicken, broiled eels, tomato stew, ham salad, fish in soy sauce, and soup. We ate plenty of eggs—fresh at first, then powdered. And much, much rice.

For evening snacks there were dried biscuits and sometimes milk or noodles, or *"zenzai"* (beans cooked in sweet fashion for a treat) and tinned fruits. We drank very little coffee, but lots of green tea. Our average daily intake was 3300 calories, far above the Japanese national average. It was high in protein, but I think it lacked in fats.

At Rabaul, while I was there, submarine crewmen used to take rice, cigarettes and soap ashore to the native villages and trade these for fresh fruit. Once in a while, when the crew was very tired, I would allow an issue of *sake* or whiskey. Overdrinking was strictly not tolerated.

Despite the best efforts of shipyard workers, *I-47* fell far short of what I desired in a submarine. This was due to a basic defect in our submarine construction program—tinkering! Americans adapted one type of submarine to their every need, and I felt Japan should have done the same. Another basic defect that led to tinkering was the lack of a strong working relationship between what we might call the *operators* and the *engineers*. In fact, in Japan, a great barrier actually existed between those two groups.

In America, civilian scientists and technicians were brought in to assist with strategic planning. They were then able to develop weapons and techniques to meet changing situations. For instance, building small escort aircraft carriers on merchant ship hulls. And constructing great numbers of destroyer escorts, instead of a limited number of destroyers which were more costly. Destroyer escorts did not have to be as rugged and powerful as destroyers.

In Japan, the military "operators" simply laid down requirements for certain weapons and equipment, then handed these to the civilian "engineer." Some of the requirements were not technically feasible. Others were just impossible. Many included demands for speed in fulfilling them that just could not be met.

The civilian engineer had little reason to give much thought to what use the weapons might have and little knowledge of how they actually served in battle on which to base improvements. He had no chance to originate suggestions. It took all of his energies just to produce what was demanded.

Radar was the outstanding example of this poor relationship. Our engineers were so engrossed in keeping up with operator demands, that they had no chance to maintain the level of electronic knowledge the American engineers could. So, when radar was suddenly demanded of them, they could produce only crude, unreliable systems, at least two years behind those of the U.S. in efficiency.

In the spring of 1944, however, I could not spend too much time worrying about that. My submarine was scheduled for completion in the summer. I had to have my crew ready, so I heaved myself into that task as May began.

The campaign for the Marianas also opened in that month, a struggle that would just about break the back of Japan's submarine force. In three months we were to lose more boats than in the entire first 18 months of the war.

* * *

Chapter 15.

THE MARIANAS CAMPAIGN.

Construction of *I-47* was not completed until July 10, 1944. During the final phase of her construction, I learned that some of the things promised me in Tokyo would be forthcoming. *I-47* was off the ways before I got them, but workmen installed an air search radar set of the Mark 13 type, plus a *schnorkel*. The breathing apparatus was an older model, inferior to what the German U-boats were using at that time. As for the radar set, my engineering officer, Lt. Kikuichiro Tokuzawa, had to give up his sleeping space for installation of the control panel.

The enemy troops had leap-frogged General Adachi's positions in New Guinea and his forces were ill-fed and sickly. He had no naval support. By May 1 our high command had written New Guinea off strategically. Adachi's orders were to hold on as long as he could and make it as costly as possible for the enemy to get past him and into the Philippines.

Our Combined Fleet commander, Adm. Soemu Toyoda, had a big problem handed to him when promoted to the top post. He had to answer a vital question—where would the enemy strike next? Like Koga, Toyoda wanted to husband his naval strength until he could meet the enemy in one decisive battle. His plan for this battle was called "*A-Go*." It called for waiting for the enemy to commit himself somewhere in strength, at which time our surface forces would rush out from the Philippines and Singapore to add their weight to attacks made by our planes. With MacArthur enjoying success in New Guinea, it was thought that the next point of enemy attack might be the Philippines. Or it could be the Marianas, now that Nimitz had the Marshalls secured and could jump off from them.

To find out what the enemy was doing, Vice Adm. Takagi was ordered by Adm. Toyoda to set up a submarine sentry line across the path the enemy would take moving north from Australia toward the Philippines. In addition, 6th Fleet was to send submarines into the Marshalls, where we knew the Americans had some of their aircraft carriers.

Takagi sent *I-10*, *I-38* and *RO-42* eastward. But, since the greater danger (and closer one) seemed to be MacArthur, Takagi sent 10 submarines down to an area north of the Admiralty Islands. These were *I-41*, *I-44*, and *I-53*, supplemented by seven medium-type submarines. As we shall see, the smaller boats did little more than provide excellent targets for the proficient American destroyermen, whose antisubmarine warfare skills were improving rapidly.

The seven small submarines were *RO-104*, *RO-105*, *RO-106*, *RO-108*, *RO-109*, *RO-112* and *RO-116*, all completed since the war's beginning. Sending these boats south was not only one of the war's tragic tactical errors, but it also threw strategic moves off. The boats were skippered by men not long out of submarine commanders' school. They had been ordered to the Indian Ocean almost immediately after graduation to give them some seasoning and increase the effort in that area but, when an attack from the south seemed likely, the seven were suddenly switched to the Pacific. Five of them were lost within a few days.

On May 1 the enemy attacked Ponape, in the Carolines. Four days later Jaluit (in the Marshalls) was hit. On May 15, another leap-frog landing on the north coast of New Guinea was made. And, on the same day, an enemy carrier force suddenly appeared behind one of our major defenses, the Malay Barrier (the islands through which one must pass when heading for Singapore and the Orient from the west) and launched strikes against our holdings on Java. This shocked the high command. It gave evidence of the enemy's growing strength, that he could hit places so widely separated from one another.

On May 15 the only submarine we had that was equipped with radar, *I-44*, left Kure for her sentry work in the south. The radar set was defective and *I-44* was nearly sunk by air attack while relying on it. She suffered severe damage on May 21 and had to retreat. Up until that time *I-44* had been the anchor of an eight-boat sentry line north of New Britain and New Ireland, with *I-44* at its northeastern end. The rest of the line ran to the southwest in the following order: *RO-106, RO-104, RO-105, RO-116, RO-109, RO-112* and *RO-108*. There were about 30 miles between boats.

At this time, Adm. Koga estimated that the enemy had five powerful task forces at this disposal, each one including aircraft carriers. There was at least one in the Marshalls, one near New Guinea, and reports had come in on three others in the Carolines. However, Toyoda had no idea where any of them would strike. The main thrust could come across the Pacific from the east, into the Marianas; or it could come up from New Guinea, against Palau and the Philippines. A single American destroyer escort, USS *England*, catapulted Toyoda into making a wrong decision.

On May 16 our submarine *I-16* departed Truk with a cargo of supplies her captain, Lt. Cdr. Yoshitaka Takeuchi, was supposed to take into Buin, Bougainville. Takeuchi was sighted by an American plane. Three U.S. destroyer escorts, *England, George* and *Raby*, were sent up from the southeastern Solomons to intercept him. Five days after leaving Truk, *I-16* was picked up by *England*, steaming in a sweep with her sisters. The destroyer escort attacked, and sent *I-16* to the bottom.

Our 6th Fleet had now come up against the deadliest enemy it ever met during the war, Lt. Cdr. Walton B. Pendleton and the 200 men of his crew, manning a ship that was about half the size and fire power of our own first-line destroyers. That was USS *England*.

The three enemy ships continued sweeping westward, and missed *I-44*. This boat was later attacked and damaged by another force. The trio did discover *RO-106*. Lt. Eyasu Uda had taken this boat out of Truk on May 6. On May 22 he was lit up in the glare of enemy searchlights after trackers got him on radar. When one of her sisters missed, USS *England* sank *RO-106*.

The advice of myself and other submariners had not been taken. Our submarines had not been scattered as we suggested, and we had also urged that they *not* be arranged in sentry lines. So, moving further west, the American ships found the next boat in line, *RO-104*, that same day. She had left Truk on May 17 under Lt. Hisashi Izubuchi, and survived the first attack made upon her. But the following day she was found again. All three American ships attacked *RO-104*, but it was *England* who got her, the third kill for this light-hulled ship in five days.

The next submarine in line was *RO-105*. She must have been submerged, where radar could not find her, and outside of sonar range, because the three ships passed her, missing her. They found *RO-116*, though. What I had warned against during my table-pounding at Truk was happening. The enemy ships had come across the sentry line and were steaming right down it, getting one sentry after another. *RO-104* was discovered less than 24 hours after *RO-116*. American accounts tell that *England* got Lt. Cdr. Takeshi Okabe's boat (which had departed Truk on May 6) and that USS *England*'s captain was beginning to "feel embarrassed" at winning all the glory while in company with other ships.

He became even more embarrassed two days later, when *England* killed off *RO-108*, the boat of Lt. Kanichi Obari. *RO-108* had left Truk with *RO-116* and lived only 36 hours longer. Again, the crew of USS *England* carried out what was becoming a familiar task. It took them only one attack to get this boat.

By this time the air was full of jubilant American messages about Japanese submarines being sunk one right after another. Our intelligence people intercepted all, decoded some, and realized that our patrol line was in danger. A warning was broadcast. Lt. Hiroshi Nakagawa, commanding *RO-109*, and Lt. Toru Yuchi, who had *RO-112*, did not wait for instructions. Both at once changed position, taking up new stations about 100 miles to the northwest of where each had been. This took them out of the sweeping path and saved their boats.

Meanwhile, word of these submarine losses got to Adm. Koga. It made him assume they had been sunk by the advance screen of an enemy task force that was proceeding north. When *RO-108* was lost, the Combined Fleet commander was almost positive, but he became certain on the last day of May, when the fifth submarine in the sentry line, *RO-105*, went down that an attack on the Philippines from the south was imminent and prepared his forces to meet it. He sent *no* ships eastward.

RO-105, the sixth submarine to be sunk by USS *England* in 12 days, had left Truk on May 17, under Lt. Junichi Inouye. It took a lot of killing to sink it. The *England* force was joined by other ships, including an escort aircraft carrier, and they found Inouye's boat on May 30. He successfully dodged their attack, but was found again the next day. *England* scored again.

The days of May were also deadly to three other Japanese submarines. *RO-45* went down on the first day of the month at a point only 20 miles south of Truk. Just 20 miles! It seems hard to believe, but it is true. Lt. Cdr. Yoshihisa Hamazumi had been at Truk when aircraft carriers attacked the atoll. He was sent to pursue them, and headed out. The U.S. destroyer *MacDonough* detected *RO-45* the following day. Attacks by this ship, USS *Potter*, and a plane sent Hamazumi and his men down.

Lt. Cdr. Sadatoshi Norita had been a passenger in Kinashi's *I-8*, taking a crew to Europe for the purpose of bringing back the second submarine Germany was giving us. He and his men completed six months of training in his new, excellent boat and, on Apr. 30, Norita took *RO-501* out of Kiel, Germany, and headed for the Cape of Good Hope. He was supposed to give a position report at 30N, 37W. On May 11 he reported having passed that location five days earlier. He was not heard from again.

Postwar reports show that Norita fell afoul a type of vessel that was to be called by American writers "the scourge of the U-boats." This was the American escort aircraft carrier, a ship built on a merchant hull and used extensively against submarines. Cruising with destroyers or destroyer escorts, these ships closed the broad gap in the Atlantic Ocean's center that could not be reached by shore-based planes trying to protect convoys, an area that German submarines earlier found so full of fruit. The escort carrier USS *Bogue* left Norfolk, Virginia, in the first week of May. During the second week one of her escorts, USS *Robinson*, found and sank *RO-501* in the Atlantic Narrows, that section of water between Recife, Brazil, and Dakar, Africa.

Buka still had some of our troops on it in May and they had to be supplied so Cdr. Hideo Okada left Truk in *I-176* with a cargo of supplies for them. The killer of USS *Yorktown* at Midway was sighted by aircraft, just as *I-16* was to be a little later, and four destroyers were sent to get her. USS *Haggard*, *Franks* and *Johnston* chased *I-176* for nearly 24 hours after making contact with her on May 15 on the east side of New Ireland. Many dozens of depth charges sank Okada's ship.

As if to mock Adm. Toyoda, on May 27, (Japan's Navy Day) the enemy chose to attack Biak Island, northwest of New

Guinea. His force was reported to contain 2 aircraft carriers, 2 battleships, 4 cruisers, and 14 destroyers. That made the commander-in-chief certain that the enemy intended to jump from Biak to Palau and the Philippines. He ordered the First Air Fleet (our carrier force) to move down and crush the enemy, pulling planes out of the Marianas for this purpose. He also ordered the 2nd Fleet (which included the giant battleships *Yamato* and *Musashi*) to stand by for a rush to the south. These were based at Tawi Tawi, our anchorage in the Sulu Archipelago, at the tail of the southern Philippines.

Toyoda was still busy deploying his forces when, on June 5, one of our land-based planes from Nauru Island flew over Majuro, in the Marshalls. This daring long-range flight resulted in a message that read "At Majuro, apparently ready to sortie, are 14 enemy aircraft carriers, 6 battleships, 14 destroyers, 4 tankers, and about 20 cargo ships."

This caught Toyoda out of position, because he was still working up to an all-out counterattack on Biak. But, he still believed that the Philippines was the enemy's next objective. Perhaps it was because he believed that MacArthur (a man whom our top leaders knew to be greatly sensitive of his person and position) was eager to keep his promise of returning to the Philippines. In any case, Toyoda ordered the battleship-cruiser force at Tawi Tawi to start southward to Halmahera, from where it could strike into Biak. Our 6th Fleet commander, Vice Adm. Takagi, moved from Truk to Saipan, in the Marianas, in order to have a better location (Truk being endangered) from which to direct our submarine operations. Again, no ships were sent eastward.

Toyoda kept his carriers at Tawi Tawi and waited for the situation to develop further.

Contact with the enemy force from Majuro was lost on June 9 and Toyoda had no idea where it was heading. Meanwhile an American submarine, scouting off Tawi Tawi, sank three of our destroyers in four days. This was excellent submarine work by USS *Harder* and her captain, Cdr. Samuel Dealey, who certainly deserved having a ship named after him later.

The loss of five sentry line submarines had given Toyoda the impression that a task force was sweeping up from the south. And the sinking of three destroyers right off his main anchorage, plus the sinking of a fourth destroyer and three tankers not very far away, plagued him further. Toyoda had to move his carriers out of Tawi Tawi soon. Otherwise they'd either be sitting ducks for attacking American planes or be trapped inside a ring of enemy submarines.

When the Americans saw this midget sub wash ashore, they assumed it to be a suicide weapon. However, the small subs were meant to be retrieved.

The *I-76* (same type sub as *I-77* upon which Captain Orita served) had a surface displacement of 1630 tons

The *I-16* (same type as *I-47*) was of the class of sub later fitted out for *kaiten* work in home waters.

The *I-400* was among the largest of the world's subs and could launch observer aircraft from its deck.

I-47 had *kaiten* men of the *Tembu* (heavenly knighthood) group. Lieutenant Commander Orita is seen here seated fourth from the left.

I-36's men, also of the *Tembu* group, were in friendly competition with Captain Orita's dedicated ship and crew.

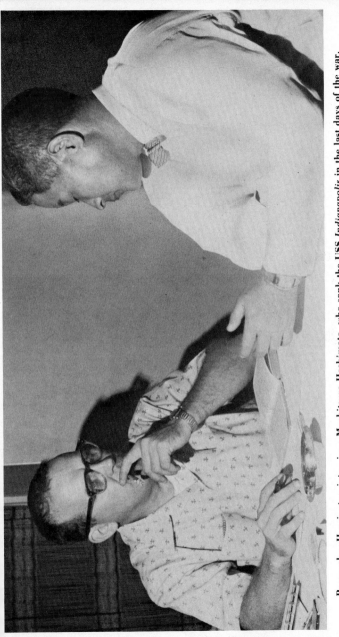

Researcher Harrington interviews Mochitsura Hashimoto, who sank the USS *Indianapolis* in the last days of the war.

Hiroshi Kuroki (left) and Sekio Nishina conceived the idea of the *kaiten* human torpedo some two years before the weapon was accepted. It was thought to be powerful enough to "roll back the sky."

Yukio Oka, left, made a drawing of the first *kaiten* success. His work was later presented as a gift to Emperor Hirohito.

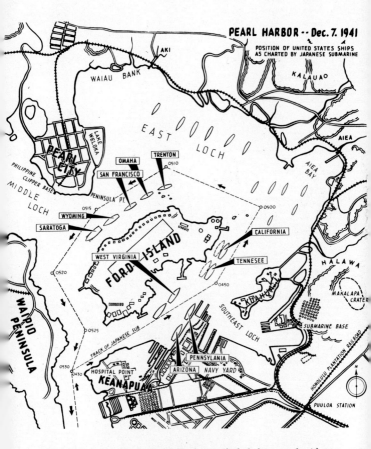

PEARL HARBOR -- Dec. 7. 1941

POSITION OF UNITED STATES SHIPS
AS CHARTED BY JAPANESE SUBMARINE

WAIAU BANK

AKI

KALAUAO

WAIPIO PENINSULA

MIDDLE LOCH

PHILIPPINE CLIPPER BASE

PEARL CITY

LAKE WELORA

EAST LOCH

AIEA

AIEA BAY

OMAHA

TRENTON

0510

SAN FRANCISCO

PENINSULA PT.

0515

WYOMING

SARATOGA

0500

0520

WEST VIRGINIA

FORD ISLAND

CALIFORNIA

TENNESSEE

HALAWA

0450

KUAHUA

MAKALAPA CRATER

SUBMARINE BASE

0525

SOUTHEAST LOCH

0530

TRACK OF JAPANESE SUB

0430

HOSPITAL POINT

PENNSYLANIA

KEANAPUAA

ARIZONA

NAVY YARD

HONOLULU PLANTATION RAILROAD

PUULOA STATION

Plans for the attack on Pearl Harbor included the use of midget
subs. They were to penetrate harbor defenses before the attack
began. When Japanese aircraft began to make their bombing runs,
the subs were to rise to periscope level, make their own strikes
against American warships and circle Ford Island, keeping to the
left, and make their escape to a rendezvous with waiting ships.

Kaiten pilots like Lieutenant Maeda (above) of the *Tembu* and *Kikusui* Groups sought to forestall the destruction of Japan by sacrificing their lives in *samurai* tradition.

An artist's sketch illustrates the attack technique used by submarines. They released *kaiten* (manned torpedoes) from their decks to do as much damage as possible to American invasion fleets and their supply convoys.

The *I-400* type of submarine was initially designed to launch attacks as far away as Washington and New York.

(top) The miniature model depicts a sub loaded with six *kaiten*, or human torpedoes. (left) The sonar room of *I-58* was typical of Japanese submarines. The lack of up-to-date radar equipment was to prove a major problem to the Japanese navy throughout the war. (bottom) The *I-47* is shown leaving for duty on Nov. 8, 1944.

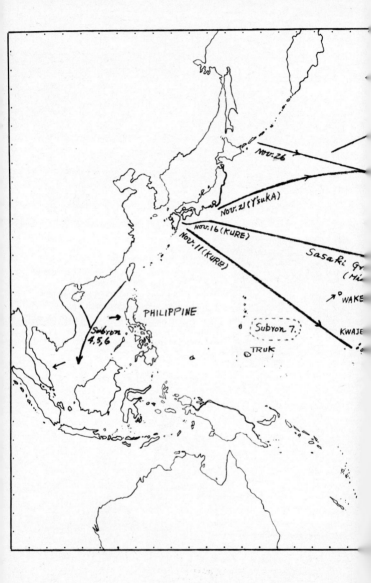

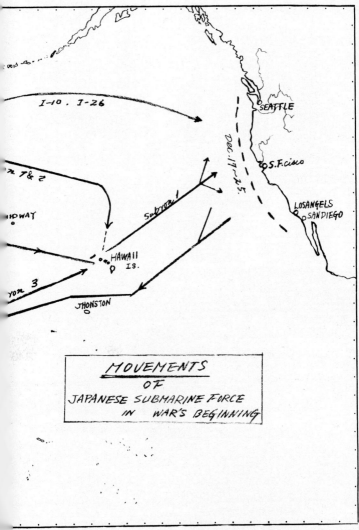

MOVEMENTS
OF
JAPANESE SUBMARINE FORCE
IN WAR'S BEGINNING

Zenji Orita's map shows the movements of submarines of the Imperial Japanese Navy between Nov. 11, 1941, when the first ships left home waters and Christmas of the same year, when Japanese submariners were patrolling off the California coast.

The very existence of Japan's two-man submarines was one of the best-kept secrets of pre-World War II. Before the fleet left Japan to attack Pearl Harbor, even very few Japanese navy officers were aware of this very important secret weapon.

Zenji Orita was a captain in the Japanese Maritime Self-Defense Forces in 1963. He has since retired from all military service.

On June 12 the carriers were still at Tawi Tawi (and Toyoda's heavy surface ships at Halmahera) when an enemy task force suddenly appeared off the Marianas, sending in planes to hit Guam, Saipan, and Rota. But Toyoda felt this was merely a diversion—an attempt to draw his forces away from the southern Philippines, so that MacArthur could land on Mindanao. Toyoda thought so little of the attack on the Marianas, in fact, that 6th Fleet sent only three submarines, *RO-36*, *RO-43*, and *RO-114* to that area to counterattack. The three boats were to operate east of the Marianas. All other submarines were to concentrate in the Carolines and in the area north of the Admiralties.

On June 13 and 14 reports came from Saipan and Tinian that enemy battleships and cruisers were bombarding them, while aircraft were bombing. On June 15 came word that American marines were landing. What Toyoda had thought was a lure was actually the vanguard of a mighty force containing more than 125,000 men!

Toyoda ordered Operation *A-Go* put into motion at once. It was actually an excellent plan. And it might have worked except for two things—the bright mind of American admiral Raymond Spruance, and American submarine men. The first battle in the Philippines Sea is called by the Americans "The Great Marianas Turkey Shoot." It might just as easily be called "The Great Submarine Success" (if looked at from the American point of view) or "The Great Submarine Disaster" (if looked at from the Japanese side).

First of all, we lost those five submarines on the sentry line. A sixth, *I-44*, was badly damaged. Then the American submarines *Harder*, *Puffer*, *Gurnard*, and *Bonefish* sank seven of Toyoda's ships. And, when Toyoda finally gave the order for his carriers to leave Tawi Tawi, the American submarine *Redfin* sighted them that very day.

Vice Adm. Jisaburo Ozawa had our aircraft carriers. He was sighted and reported when passing through the central Philippines and again when emerging from San Bernardino Strait. USS *Flying Fish* sighted him there. Meanwhile, Vice Adm. Matome Ugaki had left Halmahera with *Yamato*, *Musashi* and other heavyweights, his attack on Biak having been cancelled. The American submarine *Seahorse* sighted Ugaki's force and the enemy knew our ships were coming.

Spruance sent fighter sweeps northward into the Bonins and Volcano Islands to knock out aircraft there, thus eliminating air counterattack against him from land bases for at least a few days. Then he stood by to await the arrival of our carriers and battleships. And, before his aircraft carriers had a chance to attack ours, two American submarines scored great victories. USS *Cavalla* sank our carrier *Shokaku*, and USS *Albacore* sent carrier *Taiho* to the bottom. After that, Spruance's pilots wiped out more than 80% of Ozawa's fliers.*

Our underwater enemies chewed at the Combined Fleet before it sortied, reported it when it did, then smashed two of its most important fighting units before the main battle was even joined. What had been pre-war doctrine for both the American and Japanese submariners had been executed in a classic manner by our enemies. They did everything right, under Vice Adm. Charles A. Lockwood's direction. Our submarines, under Toyoda's and Takagi's direction, did everything wrong.

Operation *A-Go* called for land-based planes to attack the enemy's ships, land in the Marianas, rearm and refuel, then strike again on the way back to home bases. Our aircraft carrier planes were to do the same thing: strike the enemy, refuel and rearm in the Marianas, then strike again on the way back to their carriers. Operation *A-Go* was, therefore, intended to give our air forces twice their striking power.

Spruance, and American submarines, wrecked Operation *A-Go*. Our land bases were temporarily neutralized and our land planes made ineffective. Loss of two carriers meant loss of their planes while still out of range of the enemy. The remainder of our airpower, sea-based, was overwhelmed by the waves of planes from Spruance's undamaged carriers.

And, when the battle was finally joined, where were *Japan*'s submarines? Completely out of the picture, believe it or not!

When fleet forces met fleet forces, our nearest submarine was many hundreds of miles away. None was in the Philippine Sea. So sure was Toyoda that the enemy attack would be against the Philippines (thanks to USS *England*'s accomplishments against our submarines and the submarine *Harder*'s against our surface ships) that our submarines at Kure, Yokosuka, Saeki Bay, Truk and Palau received no orders from him until June 16. By that time communications with Vice Adm. Takagi, on Saipan, had been temporarily cut off and Rear Adm. Noboru Owada, heading SubRon 7 at Truk, had to take over command of the 6th Fleet for a while. He ordered 12 submarines to form three sentry lines.

I-6, I-185, I-184, I-5 and *I-41* were ordered to take station in that order about 300 miles east of the Marianas on a north-south line, with *I-6* the northernmost boat. Parallel to that line, and about 80 miles east of it, was to be a chain made up of

RO-47, *RO-42*, *RO-41*, and *RO-43*. Another 150 miles east of this second line was to be a third (also parallel) made up of *I-10*, *I-38* and *I-53*. Owada also ordered eight other submarines to deploy in waters closer to Saipan. These were *RO-36*, *RO-109*, *RO-111*, *RO-112*, *RO-113*, *RO-114*, *RO-115* and *RO-117*.

On June 16, an order came down from Toyoda's flagship in the Inland Sea that all Japanese submarines were to remain *east* of the 145th east meridian of longitude. The first battle of the Philippine Sea took place *west* of that, so the order kept our submariners well away from where they might have done the most good. The order was rescinded on June 20, but by that time it was too late. The major damage to our fleet had already been done. The enemy no longer feared our aircraft carriers, which were fleeing. His own carrier planes were available for heavy attacks on our island garrisons and for intensified anti-submarine patrol sweeps.

From Truk (on June 17) Admiral Owada gave orders for the eight RO-type boats near the Marianas to begin making attacks on the 19th against ships in that area, but they were still limited by the order to remain east of the 145th meridian, which cuts between Guam and Rota. Saipan and Tinian were in the allowed area of attack, since they lie east of that meridian. But four of our submarines were sunk before the date of attack arrived.

RO-36, under Lt. Cdr. Tatsua Kawashima, had just made a supply run from Kure to Truk and returned home safely. On June 4 she left Saeki Bay, Kyushu, with more supplies. This time her destination was Wewak, New Guinea. On June 10 the U.S. destroyer *Taylor*, operating with an escort carrier and three other destroyers north of the Admiralties, sank a submarine. Since the submarine broached after being depth-charged and was actually seen in mid-afternoon by American sailors, I assume it was *RO-36* that Taylor sank. We had no other submarines in that area at that time.

Another boat left Saeki Bay the same day. This was Lt. Cdr. Naozu Nakamura's *RO-111*. He had orders to sail for Saipan. I think that Nakamura's boat is the one sunk about 100 miles west of Saipan by the U.S. destroyers *Melvin* and *Wadleigh*, which got her on radar at midnight of the 15th. *RO-36* could have been in that area, because the 145th meridian order had not yet been sent when the American ships made their contact.

The third submarine lost was *RO-117*, under Lt. Cdr. Yasuo Enomoto. He left Truk on June 5, heading north. On June 16 he was ordered to take station northeast of Saipan, and was still working his way into position when an American heavy bomber flying antisubmarine patrol out of Eniwetok (in the Marshalls) sank him.

RO-114 left Saeki Bay under Lt. Yoshihiro Ata on June 4, to patrol in the Marianas area. She was never heard from again. I think she is the submarine sunk on June 13 by the destroyer *Melvin*, east of Saipan. This ship got a radar contact not long after midnight, closed in, illuminated, and opened fire. *RO-114* dived, but was sunk by depth charges slightly north of the patrol position assigned to her.

During the campaign for the Marianas we sent a total of 26 submarines there on various missions and lost 11 of them. American and Japanese records disagree as to the times and places some of them were sunk. Having made a careful study of the missions assigned, positions assigned, dates of leaving port, plus the dates and positions from which last heard, I am sure that my accounting of the lost submarines is the most accurate one available, especially since "official" American accounts were written and published long before many valuable records were unearthed in Japan and elsewhere.

There is no disagreement, however, on the two submarines we lost in the Marshalls during this period. They were *RO-42* and *RO-44*. Lt. Cdr. Mochitsura Hashimoto gave over command of *RO-44* to Lt. Cdr. Sadao Uesugi just before it left Kure on May 15 for Saipan. From Saipan it went on to the Marshalls and checked on enemy activity around Eniwetok. After a second scouting of Eniwetok, *RO-44* headed for Bikini. On June 16 it met up with the destroyer escort *Hastings* at about 3 A.M. Uesugi and his men died not long afterward.

By then, *RO-42* had already been lost. She left Kure the same day as *RO-44*, and went straight to the Marshalls, from where she sent back situation reports. On June 10 she appeared on the radar screen of destroyer escort *Bangust*, east of Kwajalein, a little before midnight. Lt. Yoshonosuke Kudo and his crew never saw another dawn.

After a while, Rear Adm. Owada passed the command of 6th Fleet on to Vice Adm. Shigeyoshi Miwa, at Kure. This happened after Owada had given two more general orders. On June 19 he ordered all available submarines to make attacks in the Saipan area. The next day Adm. Koga's limiting order was rescinded, giving the boats freedom of action. But it was then too late to help our Combined Fleet, which had retreated. On June 22, Owada ordered all but six boats to pull out of the Marianas area. *I-6*, *I-38*, *I-53* and *RO-47* were to continue to attack when and where they could. *I-10* was to make for Saipan to evacuate Admiral Takagi and his staff. *I-41* was to head for

Guam, where waited many pilots and airmen whose planes had been destroyed on the ground. The Naval General Staff wanted them brought back to Japan so they could fight again.

Nakajima had to get *I-10* in past more than 100 ships and get Takagi out. I cannot account for the sinking of *I-10* on a specific date, but I am sure she was lost no later than June 28 and most likely to an enemy plane. American sources list her as being sunk on July 4. I cannot agree, mainly because Admiral Miwa had already given her up for lost by June 28, the date on which he ordered *I-38* to take over *I-10*'s mission.

Only one submarine appears to have had any good fortune during the Marianas campaign. And even she did not achieve positive results. Lt. Hisashi Watanabe took *RO-115* out of Kure in mid-May with a cargo of supplies. He stopped at Truk, then Wewak and Palau, after which he was ordered to move in close to Saipan. On June 19 he was west of Rota, and fired four torpedoes at a Wasp-Class aircraft carrier. That exhausted his offensive capability and he returned to Japan. No American carrier was reported as receiving torpedo hits on that day.

On June 22 the pilots and airmen at Guam were picked up by *I-41*, and taken safely to Japan. Lt. Cdr. Mitsuma Itakura brought off this coup after a strange plan was abandoned. I have already mentioned that Itakura made a much-needed supply run to Buin, despite the danger, when he could have gone back to Japan for a special mission. His was the last Buin run made. Itakura then rendezvoused with *I-36, I-38* and three other submarines in the Inland Sea, south of Kure. Someone had conceived an idea nearly as weird as the wooden torpedoes Hashimoto had been ordered to test in 1942.

The six submarines were supposed to carry amphibious tanks from Kure to Bougainville and put them ashore. The tanks were equipped with, of all things, torpedoes! They were to go ashore, make their way overland, go into the water near the enemy beachhead, and *make a torpedo attack on enemy ships!*

This would be called the "*Tatsumaki* (tòrnado) Operation." The submarine captains were astonished to think that anyone was really serious about this new thing. First, submarines would have to get in near Cape Torokina, which none had been able to do so far. Then they would have to surface in this perilous area for at least 20 minutes to get the tanks away. That is, if the tanks' motors would start, after being underwater for so long. Then the tanks would have to reach land safely, cross it, and enter the sea again. They made a monstrously-loud noise and could only achieve a maximum speed of *4.5 knots!* Were enemy sailors supposed to sleep through all this din while these creeping caterpillars closed in on them? The project was finally abandoned. I think it was laughed out of existence!

Itakura was then sent to the Admiralties as a sentry during the period when USS *England* killed off six of our submarines. He sighted nothing, and nothing sighted him. *I-41* was ordered into Guam, and evacuated 106 men from there, putting them ashore at Oita, Kyushu (near Beppu) on June 30. Itakura then went to Kure, where he received orders to help establish a *kaiten* organization.

On the same day Itakura evacuated the pilots in *I-41*, we lost another submarine, Lt. Cdr. Jun Arai's *I-185*. She was en route from Kure to Wewak when ordered to intercept the enemy instead. On June 22, Arai spotted a convoy near Saipan bringing in reinforcements for the assault on that island. But the convoy's escort also spotted *I-185*. Destroyers *Newcomb* and destroyer-minesweeper *Chandler* sent Arai's boat to the bottom.

Another diverted submarine, *I-184*, had been sunk three days before that. On May 20 the boat of Lt. Cdr. Matsuji Rikihasa left Yokosuka with supplies for Mili, an island whose story is one of the war's saddest. Counting the troops who fled there from Majuro in January, over 4500 men were marooned on this tiny island. For 20 months thereafter they were subjected to bombing and shelling by passing ships and planes, even providing an occasional bit of target practice for new American units just arriving in the combat area. Except for the meager supplies a few submarines took to them, this garrison had nothing. Over 1600 men died from starvation, and from sicknesses brought on by lack of food. Another 900 succumbed to enemy attacks. The rest were all serious hospital cases at the time of final surrender.

Rikihasa arrived at Mili, unloaded his supplies, and left there on June 12. On June 15 he received word to close in on the Marianas. Before he could get there, a Grumman torpedo plane from the escort aircraft carrier USS *Suwanee* downed him with depth charges.

I-6 was one of the boats that Adm. Owada, while temporarily commanding the 6th Fleet, had told to stay in the Marianas area when the other boats left it. On June 30 she fired torpedoes at an aircraft carrier only 10 miles east of Saipan. I think that Lt. Shozo Fumon retreated after that attack and waited for a chance to strike again. On July 4, a group of American escort carriers and tankers was east of Guam. Part of their screen located a submarine that evening. Destroyer escort *Riddle* and destroyer *Taylor* made a depth charge attack, and reported sending it to the bottom. I am convinced that it was *I-6*.

No American sources are correct on the other three submarines lost in the June-July period of the Marianas fight—*I-5, I-55,* and *RO-48.*

Lt. Cdr. Takeshige Doi left Truk in *I-5* on July 6 for a supply run to Ponape, in the Carolines. He got there safely on July 11, unloaded, and made for Truk. Three days later, Doi radioed that he was attacking some enemy ships about 300 miles east of Saipan. We never heard from him again. The ships he attacked were a group of hunter-killers, especially searching out submarines. The destroyer escort *Wyman* sank *I-5* after Doi's ship had been picked up on radar in the darkness.

Three different submarines tried to tow *"unpoto"* to Guam, to help our beleaguered forces there. Cdr. Toshio Kusaka left Kure on June 27 with *I-26* and, after many attempts to pierce the antisubmarine defenses unsuccessfully, finally got through them and unloaded his cannon carrier on July 7. Then *I-45* and *I-55* were sent to try, leaving Yokosuka on July 7. Chased off several times by alert enemy patrols, *I-45* had the misfortune of seeing her *unpoto* washed overboard in heavy seas. She had to return to Japan. This was the second piece of bad luck for *I-45* in a short period. On her previous mission (to the Marshalls) she had been bombed and heavily damaged by an enemy aircraft. The sub barely made it back to Japan, with a wrecked stern.

Cdr. Monshiro Izuzu had *I-55.* He also kept trying to get in to Guam with an *unpoto.* Finally, word was sent him to abandon his mission and head for Tinian where airmen waited to be evacuated. Izuzu cast loose the *unpoto,* and acknowledged this order late on July 13, saying he expected to arrive at Tinian on the 15th. He must have been still sending this message when an American plane sighted *I-55* about 80 miles west of Saipan. An ambush was laid and the destroyer escort *Miller* picking up *I-55* on radar next morning. *Miller* was still making depth charge attacks when her crew heard a great explosion. It was *I-55*'s death cry.

RO-48 was the 11th of our submarines to be sunk in Marianas operations. She left Kure on July 5 under Lt. Cdr. Seita Kazutomi. On July 14 she reported undergoing a severe depth-charging only 30 miles east of Saipan. It was the last message received. I think that Kazutomi limped away from that attack and tried to make battle repairs. Then, shortly before sunset on July 28, a hunter-killer group built around the escort carrier USS *Hoggatt Bay* found *RO-48*. Destroyer escorts *Wyman* and *Reynolds* sank her quickly.

After being raised at Truk, refloated, and towed home, *I-33* was refitted. Lt. Cdr. Mutsuo Wada was given command of her, and in June was giving refresher training to his crew in the Inland Sea, as well as shakedown training. On the 13th, at 8:40 A.M., Wada ordered a sudden dive. *I-33* did not come to the surface again until 9 years later, when it was salvaged and the bones of Wada and 89 other submariners recovered. The reason for the sinking of *I-33* was the same as that for the sinking of *USS Squalus* in 1939 (the American submarine that was recovered and refitted to fight against us as USS Sailfish). The main induction valve had not closed. This is the opening through which submarines of that period "breathed" while running on the surface. It had to be closed when they dived. If not, a great column of sea water poured into the submarine, weighing her down.

USS Squalus was found and the McCann diving bell was used to rescue those of her crew who were still alive. In the case of *I-33*, she was located, but we had no method of saving her men, even though they were in only 180 feet of water, a much shallower depth than Squalus. Wada and his crew must have suffered awfully, before suffocation finally brought them death.

I-52 was lost in the Atlantic. She had gone there under Cdr. Kameo Uno, carrying a cargo of rubber, tin and tungsten. She met a U-boat off Biscay Bay, but no report of her arrival in Europe ever got to Japan. After the war we learned that *I-52* was the victim of airborne radar and a weapon called the "sonobuoy."

The sonobuoy, when dropped into the water from an aircraft, acted both like a sound detection station and a radio station. Its sonar portion established the range and bearing of an underwater object, and its radio portion sent this information to aircraft in the sky. Three aircraft from the U.S. escort carrier *Bogue* discovered, depth-charged and sank Uno's boat on June 24, 1944.

In July we lost a submarine to a British submarine. *I-166* was summoned east from the Indian Ocean, so Lt. Cdr. Shoichi Nishiuchi took her out of Penang on July 16, heading for a rendezvous with Fleet units off Singapore. *I-166* was ambushed the following night by HMS *Telemachus*. Nishiuchi, fortunately for him, was on the open bridge when the enemy's torpedoes hit. *I-166* sank from under him. He and a few others were picked up by a friendly craft in the Malacca Strait.

I-29 was sunk by a submarine also. Under Cdr. Takaichi Kinashi, the ace of our submarine fleet, she had gone to Europe. Kinashi brought his boat back safely as far as Singapore, loaded with machine tools and other valuable devices for our war industry, plus new weapons. He departed Singapore for Kure on July 22. Four days out, he was sunk by USS *Sawfish* south of Formosa. Some of *I-29*'s crew survived, but Kinashi did not. He went down with his ship.

Organized Japanese resistance on Saipan ended July 9. Admiral Takagi and his staff had perished two days before that in a *banzai* attack. Vice Adm. Chuichi Nagumo, who had led our aircraft carriers at Pearl Harbor, in the Indian Ocean, at Midway, and in the Solomons, committed *seppuku* on Saipan at that time.

Tinian men continued to fight as units until Aug. 1. And Guam, after being pounded by enemy ships and planes for a month, was invaded on July 21. The Marianas were lost and the Tojo Cabinet fell. At Kure, late in July, our new commander of submarines, Vice Adm. Miwa, held a conference to study what had happened to our boats in the 12 weeks since the Naval General Staff had handed down preliminary orders for Operation *A-Go*.

Those captains who had been badly battered by the Americans and barely returned to Japan alive had plenty to say. They pointed out that 9 of the submarines lost in the Marianas had been pulled out of the Indian Ocean, were manned by men just out of submarine school, or both. Captains of such submarines, they said, had no knowledge of the latest American developments and techniques in antisubmarine warfare. Lt. Hisashi Watanabe, CO of *RO-115*, was most vehement. He attacked the Kure school staff for adhering to obsolete curricula and making no change in their approach to tactics. "These people are too slow in developing means for use against the enemy!" he said.

Rear Adm. Keizo Yoshimura, chief of staff to Admiral Ozawa, who commanded *our* aircraft carriers in the Philippine Sea battle, was caustic in his reply to Watanabe. "In the Marianas battle," he said, "the American submarines performed brilliantly. Where were Japan's submarines? What were they doing to help us?"

Watanabe would have none of this, even from an officer so much senior to himself. He and his friends had fought too hard. His tongue was just as sharp as Admiral Yoshimura's as he answered: "You know very well, Admiral, that Admiral Toyoda himself ordered us to stay out of waters that were expected to be the battlefield. Therefore, you must know very well why we could not meet and strike at the enemy!"

Having gone this far, Watanabe felt that he might as well go all the way. "Before criticizing us submariners for supposedly having failed you," he said, "you may first reflect on the defeat of your own air and surface forces, and on how well American submarines were able to perform against you. If our submarines are to enjoy any degree of success in the future, you will have to stop underestimating the ability of men the enemy sends against our submarines. It is excellent! You think of nothing but the clash between two great surface fleets. You completely ignored us *and* the men who fought against us!"

After that there was a great commotion in the conference room, but Watanabe had made his point. Had our submarines been ordered *west* of the Marianas, we might have been able to make inroads on the enemy's strength, just as his submarines had been able to slice away a great deal of ours. We might have avenged the carriers *Shokaku*, *Taiho* and *Hiyo*, which were lost in the Philippines Sea battle. And the enemy might not have then been able to turn the full force of his power against Japanese submarines, the only sea force that opposed him in the Marianas after June 20.

Everyone began shouting opinions, charges, and counter-charges when Watanabe finished talking. Nothing could be resolved, and the meeting adjourned on an angry note. It was some days before a new policy was drafted and a statement issued. I learned of it while putting *I-47*'s new crew through shakedown training.

In summary, the 6th Fleet's new policy was:

1. Because of the small number of submarines now remaining, sporadic, separated Fleet attacks will not be made. Submarines will operate en masse, attacking enemy forces in conjunction with our air and surface forces. Until the enemy has approached nearer to Japan, our submarines will remain in home waters, refitting and undergoing extensive training, so as to achieve maximum capability.

2. Submarines especially designed for transport duty are now being completed in rapid succession, one after another. They will increase the frequency of our supply missions to the defenders of our Pacific outposts.

3. *Kaiten* are now being built, and *kaiten* pilots are now being trained. A number of submarines will be assigned to

kaiten operations.

When the U.S. 5th Fleet smashed Ozawa's carrier force, it wrecked all chances of Japan's ever mounting enough naval air strength to score a decisive sea victory. Our island air strength was also in pieces and, although we could still manufacture aircraft at a high rate, we did not have the time to turn out high-caliber pilots to man them.

The Combined General Headquarters, Tokyo, admitted to the loss of only one aircraft carrier during the May-June period, while claiming to have sunk 1 battleship, 3 cruisers, 1 destroyer and 1 submarine; and to have sunk or damaged "more than 5 enemy aircraft carriers."

The truth, however, was that our navy in the air, on the surface, and under the sea had suffered what was very nearly its death stroke. Our hope now lay in a desperate measure. At last, two years after Hiroshi Kuroki and Sekio Nishina first thought of their human torpedo (the weapon that might "roll back the sky") it was accepted. Word came down from the Naval General Staff in June to rush ahead with mass production of *kaiten*, and to commence training men to man them. I, Zenji Orita, would have much to do with this weapon.

Chapter 16.

SPECIAL SUPPLY SUBMARINES: THE PHILIPPINES:
KAITEN.

I had almost finished the final phase of surface shakedown training with *I-47* and was about to commence the underwater phase when the Americans assaulted Saipan. My submarine was not ready for battle yet, so I concentrated on three months of arduous training. Things were quiet for the 6th Fleet in August and September, as nearly all boats were being held in Japanese waters for a major effort. We lost no submarines in August and only two in September. One of these was engaged in supply operations.

The big B-29 bombers had been appearing over Japan since June, but our submarine construction program was not interrupted. *I-362* was the first submarine of the *I-361* transport class of submarines to be completed. She was finished on May 23, and was followed by *I-361* (May 25), *I-364* (June 14), *I-363* (July 8), *I-365* (August 1), *I-366* (August 3) and *I-367* (August 15).

These boats had no torpedo tubes. A pair had been built into some of the first ones but sea tests showed that this arrangement caused an enormous bow wave when cruising on the surface, easily detected from a great distance. The tubes were removed, and the length of the boats increased 6½ feet, to fair out the hull line. The original conning tower was also altered, from the Japanese traditional block shape to a sort of cup shape, narrower at the bottom than the top. Some of these *I-361* Class boats served as underwater tankers, carrying gasoline home to Japan. And some never got into transport work at all. They were assigned to the *kaiten* squadron upon completion.

The first of these boats to leave Japan on a supply mission was *I-362*, which left Yokosuka for Nauru on Aug. 21 carrying 80 tons of food. Lt. Cdr. Einosuke Nakajima got his boat to Nauru safely, then made for Truk. He got back to Yokosuka on Oct. 3, with 83 plane-less airmen as passengers. That had become an important function of our submarines, bringing back airmen to man the defenses of our homeland.

Next transport submarine out was *I-361*, leaving Aug. 23 for Wake with 80 tons of goods and bringing back 30 evacuees.

Then it was *I-364's* turn. Lt. Cdr. Takeo Makino set out with another boatload of supplies for Wake, but never got there. He left Yokosuka on Sept. 14, and was sunk that very same day by the American submarine *Sea Devil*, which was lurking outside Tokyo Bay.

The Americans were hitting the western Carolines often, by that time. On Sept. 15 enemy marines landed on Peleliu, in the Palaus. Palau had been the headquarters of our South Seas Administration ever since Japan had been given a mandate over Pacific Islands by the League of Nations. The Americans wanted the Palaus for a base to cover their planned invasion of the Philippines. The Allies had abandoned Formosa and the China coast as objectives by this time. It had been decided to take the Philippines, then islands between the Marianas and Tokyo, with a final assault to be launched against the Japanese homeland from Okinawa after it, too, had been taken.

RO-47, under Lt. Nagao Ishikawa, tried to counterattack the enemy amphibious force off the Palaus. Leaving Kure on Sept. 18, she was sunk 8 days later by the destroyer escort *Reynolds*. Hedgehogs got her.

With hedgehogs a destroyer could track at slow speeds, get a submarine on its sonar, and keep it there. It could stand off, calculate target position precisely, and fire hedgehogs. These missiles made no noise if they missed, so the destroyer's sonar remained effective during the attack. If a hedgehog hit and exploded it registered well on sonar·and also punched a serious hole in the submarine's hull. Once a Japanese submarine was located by an American ship armed with hedgehogs, its life was usually measured in minutes. Once a hedgehog hit, depth charges could finish the job easily.

By Aug. 10, all organized resistance on Guam came to an end, although some surviving men would hold out there for many years, refusing to believe (even long after the war ended) that Japan had been defeated.

A *kaiten* base had been set up on Otsujima Island in Tokuyama Bay, Yamaguchi Prefecture. Its commanding officer was Lt. Cdr. Mitsuma Itakura, who had served well in submarines. The chief instructors at Otsujima were the *kaiten's* co-inventors, both of whom had been promoted; Lt. Hiroshi Kuroki and Lt. (jg) Sekio Nishina. About two dozen men were being trained. A lot more would be needed as *kaiten* came rolling off assembly lines, so the Naval General Staff set about getting them.

Volunteers were sought at two naval air training bases; Nara (not far from Otsuka) and at Tsuchiura (northeast of Tokyo). A total of 200 were wanted, 100 from each base. Petty Officer Yutaka Yokota, with whom Mr. Harrington has written a book telling the story of *kaiten*, was a member of the 13th Flying Class, numbering 2000 men. On Aug. 25, 1944, he and his comrades were assembled before the main hangar at Tsuchiura and addressed by Capt. Kenjiro Watanabe, commanding officer of the base.

"It grieves me very much to tell you this," said Watanabe, "but the news from our Navy comrades on the front lines is not good. The difference between our power and the enemy's grows ever greater. In spite of the gallant fight our countrymen make, Saipan is in enemy hands and we are having great trouble supplying our forces at Rabaul and other outposts."

Then, without telling what it was, Watanabe revealed that Japanese technicians had developed a weapon of overwhelming strength, and asked for volunteers to man it. He warned the student pilots beforehand that it was a "no return" weapon, causing a gasp to go up from the ranks. This was the first more-or-less public mention in Japan of a *tokko* weapon that was actually *designed* to be a *tokko* weapon. The public had read many accounts of men dying in last-gasp heroics, even early in the war. Several Americans, in fact, crashed their aircraft into Japanese ships when they were already shot and dying and wanted to get in a final blow at their enemy. The well-known *kamikaze* were not organized until two months after Capt. Watanabe's speech.

Yokota was one of those who inscribed two circles on a piece of paper, signifying eagerness to volunteer. Men volunteered in such numbers that they had to be screened. No married men were taken, which eliminated a number. Yokota, 19 and single, was one of the 100 accepted. Three days later he entrained for Kure, where he took a boat to Otsujima. There were 30 men already in training when he arrived. Yokota and his comrades were given an introduction to the new weapon, and began at once attending classes on its construction, maintenance, and control. I may as well say at this point that *kaiten* had no escape device, as mistakenly stated in the American naval history of the war. That work says there was a device in each *kaiten* to throw a *kaiten* pilot clear while he was still short of his target. It is true that when the Naval General Staff first gave its permission to build *kaiten*, it was on condition that such a "throwing" device be included. But, during manufacture and testing, it was decided that this would interfere too much with design. At the strong urging of Kuroki and Nishina, it was eliminated.

Lt. Kuroki, co-inventor of the *kaiten*, died at Otsujima on Sept. 6, when his weapon took a sudden dip and struck the bottom of Tokuyama Bay. This cracked a hole in the giant torpedo. It flooded, drowning Kuroki and the man who was riding tandem with him, Lt. Takashi Higuchi. The weapon was later recovered, and both men cremated. Nishina vowed to carry Kuroki's ashes with him on the first *kaiten* mission. I helped Nishina keep his vow. From my submarine, *I-47*, the first human torpedo was launched in combat.

Eight days after the Americans landed on Peleliu, they put Army troops ashore at Ulithi, in the Carolines. They met no opposition because our troops on Ulithi had already moved to Yap. By then my old ship, *I-177*, was four days out of Kure under Lt. Cdr. Masaki Watanabe, heading for the Palaus to hit the enemy there. The commander of SubDiv 34, Capt. Kanji Matsumura, was on board. *I-177* was sunk on Oct. 3 by the destroyer escort *Miles*, part of the hunter-killer group. Three other submarines sent to the Palaus (*RO-41, RO-43,* and *RO-46)* got back to Japan safely.

Enemy aircraft carriers carried out heavy attacks on the Philippines and Formosa in early October. On Oct. 11 a task force that included 17 carriers, 5 battleships, 15 cruisers and 58 destroyers struck at Okinawa and other islands of the Ryukyus chain. Those areas were considered a part of the Japanese homeland. An attack there could not be tolerated for fear of its effect on our civilian population, so Adm. Toyoda told Vice Adm. Miwa that an all-out submarine attack should be made on this roving enemy fleet. The pursuit of it eventually cost us 6 first-line submarines from the 16 Miwa had available. The struggle for Leyte Gulf, in the Philippines, would cost Japan more than 40 warships. When that fight ended, our Navy would no longer be a fighting force. From then on, the emphasis would be on *tokko* weapons and tactics.

When Toyoda ordered this all-out submarine attack, our 6th Fleet table of organization showed that we had 55 submarines. This seems like a formidable force, but let me state that we had 55 boats—only on paper! First of all, 15 of these boats were in use only for training. All were obsolete but *RO-500*, the German gift. That reduced our effective numbers to 40. But the 7 boats of SubRon 11 were undergoing shakedown training, which left 33. SubRon 8 was in the Indian Ocean, under Rear Adm. Kisao Ichioka. It had 4 boats; *I-18*, *I-165*, *RO-133*, and *RO-155*. This brought us down to 29 boats, but 7 of these were under Rear Adm. Owada in SubRon 7, and all were of the *I-361* transport class, without torpedo tubes. Of them *I-364* was missing.

So, the 55 boats were really only 22. *I-12*, under Kaneo Kudo, had left for independent operations in the central and eastern Pacific, so that left 21. These boats were in SubDiv 15, to which my ship belonged, and in SubRon 7. Capt. Kiyotake Ageta commanded SubDiv 15. We had 12 boats, but three were already earmarked for *kaiten* work, and my boat was one of them. That left only 9 boats for action against the enemy if Toyoda's all-out submarine attack were to be launched, plus 9 more in Capt. Kanji Matsumura's SubDiv 34. And two of his boats, *I-177* and *RO-47*, were missing. In fact, Matsumura himself was missing, too. So it was that 55 submarines on paper became only 16 that could actually sortie out through Bungo Strait against the enemy.

Miwa formed 14 of these boats into three groups, and ordered them to sortie as quickly as possible. By Oct. 15 four of them, *I-26*, *I-45*, *I-54*, and *I-56* were on their way. On Oct. 17 the Americans made landings on the islands at the entrance to Leyte Gulf in the Philippines. The enemy's intentions were now clear, so all submarines were ordered to head for Leyte. By Oct. 21, eight more submarines had followed the first four out. These were *I-38*, *I-41*, *I-44*, *I-46*, *I-53*, *RO-41*, *RO-43* and *RO-46*. Then *RO-109* left on Oct. 23, with *RO-112* following her three days later.

The Battle for Leyte Gulf began on Oct. 23, with American

submarines drawing first blood. We had a Northern, a Center, and a Southern Force. The Northern Force was composed of almost plane-less aircraft carriers. It was supposed to work only as a lure, drawing the American admiral Halsey's carriers away from their task of providing air cover to ships off the new beachhead. Once this was done, our Center Force of battleships and cruisers was to emerge from San Bernardino Strait and turn south toward Leyte. There it would be joined by our Southern Force, a group of battleships and cruisers that was rounding the southern end of the Philippines while the Center Force was steaming through the central Philippines. They would form a pincers to crush the American support ships with their vital supplies, fuel and ammunition. Air cover for our forces would be provided from bases in the Philippines.

On Oct. 23 the U.S. submarine *Dace* sank heavy cruiser *Maya* and the submarine USS *Darter* sank heavy cruiser *Atago*, while our Center Force was beginning its approach through the middle of the Philippines. These two submarines also reported that we had large ships on the move, warning Halsey. Pilots from Halsey's carriers who had already wiped out most of the land-based Japanese aircraft that were intended to support our Combined Fleet hammered away at our Center Force after that, sinking mighty battleship *Musashi* the following day.

Early on the morning of Oct. 25, our Southern Force ran into a Surigao Strait ambush, composed of PT boats, destroyers, cruisers and battleships. The enemy's smaller ships did most of the damage, with two of our battleships and three of our destroyers going down. More ships were picked off by U.S. aircraft as they retreated from the battle scene.

The Northern Force was a successful lure, all right. It drew Halsey off, but at the cost to us of four aircraft carriers, a cruiser and a destroyer. Our Center Force was able to break through and attack enemy forces off Leyte, but all it accomplished before beating a retreat was the sinking of an escort carrier, two destroyers and a destroyer escort. Halsey, after sinking our carriers, raced to get into striking range of the Center Force. His planes sank three of its cruisers.

And, during the retreat, American submarines scored two more successes. This destruction wrought on our Fleet provides the background I must use when placing the operations and losses of our submarines in the Philippines, to show how great a defeat the Americans inflicted on us.

I-26 lived for only 11 days after leaving Kure. Her skipper, Lt. Cdr. Shoichi Nishiuchi, hoped to repeat his accomplishments in the Solomons, Indian Ocean, and Australian waters. On Oct. 20 Nishiuchi was ordered to take station southeast of Leyte Gulf. Four days later, he reported sighting four aircraft carriers. One of their screening ships, USS *Rowell,* sank *I-26* before Nishiuchi could attack.

Of those submarines we had ranged off the eastern approaches to the Philippines, the second to go down was *I-54.* Lt. Cdr. Denshichi Nakayama acknowledged an Oct. 20 order to change his station, but was never heard from after Oct. 23. Five days later he was sunk while trying to penetrate a screen around American aircraft carriers. *I-54* was detected and the carriers made off while destroyers *Helm* and *Gridley* hunted down and sank this (one of our newest) submarine.

I-45 was lost the same day. Lt. Cdr. Mamoru Kawashima sighted a warship early that morning and opened fire, sinking the destroyer escort *Eversole* with two torpedoes. When rescue ships came to pick up the American survivors, one of them found our submarine. It was USS *Whitehurst* which sent *I-45* to the bottom.

Our other submarines, meanwhile, were not idle. Lt. Cdr. Masahiko Morinaga fired three torpedoes from *I-56* at the enemy convoy on Oct. 22 and sank one cargo ship. On Oct. 25 he was able to locate other enemy ships by his radar. He attacked, and radioed he had sunk one escort carrier and one destroyer. But the escort carrier, *Santee,* did not sink. Then, on Oct. 26, Morinaga met up with another convoy and reported sinking three cargo ships. Out of torpedoes at last, he headed for home, arriving at Kure on Nov. 4.

I-41 was Lt. Cdr. Fumitake Kondo's boat. She left Kure on Oct. 19 and scored on an enemy cargo ship eight days later. Kondo thought he sank an escort carrier and a destroyer on Nov. 3 and so reported by wireless on Nov. 12. It turned out later that he had damaged the light cruiser *Reno.* Down sharply by the stern, this ship had to be towed to the rear area for repairs. Later in the month the Americans sought to shut off Ormoc Bay, on the other side of Leyte from their first beachhead, so Japanese reinforcements could not be put ashore on Leyte Island from there to join the fight, as we had done from islands in the Solomons. Kondo tried to attack enemy ships in Ormoc Bay on Nov. 28, but a patrolling aircraft warned of his approach. *I-41* was sunk by four destroyers, *Pringle, Waller, Saufley,* and *Renshaw.*

Lt. Cdr. Kosaburo Yamaguchi (with whom I had visited Tokyo to make reports during the previous February) left Kure on Oct. 19 in *I-46,* a new boat like mine. As skipper of *I-*

176 he had sunk an American submarine, but now was after bigger game. Yamaguchi was still searching out targets when, on Nov. 17 he was spotted by a radar-carrying aircraft. USS *Taylor*, a destroyer summoned to the scene by the airplane, kept attacking until *I-46* was sunk.

On Nov. 12 we lost another of the submarines sent to the Philippines, although she was not lost in the Philippines area. Lt. Cdr. Kichiro Shimose took *I-38* out of Kure on Oct. 19, and patrolled off Leyte and Samar until Nov. 5, when he was ordered to make a reconnaissance of the Ngulu Islands. These lie between the Palaus and Ulithi. Our high command wanted to know whether the enemy had any ships based in the Ngulu Islands' excellent lagoon. While acknowledging this order on Nov. 7, Shimose did not include any sinkings claims with his message, so I do not know whether he downed any enemy ships after leaving Japan. *I-38* crossed the path of U.S. warships that were heading from Ulithi to the Palaus on Nov. 12. USS *Nicholas* detected *I-38* with radar in the evening darkness and sank her.

There is still much doubt in the minds of former members of the Japanese 6th Fleet as to how much our submarines actually accomplished in the Philippines campaign. Lt. Cdr. Masao Kimura left Kure in *RO-50* on Nov. 15. He claimed the sinking of an escort carrier and a destroyer on Nov. 25, but the official American naval chronology shows no such ships being either sunk or damaged on that date. Yet, as of Nov. 15 our 6th Fleet commander, Admiral Miwa, officially estimated that his submarines around the Philippines had sunk 3 aircraft carriers, 7 destroyers, and at least 5 cargo vessels. The American naval chronology confirms only the sinking of USS *Eversole* and the damaging of *Reno* and *Santee*. We did get an American destroyer in the Palaus before our submarines went to the Philippines, though, and the incident caused the enemy to sink one of his own submarines!

On Oct. 3, near Morotai, Lt. Yoshikuni Honda was cruising in *RO-41*. He put up his periscope, and saw an American destroyer, USS *Shelton*, which he hit with a torpedo shortly afterward. *Shelton* later rolled over and sank while being towed to safety. *RO-41*, meanwhile, eluded another ship that was depth-charging her and got away. But an alarm had been raised and this second ship, USS *Rowell*, which had come to aid survivors of the *Shelton*, was called away from *Shelton's* side by airplanes that had sighted a submarine. Racing to the spot indicated, *Rowell* kept attacking until the submarine was sunk. It turned out later to be USS *Seawolf*.

We lost one more submarine in November. *I-365*, under Lt. Cdr. Motoo Nakamura, had made a run to Truk with a load of supplies and was on the way home when the American submarine *Scabbardfish* sighted it less than a day's travel from Yokosuka. All hands but one in *I-365* were lost on Nov. 28, the survivor being captured by the enemy submarine.

On Oct. 10, when the Americans bombed Okinawa, Admiral Miwa had 16 submarines actually available for attack operations. By the end of November he had only 10. In the group to which I belonged, there were only 3 boats left, besides those set aside for *kaiten* action. In SubDiv 34 there were 7 others, all RO-boats. *I-12* was still out on a mission from which she would not return. There were another 3 boats soon to join Miwa's active force, but that would give him only 13 to pit against the thousands—yes, *thousands*— of enemy ships that were converging on our island homeland. Thanks to our planners' inflexible unwillingness to change, and the ability of the American planners to change and adapt, the defeats suffered by the 6th Fleet in the Marianas and Philippines wrecked it as an effective fighting force. We would fight on for another 9 months with what we had, but with never a hope of victory.

Between Aug. 21 and the end of 1944, a total of 10 submarine loads of food, fuel and ammunition left Japan for outlying island posts. I have mentioned three. The fourth was *I-363*, which left Yokosuka on Oct. 9, for Woleai, via Truk. She took out 75 tons of food, 5 tons of clothing, 5 tons of heavy oil, and 5 tons of miscellaneous items, returning on Nov. 19. *I-361* left on Oct. 17 for Wake, and returned safely home on Nov. 9 after delivering 67 tons of food and ammunition. The sixth transport run was made by *I-365*, which was sunk on the way home by USS *Scabbardfish*. *I-366* made a run then, from Yokosuka to Pagan Island. She left Dec. 3 with 51 tons of food, and brought back 49 passengers on Dec. 28.

I-367 left on Dec. 4 for Wake with 81 tons of food and ammunition. When she got back she was ordered into the dockyard for fitting of *kaiten* racks. *I-363* successfully reached Marcus Island on Dec. 17 with 108 tons of cargo, mostly food, and got back to Yokosuka with 60 passengers nine days later. The last transport run of the year began on Dec. 30, when Lt. Cdr. Yasuo Kamijukoku took *I-371* out to Woleai, via Truk. *I-371* got back to Truk, and left there on Jan. 31. She was not heard from again. The American submarine *Lagarto* intercepted and sank *I-371* on Feb. 24, we learned after the war. Thus did we lose three out of eight special transport submarines to enemy submarines.

I was still training my crew in the Inland Sea when the Philippines fighting started. *I-47* was to be ready for battle in just a few days. I was at Yokosuka naval shipyard, getting final checks and was summoned to Kure soon afterward. There I went on board *Tsukushi Maru* for a conference. Attending it were: Capt. Kiyotake Ageta, the commander of my submarine division; Lt. Cdr. Nobuo Kamimoto, CO of *I-37;* Lt. Cdr. Iwao Teramoto, CO of *I-36;* and myself. We were joined by Cdr. Shojiro Iura and Lt. Cdr. Kennosuke Torisu of Admiral Miwa's staff. After green tea had been served, Iura gave us a full briefing on the fighting in the philippines area up to that time. Not a bit of the news was good.

"In order to turn the tide of war in our favor," Iura said, "Combined Fleet and 6th Fleet have decided to load special weapons, called *Maru Roku Kanemono*, on board large-size submarines and attack advance enemy anchorages with them. The plan is already under way, and the first attack will be made about the middle of November, using *I-36, I-37* and *I-47*. Without waiting for formal orders you are to go ahead and make preparations."

"What" said Kamimoto and I, almost simultaneously, "are *Maru Roku Kanemono*?"

Torisu joined in, and explained that "Circle 6 Metal Fitting" was a cover name to maintain high security for a manned torpedo. This was the Model 93, he said, converted to be steered by a man. "The pilot will be the torpedo's eyes, and steer it directly into a target. Once it is released from a submarine there is no way to recover it, or its pilot. It is a *tokko* (suicide) weapon designed especially for water use."

"Where are the pilots?" asked Kamimoto.

"Training at Otsujima, Tokuyama Bay." answered Torisu. "Experimental attacks have been made—using *I-36*. Results have been very favorable, so far."

"Are the weapons ready?" I asked.

"Kure Naval Arsenal is producing them right now." replied Torisu.

An hour later I saw my first *kaiten*. Its structure and capability was explained to me and I was told of the young men who invented it.

There are times when words just escape a man. As I walked along with Kamimoto a little later, all I could do was fall back on more-or-less standard statements. "Things must be really bad," I said, "if we have to resort to this!"

"I agree." he said, "The pilots will certainly have to have the *tokko* spirit. But so will we submarine crewmen, if we are go-

261

ing to help them do their jobs."

From that day on, the thought of life-versus-death rarely left me. While in *I-15*, *RO-101* and *I-177*, I had not once dwelt on the possibility of my dying. And I thought whether any of my officers and men did. I think that all felt as I felt, that they would survive combat, even if every other ship and man in the 6th Fleet were lost. During training, as well as when out on missions, they always believed that they would make a safe return to port.

Now, in my new work, I would be taking to sea men who were determined to die and I had always felt it my duty, up until that time, not to let even one man under my command die if I could do anything to prevent it. I was going actually to have to order men to die. I would have to direct them into their *kaiten*, and send them against the enemy. I would, in a sense, be an executioner. Also, never before had submariners taken such risks as I was going to have to take. I would have to maneuver closer to the enemy than anyone had so far while he was gathered in great strength. One mistake might mean the loss of my ship and its crew. So, I was in a dilemma; having to provide some men the means for death, while at the same time keeping in others a hope of life. It caused me many torturous moments, but I finally came to a solution. My duty was clear. I had to get those *kaiten* men to their launch points! So, while doing that, I had to put out of my mind any thought of the lives of my crew. After the *kaiten* were away, I rationalized, I would reassume the responsibility for my crew.

The next three weeks were busy ones. Four *kaiten* racks had been installed on *I-47's* deck, two forward and two aft. The weapons were to rest in these, each secured by four wire bands. Two of the bands could be released from inside the submarine's hull, but we would have to surface to release the other two. In training, off Otsujima, we used torpedo boats and other small craft as our practice targets. Workmen painted the upper half of each *kaiten* white, so that observers on the target ships could see results achieved by the pilots, each of whom set his depth so as to pass under the vessel he was using as his target.

Our pilots trained with us. The four who were to go out in *I-36* were Lt. Kentaro Yoshimoto, Ens. Taichi Imanishi, Ens. Kazuhisa Toyozumi, and Ens. Yoshihiko Kondo. Those to go in *I-37* were Lt. Yoshinori Kamibeppu, Lt. (jg) Katsumi Murakami, Ens. Shuichi Utsunomiya, and Ens. Kazuhiko Kondo. In *I-47* I was to have the co-inventor of the *kaiten*, Lt. (jg) Sekio Nishina. He was a very intense young man, full of courage, determination, and faith in the weapon he and his friend had devised. The 54-foot torpedo could run for 60 minutes at 40 knots, and Nishina often told the men he was training that no warship in the world could outrun it. With Nishina in *I-47* were to be Lt. (jg) Hitoshi Fukuda, Ens. Akira Sato, and Ens. Shozo Watanabe. The senior *kaiten* pilot in each submarine was a graduate of Etajima.

The target given two of us was Ulithi Atoll, which had become the major advance anchorage of the U.S. fleet. The enemy had all kinds of ships there from fleet tugs to mighty battleships. Japanese pre-war strategic predictions were being borne out, but not along the lines Japan's planners had hoped. The Americans were pressing westward from island to island, all right, but we had failed to stop them. At Midway, the Solomons, the Marianas, and Leyte, we had failed to win the one great battle that was supposed to stop the enemy in his tracks and send him home sorely wounded. The enemy had successfully seized our former bases, and was using them against us. Just as Kuroki and Nishina had said in their original presentation of the *kaiten* scheme, we might be able to attack him successfully in those anchorages. The *kikusui* Mission would tell.

About 800 years ago in Japan, there was an Emperor named *Go Daigo*. Well-read and intelligent, he felt that an Emperor should rule, rather than sit in polite, idle seclusion while the *Shogun* (the "barbarian-conquering chieftain" whose chief responsibility it was to keep Japan inviolate from invasion, peaceful or otherwise) ruled for him. But, when Emperor Go Daigo tried it, *Shogun* Takauji Ashigara banished him. There was at the time, however, a brave retainer of Go Daigo who agreed with his ruler. His name was Masashige Kusunoki. He was lord of the Kawachi district, south of Nara, our ancient capital. Kusunoki raised an army, defeated and deposed Ashigara, and restored Emperor Go Daigo to his throne.

But Go Daigo then made the same mistake as did King Charles II of England when noblemen brought him back from exile to the throne of his homeland. Instead of rewarding those who had fought and bled for him, Go Daigo favored fawning courtiers who had done little or no fighting. So, not too many years passed before he was deposed again.

Masashige Kusunoki fought for his Emperor once more, but his force of 300 warriors had to face 10 times that many at the Battle of Minatogawa, near Kobe. He died in the unsuccessful battle. No emperor ever held any real power after that until Meiji, grandfather of Emperor Hirohito, was "restored" in

1868.

Kusunoki has traditionally been revered as the perfect Japanese model of loyalty to the throne. Our mission against Ulithi was given the name *Kikusui,* in honor of the Kusunoki family crest. It consists of *"kiku"* (chrysanthemum), and *"sui"* (water), which combine to make the phrase "floating chrysanthemum." The *kanji* ideographs making up the Kusunoki family crest were painted on the conning towers of all three submarines in white when we went out on the first *kaiten* mission. Some American writings mistakenly use the word *kikusui* to describe some of the aircraft *tokko* missions. The only employment of this expression in Japan was to designate the first *kaiten* sortie. Other sorties, had other names.

After intense practice, our pilots were pronounced ready. The date for the attack on Ulithi was set for Nov. 20; the date for our departure from Otsujima for Nov. 8. On Nov. 7 we had a visit from Vice. Adm. Miwa. He addressed all the *kaiten* trainees, telling them how much Japan's hopes now rested on them and the weapon they had chosen. Our largest-sized Imperial Navy flag, with its eight red rays, hung from a nearby flagpole. The admiral saluted it and pivoted to face in the direction of Tokyo, whereupon all present bowed very deeply to the distant Emperor. Then Miwa directly addressed the *kaiten* pilots who would go out with us. They were standing in a row, wearing their best uniforms. Miwa presented each with a brand-new short ceremonial sword and wished him well. Such swords had special meaning. In the old days they were used by the *samurai* to disembowel themselves in *seppuku* (which Westerners usually call *hara kiri*) when they failed their lord in their duty.

We threw a big party for our 12 heroes that night, with Admiral Miwa attending. *Sake* flowed freely, and the food was the best that could be served. The traditional festive *tai* (redfish) was the main dish, accompanied by *kachi kure* (victory chestnuts), as well as all other delicacies our commissary staff could assemble.

Next day at 8 A.M. all hands mustered again and sang "Kimigayo," our national anthem, after which the *kaiten* pilots made a brief visit to a shrine built specially for them. Then, having made sure that bits of hair, fingernail parings, and all earthly possessions had been packed for shipment to their loved ones, the 12 men marched proudly between two files of *kaiten* trainees to boats that took them out to the three waiting submarines. Each pilot stood proudly on his *kaiten*, waving his sword about his head, as *I-36, I-37* and *I-47* moved slowly out of the harbor. A great flotilla of small craft milled about us. Many displayed great white banners with fiery slogans written on them. The crews and passengers shouted good wishes and cheered, until they had to turn back in order to conserve the fuel so precious to Japan at that time. American submarines, ironically, were reducing the amount of fuel available to Japanese submarines and the small boats that aided us, by sinking tanker after tanker.

The few aircraft still at Truk were assigned responsibility for making a reconnaissance of Ulithi for us. On Nov. 16, one of them flew over the atoll. Next day I received a wireless report of what it had seen. The nine mile-long lagoon had room enough to hold most of the U.S. Fleet, and much of it was there. "To the north there are about 30 ships, including battleships," the report read, "In the center anchorage there are about 100 transports and other auxiliaries, in two groups. To the south there are about 50 warships. These appear to be the task forces. They include battleships and carriers."

When I showed this to Nishina, he gasped. He was elated and disappointed at the same time. It meant plenty of targets for himself and his comrades, but it could have meant much more to Japan, as he saw it, had the high command listened to him and Kuroki when they first submitted their proposal. "All those ships," he exclaimed, "and we have only eight *kaiten* for an attack! What an opportunity this could have been!"

Nishina may have been right. If the Naval General Staff had accepted the *kaiten* idea in 1943 instead of 1944, Japan might have had hundreds of *kaiten* ready at Tarawa, Makin, Kwajalein, Eniwetok, Majuro, Guam, Saipan, Tinian, and Leyte. The monstrous defeats we endured might have been glorious victories instead. As it turned out, *kaiten* were based ashore in Japan during the final months of the war. They could just as easily have been stationed at island outposts earlier, before the American assault was mounted in full strength.

All this, of course, is mere conjecture. Still, the fact remains that Kuroki, Nishina and an excellent technician, Mr. Hiroshi Suzukawa, had plans for a workable *kaiten* weapon ready in January, 1943, when Japan's war fortunes were still at a fairly high point despite the Solomons losses. *Kaiten*, in fact, might well have been used with telling effect in that area itself.

Only two of our submarines (*I-36* and *I-47*) were to attack Ulithi. Cdr. Kamimoto was to head *I-37* for Kossol Strait, in the Palaus. We knew the enemy had much shipping there, and Kamimoto was supposed to sink four large ships with his *kaiten*; then sink what else he could with conventional torpedoes. A plane sighted *I-37*, however, while Kamimoto was maneuvering for his final approach. Destroyer escorts *Reynolds* and *Conklin* were sent out from the Palaus to find the submarine. They did, just about 12 hours before Kamimoto's pilots were to have mounted their weapons for the final run-in. *I-37* was sunk.

Before I headed south at a smooth 20 knots, our Imperial General Headquarters released communiqués making some fantastic claims. One said that our troops had killed or wounded 18,000 enemy troops on Peleliu, while destroying or disabling 200 tanks. Also claimed were the sinkings of a cruiser, two destroyers, a submarine, and more than 60 landing craft. Another communiqué covered the attack on Okinawa that had triggered Adm. Toyoda into ordering an all-out submarine attack. It claimed the sinking of 11 enemy aircraft carriers, 2 battleships, 3 cruisers and 1 destroyer. Another 8 carriers, the communiqué said, were damaged, along with 2 battleships, 4 cruisers and 1 destroyer. As for the Philippines, where the Combined Fleet received its death blow, three communiqués claimed a total of 14 carriers sunk, along with 6 cruisers, 3 destroyers, and more than 10 transports. With reports like these it is no wonder that, right up to the final months, most Japanese citizens truly believed that Japan was winning the war!

I had both of *I-47's* radars working while surfaced and (being especially fearful of enemy submarines and aircraft) had 6 lookouts posted on the bridge. But, aside from this special alertness, we were a fairly relaxed group. I teased my medical and engineering officers because they seemed to have little work to do. "It is good, though," I told them, "that you two are idle. It means I don't have much to worry me. But, when you are very busy, I know I am in trouble!"

We also teased *kaiten* pilot Fukuda, who was squirming uncomfortably after being at sea a full day. He had not used *I-47's* complicated toilet because he was too embarrassed to ask someone how it worked.

Chief Petty Officer Yukio Oka helped keep spirits up. The son of a Tokyo fish market operator, Oka was a cheerful man of highly competitive spirit. He did not like to lose at anything. He was also quite talented. Besides being very proficient in his main duty as assistant diving officer, he was an accomplished singer who had learned a number of traditional chants handed down in his family. He would often sing them for us. Oka was also something of an amateur artist.

Because of his tremendous professional skills and his bright approach to any subject or problem, the crew had great faith in Oka. But he, too, came in for share of teasing. While inspecting our *kaiten* one day, his lifeline parted and he was washed overboard. We had to stop ship and recover him. Lt. Nishina, who kept a daily diary, noted that "Oka, in charge of submerged navigation, was too eager, and swam 10 minutes in the Pacific Ocean today." When they were not studying the chart of Ulithi Atoll, or recognition silhouettes of enemy ships, the *kaiten* men and my officers played chess, cards, and *go*.

At 3 P.M. on Nov. 17, while running submerged, we picked up propeller sounds. A look through the periscope revealed an American destroyer heading northwest, away from us. At sunset of Nov. 18 I surfaced *I-47* about 50 miles west of Ulithi Atoll. For all my years at sea, the moment was one I will never forget. The sea, sky and submarine seemed to be dripping orange from the brilliant light on the western horizon and soon the symmetrical Southern Cross appeared in the sky. While the navigator checked our position by celestial observations and my lookouts kept careful watch, *kaiten* pilots and their maintenance men carefully loosed the first and fourth hold-down band on each weapon. These left only the two center ones to be freed, which could be done by us from inside *I-47's* hull. The maintenance men were Petty Officers Kanzo Iwano, Tokizo Kameishi, Fumio Kurokawa, and Seaman Masao Mori. These four men had embarked as technical specialists to make sure that all weapons were kept in good condition.

I then steered toward Ulithi and was reminded of my days off San Francisco in December, 1941, when the eastern sky had lit up before us. The ships inside Ulithi's lagoon must have been well-illuminated, to cast such a glow into the sky.

One hour before sunrise on Nov. 19, I submerged to 180 feet, so as to avoid detection from the air. I then edged *I-47* in until (at 9:30 A.M.) we were four miles off Zowariyau Channel, the southwest entrance to the lagoon. I came up to periscope depth, made a swift sweep, and called out the bearings of three cruisers inside the lagoon to my navigator. Then we dived and did not come up to periscope depth again until just before noon. After checking with radar for planes and noting none, I raised the periscope about 4 feet above the surface for a good look. I was then just outside Ulithi's reef.

The nearest cruiser was only about 3 miles from me. Beyond her were several battleships and some more cruisers. Beyond those I could see aircraft carriers, with two carrier-type planes and a twin-engined seaplane circling above the ships. These were all in the southern area of the lagoon. I could see ships in the central section, moored in several rows. There were ships beyond those, too, which I couldn't actually see through my periscope, but whose presence was indicated by thin rising columns of smoke.

"Here, Nishina," I said to the senior *kaiten* pilot, "take a look." He, Fukuda, Sato and Watanabe all took turns at the periscope. They were very elated by what they saw. "A fleet that size could not possibly move out of here in a night!" one of them said, and Nishina's diary for that day commented on "the golden opportunity to use *kaiten*."

I-36 was northeast of Ulithi, ranging to within four miles of another entrance to make observations, while I was west and southwest of the anchorage. Having finished my visual checks, I ordered *I-47* taken to 180 feet once again, and moved out to sea south of the atoll. Although it was time for lunch, I could not eat. I retired to my cabin to meditate for a while. When I left there I paused at the ship's shrine, located outside my cabin door, before summoning department heads and the *kaiten* pilots to the wardroom.

"We will launch *kaiten* in the morning," I said, "from a point about 4 miles off the eastern opening of the atoll. They will enter through the westernmost of the two channels. Targets will be the large-size aircraft carriers in the southern anchorage, or the battleships.

"In order to avoid having two *kaiten* attack the same target, and so we can make simultaneous attacks, Lieutenant Nishina will be launched at 4 A.M. He will penetrate the anchorage and go straight ahead as far as he can. Ensign Sato will go off at 4:04. He will move off to the right just after entering. Ensign Watanabe will follow five minutes after that. He will go left. And Lieutenant Fukuda, five minutes after Watanabe, will seek as large a target as possible near the entrance."

Lt. Nishina then gave detailed instructions to his comrades on navigation, depth setting for attack, etc. , and the pilots retired to their quarters. Lt. Fukuda's assistant gave him a haircut. Ens. Sato shaved off what had been a beautiful beard. Ens. Watanabe, who had been quite a dandy at Keio University, devoted his time to becoming extra neat and clean. I let all four use some of our precious fresh water for showers. Then they dressed in neatly-ironed shirts, and bound white sashes over their uniforms, around their waists.

Joining me in the wardroom, the four men wrote the last words each wanted to leave behind. Chief Oka then produced a sketch he had been making, drawn with soft black pencil in varying shades. It showed an American aircraft carrier breaking in two as a *kaiten* collided with it. More than a dozen planes were sliding off the flight deck into the sea. The *kaiten* pilots were most pleased with this surprise. All autographed it, and Nishina wrote *"Gochin"* meaning "instantly sunk" under his signature.

That evening at dinner a fine *sake*, a gift from the Emperor, was served in specially prepared lacquer-ware cups. Then the pilots retired to get what rest they could. I waited until 90 minutes after sunset, then took *I-47* to the surface. At a speed of 12 knots I approached Ulithi. There was no need to take a star sight. The atoll sky was bright, like a coastal city's in peacetime. While *I-47* recharged batteries, I told myself that the presence of all those lights meant the enemy had no idea we were anywhere near.

* * *

Chapter 17.

KIKUSUI: KONGO.

Countless pale stars glittered in the sky and a soft breeze caressed my cheek as I moved *I-47* in closer to shore. The enemy was repairing damage done to his ships at Leyte, obviously. Even at midnight I could catch the sparkle of welding torches. A half-hour later I gave the order "Pilots, stand by to board *Kaiten* Three and Four!" These two giant torpedoes could only be boarded from on deck. The other pair could be reached via access tubes from the hull.

Ensigns Sato and Watanabe walked up to Nishina at that time. "I am ready to board!" each said, saluting. Both were wearing short swords and had white *hachimaki* tied tightly about their foreheads.

"I appreciate your excellent conduct and spirit while under my command." said Nishina crisply. "Keep your spirit high, right up to the target. I will shortly meet you in the world to come. Good luck!"

The three of them came to the bridge. "Conditions inside

the lagoon appear to be unchanged," I told them. "There seems to be the same number of ships present as we saw before and the enemy does not appear to be taking any extra precautions. I intend to follow our original plan. I hope that you men will be able to demonstrate the full power of the *kaiten*."

Sato and Watanabe shook hands with me then, saluted, and hurried aft to where the weapons rested in their racks. Assisted by Nishina and the technicians, they climbed into the torpedoes. Both took one look at the sky and one deep breath of fresh air before the hatches closed over them. It was 1 A.M. We were about 5 miles from our launch point. I dived *I-47* and moved at slow speed. At 3 A.M. I ordered the two remaining pilots to board their *kaiten*. Nishina congratulated my crew and myself on having gotten so close to the enemy without detection and thanked us for our help. "Please do not endanger your ship in observing our results, sir," he said, "*Kaiten* operations should always remain a mystery to the enemy, if possible." He hoped that we would leave the area without being detected, so that the Americans would have difficulty puzzling out the source of this attack.

Nishina then headed for his access tube in the main engine room and Fukuda for his in the machinery compartment. Both shook hands with *I-47* crewmen along the way. Nishina had Kuroki's ashes in an urn with him.

My navigator manned a telephone in the conning tower that connected him with all four pilots. "Are you lonesome up there?" he asked Sato and Watanabe. "You have been waiting a long time." Both had by then been confined in their narrow chambers for two hours. "Not I!" said Sato. "I have been singing!" Watanabe was equally nonchalant. "That ice cream you served us at dinner was very good." he said, calmly. "Thank you very much for your thoughtfulness."

I have often thought, over the years, of how calm those young men, the flower of Japan's manhood, were. Death was only minutes away, but they were acting as though everything was routine.

At 4 A.M., *I-47* was off Lossau Island, Ulithi Atoll. By running directly northeast, all four *kaiten* would pass between Lolang and Mangejang (two small islets) and be in the deep anchorage water. *I-36* was about 7 miles northeast of me, off Gielap Island. Her *kaiten* had a straight run west, through Mugia Channel, the broad eastern opening to Ulithi lagoon. *I-47* picked up a destroyer on its sound gear about 3:30 A.M., but he moved away without attacking us.

A rapid series of orders poured from our navigator as the

kaiten pilots set their compasses to line up with *I-47's* and rechecked their depth settings against ours. "Stand by, Number One!" I ordered, then asked Nishina if he wanted to speak any final words. "Yes." he said. "My thanks to all. Good luck to those *kaiten* that follow me. And good luck to *I-47!*"

"Go!" I ordered. It was 4:15 A.M.

The third band had already been loosed. Now the fourth was let go. As I heard Nishina's engine start, I moved to my periscope. A line of white bubbles obscured my view. It was the wake from *Kaiten 1*. Nishina was away. Next was *Kaiten 3*, with Ens. Sato. He was aft, on the starboard side of the deck. "I will try to strike one of those large ships for you, Captain!" were his last words. Ens. Watanabe, aft on the port side, had *Kaiten 4*. "Long live the Emperor! Long live *I-47!*" he shouted. This moved me very much, and I shouted "Ensign Watanabe, *banzai!*" The time was 4:25 A.M.

Lt. Fukuda was the last to go. His *kaiten* had been having trouble with its steering apparatus. "Can you steer all right?" I asked over the telephone.

"It seems satisfactory, Captain." he replied. "I am ready to go."

"Good!" I said, "The other three torpedoes are running smoothly. There are lots of targets. Take your time and attack the best target you can find. Do you have any final words?"

No sound came from him. I thought the telephone line might have parted, but it had not. Fukuda was simply speechless. Then, just after his engine started, and just before his telephone line parted, Fukuda cried *"Banzai!"* It came over the telephone so loudly that all in the conning tower could hear it. All four *kaiten* were gone, four men seeking out targets more than 1000 times as big as their weapons.

Releasing them made *I-47* lighter. She bobbed gently to the surface, less than three miles from the nearest enemy ship. Fortunately, darkness covered us. I swung about on a southeasterly course and made away at 20 knots. Although Nishina had pleaded me to concentrate solely on escaping, I intended to stay near enough to note results. The *kaiten* were due to reach their targets shortly before 5 A.M. I wanted to be on the surface holding binoculars, not underwater looking through a night periscope, when they struck.

Time ticked by. "Five o'clock, Captain!" the signals petty officer told me as I stood on the bridge, peering out over the stern. More time went by, until the signals petty officer, after lookout and I, all shouted, simultaneously, "There!"

A great, reddish-orange light flared like a lightning burst in the center of the American anchorage. Then a column of fire shot up from the water's surface, quickly developing into a large fire. "A direct hit!" the signals petty officer shouted down into the submarine. I could hear crewmen shouting and cheering below me. The time was 5:07 A.M.

At 5:11 A.M. there was another flash, another flame, and another column of fire. "Second hit!" the signalman shouted to my crew. It was almost daybreak then, but I wanted to wait a little longer. I felt that I owed it to the men who had worked so hard at Kure and Otsujima, to take news of a third hit back to them.

This was prevented when one of the lookouts shouted a warning. "Destroyers, Captain! Right, five degrees! Range, two miles! Approaching!"

"Emergency dive!" I ordered. All eight of us on the bridge got below swiftly. "Take her down to 170 feet!" I called out, "Down angle, fifteen degrees!" In a submarine, this can sometimes make you feel as though you are plunging vertically. All hands clung to whatever they could as *I-47* plummeted. When nearly 30 minutes passed without any depth charges coming down, I went up to periscope depth. The destroyer was far away, between us and Ulithi, apparently heading inside the lagoon to investigate the explosions. We were out of danger, at least temporarily. Then, at 5:52 A.M., we felt a mild shock. "Small explosion inside the lagoon!" said my sound operator. I peered through the periscope and made a quick sketch of what I could see, to be filled in later. At 6 A.M. I ordered all hands to maintain silence and spend a minute in prayer for our departed comrades. Then I swung *I-47* north, making for the Leyte area.

I-36, meanwhile, had also safely approached Ulithi. Capt. Kiyotake Ageta was using her as flagship for the *Kikusui* Mission. Cdr. Iwao Teramoto had made his preliminary scouting, as I had, then moved into attack position, dodging prowling aircraft several times just before they might have sighted him. When *I-36* surfaced, Ens. Imanishi and Ens. Kudo boarded their *kaiten*. Hours later, at 3 A.M., Lt. Yoshimoto and Lt. Toyozumi crawled into the others via access tubes. Teramoto had his submarine 9.5 miles from Mas Island (which marks the right-hand side of Mugai Channel) at 4 A.M. At that time he discovered that *Kaiten 1, 2* and *4* had jammed in their racks and could not be fired.

In his later report, Cdr. Teramoto wrote "Lt. Yoshimoto and Lt. Toyozumi could not be fired, so I had to call them back into the submarine. I sent Ens. Imanishi away in Number 3, but something went wrong with his telephone connection at the last moment. I have no idea what his final words were. He was launched at 4:54 A.M."

The fourth *kaiten* gave Teramoto trouble, too. He had to surface, and take Ens. Kudo back into the hull. Then he dived, and listened for explosions. His sound equipment picked up one at 5:45 A.M. and another at 6:05 A.M. Both appeared to be south of Mog Mog Island, which would place them in the northern section of the lagoon. *I-36* then had to spend all day submerged, while soundmen picked up the noises of more than 100 depth charge and bomb explosions, none of them near the submarine. At 11:40 P.M., his batteries nearly exhausted, Teramoto had to chance surfacing. In spite of a tight enemy watch, he was able to recharge batteries and get away on the surface. Like myself, he headed for the Leyte area, where both submarines were to operate with our conventional torpedoes against enemy shipping.

I made my report by wireless to Kure on Nov. 22. It was quite a long one. *I-36* sent hers early on Nov. 23. On Nov. 24, our orders to Leyte were cancelled and we were summoned home. After a stop at Otsujima, we made Kure on Nov. 30. Two days later, a meeting was held at 10 A.M. on board *Tsukushi Maru* to evaluate the *Kikusui* Mission. There was much argument over whether the operation should be kept secret or announced. I was in favor of the latter (although I knew Nishina had not been) and I argued for my point of view. "The enemy knows about it, I am sure." I said. "What value is there in keeping it secret?"

By getting the feat announced, I hoped to see the tactic of attacking anchorages discarded. Besides air and sea patrols, there were nets and reefs barring the way to *kaiten*. I knew that the staff members of 6th Fleet and the submarine school instructors were ardent advocates of attacking enemy supply lines, so I hoped they would support my argument. They didn't. I was argued down even before the formal portion of the meeting commenced.

More than 200 persons were present at this conference, including some from Tokyo, 6th Fleet staff, submarine school instructors and students, plus officers from the Kure Naval Arsenal. Cdr. Shojiro Iura explained the original operational plan. Then Teramoto and I told of the actual mission. A study and discussion period followed, after which Lt. Cdr. Bunichi Sakamoto, 6th Fleet communications staff officer, summed everything up. Based on the two columns of fire I had seen, the two large explosions heard by *I-36*, the plan of each *kaiten* pilot launched, periscope observations, and comparison of aerial photos taken before and after the attack, Nishina was credited with an aircraft carrier, as were Fukuda and Imanishi. Sato and Watanabe were each credited with a battleship.

Americans reports differ greatly from the conclusions reached at that conference. They say that one *kaiten* blew up the fleet tanker USS *Mississinewa*. That ship was carrying 405,000 gallons of aviation gasoline, plus nearly 100,000 barrels of diesel and heavy oil. A *kaiten* near USS *Pennsylvania* is supposed to have been rammed and sunk, a third near the cruiser USS *Mobile* was depthcharged and sunk, and another downed by Marine Corps aircraft. A fifth *kaiten*, according to one version, was found wrecked on a reef.

Whether accurate or not, the American version had no effect on Japanese thinking or planning. But I still did not like the tactic of attacking anchorages. After the conference I took Lt. Cdr. Itakura aside, and told him I hoped something could be done about training pilots for attacks in the open sea, where submarines had a better chance of launching *kaiten* without being detected. A few days later I accompanied Capt. Ageta to Tokyo, where he made a full report to the Naval General Staff. On Dec. 12 he had a personal audience with the Emperor, to tell him about the mission. At that time Ageta presented our ruler with the pencil portrait done by Chief Petty Officer Oka.

On the day *I-47* left Japan on the *Kikusui* Mission, *I-372* was completed. She was originally designed to carry no armament at all, but ended up with a 140mm deck gun forward, and two 25mm disappearing-type machine guns aft. *I-372* and her two sister boats also mounted one landing craft each, and could carry a total of 110 tons of cargo, 10 tons of it on deck. Although intended for transport duty, these three submarines were converted to *kaiten* work instead, despite their dragging, 13-knot cruising speed. All guns were removed.

Three days after I left, the aircraft carrier *Shinano* was completed. Contructed on a giant hull like those of battleships *Yamato* and *Musashi* (largest ships of their type ever built by any nation) *Shinano* was completed as a carrier to help restore some of our lost naval air power.

Shinano was 861 feet long, displaced 72,000 tons, and could carry 87 aircraft. An American submarine got *Shinano* just 17 hours after she left Yokosuka shipyard for the Inland Sea. Workmen were still on board her, finishing up, when USS *Archerfish* put four torpedoes into her. She sank at 10:56 A.M., taking down 500 of the 1500 sailors and workers on board.

RO-56, last of the *RO-35* Class, was completed on Nov. 15. This type submarine was much favored by Japanese captains. In 1935 and 1937 the *RO-33* and *RO-35* were built as experimental boats, for rapid expansion of our forces in case of war. The pair proved highly maneuverable and seaworthy, so 80 improved versions, titled the *RO-35* Class, were authorized. Only 18 were actually built—*RO-35* through *RO-50*, plus *RO-55* and *RO-56*. They were 280 feet long and could make 19.7 knots on the surface, 8 submerged. Range was 5000 miles at 16 knots, or 11,000 miles at 12. Underwater endurance was 45 hours at 5 knots. *RO-35* Class subs mounted four bow torpedo tubes and , although not originally designed to have a deck gun, mounted a high-angle 80mm gun forward, plus a twin 25mm on the after end of the conning tower. All but one of these boats (*RO-55*) were lost in the war.

Three other submarines that are part of an unusual story were completed before I next launched *kaiten* at the enemy. They were *I-13, I-400* and *I-401*. *I-13* was supposed to be of the *I-9* Class, but when work lagged on the giant *I-400* boats, this and one other plane-carrying submarine, *I-14*, were enlarged and modified. They were given the designation "*Kai-Ko*" (Modified Type A) and displaced 3604 tons when completed. Surface speed was 16.7 knots, range was 21,000 miles at 16 knots. The hangar was expanded on these so that each could carry two aircraft instead of one and the supply of 18 torpedoes for the 6 bow tubes was reduced to 12, so that aerial bombs and aerial torpedoes could be carried. Special "blisters" were added along the sides of the hull, to provide stability for the added displacement. A 140mm deck gun aft, plus two triple and one single 25mm machine gun mounts rounded out *I-13*'s armament.

I-13 was completed on Dec. 16, 1944. *I-400* was finished two weeks later, and *I-401* nine days after that. Only five of the proposed 18 boats of the *I-400* Class were laid down. They were "*Sen-Toku*" (Special Submarines), intended for the bombing of Washington and New York but that ambitious plan was discarded. The new intention was to send the monster boats at the Panama Canal so they could destroy its locks and shut off the flow of ships that seemed to increase the enemy's Pacific Fleet almost daily.

Final size of the *I-400* Class boats was 403 feet in length. They displaced 5222 tons on the surface. Range was 37,500 miles at 14 knots. An interesting feature of this class of boats was that each had two *hulls*, the "spectacle" shape helping to provide stability while maintaining a low silhouette on the surface. Going aft from bow, one encountered a catapult track 86 feet long, then a massive hangar 100 feet long. On these boats (as well as on *I-13* and *I-14*) the conning tower was mounted out of the way to port, so room could be made for aircraft stowage along the centerline.

The "underwater aircraft carrier" construction program had been pushed forward as rapidly as possible, but it would be months before a squadron could be made up. Meanwhile, my *I-47* was refitted and replenished at Kure and I started training more *kaiten* men at Otsujima. Before long, a second mission of human torpedoes was ordered. It was to be called "*Kongo*."

Kongo, in Japanese, means "steel." In the Buddhist religion, it also signifies great strength or power. In addition, it is the name of a mountain in the Kawachi district, south of Nara, where the Kusunoki family lived. Masashige Kusunoki trained his army near *Kongo-yama*.

Elated over the success at Ulithi, 6th Fleet planners ignored the loss of *I-37*. A second, heavier strike was planned, with six boats ordered out on it—*I-36, I-47, I-48, I-53, I-56* and *I-58*. All of the other captains but one (Teramoto of *I-36*) had been classmates of mine at Etajima. We were to carry a total of 24 *kaiten* into battle.

Lt. Cdr. Masahiko Morinaga commanded *RO-34* and *I-5* before taking over *I-56*. He scored well with her in the Philippines. Originally a destroyer man, Morinaga entered the submarine service in 1940 and quickly mastered the tasks and skills necessary to becoming an excellent submariner.

Morinaga's target was to be Manus Island, in the Admiralties. It was an excellent anchorage and a place where the Americans astounded Australian allies with their ability to fit out a base rapidly after its capture.

Lt. Cdr. Seihachi Toyomasu, the principal of a high school in northern Kyushu after the war, had *I-53*. At Etajima we had always called him "Sister Gandhi" because his utterances were so like those of the great Indian leader. And, like Gandhi, Toyomasu was a mild man, but absolutely without fear. His target area was Kossol Strait.

I-48 and *I-58* had just completed shakedown training. Lt. Cdr. Zenshin Toyama had *I-48*. He was from Okinawa and had been a top scholar at Etajima. He had also excelled in *sumo*, swimming, and *judo*. Our common love of sports (mine being chiefly football and rowing) had made a bond between Toyama and me in those early days and we became fast friends. Toyama's target in the *Kongo* Mission was to be Ulithi and I feared greatly for him, since he would be going up against Americans who were now alerted.

Lt. Cdr. Moschitsura Hashimoto had *I-58*. He took command of her after leaving a boat with a confusing hull number, *I-158*. *I-158* was an obsolete boat in which Hashimoto carried out experiments in communication. Now and then one reads of "low frequency underwater transmissions" being used in submarine work. Hashimoto, who, after the war directed the building of submarines for Japan's Maritime Self-Defense Force at Kawasaki Heavy Industries, Kobe, may be considered one of the pioneers in this field. While operating submerged off Beppu in early 1944, he sent a message that was picked up at Nagoya, 600 miles away, having traveled through water all that distance. Hashimoto's *kaiten* assignment was Apra Harbor, Guam, another location of much enemy shipping.

The only skipper on the *Kongo* Mission who had not been a midshipman with our class at Etajima was Cdr. Iwao Teramoto, of *I-36*. He was to attack Ulithi a second time. The attack dates for all boats (with the exception of *I-48*) was to be Jan. 11, 1945. Toyama was not to attack until 10 days after Teramoto did.

As for myself, my destination was to be Hollandia, New Guinea, where heavy concentrations of enemy ships were constantly being reported. My *kaiten* pilots were Lt. (jg) Teruo Kawakubo, Lt. (jg) Toshiro Hara, Petty Officer Minoru Muramatsu, and Petty Officer Katsumi Sato. The latter had been aviation trainees. Kawakubo led the four-man group and he was very dear to me, not only because he was an Etajima graduate but because his older brother, Naotada, had been in my *buntai* (squad) at Etajima. As I explained earlier, 10 men from each yearly class were organized into vertical composite groups for athletic competition. Naotada Kawakubo, Toshitada Tokutomi (who died as CO of *RO-61* in the Aleutians), Tadayoshi Miyake (killed early in the war on board a minesweeper off Sumatra) and I had led our squad to many athletic victories. Naotada went into naval aviation upon graduation and was killed in June, 1936, while in combat over Amoy, China. Now I was taking his younger brother out to meet death in combat.

I-56 departed Otsujima for Manus on Dec. 21. I took *I-47* out on Christmas Day. Three more submarines followed us out on Dec. 30, and Toyama took *I-48* to sea on Jan. 1 for the Ulithi follow-up attack. Of our total of 24 *kaiten*, only 18 were fired. Lt. Cdr. Morinaga got close to Manus, all right, but not close enough. Mr. Harrington (who has been to Manus) tells me that ships moor a great distance in from the channel's entrance. Morinaga found this entrance completely blocked by well-laid antisubmarine nets. He tried again and again to get past them, without success. At one time he became stuck fast in the nets and had much difficulty getting free. Finally, he had to give up and head for home with his *kaiten*. That left 20 others that could be used.

Hashimoto moved in on Guam. He fired his four *kaiten* from a point 11 miles off Apra, and observed columns of smoke later. Teramoto managed to get *I-36* undetected in close to Ulithi for the second time and this time all of his *kaiten* were operative. But *I-53* had poor luck. Toyomasu got in past the screening patrols around Kossol Strait, but one of his *kaiten* was unable to get its motor started. He fired another, but it mysteriously exploded almost immediately after launching, giving the submarine a monstrous jar. The pilot of that torpedo, Lt. (jg) Hiroshi Kazumi, must have accidentally hit the special detonator switch in the operator's compartment. Captain Toyomasu got the other pair of *kaiten* away without incident.

My old friend Toyama must have made his attack successfully. American writings tell of a giant torpedo exploding near the ammunition ship USS *Mazama* on Jan. 20, but they tell of no similar occurrences at Ulithi on that date. And, on the following day, *I-48* was sighted. Apparently Toyama had hoped that his attack on Ulithi, following two others, might panic some large ships into sortying so he could pick them off as they passed by. So he remained in the general area. In the evening of Jan. 21, an aircraft reported his presence. Three destroyer escorts, USS *Conklin*, USS *Raby* and USS *Corbesier*, were sent to hunt for the submarine. Early in the morning of Jan. 23, his batteries exhausted, Toyama was forced to come up to the surface to recharge. The ever-ready radar pinpointed him and *I-48* was sunk before noon.

As for *I-47*, we were lucky again. My crewmen attributed this to a good omen, the rescue we made just five days out of the Inland Sea on Dec. 30. *I-47* was on the surface and I was just about to give a diving order when one of my lookouts shouted "Raft!"

We approached, and found on board it an Ensign, Chief Petty Officer and 6 seamen of the Imperial Navy, all nearly dead. They had the strangest story to tell. Although communiqués out of Tokyo had stated that all our remaining men on Guam had been annihilated while making one last glorious *banzai* attack, these men said that some 4000-5000 men were still alive in the island's southern section.

"We were ordered to go around the enemy lines," they said, "and make a *tokko* attack on installations and aircraft. We made a raft of empty fuel drums and set out on Nov. 28. But the current and wind were against us. We were gradually borne far out to sea."

The eight men had been adrift for 32 days in the open ocean when we found them. They had subsisted on seagulls shot with their rifles, and on fish caught with hand-made hooks. Their only water came from sporadic rain squalls which occurred daily in that part of the Pacific. When we called out in Japanese to them, they could barely wave. All eight thought their rescue was a miracle, as did our *kaiten* pilots.

"Those men have been saved to take our places in this life," said *kaiten* pilot Kawakubo. He and his men showered the remains of their personal possessions on the survivors. "They need them," the *kaiten* men said. "In a few days, we will not."

My crewmen caught this spirit of the miracle and morale soared higher that it had ever been. The trip continued without incident, only one aircraft being sighted. That was on Jan. 1, the great holiday of Japan. I was on the bridge, meditating, when a lookout called "Aircraft!" His shout interrupted a silent prayer I was saying for the four *kaiten* men I had launched at Ulithi six weeks before.

We got *I-47* submerged within 40 seconds and I congratulated the crew on their performance. The plane had not noticed us, for no bombs or depth charges followed us down. On Jan. 4 we received wireless orders changing our attack date to Jan. 12. It gave us an extra day, so I took advantage of that to slow down the boat and let the crew hold an Equator-Crossing celebration. Our leading quartermaster, who had crossed The Line 32 times in his naval career, was made God Of The Equator, with red-and-white *"mochitsuki"* (rice cakes) offered him as tribute by his "subjects."

At midnight of Jan. 10, 1945, I was 50 miles north of Humboldt Bay, Hollandia, New Guinea. Three days earlier a wireless report had said that 50 enemy ships, including cruisers, destroyers, cargo ships and tankers were anchored there. It was the rainy season in New Guinea. The sky and the sea were black. Everything that moved in the water gave off a luminous glow. *I-47* had to go ahead with care, keeping our wake to a minimum. By 2 A.M. I could see a glow in the sky ahead like the one that had shone over Ulithi. Shortly after that, in a rain squall off to port, I could see a light blinking. Was it gunfire?

Or a searchlight? I couldn't tell.

We were now inside the enemy's offshore patrol area. I swung *I-47* to starboard, presenting the smallest silhouette possible, just in case a ship was in that squall ready to open fire. The lights were repeated. "Stop engines!" I ordered. If I dared run away or try to submerge, it would only arouse suspicion. "Blink all navigation lights!" I called out.

This was done, and what turned out to be an enemy patrol boat steamed away. My ruse worked! Had I dived, he would have gotten *I-47* on his sonar in an instant. My lookouts were doubly watchful after that.

Before dawn of the 11th, I submerged. At 1 A.M. I was three miles off the peculiarly shaped mouth of Humboldt Bay, the green Stanley Range clear in my periscope. We gave Cape Soeadja the nickname of "Cape *Kongo*," after our mission. There was one LST in sight (to the left) and two small ships patrolling nearby, so I dared not let the top of my periscope get more than 30 inches above the surface. I summoned the four *kaiten* pilots to the conning tower, and let each take a look. "All you have to do," I said, "is go around that cape, and turn right. You will then have your choice among 50 targets!" After about 20 minutes, I turned *I-47* around and made for the open sea. It was time to make final preparations for the attack.

That afternoon my officers and I invited the *kaiten* pilots to a departure ceremony. A special tea was served, prepared in the ceremonial Japanese manner. Such tea is thick and bitter, so we served the traditional "*yokan*" (sweet bean pastry) to harmonize with it. The atmosphere of our gathering was quiet, almost serene, although the conversation was more animated than one might expect on such a solemn occasion. The eldest of the *kaiten* men was only 23 years old and I marveled (as I have before and since) at how such fine, strong young persons could maintain the calm cheerfulness they did in those last days and hours of their lives.

One hour after sunset, I took *I-47* to the surface and headed back toward Humboldt Bay at 9 knots. The sea was flat and glassy. I felt sure that none of the other submarines was encountering conditions so ideal for *kaiten* operations. Hollandia still threw a glow into the sky, I noted. At 1 A.M. I called all pilots to the conning tower. "We will be four and one-half miles north of Cape *Kongo* by 4 A.M." I said. "We have a dead calm sea and there is no evidence that the enemy is suspicious. Lieutenant Kawakubo will be launched at 4:15, then Muramatsu, Sato and Hara, at five-minute intervals. You will steer a course of 180 degrees until you have the tip of Cape *Kongo* abeam to starboard. After that, you are on your own. Select the best possible target. Try to make your attacks simultaneously, keeping to the time schedule if possible. I wish you success."

All four repeated my instructions. Then Muramatsu and Sato went out on deck and climbed into their weapons. Kawakubo and Hara entered theirs through the access tubes at 2:30 A.M. For many years afterward I could recall vividly how they looked, all wearing short-sleeved khaki shirts and khaki shorts. All wore white *hachimaki* about their heads, bearing the *Kanji* ideographs "*Shichi Sho Ho Koku.*"

In past ages, *samurai* warriors wore white headbands to keep sweat from their eyes during battles or duels. School children wear them in Japan these days, on athletic field days, as do union workers when conducting a strike. *Hachimaki* are considered the mark of great striving, great determination. Translated into English, the *Kanji* writings meant "Seven Lives To Serve Country," and their meaning in Japanese is "Born seven times to serve the homeland." Americans might understand this hundreds-of-years-old saying who remember what their Revolutionary War patriot Nathan Hale said just before he died.

We were still a few miles short of the launch point when the sonar buzzer sounded in the conning tower. Screw sounds were reported. I raised the periscope and took a look. There, about five miles away in the mist, was a large ship. "Stand by to load the forward torpedo tubes!" I called out, and ordered all hands to battle stations, submerged. I planned to send our four *kaiten* away on their mission, then attack this ship with torpedoes. But, as I kept watching her, I saw that she had all her lights on. I could soon make out a giant red cross painted on her side. "Hospital ship!" I told my crew, and ordered all torpedo preparations halted. The men were disappointed at being cheated of their target. And so was I.

At 4 A.M. I ordered the pilots to stand by for launching. They checked compass settings and depth gauges, then opened the pressurized oxygen valves and fuel cocks in their weapons. At my order, crewmen would release the final tie-down as the pilot reached behind him and pushed a starting lever. Seconds after that, he would move out and face eternity. At 4:10 A.M., as a tribute to those four brave lads, I ordered all of my officers and men to join me in singing "*Gunkan Kaigun,*" the Imperial Navy's marching song (the Japanese counterpart of "Anchors Aweigh"). The *kaiten* pilots, telephone mouthpieces pressed to their lips, sang along. Some of my crewmen dissolved in tears and could not finish the song.

At 4:15 I asked Kawakubo if he was ready. "Ready, Captain!" he answered in a clear, ringing voice. "Good luck to all in *I-47*!" Then, calmly, he added "Goodbye." His weapon moved away smoothly, as did the other three in their turns. As soon as the fourth one was gone I trimmed ship, put about, surfaced, and headed north at full speed. The hospital ship we had to pass was very near, moving in the opposite direction. I could have sunk her easily. Later I was to receive a severe tongue-lashing from a high-ranking officer for not attacking that hospital ship. He would chide me almost hysterically, "Why didn't you sink it? Less than two months later an American submarine sank our hospital ship *Awa Maru* in the China Sea, didn't it?"

My answer was that I had as much fighting spirit as anyone, but I just could not bring myself to torpedo a hospital ship at the same time I committed four fine young men to death.

Such are the quirks of a man's mind. Perhaps I might have attacked that hospital ship if I had met her before I became a *kaiten* submarine captain, or maybe I would have attacked in the final, desperate months of the war. I truly cannot say. But, if I had, one thing is certain. I would not be telling this story. I would have been hanged or shot by the International Military Tribunal after the war.

The same morning mist that had shrouded that hospital ship now hung over the shoreline, obscuring visibility, when my watch showed 5 A.M., the time appointed for simultaneous attack. I waited anxiously for explosions. I was still waiting at 5:05 and at 5:10. Then, at 5:11, a yellowish-red flash of enormous size tore away some of the mist over the enemy anchorage. I watched for more, but my radioman shouted up through the conning tower that he was intercepting an enemy plain language submarine warning message. At least it sounded to him like that, he said. It was "From Commander, Naval Base, Hollandia, to all Allied ships . . . S . . . S . . . S . . . S . . . S . . . ." I agreed with the radioman, and dived the boat at once. There was no trouble during our escape. We were back at Kure on Feb. 1.

Another evaluation conference was held. The 6th Fleet staff members determined that 18 ships had been sunk for the 18 *kaiten* expended. This made a total of 23 ships, including 4 aircraft carriers and 2 battleships according to them, at the cost of 2 submarines (*I-37* and *I-48*), in two missions. Many present were elated over this, but I was not. *I-56* had been turned back, and both *I-37* and *I-48* had been sunk, probably close to their targets. Then, too, there was that plain-language submarine warning. Hollandia suspected submarine presence, no doubt of it. And, too, I had been sighted on the way in, by that patrol vessel. Anchorage attacks were bound to become more difficult to make—perhaps even impossible. I pressed for a change in policy, for a chance to make *kaiten* attacks in the open sea, where odds against us were not so great. So did some of the other submarine captains and this new policy was given tentative approval. But it would be changed and rechanged later.

High officials in the Japanese government tried to keep a bright face on things, despite the war's worsening. And the weather worked for us on Dec. 18, when a typhoon struck the U. S. fleet east of the Philippines and sank 3 destroyers and damaged 20 other ships, including 7 aircraft carriers. But U. S. Army planes from the Marianas began hitting Tokyo three weeks before that.

People at home were beginning to worry. I could tell that Hisako was concerned, although she tried to hide it from me like a good Navy wife. I never told her anything of my missions. Each morning she and our son would bid me farewell at the door of our house. Each evening they would greet me on my return. When there was a mission starting, I would leave as I did on any other day, giving no sign that anything special was to happen. When I did not get home for several days, she knew that I was at sea and would wait patiently until a communications aide from the Kure naval base would come to the house and tell her that *I-47* was heading up the channel. Then she would show her joy and relief by cooking very special meals and being more than usually kindly toward me. I am sure that nothing totally reassured her but my short figure striding up the path to our house. Not even the Emperor's address to the National Diet on its Dec. 26 opening: "The war situation is growing more critical," he told our legislators, "but our army and navy are destroying the enemy wherever he is met."

The Americans took the Philippine island of Mindoro as a jumping-off place for their thrust at Manila in mid-December. Resistance on Leyte was almost completely wiped out a few days after that. American cruisers and destroyers were shelling Iwo Jima regularly when I headed for Hollandia and the 1944 total of merchant ships sunk by Japanese submarines was a dismal sum. Only 58 enemy ships were sunk in the areas where

Japanese submarines were operating, many of them by German U-boats covering the Cape of Good Hope. Only 8 of the ships were sunk in the Pacific!

As a matter of fact, in 1944, *Japanese submarines actually sank fewer enemy ships than the number of submarines we lost!* Our underwater fleet, once ranked with the world's finest, had deteriorated into a *tokko* weapon, flung at the enemy with no hope of victory, only an outside chance of slowing him down.

The Americans landed at Lingayen Gulf, Luzon, in the northern Philippines, on Jan. 9, then started their sweep down the Luzon Plain into Manila, the same route taken by the Imperial Army in its successful invasion three years earlier. We had not one I-boat left in the area with which to attack their amphibious forces. *I-8* and *I-165* were in the Indian Ocean. *I-12* had been lost somewhere in the enemy's rear area. This submarine left Kure on Oct. 4 for a solitary patrol in the eastern Pacific. A very fanciful report claims that two American ships sank one of our submarines there on Nov. 13, but I'm afraid that all that they got for their effort was a whale. *I-12* sank the American SS *John A. Johnson*, northeast of Oahu, and continued to cruise until after the end of the year. She was commanded by Cdr. Kaneo Kudo, a very gentle man, extremely thoughtful of others, who appreciated life's finer things. His boat was last heard from on Jan. 5, 1945, so she was either lost operationally or to a ship or plane that never got credit for the sinking. Long after the war I learned of an incident that took place in the last days of 1944. It concerned a large training ship (a four-masted sailing vessel) which was running supplies between New Zealand and San Francisco. The crew was surprised one day, when a Japanese submarine suddenly surfaced, almost alongside. Its gun crew poured out of the conning tower, and in seconds trained their weapon on this relic of earlier days.

The submarine slowly cruised in a circle around the sailing vessel, whose crew fully expected to be blown out of the water at any moment. Then, suddenly, the deck crew abandoned their gun and went below. A blinker light on the submarine's bridge flashed out, "A very beautiful ship. Good luck on your voyage." Then the submarine dived, and was not seen by the sailing ship crew again. *I-12* was the only submarine we had within thousands of miles of that spot at that time and, knowing Cdr. Kudo, I am sure that he could not bear to blast such a beautiful ship into the sea, so he let her go on her way unmolested.

All that Admiral Miwa had available to send against the

enemy in the northern Philippines were his medium (RO-type) submarines. Of those he sent down, four were lost. Lt. Cdr. Teruo Sugayoshi brought *RO-49* back safely, claiming damage to an Idaho-Class battleship, while Lt. Masahiko Tokunaga claimed he sank two cargo ships with *RO-46*. *RO-50* claimed hits on an aircraft carrier, a cruiser, and a destroyer. The Americans admitted only a damage to the transport USS *Cavalier*, the loss of destroyer *Renshaw*, and the loss of an LST that had to be sunk by her own forces after suffering heavy damage from a submarine's torpedo. Whatever we did accomplish in this sortie, it cost Japan four boats.

RO-115 was the first to go down. Lt. Chuzo Chikuma's boat was summoned from the Indian Ocean and sent into the Philippines. She departed Singapore on Jan. 22 and ran into the screen of a U.S. task force, west of Mindoro, 10 days later. Destroyers *Bell, O'Bannon* and *Jenkins*, plus the destroyer escort *Moore*, teamed up to sink her.

RO-55 was lost on Feb. 7. Lt. Cdr. Koichiro Suwa and his crew were not long out of a shakedown training when they left Kure on Jan. 27. The last word received from Suwa was on Feb. 2. Five days after that, west of Manila, he tried to attack a convoy of ships heading for Leyte Gulf. The destroyer escort *Thomason* picked him up on radar and sank his ship.

The other two submarines lost in this counterattack were trying to carry out evacuation missions. Adm. Halsey's pilots had been so terribly effective in sweeping our Philippines airfields clear of planes that we had a great number of airmen grounded, their planes destroyed, in the archipelago. As in other places, submarines were sent to return them to Japan. At the end of January four submarines were ordered to northern Luzon for this work.

RO-46 was the only submarine that successfully brought passengers home.

RO-112 and *RO-113* (the second of which had been pulled in from the Indian Ocean) were at Takao, Formosa, taking aboard fuel and supplies. They departed there on Feb. 9 and ran into the prowling American submarine *Batfish*. Lt. Toroo Yuchi was taking *RO-112* to Aparri, and was just entering Babuyan Channel when another technique new to us was used against him—radar-controlled torpedo fire. This shows how far ahead of us in equipment development American boats were. USS *Batfish* had radar so dependable she could use its ranges and bearings in solving the ballistic problem associated with firing of torpedoes, while the radars on our submarines, even at the end of the war, were so primitive that they might be referred to in American slang as the "Model T" brand.

RO-112 went down on the night of Jan. 11, and Lt. Kiyoshi Harada, who was trailing behind in *RO-113*, lost his ship and his life to *Batfish* a little more than 24 hours later. USS *Batfish* claims to have sunk a third submarine before getting those two, but I think American crewmen interpreted a premature explosion as a hit. We lost no other boats in that area at that time.

To shrivel our forces more, we lost two transport submarines in January. The first was *I-362*, which left Yokosuka for Woleai on Jan. 1. She was due at her station, midway between Truk and Palau, on Jan. 21. Lt. Cdr. Einosuke Nakashima had already made successful supply runs to Wake Island and Marcus Island, but his luck ran out. He was picked up on the radar of the destroyer escort USS *Fleming* in the darkness of Jan. 18, and sunk.

I-371, as I have already mentioned, was lost to USS *Lagarto*, a submarine, off Bungo Strait, on the way home from a successful supply run to Woleai.

By the middle of February, 1945, the 6th Fleet was down to a total of 7 RO-boats (including the new *RO-56*) and 6 I-boat *kaiten* carriers. Half of our Indian Ocean force had been lost in the Philippines, so *I-8* and *I-165* were called home. *I-351* was completed, but had to be put into use as an underwater tanker, so critical was the shortage of fuel in Japan at the time. The situation seemed hopeless, our problems insurmountable. Then, to make things worse, the American marines landed on Iwo Jima on Feb. 19.

* * *

Chapter 18.

IWO JIMA; OKINAWA.

In September, 1944, the Imperial Navy officially formed a submarine unit with the designation *Tokko* Squadron I, based on Ourazaki, about seven miles southeast of Kure, in the Inland Sea. Rear Adm. Mitsuru Nagai headed this first suicide organization of World War II, which was in existence more than a month before Vice Adm. Takejiro Inishi formed *kamikaze* units in the Philippines. Nagai had three staff officers, one of whom was Lt. Cdr. Mitsuma Itakura, who served as torpedoes and operations officer as well as commanding officer of the base. Ourazaki was base for *kuryu* (midget submarines), which were ordered produced in great numbers, while Otsujima, Hikari and Hirao (all not very far away) were for the training of *kaiten* pilots.

In February, 1945, *Tokko* Squadron II formed, with Rear Adm. Noboru Owada commanding. There seemed at that time no way to stop the enemy short of the homeland's shores, so preparations were made to smash him when he did try to invade Japan itself. A great number of *kaiten*, *koryu* and *shinyo* (high-speed small craft), together with torpedo boats, were scattered at hidden places all along our coastline. They had orders to train and keep developing their proficiency until the enemy was actually in sight of Japan. Then, one great assault would be made on the enemy fleet.

The *shinyo*, of which thousands were produced, were light plywood boats that could carry either two depth charges or an explosive charge in the bow. The method for using depth charges which some *shinyo* employed in the Philippines was to run close to an enemy ship in the darkness, push over depth charges set to detonate at a very shallow setting, then race away. The exploding depth charges would blast in the side of a ship if dropped close enough to it. With a charge set in the bow, of course, *shinyo* could act like *kaiten*, ramming into a ship, then exploding.

The eastern and southern shores of Kyushu (the island where the enemy would most likely make his first landing) were dotted with clusters of these weapons. More were located along Kii Strait (just south of Osaka), in Ise Bay, (south of Nagoya), and along the shores of Sagami Bay (into which Tokyo Bay flows before reaching the Pacific Ocean). We also had them on the eastern shore of Chiba Peninsula (near Tokyo), the east coast of northen Honshu, and on Hokkaido, our nothernmost main island. After the war, we learned that the Allies did, indeed plan to land on Kyushu and follow up with a landing at Chiba.

I-361 made a supply run to Wake Island in January, and right after that was rigged for *kaiten* work. The same was done with *I-363* after it made a run to Woleai and two runs to Marcus Island. *Kaiten* racks were also fitted to *I-366* and *I-367* after each had made a pair of successful supply runs. *I-368* and *I-370*, although designed as supply and transport submarines, were completed as *kaiten* carriers. The new *HA-101* Class of submarines was to replace these larger boats in the transport effort.

Plans had been approved for building 100 of the *HA-101* boats, but only 12 were actually laid down. They were only 147 feet long, and displaced 429 tons. They made 10 knots on the surface, 5 submerged. All had a cruising range of only 3000 miles, but that was considered sufficient for the work they were to do. Each could carry 60 tones of cargo and had a single 25mm machine gun on the bridge for armament. None had torpedo tubes.

In the Japanese phonetic alphabet "*I*" and "*RO*" are the first and second characters, and "*HA*" is the third, so these HA-type boats were our Class "C" ones. On Jan. 29, 1945, the beginning was made on another Class C type of submarine. That was the day *HA-201* was laid down, at Sasebo. Nearly 100 of these were planned, but only 37 hulls were laid down (of which 10 were completed). Had they been ready earlier in the war, they might have been a very effective weapon for Japan. Part of our new emphasis on small ship construction, the *HA-201* Class subs were only 175 feet long and displaced but 377 tons. They could make 13 knots either surfaced or submerged and their designed range of 3000 miles turned out to be 5000. They were called "*Sen-Sho*" (submarine, small), and carried 4 torpedoes for firing through two bow tubes. Deck armament was a 7.7mm machine gun on the bridge. *HA-201* subs were prefabricated in shops, then assembled on the ways, with electric welding used throughout. Construction time was only 12 weeks and we hoped to build 14 a month once production got rolling. Crew strength was 22 men and the boats could dive to 330 feet.

We used the *I-200* series to number our high-speed submarines. The *I-201* Class, built after much study of RO-500 (given us by the Germans) was a revolutionary type. *I-201* herself was completed on Feb. 2, 1945. She was a new thing in submarines, completely streamlined (even her two 25mm machine guns on deck were the disappearing type). Called "*Sen-Taka*" (submarine, high speed), she had nearly a 12-1 length-to-diameter ratio, which made her very sleek. Displacing 1291 tons, these boats would make 15.8 knots on the surface. Once underwater, though, they could make a phenomenal *19 knots*! They could maintain this rapid pace for 55 minutes, then continue underwater for 12 more hours at 3 knots. Or, alternatively, they could move underwater for 45 hours at 3 knots. *I-201* Class boats could dive to 365 feet and carried 10 torpedoes for firing through 4 forward tubes. Eight of these boats were laid down but only three were completed, all of them at Kure.

When Iwo Jima was invaded, the third *kaiten* sortie was made. This was the *Chihaya* Group, named for *Chihaya-jo*, the castle where the Kusunoki family lived. Three boats took 14 *kaiten* to Iwo Jima. *I-368*, under Lt. Cdr. Mitsuteru Irisawa, mounted five, as did *I-370* under Lt. Suzumu Fujikawa. Lt. Cdr. Genbei Kawaguchi's *I-44* carried four of the human torpedoes.

The first two boats left Otsujima one day after the Americans landed on Iwo Jima. *I-44* followed three days later. *I-370* tried to attack a convoy of transports south of Iwo Jima on Feb. 26. The destroyer escort *Finnegan* picked her up on radar before dawn and sank her. She may have launched *kaiten* before being sunk, because our Iwo Jima garrison reported seeing several tall columns of fire out to sea. *I-368* was sunk the following day by planes from USS *Anzio*, an escort carrier that was the nucleus of a hunter-killer antisubmarine group protecting the American amphibious force.

We also lost *RO-43* on Feb. 26. Lt. Seiki Tsukigata had taken this boat out of Kure on Feb. 16. Five days later he torpedoed and badly damaged the destroyer *Renshaw* off Iwo Jima. The enemy ship had to be towed away to safety. *RO-43* got away from surface attackers and escaped their onslaughts again a few days later. But, on the 26th, a plane from USS *Anzio* found and sank Tsukigata's boat.

As for the third of the *kaiten* carries, *I-44*, she was kept down for nearly 47 hours by ships and airplanes, so tight were the patrols around Iwo Jima. When his crew seemed near exhaustion and suffocation, Lt. Cdr. Kawaguchi decided to break off his mission. He headed for home. This so infuriated Admiral Miwa that the 6th Fleet commander ordered Kawaguchi relieved immediately upon return to port. An unjust action, surely, but it points up how desperate the situation was and how desperate men had become. Although *I-44* would almost certainly have been sunk without doing any damage to the enemy had Kawaguchi pressed on, Miwa still felt that he should have.

Other submarine captains, myself included, felt that *I-44's* captain had done the proper thing. Only four men in that boat had death as their mission, not the entire crew. It is much easier to make decisions in the rear area than at the periscope of a submarine in the battle zone. In battle, all responsibility lies with the captain. His judgment, after all his years of training and experiences, must be trusted.

The Americans had planned to land on Formosa and the coast of China and launch a direct invasion of Japan from there. However, our land forces in China had staged a great offensive and overrun some of the air bases from which the Allies had intended to bomb Japan. So they changed their strategy. After the northern Philippines were secured, their new plan was to take Iwo Jima, then Okinawa—each area captured providing support for the next to be taken. Our planners expected something like this so, toward the end of 1944, Iwo Jima and Okinawa were heavily fortified. The defenses were mainly inland, rather than at the beaches. The idea was to fight the enemy at his beachhead at first, then to hit him again and again, much harder, after he had made his way inland.

The fourth *kaiten* sortie to go out(and the second aimed at Iwo Jima) was the *Shimbu* Group. *"Shimbu,"* freely translated, means "The Way Of God's *Samurai.*" Only two submarines made up the *Shimbu* Group, *I-36* and *I-58*. *I-36* was commanded by the youngest man to captain a first-line Japanese submarine, Lt. Cdr. Tetsuaki Sugamasa. He was only 29 years old at the time and 8 years out of Etajima, from which he was graduated in 1937. Each boat carried four *kaiten.* My classmate, Hashimoto, left in *I-58* on March 1. Sugamasa left two days later. *I-36* was called back, due to a change in plans, but *I-58* continued to the attack. Hashimoto did a remarkable job of getting almost to his launching point but he was diverted to take station off Okino Shima in order to provide a radio beacon for two-engine *Ginga* bombers making a long-range *kamikaze* strike from Kyushu against B-29 bomber facilities on Saipan.

On the night of March 10, while Hashimoto was still out, Tokyo was fire-bombed on a raid for which the American air general, Curtis LeMay, did not have official approval or permission. Wave after wave of stripped-down B-29 bombers came in at low level, scattering incendiary bombs. What ensued was what safety officials in Tokyo always have feared most—a fire storm. The fires generated high winds through excessive heat and these winds swept flames across the city, above the ground and buildings—consuming the oxygen beneath them. Japanese died where they stood or sat, not a mark upon them. They simply perished of suffocation. (A similar thing had happened in The Great Kanto Earthquake of Sept. 1, 1923, which was followed by fire storms.) In that 1945 fire, in one night, more Japanese died than the total in atomic bombings of Hiroshima and Nagasaki. Over 125,000 lost their lives, and another 1,000,000 people were left homeless.

This bombing worried me and made it difficult to concentrate on my duties. Hisako was pregnant with our second child and living not far from the base, which American carrier planes hit on Mar. 19. She tried not to show me her fears, and had even made me a *"sen-nin bari haramaki,"* to preserve me in danger. Translated literally, this means "thousand-persons-stitches-stomach-wrapper." Wives, mothers, and sweethearts gave them to their men in war. Worn wrapped about the waist, they were supposed to give a man the protection of the gods. A woman tried to get 1000 different persons to sew one stitch apiece into this band, signifying that the hopes and prayers of 1000 people accompanied it. It was a common sight during the war to see women standing on the street corners for days, until enough passers-by had stopped to complete one. To please Hisako, I wore this *haramaki* together with a small amulet in a brocade sack which she had obtained at a shrine.

On Mar. 13 I met the next group of human torpedoes I was to take into battle. Four submarines were assigned to the *Tatara* Group. These were *I-36, I-44, I-47* and *I-56.* Our mission was named for *Tatara,* a beach near Fukuoka, in northern Honshu where, in the 15th century, a *kamikaze* ("divine wind"), helped hero Tokumine Hojo defeat a Mongol fleet that was attempting to invade Japan.

All four submarines had been re-rigged to carry six *kaiten* each instead of four. And all now had access tubes through which pilots could enter the *kaiten* directly from the submarine's hull. Although I had given up all hope for a Japanese victory, I still had my duty to do it. And my six human torpedoes would have a better chance to do theirs, too, if I could remain underwater during launching operations. No distance from Iwo Jima could now be called safe for surfacing my submarine, so heavy were American ship and air patrols.

Heading my group of *kaiten* pilots was Lt. (jg) Minoru Kakizaki. An Etajima graduate, he had gone to Manus Island in *I-56* with the *Kongo* Group and found nets barring the way to enemy ships. He had also gone out and been called back in *I-36* of the *Shimbu* Group. Two of the other *kaiten* pilots were long-time Navy men, Petty Officers Shigeo Yamaguchi and Hichiro Fukugawa, both of whom had been out twice before. The replacements were both former aviation trainees, Petty Officers Kikuo Shinkai and Yutaka Yokota. These last two men had been in a four-man unit supposed to go out in *I-368.* They replaced two dead men.

I had given the quartet a practice launch on March 16, from *I-47.* Petty Officer Yoshito Yazaki died that day, overcome by fumes that leaked back into his pilot's compartment. Lt. (jg.) Mamoru Miyoshi died a few days later, when his weapon hit the sea bottom after shearing off part of its periscope when striking a target ship. He drowned.

I picked up my six new pilots at Hikari, a second base that had been established not very far from Otsujima. A third base, Hirao, had also been added but most of the men who were trained there were to be shore-based in *kaiten* to meet the final assault on Japan.

I-14, the second enlarged *I-9* type built to buttress the *I-400* submarines, was completed at Kawasaki on Mar. 13. On the 19th, carrier planes hit Kure and we lost *I-205* in the attack. A hit capsized her. She was later righted, but was only 80% completed when the war ended.

On Mar. 21 the first *"Aki"* suicide bomb was used against
enemy ships. This was an aerial *kaiten*, a human bomb slung
beneath the fuselage of an airplane. It was carried out to a
launch point, after which a pilot used its rocket engine for diving into a target. *Aki*, in Japanese, means "autumn," and its
poetic significance was "falling leaves," because it was to shower down on Japan's foes. The enemy called it the *"baka"*
(stupid, or fool) bomb.

On Mar. 18, the Americans began making daily strikes
against Okinawa with carrier planes and continued this daily
until Mar. 23. Admiral Miwa ordered five submarines to go
and sink the enemy carriers—*I-8, RO-41, RO-46, RO-49*, and
RO-56. All were lost.

First to go down was *RO-41*, on Mar. 23. Lt. Yoshikuni
Honda left the Inland Sea with her on Mar. 18, and was
sighted when trying to attack a U.S. carrier task force. The
destroyer *Haggard* dropped depth charges and *RO-41*
broached.

American sources say that Haggard rammed the submarine.
Japanese records say that *RO-41* tried a suicide ram of the
destroyer. Whichever version is true, *RO-46* sank after the
collision, and *Haggard* was so badly damaged that she had to
retire for repairs.

Lt. Cdr. Shigeo Shinohara, who survived the accidental
sinking of *I-169* at Truk a year before, had *I-8*. He did his best,
but it was not good enough. All of *I-8*'s crew went to the bottom on Mar. 31 except Petty Officer Takamasa Mukai. Here is
his story.

"On March 30, in the afternoon, we sighted a convoy and
began pursuing it at first on the surface and then submerged.
At 11:30 P.M. we saw a destroyer coming at us. Captain
Shinohara quickly dived the ship. As we passed the 100-foot
level, depth charges exploded in a cluster near our stern. That
was the first of many depth charge attacks we endured in the
following four hours. Water leaked into the boat, making us
sink almost to the 500-foot mark. In order to keep *I-8* from
plunging still further, we blew the main tank. This gave off a
trail of bubbles that betrayed us to the enemy.

"Finally, after four hours, Captain Shinohara decided to
surface and fight it out. I gathered in the conning tower with
five other men of the forward gun crew. As soon as *I-8* broke
water I leaped out, bare-footed, with the others and headed
forward. We got one round away and had another in the
breech when enemy gunfire splattered around us, wounding

294

me in the foot. The ship took many hits and went down by the stern. I was in great pain from my wound and lost consciousness as I floated off the ship. When I came to, I was in the sickbay of an American destroyer.

"The Americans questioned me and asked the name of our ship. I asked them, 'If your ship was sunk, would you give its name?'"

The ships that sank *I-8* were the destroyers *Morrison* and *Stockton*. She was the 14th of our submarines to be lost since the first of the year.

RO-49 went down five days later. Lt. Cdr. Yasuo Go left Mar. 18 with his boat. He fired torpedoes at American ships on Mar. 26 and wirelessed a report of the action to Kure, but was not heard from again. Go and his crew were sent to the bottom on Apr. 5, west of Okinawa, by the U.S. destroyer *Hudson*.

On Apr. 5 our *HA-102* left Yokosuka with a load of supplies for Marcus Island, the first such run made by a submarine of that class. It was a hazardous mission, with only a single machine gun for offense or defense. A total of six runs were made by boats of this type before the war's end, four of them to Marcus Island. *HA-104* left Yokosuka for Marcus Island on May 10, and *HA-101* departed from the same port on June 17, while *HA-104* started its second run out of Yokosuka on June 26. *HA-103* left Kure for Borodino Island, east of Okinawa, on Apr. 17. *HA-105* departed Kure with a load for Amami Oshima on July 4. That island lies between Okinawa and Kyushu. (It shows how tight the noose was drawing—an outpost right in our territorial waters was cut off!) All boats returned to Japan safely.

In mid-March, having just finished training men in *kaiten* at Hikari, Lt. Cdr. Seihachi Toyomasu was taking *I-53* to Kure for final refitting before going to combat. Enroute, a mine exploded near her stern, seriously damaging the after electrical control panel. Toyomasu managed to get his boat into Kure, but she had to be scratched from the next *kaiten* mission.

Enemy aircraft began mining our home waters in March. They sowed the Inland Sea and its exits to the ocean with magnetic mines, pressure-detonated mines, and impulse mines. More than 12,000 mines of various types were dropped in our waters in the final six months of the war. They cost us more than 125 ships sunk and at least that many more damaged. Masts of sunken Japanese ships made an "iron forest" of Shimonoseki Strait (western exit from the Inland Sea) as they protruded from the water. In time they also became a serious navigational hazard. Bungo Strait was the only reasonably safe exit from the Inland Sea and even it was dangerous. Mines, enemy planes and enemy submarines awaited the unwary.

On Mar. 28 I took *I-47* into Hikari, where we loaded six *kaiten* on board. The pilots came out to the ship and I dived to test the structural strength of the weapons at deep levels, then conducted several *kaiten*-manning drills. Although I had fears when first given command of *I-47*, I was now proud of the ship. We had a good team. They felt lucky and felt that they had a lucky captain, knowing that two submarines had been sunk on their first mission after I turned over command.

All hands were sure I would bring them home safely from any mission. They called themselves the "Never Die Crew of *I-47*." They got this motto from our hull number. Translated directly into English, *"I-47"* means "Class A Submarine, Hull Number 47." The *Kanji* characters making up this are *"shi"* (four), *"nana"* (seven), and *"i"* (I). However, when run together they can also make up *"shinanai,"* which means "Do not die!" or "Never die!" After our two successful approaches within a few thousand yards of enemy anchorage and our escaping without making a contact, the crew felt that nothing could harm them. It made for high professional performance.

A send-off party was held for the *kaiten* men at Kikari on Mar. 28, with Rear Adm. Mitsuru Nagai attending. *Sake* flowed freely and an excellent meal was served. Lt. Cdr. Sadatoshi Toreeda, proposed the first toast to the human torpedoes. Later, we all rose and sang *The Warrior's Song* in their honor. The pilots sat stiffly at attention while the rest of us gave full voice to

"At sea we may sink beneath the waves
On land we may lie beneath green grasses
But we have nothing to regret
So long as we die fighting for our Emperor."

As the evening wore on, the Navy March and other stirring songs were also sung. Many of those present had big headaches next morning when *I-47* got underway from Hikari, because Navy men liked to demonstrate their capacity for *sake*.

A brief departure ceremony, including the presentation of swords to *I-47*'s human torpedoes, was held on shore in the morning. By mid-afternoon I had my boat heading out through Bungo Strait and ordered the bridge cleared. Everything outside Bungo Strait was now considered "enemy waters." I wanted no sightseers on deck should a prowling plane or submarine spot us. I wanted to be able to dive, fast.

This turned out to be a wise precaution. Late that same afternoon we were attacked by Grumman airplanes. My lookouts at first thought they might be covering aircraft from our base at Miyazake, in southern Kyushu. We barely got beneath the surface in time. Actually, those planes were part of the many sweeps the enemy was making to protect his ships gathering off Okinawa for an assault on it. I took *I-47* back to the surface later, and we ran southeast in the darkness.

Next morning, just before 3 A.M., my lookouts sighted what they thought to be two enemy cruisers. I dived *I-47* at once. We were then much south of Kagoshima, at Kyushu's lower end. I ordered "Stand by to load torpedoes!" and eased the boat up to 55 feet. Sound reported a ship 40 degrees off our port bow, sound intensity 3. I wanted a look at this target, so I ordered "Up scope!"

Seconds later I was shouting "Down scope! Dive! Take her down to 200 feet!" What my lookouts had thought were cruisers were a pair of destroyers. They were racing in to attack!

Sound now had both of them on its equipment. Before long the first depth charges (10 of them) came tumbling down. I was able to swing about and present our stern to them before they exploded. Damage to the boat was only minor. No more depth charges came down, surprisingly, even though the enemy did pass directly overhead again. And they remained within sound range for more than 9 hours. I kept easing *I-47* northward, trying to move as silently as possible. The closer I could get to Kyushu, the sooner those destroyers would break off their attack, for fear of our planes at Kyushu bases.

At 1 P.M. my soundman reported no more traces of the enemy on his equipment, but I kept *I-47* down until after dark. At 8 P.M. I surfaced the ship and headed for Tanegashima, a small island just to the south of Kyushu. The first Westerners ever to visit Japan had been cast away there more than 400 years before. I wanted to moor in Tanegashima's habor and survey any damage to my ship and our *kaiten*. On the way to Tanegashima we were once more attacked by aircraft and had to dive again.

On arrival in the harbor, I inspected the *kaiten*. They were badly battered, with great dents from depth charge explosions. *Kaiten* did not have the structural strength of submarines. Their skins were only one-quarter of an inch thick. And the external inspection of our hull disclosed a considerable leak in one of our fuel tanks. I had no choice but to go back to Kure for repairs, and to Hikari for repair or replacement of the *kaiten*. The latter news was disquieting to the *kaiten* pilots when I announced it, and Petty Officer Furukawa pleaded so long and so loudly that Lt. Kakizaki berated him for insubordination. Through clenched teeth I finally said "That's enough, Furukawa!" although I understood and sympathized with his feelings. This would make the third time he'd return from an unsuccessful *kaiten* mission, but there was no arguing with the long streak of oil that marked *I-47's* wake as we put back into port on Apr. 2.

I-58 followed us out in two days, and *I-56,* under Lt. Cdr. Keihi Shoda, left Otsujima on that same date, Mar. 31. *I-44* had a new captain, too, Lt. Cdr. Kiyoshi Masuzawa. He left Otsujima on Apr. 3.

While *I-47* was at Tanegashima and Furukawa was pleading with me, the Americans invaded Okinawa. In spite of the Imperial Navy's hopes and efforts, the U.S. war machine had reached full power. More than 1200 enemy craft, the most powerful armada in world history, assembled off that island, carrying nearly 250,000 troops. The bloodiest battle in history soon followed and the name of my old military mentor at Kagoshima Middle School burned itself into the history of the U.S. Marine Corps.

Mitsuru Ushijima, the man who urged us to enter the service academies so we could later become Japan's military leaders, had become a Lieutenant-General. He commanded Okinawa's defenses. Although Ushijima died and many Imperial Army and Navy men died fighting alongside him, he made the enemy pay a bitter price for this, our last island bastion.

The fourth of the RO-boats sent against enemy forces off Okinawa was sunk on Apr. 9, only three days after leaving the Inland Sea. Lt. Cdr. Masao Kimura's *RO-46* had scouted Ulithi five months earlier, a few days before our *Kikusui* Group of *kaiten* made its attack there. Off Okinawa, Kimura showed the same skill he displayed off Ulithi. He got well inside the screen of escorts that surrounded the enemy aircraft carriers before being detected and was getting ready to launch torpedoes when he was picked up on sonar. The destroyers *Monssen* and *Mertz* sank *RO-46*.

RO-56, under Lt. Masateru Nagamatsu, was the fifth of the submarines sent against enemy forces off Okinawa (besides the *kaiten* carriers of my *Chihaya* Group). She was never heard from after leaving port. USS *Sea Owl* is credited by the Americans with sinking *RO-56* at Wake Island on Apr. 17. Impossible! *RO-56* was nowhere near Wake Island at that time. *I-*

372 was, but she arrived back safely in Japan on the Emperor's birthday, Apr. 29. I think RO-56 either was sunk by a ship or aircraft that never received credit, or that she was damaged in an attack, then kept down by heavy enemy patrols until her crew suffocated. Records of many enemy ships would have to be re-checked, to pinpoint which one might have sunk *RO-56*.

After *I-47* was forced back to Kure for repairs, two of the other three submarines in the *Chihaya* Group were lost. *I-56* was spotted while moving in on a carrier task force. Shoda's boat was overwhelmed by aircraft from the light carrier *Bataan,* plus destroyers *Uhlmann, Heermann, Mertz* and *Collett,* on Apr. 18. Under her new captain, Lt. Cdr. Kiyoshi Matsuzawa, *I-44* went down on the Emperor's birthday, a victim of aircraft from the carrier *Tulagi.*

As for *I-58,* Hashimoto again penetrated the American defenses in spite of many attacks by enemy aircraft along the way. Then, while making for his launch point, he was suddenly diverted to join the battleship *Yamato.* Our great behemoth of a battleship had sortied from the Inland Sea with light cruiser *Yahagi* and 8 destroyers. She was on a *tokko* mission, carrying only enough fuel to get her where she was going, but not back home. *Yamato* had orders to beach herself on Okinawa and add her great 18-inch guns to its defense.

Before *I-58* could rendezvous with *Yamato,* our greatest battleship was sunk, along with *Yahagi* and 4 of the 8 destroyers. More than 300 American carrier planes overwhelmed this force, attacking again and again in waves. The final torpedoes were fired into *Yamato* while she was still rolling over, so concentrated and fierce was the attack. One can probably understand America's growing capacity for war if he considers that she sent as many planes against *Yamato* as we had sent against her great fleet at Pearl Harbor just 40 months before—and had hundreds more to spare for work elsewhere in the western Pacific against us.

Vice Adm. Seichi Ito went down with *Yamato.* He had almost expelled me from Etajima the night before my graduation.

During my final year at the Academy, Ito was a Commander, and director of the Midshipman Corps. Slender and tall, with a slight stoop, Ito smiled a lot. At the same time he was very tough and stern. On the night before our graduation, several of us decided to have a little *sake* celebration. Ito caught us and immediately ordered the entire graduating class to assemble. Then he berated us for not having perseverance. "I have no desire to tell a man that he cannot drink," he said, "but I am stunned and amazed that some of you would violate one of our most stringent regulations on your very last night here! You must realize that the Imperial Navy has many other rules and regulations that also may not be violated under any circumstances. A man must have will power and discipline to observe *all* of them, at *all* times! Yet, some of you are so weak-willed that you could not observe the Etajima no-drinking rule for just one more day. The Navy has no place for men who cannot discipline themselves!"

We were quivering and shaking by the time he finished and had learned our lesson well. So, he decided to let us off without expulsion or other punishment. Fourteen years later, Admiral Ito proved himself to be the man he had been in 1931, one who practiced what he preached. Ordered to take *Yamato* and her escorts to Okinawa, he knew he had no chance of getting there, but was not deterred. He knew the underlying purpose of this sortie. *Yamato* was a great prize that the enemy wanted at the bottom of the sea. Once she was sighted, every available aircraft would be launched against her. This would give our planned *kamikaze* attack a better chance against ships whose overhead shield would be thinner.

Ito did not flinch. "I understand fully," he told the Naval General Staff's special courier who brought him the special orders. "Leave everything to me." *Yamato* went down, but she drew off enough enemy aircraft so that our *kamikaze* got through to hit nearly 30 American ships that day.

While depth charges were falling about *I-47* on Mar. 31, Leading Petty Officer Fujisaki of my crew had teased the *kaiten* men, saying "Your *Tatara* Group is '*tatararea.*' " In Japanese that expression means to have a day filled with misfortune. Still, four of the six pilots soon would have the kind of luck they hoped for. On Apr. 20 I was to take them out again, and four men would be launched at the enemy in their steel projectiles.

Before I took *I-47* to sea, three other submarines left the Inland Sea. These were *RO-57, RO-58,* and *RO-59*—obsolete craft that, after their early work in the Wake Island campaign and defense duty in the Marshalls, had been brought back to Japan. They had served as training boats for crews of new ships under construction. They operated only in Tokyo Bay and the Inland Sea, under strict orders not to venture into the Pacific where they might be mistaken for prowling enemy submarines. By April, 1945, however, even the Inland Sea was no longer a completely safe training area. Enemy planes and enemy-laid mines had made it hazardous, so this trio of boats was ordered to a new training base in Anamizu Bay, on the Noto Peninsula. This is on the west coast of Honshu, in the Sea of Japan, out of range of the big enemy bombers operating from China and the Marianas. These bombers were hitting the homeland often and hard now, wreaking havoc not only with our means to fashion the tools of war, but on our ability to transport within Japan the necessities of life. An enormous black market had built up because of ever-stricter food rationing. City people travelled far into the countryside to buy food from farmers. Many a family bartered its treasured family possessions for enough food to keep a young child or aging relative alive.

Two ships made up the *Tembu* ("heavenly knighthood") Group, *I-36* and my *I-47* boat. Great competition existed between the crews. Each boat had launched *kaiten* twice (on the *Kikusui* and *Kongo* missions) and each had one *kaiten* mission cut short. Now both would have a chance to do what I and other submarine captains had long been advocating. Instead of attacking great assemblies of closely defended warships at anchor, the pair of us were ordered to use our *kaiten* and torpedoes against the enemy's thinly guarded supply lines. We were to patrol along the Ulithi-Okinawa line and ambush ships carrying men, food, oil and ammunition to the Americans on and near Okinawa. The future of the *kaiten* would depend on how well we did.

I left Apr. 20 from Hikari, just 9 days before Hashimoto returned with *I-58*. When he could not rendezvous with *Yamato*, he was given orders to "rush in and fight to the death." Again Hashimoto performed the amazing feat of piercing the enemy screen and got ready to release his *kaiten*. And again, a few hours short of his launch point, he received another change of orders, "Put out into the Pacific, and attack enemy supply lines."

I-58 was then to the west of Okinawa and patrols were so heavy that steering directly east was simply out of the questions. Hashimoto had to run south along the China coast (all the way past the southern tip of Formosa) before daring to swing east. He then started north to attack the enemy off Okinawa, but was summoned home while enroute. Upon arrival he reported having been attacked by enemy aircraft no less than 50 times in the 29 days he spent at sea.

One more submarine was lost during April, five days after I sortied in the *Tembu* Group. It was *RO-109*, Lt. Cdr. Kazuo Ebato, which had left Sasebo for the Okinawa area on Apr. 12. She and *RO-50*, the only two medium type submarines remaining in Vice Adm. Miwa's forces, were ordered to patrol east of Okinawa. Ebato was intercepted on Apr. 25 by the high-speed destroyer-transport USS *Bass*, and sunk.

The American president, Mr. Roosevelt, died during the second week in April. Some Japanese took hope in this but most realized that the war machine could not be stopped by just one man's death. On Apr. 8, a new Cabinet had taken over our government, under Baron Kantaro Suzuki, a naval officer. Although none of us knew it, he was under personal and direct orders from the emperor to seek some way of ending the war.

By the end of April the 6th Fleet was in a terrible state. We had more submarines in our training divisions than we had on our active, combat-ready list. There were 17 training boats. These included the two old minelayers *I-121* and *I-122*, the six old cruiser types *I-155*, *I-156*, *I-157*, *I-158*, *I-159* and *I-162*, the eight obsolete medium types *RO-57*, *RO-58*, *RO-59*, *RO-62*, *RO-63*, *RO-64*, *RO-67* and *RO-68*, and *RO-500* (which we had received from the Germans).

Available for active duty were 14 submarines. *I-351* was a gasoline tanker. Three other submarines (*I-369*, *I-372* and *I-373*) were also engaged in transport work. *I-36*, *I-47*, *I-53* and *I-58* were *kaiten* carriers, with *I-361*, *I-363*, *I-366* and *I-367* soon to join us in this work. *I-165* was being converted also. Plans were ready to convert the six old cruiser types I mentioned to this work. Actually, Japan had one lone submarine left *(RO-50)* ready to fight the enemy in the old manner with conventional torpedoes only.

True, we had four large submarines being made ready that could carry a total of 10 special-type bombers out against the enemy, but these were of no use to us at the moment. Fuel was in very short supply and the planes and pilots for those boats were not ready or trained. Nor were any of the high-speed *I-201* Class boats yet available. As for the HA-types, they totalled very little in offensive power. The mighty submarine fleet of Japan, like its mighty surface fleet, had been pared down to a thin and desperate skeleton.

So I departed Hikari with mixed feelings. Behind me at home were a son and pregnant wife whom I feared faced tremendous hardship, who might have no future the way things were going. And, in *I-47*, I had an odd morale situation. The six *kaiten* men were filled with renewed hope, their spirits were high and they were determined to send six large enemy ships to the bottom. All wanted to die. Any possibility of not dying might throw them into a panic, as it had Fukugawa at Tanegashima. My crew were also eager. They wanted to help these *kaiten* men kill six enemy ships; wanted to kill others with our torpedoes. They wanted to outdo *I-36*, then to come back and boast about it. So I had men who wanted to die, and others who wanted to live. I suppose that I, being in command, was probably the only man on board who thought at all of the general situation; who gave thought to the future's darkness.

Chapter 19

DEFEAT BECOMES CERTAIN.

It was *"sakura no jiki"* (the time of cherry blossoms) in Japan when *I-47* left Hikari in the *Tembu* sortie. Our *kaiten* pilots stood on their weapons, *hachimaki* about their foreheads and cherry blossom branches in their arms as we left port. During the first week of cruising we sighted no enemy ships. I spent much of the time conducting loading drills for the pilots. I would usually order these without warning in the morning. At the command "Man all *kaiten!*" the pilots would race for their access tubes. The technicians managed always to be loitering near these. Each would follow his pilot through the tube to the weapon's lower hatch. Once the pilot was in, the technician would secure the hatch, retreat through the tube, and close another hatch in our hull.

I kept a stop watch in my hand, letting it run until the last pilot reported "Manned and ready!" over his telephone. After many drills, they reduced their manning time from 2 minutes to 30 seconds. This pleased me. Not only did the drills keep the pilots from fretting, but the speed they attained could prove useful should we make a sudden contact. The access tubes were kept full of sea water while we cruised and were blown free of water when a drill started, so pilots could crawl through them. In actual attacks they had to be flooded once the weapons were manned, to break suction and let *kaiten* get free of the racks easily.

I-36's crew had a great rivalry going with mine. They, too, had a nickname for their boat. They ran together the characters *"i"* (I), *"sa"* (three) and *"mu"* (six), to make *"isamu."* That means "good luck." Late in the afternoon of Apr. 29, after we had conducted Emperor Worship to honor our ruler on his birthday, the wireless operator handed me a message he had intercepted. It was a report from Sugamasa's boat, telling of an attack *I-36* had made two days before. Our Navy's youngest submarine captain had come across a convoy of 30 ships, and fired only four *kaiten,* the other pair being inoperative. Sugamasa reported sinking four transports.

This was great news to me. It bore out my contention that submarines and *kaiten* were better suited for operations against the enemy's supply lines than against clusters of warships. But the news was dismaying to my crew and the *kaiten* pilots. *I-36* was now ahead of us in ships sunk. We had not yet sighted any targets. The pilots were especially edgy. The desire to down an enemy had been building in them for months.

Some days earlier I had held a send-off party for the pilots, knowing that there would be no time once we sighted an enemy. My officers provided the best selections from our stock of tinned foods, plus some beer. The six young gentlemen seemed outwardly cheerful during the proceedings, but you could read in their eyes their great desire. For more than seven months they had been training to leap into eternity, taking hundreds (or even thousands) of the enemy with them. Waiting until we sighted targets became unbearable for them, especially since their earlier disappointments.

We finally made a sighting, on May 1. It was in the evening, about an hour after sunset. We were then east and south of Okinawa, well outside the thick screen of enemy warships. One lookout sighted a ship at 12 miles, getting it in his binoculars even before our surface radar gave an indication. After confirming the sighting visually myself, I ordered full speed on the surface in an attack approach. As we moved in, my radarman called out "Targets on the scope!" and I dropped to the radar room for a look at the screen.

"Load all forward tubes!" I ordered when I returned to the conning tower. *Kaiten* were of little effect in the darkness. The pilots were not likely to see much, and once launched they were gone forever. I was back on the bridge in a few seconds, unable to believe what lay before me. There were more than a dozen ships in convoy, and not one seemed aware that we were near. I decided that either the enemy's antisubmarine successes had made him over-confident and slack, or that his intelligence sources were faulty and made him think he had nothing to fear from Japanese submarines.

Nonetheless, I took no chances. I dived *I-47* and kept moving in. Lt. Kawamoto took turns with me at the night periscope as the range shortened to 2 miles. By that time we had a good torpedo firing setup, with the targets to pass before us from right to left. My torpedoes would run less than 1 mile. I slowed *I-47* until she was almost dead in the water and told the torpedo men to stand by.

"Fire One!" I called out, and pressure in the boat changed slightly as the first Model 95 raced away. Three more followed in quick succession. Lt. Kakizaki and the other *kaiten* pilots stood near the conning tower, listening. Time ticked away and we heard an explosion, followed soon by another then, after a while, a third. I reported to the crew that *I-47* had scored three hits, and ordered the submarine taken down to 250 feet while the sound watch listened for enemy propellers. By back tracking in the direction from which the torpedoes had come the escorts could start their search for us. No high-speed screw sounds were picked up, however. Either there had been no escorts or they were too busy assisting the ships we had hit. *I-47* glided away unmolested.

At dawn of the next day I was on the surface, charging our batteries for a day's run underwater. I had not forgotten lessons learned in the Solomons. We submerged after a while and were underwater about three hours when Lt. Kawamoto, at the periscope, sighted more ships. The crew went rapidly to their battle stations, and I ordered all *kaiten* manned. The pilots dashed for their access tubes. Soon all six reported manned and ready. Half of the tie-downs had long since been loosed. Any or all *kaiten* could now be released from within the hull upon my signal. With *I-47* at periscope depth, each *kaiten* would launch at a depth of 35 feet.

So far as I could make out, there were only two targets in sight, a cargo ship and a destroyer. I launched Lt. Kakizaki and Petty Officer Yamaguchi at them, in *Kaiten 1* and *4*. Then a third target, a destroyer, came into view. I launched Petty

Officer Furukawa, in *Kaiten 2*, at this ship. Each man had been given the course he was to follow, my navigator having worked out the interception problem in the conning tower. After running along at 35 feet for a specified number of seconds, each was to come up to a depth of 6 feet and raise his periscope. If all went right, he would find himself about 400 yards off his target's beam. He could then shift to his final course, line up with the center of his target, crank down his periscope, and race into the enemy's side.

Soon three large explosions were distinctly heard by all hands. I reported three *kaiten* hits to the crew. They were overjoyed. They began cheering and singing. With no more targets in sight, I ordered the three remaining pilots back into the hull and began clearing out of the area. I knew only too well how rapidly the Americans could respond to a sinking or a submarine contact. The area would be jammed with enemy ships and planes before long, just as in the Solomons whenever I had been detected there.

We patrolled along the Okinawa-Guam line for three more days without sighting any more enemy ships. I made a wireless report of the May 2 action and kept searching. Then, on the morning of May 6, we sighted a British cruiser of the *Leander* class. I launched Lt. Maeda at this ship, and was so sure he made a hit that I reported it to 6th Fleet via radio. They acknowledged my report, and ordered *I-47* home. As I entered Kure on May 12 I was filled with satisfaction. I was sure I had sunk six enemy vessels. Sagamasa's *I-36* was already back, claiming eight sinkings, four each with *kaiten* and conventional torpedoes. Fourteen ships, and both submarines safely back! Japanese submarines hadn't done this well since the early days of the war. Hope rose within me. Perhaps 6th Fleet would not realize that behind the enemy's lines was where it should be sending its submarines, not charging into his best ships, men and equipment.

Vice Adm. Tadashige Daigo was Commander, 6th Fleet, when *I-47* got back, having relieved Miwa on May 1. One of our best submarine commanders did not live to serve under him. This was Cdr. Eitaro Ankyu, who had made a name for himself in the Indian Ocean, and also made the top number (16) of transport runs from Rabaul to New Guinea.

Besides his formal reputation as a cool planner and a bold fighter, Ankyu had an informal one among submarine men. He was considered our best drinker. When at home in Kure, where his family lived, he was a model father and husband. But away, he could outlast any of us in a drinking bout. Only

Tsuso Inaba, who had commanded *I-6* and *I-36*, could come anywhere near our boisterous comrade. The rest of us would be long asleep while Ankyu was still drinking toasts to the Emperor.

It was sad that Ankyu, after facing so many perils far from home and surviving them, should die in the Inland Sea. It happened on Apr. 12. Ankyu had been transferred from command of *I-38* to an instructor's post at the Kure submarine school. He was out on a training run in *RO-64*, the obsolete sub captained by Lt. Cdr. Keigo Muto. Besides the crew of 50 men, there were 30 trainees on board at the time studying attack tactics under Cdr. Ankyu, when *RO-64* hit an American-laid mine. She sank at once and came to rest in 140 feet of water, where all on board died. The ancient submarine did not have any escape device in her and we had no submarine rescue vessels. There might have been an outside chance to raise *RO-64*, if large ships could have brought into use, but mines barred them. The route between Kure and the spot where *RO-64* went down was littered with them.

Some American accounts state that *RO-67* was lost in a similar manner a few days later in the same area. That is amusing. *RO-67* survived the war, and her hulk was later put to use as a pontoon at Sasebo, a base used by the U.S. Occupation Forces. Her commanding officer survived the war and later held the post of second-in-command at Kure when the Japanese Maritime Self-Defense Force was developed.

Operation of midget submarines *(koryu)* ended at Okinawa before I went on the *Tembu* Mission. I may as well tell here about those in the Philippines, too.

In the summer of 1944, when the high command felt that an enemy attack on the Philippines was due to come soon, 10 midget submarines were sent to the island of Cebu and placed under the command of Rear Adm. Kaku Harada. Earlier, in command of submarine transport operations out of Rabaul, Harada had taken over the 33rd Base Force at Cebu. Midget submarines were something of a speciality with him. As CO of IJN *Chiyoda* before the war, he oversaw their development and trained men to operate them. Forty-two men reported to Harada and commenced training.

In December, 1944, the midgets went out on many sorties, first being alerted by a lookout station on the northern tip of Mindanao whenever enemy ships were passing through the Philippines. One *koryu* was lost and 4 damaged beyond further use in this effort, while Harada claimed the sinking of 11 cargo ships, 4 destroyers, 2 cruisers, and 1 carrier. When the enemy took Cebu on Mar. 28, 1945, the remaining *koryu* were scuttled and their crews, together with the technicians, retreated to the mountains to fight on with Army troops.

Koryu were sent to Okinawa in January, 1945, as were hundreds of *shinyo,* the *tokko* motorboats. Also sent were nine *kaiten* under Lt. Fujio Kawai. These last never arrived. Pilots, crews and technicians were lost enroute, when the ship transporting them was sunk.

When the enemy assaulted Okinawa, the 33rd *Koryu* Group was there, with 6 midget subs and 130 men. Three midgets went out to attack enemy ships on Mar. 25. Only one returned, its captain reporting that he had hit an enemy ship with two torpedoes. The next day two midgets went out, with one coming back. It reported hitting an American cruiser. This may actually have been the destroyer *Halligan,* which was torpedoed and sunk that day. Either the midget, or *RO-49,* about which I speculated earlier in this chapter, got that ship.

The Americans wiped out our nest of *shinyo* (our suicide surface craft) when they landed on Kerama Retto, next to Okinawa, to set up artillery for shelling the larger island. The only other sorties by *koryu* from Okinawa were made on Mar. 30 (when one went out) and on Apr. 5 (when two went out). All three reported that they made no hits. By Apr. 7 the enemy was on Okinawa in great force and closing in. The remaining *koryu* were scuttled and the 33rd Group wirelessed 6th Fleet that its members were joining Army troops. Nothing was ever heard from them again.

At home, submarine construction continued. *I-373* was completed on Apr. 14 at Yokosuka. She was destined to be our last submarine sunk. *I-352* was launched at Kure on Apr. 23, but was destined never to reach completion. And, at Kure, the building of midgets went ahead so rapidly that at war's end we had a massive drydock filled with them, almost ready to go.

I-351 left Kure on May 1 for Singapore, under Lt. Cdr. Noboru Okayama. She took out clothing, ammunition, and aircraft spare parts, arriving May 15. The enemy landed on Borneo that day, his aim being to cut us off from a great supply of oil that was so pure in its natural form that the Combined Fleet used to pipe it, without refining, directly into the bunkers of our warships.

Germany surrendered early in May, and Japan found herself standing alone against the world. A one-ship *kaiten* sortie was made on May 5, when Lt. Kunio Taketomi left Otsujima with *I-367.* He launched one *kaiten* bearing Petty Officer Masaaki Ono at the enemy, but no others. Upon returning to port June 3 he reported that two of his remaining *kaiten* had suffered mechanical failure, one had rudder trouble and the fifth suffered leakage into the pilot's chamber. This one-ship mission had the name *"Shimbu."* Made up of different ideographs than the name of the earlier *Shimbu* Group, this latter designation translates into English as "advancement of the *samurai* way."

On the day before *I-351* arrived in Singapore, I gave over command of *I-47* to Lt. Cdr. Masakichi Suzuki. The death of Cdr. Ankyu in *RO-64* had left a gap in the ranks of combat-experienced instructors at the submarine school, so I was transferred into his place. When I arrived at the school, on the north side of the Kure base, there were already two classes awaiting me. Each contained 30 officers. The HA-Class of submarines were being completed then and these men had to be trained quickly.

I took over the attack section of the school's curriculum, which covered most of the 15-week training course. Classroom sessions included lectures and blackboard illustrations in the theory and principles of submarine attack. They were followed by laboratory sessions, during which students trained on simulators and attack training devices. After that, I could take groups out in one of the training submarines moored nearby. I then conducted approach and attack exercises, using small craft as practice targetships. All drills were repeated over and over again as each student took his turn at the duties he would have in a combat situation. Most of our operations were conducted in Hiroshima Bay. We also used Iyonada Bay, near the western end of Shikoku Island in the Inland Sea, until enemy activity became so frequent that we even had to get out of the Inland Sea for a while.

While I still had my first class of students under instruction, four more *kaiten*-carrying boats went out. It was the *Todoroki* Group. In Japanese this means "great roar," like the sound of a cannon. Two transport submarines, *I-361* and *I-363*, joined with *I-36* and an obsolescent boat, *I-165*, to make up this sortie. The last boat carried only two *kaiten*, and left port well after the other two ships had departed. One of them, in fact, had already been sunk by the time *I-165* sailed.

Lt. Masaharu Matsuura took *I-361* out of Kure for the Okinawa area on May 24, carrying five human torpedoes. She was never heard from again, and was sunk on May 30 by aircraft from the escort carrier USS *Anzio* without, I think, ever firing either *kaiten* or other torpedoes. As for *I-363*, Lt. Sakae Kihara brought her back to port after 31 days at sea without a

310

victory. He sighted enemy ships on several occasions, but *I-363's* sluggish 13-knot speed could not get him into position for making a launch.

I-165 left Hikari on June 15 for a patrol east of the Marianas. We never heard from her again, but Japanese radio intelligence indicated to the 6th Fleet that she achieved good results before land-based aircraft from the Marianas downed her on June 27. Lt. Yasushi Ono commanded this ship.

I-36 left Hikari on June 4, carrying six *kaiten.* She met an enemy convoy on June 24, but when two successive *kaiten* failed to operate, Sugamasa became disgusted. He fired a spread of conventional torpedoes, later reporting that he had hit a transport that seemed damaged at first, then quickly picked up speed and ran away. On June 28, Sugamasa launched one *kaiten* at a transport or cargo ship, but was quickly pinned down by its counterattacking escort. *I-36* seemed doomed when two *kaiten* pilots volunteered to be launched against the prowling destroyers overhead. Although he wasn't sure *kaiten* could be released from a depth of more than 200 feet, Sugamasa tried. His crew heard one loud explosion and several small ones and *I-36* was able to get away during the confusion. She claimed at least one destroyer for the day's action. Sugamasa's remaining *kaiten* pilots had to return to port with him when their weapons failed to function. *I-36* was certainly the *"isamu"* (good luck) ship her crew had named her. She not only survived heavy damage from the depth-charging she received on June 28, but also just barely missed being sunk right in Bungo Strait on the way home. The American submarine *Gunnel* fired four torpedoes at her shadowy shape in the blackness of July 6, but they passed astern of her and exploded against the shoreline.

The plan to bomb Washington and New York with planes from the massive *I-400* Class submarines was abandoned and replaced by one to bomb and torpedo the locks of Panama Canal. Only 5 of the proposed 18 giant boats were laid down. Construction of *I-405* was halted in January, 1945, when all emphasis was placed on smaller craft of the *tokko* type. So only four were left. By May two of the big boats, *I-400* and *I-401*, were ready. These, together with *I-13* and *I-14*, were formed into SubRon 1, under Capt. Tatsunoke Ariizumi. But, they could not yet go out to fight. The construction of special *Seiran* float aircraft for them had been delayed by bombings of the Aichi Aircraft Factory, in Nagoya. Another delay was in providing pilots for these planes. The men trained at Kasumigaura (near Tokyo) in other aircraft types, but had no practice in the kind of special operation intended. Then enemy B-29's took a hand, laying mines so thick in the Inland Sea that there was not even enough cleared area in which submarines could practice.

In early June, just after *I-351* got back from Singapore with 132,000 gallons of high octane gasoline, some of our training submarines, plus the two giant boats, were ordered to proceed through Shimonoseki Strait to Anamizu Bay, on the west coast of Honshu. *I-13* and *I-14* were to train at Ominato, near the very northern tip of Honshu.

During this transfer of ships we lost the old minelayer submarine *I-122*. A group of American submarines (a wolfpack nicknamed "Hydeman's Hellcats") had slipped through Tsushima Strait in a daring move. They then operated in the Sea of Japan against the shipping between Korea and Honshu. One of them, USS *Skate*, put two torpedoes into Lt. Sosaku Mihara's boat and *I-122* went down on June 10, an event that put a damper on the good feelings I had at the time.

HA-201 and *HA-202* were completed at Sasebo on May 31, and on the following day I went to Tokyo with the 6th Fleet chief of staff, Capt. Hankyu Sasaki. There Admiral Soemu Toyoda, commander-in-chief of the Combined Fleet, heaped praise on me for my operations with *kaiten*. He then presented me with a sword and the Medal of Merit, Double. A Medal of Merit, Single, was honor enough for any naval officer, so I was overwhelmed to receive the double. During the days following, naturally, I was in very high spirits.

On June 5 a typhoon hit the American fleet off Okinawa, damaging 34 ships. Our *kamikaze* also struck it, damaging another 5 ships, but neither "divine wind" had an appreciable effect on the enemy's ability to wage war against us. Destroyers had already shelled Paramushiro, out of which our submarines operated against the Aleutians. And carrier-based aircraft were becoming a common sight in the skies over Kyushu. The enemy had started his campaign of attrition against our aircraft there, in preparation for the invasion of Kyushu.

With American submarines roaming about in the Sea of Japan, that area was no longer a safe place where young submariners could learn the arts of war. I took up duties at Otake, a base at the extreme western end of Hiroshima Prefecture, facing the Inland Sea. Until the war ended, we confined our training cruises to the swept waters just off Kure. And we never dared take a boat into those, really, until the minesweeping command reported the area clear.

On June 22 we lost two more of our dwindling force of submarines when B-29's showered their bombs on Kure. *I-204* and *I-352* were almost completed. Both were hit and neither was completed by the time the war ended. For all practical purposes, the enemy had sunk these two submarines.

On that same day the Emperor held an Imperial Conference at which he told our top people that the war had to be ended. The Japanese people were suffering severely, he said, and could not endure much more hardship. Also, he added, he wanted the widespread destruction brought to a halt before Japan became weakened beyond the point of possible recovery. On that day, also, all organized Japanese resistance on Okinawa ended. My old teacher and inspiration, Lt. Gen. Mitsuru Ushijima, took his life in *seppuku*. More than 115,000 of his men had died in the 82-day struggle to beat back the enemy.

On the next day an Imperial message went out, stating that the crisis for Japan was "unprecedented." But die-hard Army leaders over-rode it with one of their own, urging all Japanese to continue the struggle until victory was won. They predicted that we would slay the enemy to the last man if he dared set foot upon our beloved homeland.

One week later the B-29's came over again, making a night fire-bombing raid on Kure. Two-thirds of the city and most of the great naval arsenal of which Japan was so proud, were wiped out. More than 2000 people died. I was then at Otake, but my family lived in Kure and it was nearly 36 hours before I could get away from the base to search for my pregnant wife and our son. I found them, dazed, among the ruins of our house, from which wisps of smoke still rose. They had rushed to an air raid shelter when the alarm sounded and so had suffered no physical injury. My heart sank when I saw the sadness in Hisako's eyes. This tender girl, whom I had first met when she was 16 and I was 23, was a picture of forlorn misery.

Hisako's and my "first confrontation" had come as a surprise to me on January 7, 1933. While home on leave that day, I was invited to accompany my mother and father to the home of Mr. and Mrs. Shigeru Ankyu. We were served by a very pretty girl wearing *fumisode,* the special elaborately-sleeved *kimono* worn only on formal occasions. Later, on the way home, my parents asked me what I thought of this girl, who had struck me as a very pretty, bright, and well-mannered young lady.

A surprised thought occurred to me. "Was that our *omiai?*" I asked.

My parents nodded, signifying that she was the girl they had chosen for my future wife. Next day, when I went to the train station to return to my ship, Hisako was there with her elder brother. His presence meant that she, in turn, approved of me. I thought of her often on board the battleship *Mutsu,* although I never mentioned her name to anyone. The China Incident had begun just before my graduation from Etajima and I felt that I could not ask a girl to share the life of a Navy man in those troubled times. We were at sea a great deal of the time when not studying hard in a service school, which left very little time for a family life. So I did not express my true feelings to Hisako for, it is difficult to believe, *five more years!* By then the "incident" had bloomed into a full-scale war. I had spent the intervening time at sea in the destroyer *Kaki,* submarines *RO-27, I-55, I-7* and *I-52,* and the cruiser *Nagara.* Meanwhile, in spite of the hard life of a naval officer, my classmates were getting married one after another. So, in the summer of 1938, I made formal application to the Navy Ministry for permission to get married. It was approved several months later and, on Feb. 11, 1939 (anniversary day of the Japanese Empire's founding by Emperor Jimmu) Hisako and I were married at Chindhae, Korea. I was then serving in the destroyer *Shikinami.* Five days later, my ship received sudden sailing orders, because Russian patrol craft were harassing Japanese fishing boats off Vladivostok

Hisako later confessed that she wept all the time I was absent and was sorry to have married a naval officer. In May I received orders to Torpedo School at Yokosuka, so the journey there was our delayed honeymoon. After six months at Yokosuka, Hisako and I spent another five at Kure while I attended submarine school. That was the extent of our married life together until 1944, when I was ashore fitting out *I-47.* Now I was more or less ashore again, but under what awful conditions!

After the raid on Kure, there was nothing I could do but take my wife and son back to Otake with me. Everything we owned had been destroyed in the bombing. We spent one night together at an inn, then I found a room for Hisako and Shuichi at a farm. Leaving some money with her, I returned to the school. Eleven days later, while holding a night class, I was interrupted by a messenger bearing a note. "Son born last night," it said. "Mother and baby doing well." I got time off the next day, borrowed a bicycle, and pedalled it furiously over hilly roads for three hours. The roads were rough, and I was laden down with canned milk and some vegetables, which were very hard to obtain at that time.

There, by Hisako's side, wrapped in white, lay our second son. He had been conceived while I was preparing to go out on the *Kongo* Mission, so I named him for it. In the tiny room of that lonely farm on a mountainside, I peered proudly into the infant's face, and declared that his name would be Goichi, meaning "first in strength." *"Kon"* and *"go"* (steel) meant, "metal, strong." As I spoke the name of our second son, Hisako broke down, the first time she had done so since the early days of our marriage.

"When will this horrible war end?" she cried at me. "We have no home, no clothes, nothing! There was the little money you gave me, but I could buy practically nothing with it! It took much searching in the black market just to find enough to keep us alive. You, my husband, are a naval officer. You must fight. It is your duty. But I have no willingness to struggle anymore. Nor does anyone else! No one believes that Japan will defeat the enemy when he comes to our shores, no matter what the newspapers or radio say. Our land will be reduced to ashes and your sons and I with it. Our only choice will be dying under bombs, or through starvation!"

I tried to comfort my wife, but what could I do? What could I say? My heart was breaking in two. There was my family to consider, but also my duty. I was a naval officer, sworn to defend *all* wives and children of Japan, not just my own. To do less was to be a coward, a shirker.

I calmed Hisako as best I could, left the food and some more money with her, promised to get more, then returned to the school. There I hurled myself into my tasks, impelled by a great desire for revenge. I had only one real weapon, my experience. If I could pass some of this to my students, they could better face the enemy. The next few weeks were a frenzy of work for me, broken sharply by an incident that occurred near the end of the month.

I had set out early in the morning for the western end of the Inland Sea, as tactical officer in command of four training submarines and one target boat. Lt. Cdr. Iwao Teramoto (who had *I-36* during the *Kikusui* and *Kongo* sorties) was an instructor with me at the school. He was on board the target boat. Between us, we were to direct the exercises. I would supervise the students in their approach and attack techniques and Teramoto would judge and criticize the results. In the afternoon, we would exchange positions and duties.

Training started early in the morning. In the middle of the second approach run, the wireless operator on the submarine I

315

was riding handed up an air raid warning message. I signalled all submarines to dive at once and the target boat to run for a sheltered cove along the shoreline. It didn't get there in time, though. Through the periscope I watched the Grumman fighters peel off, dive, and open fire on Teramoto's craft with rockets and machine guns. I could not help him, of course, but the lone 13mm machine gun on his boat kept up a steady fire. Still, it was clear that the target boat did not have a chance.

All of a sudden I saw flame flare from its engine spaces. When the Grummans flew away, I surfaced and went alongside. No one was visible on deck as we approached and my boarding party found several men lying about, seriously wounded. Eight others were dead. Teramoto was one of them. As he stood at his post on the bridge, three bullets had pierced him.

How strange was fate! Had the attack come a few hours later, I would have been standing in his place. Again the fortunate Orita had escaped death. No wonder the *I-47* crew had thought me a lucky captain and named their ship "Never die!"

The eighth *kaiten* sortie began departures on July 14, led by Lt. Cdr. Saichi Oba's *I-53*. He had the first of six boats in the *Tamon* Group, so-called after the "youth name" of Masashige Kusunoki's son, the name he used until adulthood. Oba had 6 *kaiten* on board, of which two failed to function. One of the others, so far as I can tell, sank the U. S. destroyer escort *Underhill*. *I-53* got back to port 29 days later with a report of successes.

Lt. Cdr. Hashimoto took *I-58* out from Hirao two days after *I-53* left, a false start that had to be repeated. My former ship, *I-47*, left Hikari on July 19, found no enemy ships, and came back on Aug. 11 without firing *kaiten*.

I-367 brought her five *kaiten* back on Aug. 16, after 28 days at sea. Lt. Kunio Taketomi had also not found the enemy. The fifth boat, *I-366*, left Hikari on Aug. 1. She was back on Aug. 16, three *kaiten* expended, two inoperative. On Aug. 9, Lt. Takami Tokioka was detected by a group of enemy warships. When attacked, *I-366* launched three *kaiten*, bearing Lt. (jg) Kenji Naruse, Petty Officer Tokuei Uenishi, and Petty Officer Hajime Sano. Although 6th Fleet thought that those *kaiten* sank three large transports, Americans credit the destroyer escort *Johnnie Hutchins* with sinking all three of these human torpedoes. I'm afraid that 6th Fleet's estimate was incorrect. Investigation showed that there were no large transports in that area at that time, only a large group of enemy destroyer escorts, bent on killing off any Japanese submersible encountered.

The last of the *Tamon* boats, *I-363*, was at sea for only eight days. Lt. Sakae Kihara left Hikari on Aug. 8, heading for waters east of Okinawa. He was soon diverted into the Sea of Japan, was strafed by enemy planes en route there, then was recalled to Kure.

Our "underseas aircraft carriers," meanwhile, had gone out on a sortie. *I-400* and *I-401*, after much delay, had finally received their aircraft. *I-401* was under Cdr. Shinsei Nambu (later an officer in Japan's Maritime Self-Defense Force). Cdr. Utsunosuke Kusaka had *I-400*. These submarines dwarfed the USS *Argonaut* and the French *Surcouf*, considered the world's largest submarines until the existence of ours was revealed after the war. Although somewhat unwieldy because of their size, both boats could crash-dive to periscope depth in 56 seconds, considered quite an achievement.

Pilots for the aircraft of these submarines trained at Kasumigaura, then at Fukuyama, in Hiroshima Prefecture. They were of the 901st Air Group, formed strictly to train aviators for these submarines. The plane they flew was a low-winged monoplane with floats. Overall length was 35 feet and the wingspread 40 feet. Hydraulic mechanisms folded and unfolded its wings and also raised or lowered the fuselage on its float struts, making for faster and simpler storage. The *Seiran's* pilot could also jettison his floats in mid-air, should he desire increased speed for a *kamikaze* dive.

There was not enough fuel available in the Kure area for the two giant boats to obtain a full load, so in mid-April they started for Dairen, Manchuria, to take on fuel. After that, they were supposed to go to the Inland Sea, and start training pilots. *I-401* hit an American-laid mine off Himejima, Kyushu, and had to put back into Kure for repairs, but *I-400* made the round trip without incident. While his *I-401* was being repaired, Capt. Ariizumi took advantage of the delay to get *schnorkel* installed. *I-13* and *I-14* also received them. Then, in June, they started for the Inland Sea again.

"It was a chilling experience, passing through Shimonoseki Strait," said Capt. Nambu long after the war, "The masts of sunken ships looked like a forest of ghostly trees. Some ships had capsized in shallow water and their bottoms had a red, rusty color. It was a tense passage. I was worried all the time. *I-401* had an anti-magnetic apparatus installed in her, but there were other types of mines that could sink us. All hands breathed a big sigh of relief when the journey was completed."

317

At Nanao Bay more delay followed, due to difficulty in training pilots. They had to make catapult takeoffs and water landings, then maneuver skillfully on the surface for pickup by the fold-away crane each big boat had on is deck. One plane crashed at sea and was lost. Another slammed into a mountainside. They had to be replaced and new pilots trained.

Forced landings at sea were another hazard, because each time its submarine had to go out and pick up both pilot and plane. According to Nambu, it was a rare moment when *I-401* had all three of its planes on board and in good condition. "We worked hard, though," he said, "and once were able to surface, unstow three aircraft, and get them away, all in 45 minutes. It was the only time, however, that we did have three planes ready for such a drill."

It was at about this time that Capt. Ariizumi proposed the destruction of the Panama Canal, saying that it would delay the arrival of the U. S. Atlantic Fleet in Pacific waters for at least three months. Since Germany had surrendered, we could expect that fleet to join the U. S. Pacific Fleet against us.

Life-sized models of the Panama Canal locks were built at Maizuru and towed to Nanao Bay. Attack drills were conducted and a sortie date set. The boats were to head east on just about the same course our 1st Air Fleet had taken on its way to attack Pearl Harbor in 1941. Once past Oahu, the giant submarines were to turn south and head in that direction until they were on the same latitude as Colombia, in South America. Then they were to turn east, run for the South American coastline and, hugging it, creep northward until within air range of the Panama Canal. Ten aircraft would then be launched, each carrying either a 1760-lb. bomb or a torpedo. A light force guarded the Panama Canal, since both the great expanses of the Atlantic and Pacific oceans were now in Allied hands. It was believed that not only would surprise be achieved, but the planes recovered as well. Capt. Ariizumi suggested this plan when the one to bomb Washington and New York was scrapped. He was infuriated when it, in turn, was scrapped in favor of an attack on Ulithi, where I had launched *kaiten* eight months before.

The Ulithi assault was to be a combination aircraft-*kaiten* attack, with the air strike force reduced from 10 to 6 planes, all to take *tokko* dives. *I-13* and *I-14* would not be launching aircraft from sea against Ulithi. Instead, they would sortie from Maizuru to Truk, each carrying two long-range *Saiun* scout aircraft, crated. These planes were to be re-assembled at our by-passed outpost, then make a swift reconnaissance flight over Ulithi. Meanwhile, *I-400* and *I-401* were to rendezvous in mid-ocean, receive the necessary information by radio, and launch 6 aircraft at Ulithi. *Kaiten*-carrying submarines lurking just outside Ulithi's reef, would attack at the same time.

Capt. Ariizumi fought this change of plans. He wanted to hit the enemy as powerful a blow as possible and felt that destruction of the Panama Canal would achieve more lasting damage.

The Naval General Staff did not agree. Its members pointed out that enemy ships were already coming from the Indian Ocean and more, from European waters, were coming via the Suez Canal. Troops were being diverted from other war fronts, too. Ulithi was an important staging point for these troops, which would soon be employed against our homeland. Damage done to the Panama Canal could not defeat what was already in Oriental waters.

"A man does not worry about a fire he sees on the horizon," staff members told Ariizumi, "when other flames are licking at his *kimono* sleeve." They insisted on his striking at Ulithi. He had to accept this third plan.

I-13 and *I-14* sortied through Tsuguru Strait on July 2. *I-13* was not heard from again. The destroyer escort *Taylor,* and planes from USS *Anzio*, are supposed to have sunk her on July 16, east of Honshu, but I don't think that is possible. The site of the alleged sinking is nowhere near where *I-13* was scheduled to be at that time. Perhaps *Taylor* and the aircraft attacked one of our *HA-101* class boats, some of which patrolled that area, manned by young officers who were disgruntled at having mere picket duty without weapons. Some of these young captains had appealed to Capt. Hanku Sasaki, asking at least that they be equipped with demolition charges, so that they could ram oncoming enemy ships. Their suggestion was still being considered when the war ended.

So, as in other cases, there probably was an American pilot somewhere at the war's end, wondering why he did not get credit for sinking a submarine. I believe *I-13* either fell victim to one of the many air patrols with which the Americans were then darkening the skies, or sank through accident. In any case, she did not arrive at Truk on July 14, as scheduled. *I-14* did, and unloaded her two crated aircraft.

I-400 and *I-401* followed these submarines out later, parting company soon after clearing home waters, on Capt. Ariizumi's orders. Each was ordered to proceed independently to a rendezvous point south of Ponape, in the Carolines, arriving on station Aug. 12. There they would await word of the attack date. To camouflage the group's mission and to make sure both submarines were not found together, Capt. Ariizumi told Cdr. Nambu, captain of the flagship in which Ariizumi was riding *(I-401)* to take his boat on a long swing east of the Marshalls. Then they ran southward a great distance before turning westward and then toward the Carolines. Both ships had excellent radar, effective up to 60 miles. It was felt that they were not likely to be surprised and sunk, as had happened to so many Japanese submarines in 1944 and 1945.

Before the rendezvous day, however, two other important dates arrived. One was July 29, when Lt. Cdr. Mochitsura Hashimoto initiated a strange series of events by torpedoing and sinking the heavy cruiser USS *Indianapolis*. And the other was Aug. 6, ever since known at Hiroshima as "the day of double-dawn."

* * *

Chapter 20.

DEFEAT; A NEW CAREER; MY FINAL SERVICE

On July 2, the American submarine *Barb* used a new weapon for submarines—rockets—against targets in the Japanese homeland. Three days later, Gen. MacArthur announced that the Philippines had been formally liberated from Japan. On the next day, *I-351* arrived at Singapore. This was Lt. Cdr. Noboru Okayama's second fuel run there. He took aboard 500 kiloliters of aviation gasoline, as before, and started for home on July 11. Three days later, *I-351* and all her crew were scorched into eternity. Torpedoes from the American submarine *Bluefish* tore into her, and the transport-converted-to-tanker blew up. Next day a force of enemy surface ships shelled our northern island, Hokkaido. The net was closing.

On July 15 the 6th Fleet added six submarines to its roster, but only on paper. They were the German submarines *U-181*, *U-862*, *UIT-24*, *UIT-25*, *U-219* and *U-195*. The first two were confiscated at Singapore, the next pair at Kobe, and the others at Jakarta and Soerabaya, respectively. We renamed them *I-*

501 through *I-506*. All were out of service when we confiscated them from our surrendered ally and still undergoing refit when the war ended.

On July 16 the world's first atomic bomb was exploded successfully at Almagordo, New Mexico, in the U. S. On the same day USS *Indianapolis*, which had been waiting for word of this, left San Francisco for Tinian, carrying a special cargo of uranium. Battleships and cruisers were shelling our main island of Honshu not long after that. On July 16th and 18th enemy carrier planes swept, one wave after another, over the Kanto Plain. Described to Mr. Harrington by a Yokosuka resident as "filling the sky in every direction you looked," they hit Tokyo, Yokohama, Yokosuka, and the nearby airfields defending our capital city. *I-372*, which Lt. Shingo Takahashi commanded, was getting ready for a sortie at Yokosuka and was sunk in the July 18 raid, all hands miraculously surviving the bomb hit that sent her down. Just before and after *I-372*'s loss, however, we scored two minor victories. *I-53* sent a *kaiten* into the attack transport USS *Marathon* on July 12, damaging her, then sent another into the destroyer escort *Underhill* on July 24. Lt. Cdr. Oba hit *Underhill* right in the middle of an attack on him. *Underhill* was so badly damaged that she had to be sunk by friendly forces.

Carrier aircraft hit Kure on July 23-24. When they flew back over the horizon, Japan had practically no navy left. Battleships *Hyuga, Ise* and "lucky *Haruna*" (the ship Americans claimed to have sunk about as often we claimed to have sunk USS *Saratoga*) settled right at their moorings, only portions of their superstructures thrusting above the surface. That left Japan with only 1 of her 12 battleships remaining, IJN *Nagato*, and she was damaged. Also, while those carrier planes were hitting Kure, Japan was being invaded—by submariners! A party of Americans had paddled ashore from USS *Barb* at Karafuto and blew up a railroad train.

I-402 was completed at Sasebo on July 24. Neither she nor her sister, *I-404*, saw action. The war was over before *I-402* completed her shakedown training, and *I-404* was sunk by bombing at Kure on July 28. She was moored offshore awaiting completion when carrier planes swooped in to give our navy its final blow. Carrier *Amagi*, ancient cruiser *Izumo*, light cruiser *Oyodo*, and destroyer *Nashi* went to a watery grave with *I-404*.

Meanwhile, in *I-58*, Lt. Cdr. Hashimoto had cruised for a week without sighting anything. On July 28 he spotted a tanker and, a few minutes later a distant explosion was heard.

I-58 surfaced for a look, but a rain squall obscured vision in all directions. Hashimoto dived his sub again, estimating there was a "very dim possibility" that he had sunk a tanker. At that moment in time, in spite of duty in a total of five submarines since the war's beginning, Hashimoto had yet to fire a conventional torpedo at the enemy. The following night, he scored Japan's last success of the war.

"A messenger waked me as I had ordered, at 10:30 P.M." he said, "The moon had then been risen for 30 minutes." Hashimoto threw some water on his face, then stopped for a few moments of meditation at his ship's shrine. This, a 10″ x 16″ box of white paulownia wood installed by workers at Kure, contained a few mementoes and charms from Ise Grand Shrine, where the Emperor's goddess-ancestor, *Amaterasu,* is venerated. Then Hashimoto went to the conning tower, accepted a routine report from his watch officer, and assumed the conn.

"Night action stations!" he ordered, and took *I-58* up from the depths to where he could scan with his periscope. He also ordered the air and surface search radar antennas elevated and, when nothing could be detected either visually or electronically, called out "Surface!"

I-58 had hardly come to rest when one of her lookouts reported seeing a ship, 90 degrees left of the bow. Hashimoto was then steering almost directly south. The sighting was to the east.

Hashimoto said he heaved his "thick body up the ladder to the bridge," to confirm the sighting personally and issued a rapid series of orders. "Dive! Level off at 60 feet! Man all *Kaiten!* Make ready all torpedo tubes!"

The enemy ship, which had been a black blob on the eastern horizon, slowly took on a triangular shape. Hashimoto began to make out a large ship with a high superstructure. It was either a battleship or a cruiser. As it kept plowing through the sea toward him, neither changing speed nor appearing to zigzag, he kept saying to himself "That ship is dead!! That ship is dead!"

All six of *I-58's* tubes were loaded and readied, at which point Hashimoto grew fearful that the enemy vessel might pass too close to him for his torpedoes to arm. Like Tanabe approaching USS *Yorktown* at Midway, Hashimoto needed to make sure the run from his tubes to the target would be long enough for his torpedoes to arm themselves, which they did after a specific number of propeller revolutions. He quickly ordered a 180°-turn made to the left. Then he ordered another, to the right. This long S-turn put him back on his original course, but along a path more to the east and somewhat more distant from the enemy's track than he had been earlier. The cruiser-or-battleship was now about 2½ miles away, angling across *I-58*'s bow from the left. Hashimoto could now make out her two towering "islands" clearly, as well as her turrets. He decided, because of her high freeboard, that she was an *Idaho*-class battleship.

The four *kaiten* men were in their weapons, all clamoring to be fired away, now that the size of the target had been announced. Hashimoto curtly told his torpedo officer, Lt. Toshio Tanaka, that the *kaiten* men could wait. He had a perfect firing setup now, and was waiting only for the range to shorten a little more before emptying his tubes at the target. If he took time to launch *kaiten,* the target might pass and be gone into the night. Also, launching human torpedoes was a noisy operation that might be picked up on enemy sound equipment. And the visibility had begun to vary. *Kaiten* pilots might not be able to see a thing through their short periscopes.

When the enemy ship was about 1500 yards away and *I-58* on a line 60 degrees off his starboard bow, Hashimoto shouted "Fire one!" In quick succession, a half-dozen Model 95's leaped from their tubes, spaced 3 degrees apart, set to run at 19 feet. Three missed, running across the enemy ship's bow. Then, one after another, the other three hit. The first slammed into the bow, and the second hit under the first turret. The final torpedo struck under the bridge, according to Hashimoto's report. He could see a third column of water in the light of explosions caused by his first two hits.

I-58's torpedo officer, gunnery officer and two communications petty officers kept scrambling for turns at the day periscope while Hashimoto was using the night one. Their cries of joy were repeated throughout the submarine. Hashimoto kept sweeping the horizon with his periscope. He could not believe that so big a ship was traveling without escorts and recalled the time off the Marshalls when a line of destroyers appeared out of nowhere while he was working into position to torpedo two aircraft carriers and a battleship. After a short while he dived his boat and turned to the westward, to keep clear of any escorts while his torpedo tubes were reloaded. An hour later he was back on the surface, sweeping the area with both radar and binoculars. The radar showed nothing and the visibility had closed down to 100 yards. Hashimoto wirelessed Kure, saying "Have just torpedoed and sunk *Idaho*-class battleship." Then he turned north and made full speed for several hours on the surface, getting as far away as possible before diving again.

On Aug. 10 the captain of *I-58* launched two more *kaiten* at enemy ships, with results doubtful. On Aug. 12, the last *kaiten* of the war was fired. Hashimoto had two remaining, but Petty Officer Ichiro Shiraki's was found defective. The other, manned by Petty Officer Yoshiaki Hayashi, was sent away at what Hashimoto thought was a large seaplane tender. Actually, it was the dock landing ship USS *Oak Hill*. Hayashi may have actually scraped this target's side with his *kaiten,* but he did not sink it. Destroyer escort *Nickel,* trying to locate the human torpedo, saw it explode about a mile astern of *Oak Hill.*

Hashimoto had set out on July 16, but had had to put about and return when several *kaiten* periscopes were found to be defective. A week after he left this second time, Japan received word of the Potsdam Declaration, which demanded unconditional surrender from Japan. To some of our high-ranking officers, this was unthinkable. A group of them, later called *kichigai* ("the insane ones"), plotted to seize rule of Japan. They claimed that this would foil the "Badoglio-type" statesmen surrounding the Emperor who, they said, were acting like the officer who had surrendered Italy to the Allies. Gen. Korechika Anami (Minister of War) was the leader of this no-surrender faction. His followers went so far as to forge an order giving them command of the Imperial Palace guard, then searched the Emperor's residence on the night of Aug. 14, trying to find the phonograph record of the surrender announcement the Emperor had made for broadcast the next day. Posters suddenly appeared everywhere, denouncing the Emperor's closest advisors as traitors and urging people to provide themselves with bamboo spears for repelling expected Allied paratroopers. *Mainichi,* one of our larger national newspapers, carried announcements of government orders that indolent workers would be punished and showed pictures of large underground factories being constructed. Workers, fearing bombs, had not been reporting for work at industrial defense plants, so threats of fines and imprisonment were used against them. Absenteeism had become a civil crime.

Then came Aug. 6, the day when "two suns," one natural and the other man-made, cast their fiery glow over Hiroshima, not very far from my place of duty. An air raid warning sounded at 8 A.M. at Otake, but I did not pay much attention to it. There often were false alarms and the radio at the time was reporting that only one lone B-29 had been sighted in the sky. I had gathered up my books and was about to head for my classroom when, at about 8:15 A.M. a terrific explosion was heard. A short time later, all the windows on the north side of my building were blown in by an air blast, the great pressure wave emanating from where an atomic bomb was first dropped on human beings. I looked toward Hiroshima. A large cloud was spreading over the city. It then seemed to zoom upward with ever-increasing speed, after which it topped off at a great height, giving it the appearance of a giant mushroom.

"Atomic bomb!"

I don't think I spoke the words aloud, but I know that I spoke them in my mind. I had heard from time to time that Japan's scientists were studying how to make atomic bombs. And the matter had been brought up for discussion in the National Diet during 1942. At once I realized that America had perfected her bomb first. Two other things came into my mind at the same moment. My family was safe, but the war was lost. Should America continue to drop bombs like that one, Japan was truly doomed.

I went on to my classroom, but had difficulty concentrating on the curriculum. *What is the purpose of what I am doing?* I asked myself. There I was, teaching students how to make a submarine attack, when B-29's were spreading mines so thickly that even Japan's fishing fleet was decimated, and could not bring food to our people. Submarines had difficulty clearing Kure, letting alone reaching and hitting the enemy. They had to pass through Bungo Strait submerged, out of fear of lurking enemy boats. And America had the atomic weapon! What chance was there for victory?

Whenever my glance moved in the direction of Hiroshima that day, I was thankful that none of my family, relatives or friends lived there.

On Aug. 7, with several other submarine school instructors, I drove into Hiroshima. We were curious to see the effects of an atomic weapon. So small was our knowledge of it, that we didn't even know about danger from radiation and rode blithely into what would be later called the danger area. Horrific sights met our eyes. Everywhere there was desolation. All that remained standing of Hiroshima's structures were the shells of concrete buildings. Everything else was flattened over a wide radius from the explosion's center. Fires were still smoking, and charred bodies of men, women, children and horses lay everywhere. A few live people, haggard-eyed, wandered about poking through the wreckage, trying to find the remains of lost ones. A sickening stench rose from everything. We soon realized that this was no time for satisfying scientific curiosity and, after offering a few of the more wretched ones our condolences, we got back into our car and returned to Otake. No one spoke during the ride back, but I am sure that my comrades had the same thoughts as I—radar, blockade, bombs, fire raids, and now this. No doubt of it, the end could not be far off!

On Aug. 8 a second atomic bomb was dropped, on Nagasaki, and Russia declared war upon Japan. The first was expected sooner or later, and the second surprised no military man. For forty years the Russians had been waiting for an opportunity to take revenge, ever since our military and naval forces had smashed them at Port Arthur and Tsushima Strait. Few of the world's white men (other than diplomats, historians and political scientists) are aware of how much that defeat rankled, especially since it had been achieved less than 40 years after Japan had emerged from a supposedly "barbarian state."

The world's colored peoples are aware of it, however. One need only discuss history for a few minutes with leaders of any backward nation before learning that scholars from such nations mark the Russo-Japanese war of 1905 as a "tide-turning," the first time in history that a colored race defeated a white one. Every Japanese military man was constantly aware of the "great bear" at our backs, ready to pounce should we ever grow weak.

In class that day, I told my students that we should fight on for Japan so long as breath was left in us. In Tokyo, the Emperor was telling an Imperial Conference that "the time has come to bear the unbearable." Lt Cdr. Yukio Inaba took *I-373* out of Sasebo on Aug. 9, heading for Formosa. Four days later the U.S. submarine *Spikefish* torpedoed and sank her, the 134th and last Japanese submarine destroyed or sunk in the war. Early in the morning of Aug. 10 our Emperor demanded the unanimous consent of his closest advisors for accepting the terms of the Potsdam Declaration. Japan, he said, must surrender unconditionally. There would be no more quibbling. And, on the next day, the American Secretary of State announced that, from the moment of surrender, our Emperor would be subject to the orders of the Supreme Allied Commander in the Pacific. This was Gen. Douglas MacArthur, who later thwarted Russian attempts to seize Japan by simply ignoring whatever the Russians requested or said.

Not knowing what else to do, I continued my submarine classes. At Otake we had no knowledge of what was occurring in Tokyo; the plots, the promises, the planned revolts. Then, at

7:15 **A.M.** on Aug. 15, we heard over the radio that the Emperor would speak to all of his subjects at noon. It was something that had never happened before; His Majesty's voice coming to all Japanese at the same time. We didn't know what to make of it, except that something of great and special importance was bound to be said.

By that time, bomb damage had hurt Japan so badly that electrical power was rationed. It required a special allotment of electricity to bring off the broadcast. When the appointed time arrived I gathered with other Otake officers and men in front of our main building, where loudspeakers had been set up. Vice Adm. Noboru Ichikawa stood facing us. None of us had any idea what was coming. I expected the Emperor either to issue an imperial order, or make a personal appeal for all Japanese to unite in one final stand against the enemy. There was a lot of static in the broadcast, making it difficult to hear, and every account I have read since states that this was "interference" caused by unknown persons who were trying to jam the broadcast. Nevertheless, all of us could make out enough of it to understand that the Emperor was telling us that he meant to end the war.

Earlier, while some of us were still in the school instructors' office, Lt. Cdr. Genbei Kawaguchi, former skipper of *I-44*, had burst through the door. In an agitated voice he said that advisors to the Emperor had told our ruler lies about the true state of Japan and overseas. He claimed that the Emperor, misled, was about to make an announcement of surrender. This was appalling news to all of us. How Kawaguchi received the word in advance, I do not know. Perhaps he had been told by representatives of the Army officers in Tokyo who were planning the *coup d'etat*. They hoped to seize control of the empire, fight on, then turn control back to the Emperor after winning the great victory they were sure they could bring off.

We became confused upon listening to Kawaguchi. The confusion increased when we later heard the Emperor's broadcast. Some wanted to fight on, including myself. But a few (again including myself) also began to think of our duty to the Emperor. He said that he was going to end the war and that made us bound to assist him, to carry out whatever orders were given toward that end. Nonetheless, August 15, 1945, was a day of insanity. No voice of reason could be heard. Anyone who dared mention the word "surrender" would have been fighting his own comrades for his life. After a lot of speculation, I and others took refuge in indecision. We decided to wait until some kind of official word was sent down through 6th

Fleet from the Naval General Staff. Meanwhile, business as usual. We returned to our classrooms.

The next day, *Gekko* night fighter aircraft from the nearby air base at Iwakuni flew over Otake, dropping handbills. Each bore a message from Capt. Yasuna Ozono. He was at the air base in Atsugi, southwest of Tokyo, and commander of the aircraft charged with defense of our capital city. Ozono refused to surrender. He had sent men to other bases, too, to take over planes from those men who were surrendering. His leaflets urged all of us to fight on with him "to a certain victory."

Only a small minority at Otake were influenced by Ozono's message. The time between the Emperor's broadcast and the dropping of the leaflets had given us a chance to think. At Hirao, Lt. Takesuka Tateyama, determined to fight on, took the old *I-159* out, with a pair of *kaiten,* and headed for the Inland Sea. But he came back in two days. On Aug. 17 I was ordered by Rear Adm. Mitsuru Nagai to take over as disciplinary commander at Otake. "You will be responsible" he said, "for calming the wild spirits of young submarine men and students. It will not be easy. You know that their spirit is the highest in the Imperial Navy. They will not want to give up."

My duties also included the burning of all official records and documents, and I also had to see to it that submarine men were released from active duty. I also had to see to the discharge of all civilian workers without incident. These were not easy tasks. Many men and women had worked long and hard in hope of a Japanese victory. Telling them that all was lost and they would no longer be needed was a hard thing to do. I had to calm many people, soothe many disturbed feelings.

Hashimoto got back to Kure with his *I-58* on Aug. 18. On the way up Bungo Strait he'd met six HA-Class submarines that had left Kure, their captains determined to fight to the death. Hashimoto, having already received the Emperor's broadcast on his radio, was reserving decision and action until he arrived in port. When his boat glided on past them, the six HA-Class boats put about and also returned.

Hashimoto reported that *I-58* had sunk a battleship. He found a very tense situation at the Kure anchorage. Submariners had earlier provisioned and fueled every boat there. A delegation of young officers, led by Lt. Akira Kikuchi, met with Capt. Shojiro Iura, of the 6th Fleet staff and asked him to convince senior officers to keep on fighting. Iura disagreed (risking his life) and reminded those men of their duty to the

Emperor. The delegation left, but a few submarine captains tried to change Iura's mind. "Let them go!" they urged, "Those men do not want to live. They can fight the enemy for as long as two more months before committing *seppuku*. They wish to die in battle, like true *samurai*. Why not let them do it?" Again Iura demurred, and it was about that time that the six HA-boat commanders took matters into their own hands and headed down Bungo Strait.

When a third group came to him in the afternoon of Aug. 18, Iura went to Vice Adm. Daigo that evening, and Daigo summoned all concerned to his headquarters the next day.

"For nearly three years," he told them, "I had official duty that put me in close attendance on our Emperor. I know what he is like. I understand his feelings. You men obviously do not understand them. He is very humane, very concerned for all of his people, not just us few in the military forces. If we continue to fight, the enemy will continue to fight. And what will happen? Many thousands of innocent ones, women and children, will die because you are so headstrong. If you sink even one enemy ship, death will shower down on the innocents who have no weapons at all. Think! Try to understand the deep sense of humanity that made the Emperor come to this precedent-shattering decision!"

Daigo's words were enough. All present apologized, and begged his forgiveness for causing him and the Emperor concern. They promised to make no more trouble. That ended the problem at Kure. Expect for an occasional raised voice, disbanding of the forces there went ahead with no difficulty. Disturbances occurred among submariners at Yokosuka, Maizuru, Sasebo, and the places where *Tokko Squadron* 11 and positioned *kaiten, koryu* and *shinyo*, but everyone eventually calmed down after a few days. Men began to think about their families, left alone to face an occupation by the enemy. They began drifting away from Otake and other bases, toward their homes.

As for Tokyo, Gen. Anami committed suicide. And one version has it that, at Atsugi, Capt. Ozono was given a hypodermic by peace-inclined people, then spirited away. The Japanese government itself later tried him, sent him to prison and did not include him years later, after the Occupation ended, on the list when pensions were given to former military men. Prince Takamatsu, the Emperor's brother, helped put things right at Atsugi, where holes were punched in fuel tanks and propellers removed from aircraft, so that the *kichigai* could not use them in *kamikaze* attacks on the approaching Allied fleet. Everything was settled before Gen. MacArthur's advance party landed at Atsugi.

One Japanese officer had an amusing experience that illustrates how rapidly the mood of the country changed. Right after the surrender he met an elderly farmer who was brandishing an ancient, rusty sword and threatening to slaughter all Americans. On Aug. 22, that officer met the farmer again. This time the sword was dripping blood. "Have you been fighting, *oji-san*?" the officer asked. "No," the old man answered, "just killing a pig. I was hungry." The pragmatic had overwhelmed the heroic. All through Japan people supported the Emperor's position, a proof of the reverence in which he was held.

After announcing the surrender of Japan, the U.S. announced the loss of the cruiser *Indianapolis*. Later events showed this sinking to be the center of a tragedy in communications. When Hashimoto's torpedoes sent the cruiser down, about 300 men died. But twice that many later died, because no rescuers came to their aid for four days. Overconfident from so many victories, the American authorities did not set up any regulation (at least in the Philippines) for action to be taken should a scheduled vessel not arrive by her designated time. The Philippines were where *Indianapolis* was heading when she was sunk. No search was made until an aircraft sighted some survivors in the water several days after the ship went down. The delay cost about 600 lives through exposure, exhaustion, sharks, and thirst.

An even stranger sequel followed. Late in 1945 Hashimoto, then involved in clearing up the debris of war, was suddenly seized by Occupation authorities and taken to America. There he appeared as a witness in the general court-martial of the officer (Capt. Charles McVey, USN) whose ship he had sunk. I do not think that such a happening has any precedent in history: summoning your enemy to testify against your own fighting men. Hashimoto, puzzled, answered the questions put to him. Later, while translating Mr. Richard Newcomb's book on the *Indianapolis* sinking into Japanese, Hashimoto realized that some of his testimony had been very poorly translated. Long afterward he still held a low opinion of the entire proceedings.

On Aug. 19 I received a letter from Hisako, telling me she was taking our sons and going back to Kagoshima. This was a bold thing for a Japanese wife to do without consulting her husband, but a brave thing as well. I had my hands full where I was, urging men to go home and arranging things for a swift takeover by Occupation troops when they arrived. On Sept. 15 the 6th Fleet was finally disbanded, one of Vice. Adm. Daigo's final offical acts being to promote me and other officers. I became a Commander (in a navy that no longer existed) and was mustered out in October.

When I left I said goodbye to the scraps of a great navy, a navy that had really been my life since I was a small boy. Of our once-mighty Fleet we had lost 11 battleships, 21 aircraft carriers, 38 cruisers, 135 destroyers and, via one means or another, 134 submarines. Eight of the submarines had been lost in *kaiten* operations, together with 80 of the young men who had volunteered to serve as human torpedoes. Another 15 *kaiten* men had died in training accidents: suffocating, drowning, or striking enemy-laid mines. About 10,000 trained submarine men had died fighting for Japan. And, after a few ships had been taken by the victors, the Allies took the remainder out to sea in February, 1946, scuttling them in Operation Road's End—the Imperial Navy's final humiliation.

As I made my way southward towards home, I found the country in a terrible state. Japan was unable to feed or clothe itself. Nor was the population able to sustain good health, medicines were in such short supply. Had not Occupation authorities rushed in massive shipments of food, much of Japan's population would not have survived the winter of 1945.

One out of every five dwellings in the country had been destroyed by bombs or fire, or had been torn down to help create fire breaks. Nearly 30 million persons had been affected by this. The lucky ones were crowded in with relatives. The rest were huddled in shacks made of whatever they could scavenge.

On my arrival in Kagoshima my brother-in-law, Kiyoshe Anraku, provided us with a house. This was most kind of him, because we were penniless. He also offered me a job in his *sake*-brewing business. But I felt I knew the sea best, so instead I took a job with a small shipping company that had managed to salvage a few light cargo carriers out of the war. But everything, including fuel oil, was in short supply during those days and for a long time afterward and my earnings could not keep place with the inflation that hit Japan. So, after four very difficult years, I finally gave up and went to work with my brother-in-law.

While still with the shipping company, I had been summoned to Yokohama by the Occupation authorities. A military tribunal was sitting there, investigating what is known as the Ichioka Case. Vice Adm. Hisao Ichioka had commanded SubRon 8 in the Indian Ocean, and the Allies were charging that atrocities had been committed by Japanese submariners in that area during the period from Mar. 1, 1943 to Aug. 31, 1944. Beginning in November, 1945, about 200 former officers and men of our submarine force were interrogated. The Allies charged that the rules of war had been violated. They said that enlisted men, officers, submarine captains and higher officers had intentionally carried out (or had allowed to be carried out without interference) inhumane acts against survivors of sunken ships. Former members of our Penang garrison were also charged with maltreatment of prisoners of war. SubDiv 14 (*I-26, I-27, I-29* and *I-37*) and SubDiv 30 (*I-162, I-165* and *I-166*), plus *I-8* and *I-10* were supposed to have been involved. As a result of the interrogations some men were arrested and the others allowed to go home. A Nisei interpreter questioned me closely for about six hours but, since there were no charges of such offenses occurring in the Pacific area, I was released.

In January, 1949, sentences were handed down. Ichioka, who had both SubDivs in his SubRon 8, received 20 years at hard labor. Vice Adm. Teruhisa Komatsu, who commanded 6th Fleet for part of that period, was sentenced to 15 years. Rear Adm. Noboru Ichizaki received 10 years, while Rear Adm. Hisashi Mito received 8 years. Capt. Shojiro Iura (whom I have mentioned in this book a number of times) had been Ichizaki's chief staff officer for a while. He was sentenced to 6 years. Capt. Nobuyaki Tadaki, commander of the Penang base, received 10 years. Cdr. Hajime Nakagawa, who had been CO of *I-37*, received 8 years, Cdr. Toshio Kusaka of *I-26*, 5 years. Two officers from *I-8*, Lt. Sadao Motonaka and Lt. Masanori Hattori, received 7 and 5 years, respectively. Five others received prison terms of 1-2 years, and 26 men were found innocent. All the convicted were sent to Sugamo Prison in Tokyo, sentenced to hard labor with other war criminals. 6 years later, all sentences were commuted and all men released on probation under Japanese laws.

Vice Adm. Tadashige Daigo was executed as a war criminal, in what I know to be a terrible miscarriage of justice. After following orders to disband the 6th Fleet and turn everything over to the Occupation authorities, Daigo retired to his home. There he was suddenly arrested in December, 1946. He was tried by the Dutch, who lusted for revenge after the humiliating and speedy defeat we had inflicted on them in 1941-42. Daigo was tried, convicted, and sentenced and executed for a crime of which he had had absolutely no knowledge whatever!

The incident occurred in Daigo's command, but at Pontianak, Borneo—while Daigo was all the way across on the other side of Borneo at Balikpapan commanding the 22nd Base Force. Daigo's tenure was from November, 1943, to August 1944. During that time some natives at Pontianak plotted to revolt against the garrison there. Its commander, a young officer, got word of this and panicked. Without permission of his superiors, he seized the plotters and executed their ringleaders. The revolt was crushed and the garrison saved, but Daigo knew nothing of it until it was all over.

The trial was very one-sided. It was evident that Daigo was free of guilt. But, in the true *samurai* spirit, Daigo was as loyal to his juniors as he was to his seniors. Even though evidence favorable to him could have been introduced, he would not allow it because it would have cast blame on others.

On Dec. 6, 1947, Admiral Daigo was shot to death in the prison courtyard at Pontianak. He declined a blindfold, sang *"Kimigayo"* (our national anthem), loudly called out three *banzai* for the Emperor, then calmly told the officer in charge he was ready. Bullets tore into his black suit and his gray flannel hat fell to the ground as he crumpled. It saddens me to think of that man and how much concern he had for all of his subordinates, including me. He was a good leader, much loved by all.

The international military tribunals caused much argument. They will provide law students of all nations much food for study in coming centuries. Many legal experts (including Americans) claim that they had no basis in law. They were simply a matter of the victors laying down the law. Had he not inflicted humiliating defeats on top British officers in Malaya, I believe it very likely that our General Tomoyuki Yamashita would have lived to a ripe old age rather than suffer execution. Two Justices of the U.S. Supreme Court said that the international military tribunals pointed the way to future "legal lynchings." Using the same principle of law applied by those tribunals, the Japanese could have "legally" beheaded General MacArthur and Admiral Nimitz had we won, for their "roles" in the slaughter of helpless drowning men in the Battle of the Bismarck Sea. Neither man was anywhere near the scene, of course, and I am sure that neither knew what was happening there when Allied planes and PT boats chopped Japanese survivors to bits.

From the shipping business, I went into the *sake* business. I became a passable salesman, despite my original distaste for business. Like most officers of the Imperial Navy, I had little money, little interest in money, and little interest in the kinds of people who liked to accumulate it. My service pay had been ample for my modest needs and my main concern had been defending my country—not getting rich.

Hisako bore us two more children after the war. Our third son, Koichi, was born on Jan. 20, 1947, and our daughter Kumiko on Sept. 29, 1950. By the latter date the Korean war had started, and MacArthur's headquarters decided that Japan should be re-armed for her own defense. In August, 1950, our Police Reserve was formed, then re-formed into a security force 20 months later, after the Japanese-American peace treaty ending the Occupation was signed. A maritime security force was also set up at that time. On Aug. 1, 1952, the National Security Agency was established to control both of these and, 23 months later, the Air Self-Defense Force came into being. The National Defense Agency was created then, to control the Air, Ground, and Maritime Self-Defense Forces. They bore these names because the constitution adoped by our government during the Occupation forbade us to have offensive military power.

During the summer of 1954 I was invited to join the Maritime Self-Defense Force. Experienced officers were needed to train the nucleus for its later expansion. The Etajima tradition does not easily die and so I accepted. I served until 1963 before retiring from active duty and taking employment with a shipbuilding company. During part of my service I commanded the submarine school, graduating 720 officers and men to crew a small but growing submarine fleet. When fine young men moved up the ranks to take command, my job was finished.

I have seen a great deal of change since entering Etajima as a Midshipman. China, once protected by America, came to hate her. Russia, once America's ally, became her chief adversary. Japan and Germany, once pitted in hate against the U.S., became her strongest trade and military partners. With a past so strange, who can predict the future?

Of the 132 men who were graduated with me in the 59th Class at Etajima, 15 were already dead when we went to war with America. Another 49 were killed in battle. Fifteen of us went into submarines—twelve had our own boats. Of the 12, only 4 survived the war. Morinaga became chief of staff for the Maritime Self-Defense Forces. Hashimoto built submarines for it at Kawasaki Heavy Industries, Kobe. And Toyomasu led the peaceful life of a high school principal at Tosu City, in northern Honshu.

People change—and are always changing. Nobuo Fujita, who fire-bombed near Brookings, Oregon, was later a guest of that city's people. I was able, in 1958, to chat cheerfully with Mayor George Christopher of San Francisco of how I had nearly given his city a "Christmas present" from *I-15* in 1941. The word "Jap" was an epithet on 100 million American tongues in 1941, but when a midget submarine was found on a reef near Pearl Harbor in 1960, the Americans raised and returned it to us with respectful ceremonies honoring the brave men who manned it.

I have memories, some of them of the 6th Fleet, which built the world's smallest, largest, slowest and fastest submarines and had a small air force mounted on its decks. And I have my children, of whom I am so proud. And Hisako, of the gentle smile.

Once a year we make a special visit to Tokyo and the Yasukuni Shrine, where the souls of Japan's war dead are venerated. There, with other former submarine men, I pray for my many departed shipmates and ask that war never again turn its ghastly face toward my beloved land.

—end—